AF531374

ADMINISTRATION OF JUSTICE IN INDIA

Ethics and Accountability

ADMINISTRATION OF JUSTICE IN INDIA

Ethics and Accountability

Dr. RAJNEESH KUMAR PATEL

Foreword by

Prof. ANIRUDH PRASAD

DEEP & DEEP PUBLICATIONS PVT. LTD.
F-159, Rajouri Garden, New Delhi - 110 027

ADMINISTRATION OF JUSTICE IN INDIA
Ethics and Accountability

ISBN 978-81-8450-343-2

Typeset by RAHUL COMPOSERS
358, Pocket-B, Phase-2, Sector-16B, Dwarka, New Delhi - 110 075

Printed in India at MAYUR ENTERPRISES
WZ Plot No. 3, Gujjar Market, Tihar Village, New Delhi - 110 018

Published by DEEP & DEEP PUBLICATIONS PVT. LTD.
F-159, Rajouri Garden, New Delhi - 110 027 • Phone : 25435369, 25440916
E-mail : ddpubs@gmail.com • ddpbooks@yahoo.co.in
Showroom :
2/13, Ansari Road, Daryaganj, New Delhi - 110 002 • Telefax : 23245122

Contents

Foreword xi

Acknowledgements xxi

1 INTRODUCTION 1

General Observations 1

Statement of Problems 8

Paradoxes in Administration of Justice: Breaking Wheels 11

The Objective of the Book 12

Scheme of the Book 13

2. HISTORICAL ACCOUNT OF LEGAL PROFESSION AND THE TRADITION OF IMPARTIAL ADMINISTRATION OF JUSTICE 15

I. History of the Legal Profession in England 17

II. History of the Legal Profession in United States 24

An Unified Bar Association also Came into Existence 32

III. History of the Legal Profession in India 34

(A) Position in Ancient India 34

(B) Position in Muslim Period 39

(C) Position in British India 41

IV. The Impact of Legal Practitioners Acts on Legal Profession 47
V. Step Towards Autonomy and Unified Indian Bar 53
(A) Report of the Chamier Committee 53
(B) The Indian Bar Council Act, 1926 54
(C) The Recommendations of the All India Bar Committee and the Law Commission 58
(D) Advocates Act, 1961: A Great Step Towards Unification and Autonomy of the Bar in India 60

3. HIGH TRADITIONS AND PRESENT STATUS OF THE LEGAL PROFESSION 76
I. Necessity of the Legal Profession 78
II. Status and Nature of the Legal Profession 82
(A) Profession of High Traditions 85
(B) Learned Profession 87
(C) A Noble Profession 90
(D) Profession of Great Honour and Dignity 92
III. Falling Standards and Degradation of the Legal Profession 94
(A) System of Legal Education 96
(B) Mushroom Growth of Law Institutions 102
(C) Lack of Service Spirit 105
(D) Problem of Over-crowding 109
(E) Lack of Training 111

4. HIGH TRADITIONS AND THE IMAGE OF JUDICIARY 116
I. Necessity and Role of the Judiciary 117
II. Status and Image of the Judiciary 122
(A) Seat of High Tradition 122
(B) Seat of Great Respect and Dignity 126
(C) Life of Judges and Expectations 129
III. Deterioration in Image of the Judiciary 133
(A) Delay in Justice 134
(B) Illusory System of Trial Proceedings 140

(C) Behaviour of the Judicial Officers 143
(D) Should Judges be Left Out of the Information Act 149

5. STATE OF PROFESSIONAL ETHICS IN ADMINISTRATION OF JUSTICE AND BENCH-BAR RELATIONS **151**

I. Professional Ethics 154
(A) Meaning and Nature 154
(B) Sources of Professional Ethics 159
II. Necessity of Codification 165
III. Problems in Framing the Rules of Professional Ethics 170
IV. Professional Ethics for the Members of Bench and Bar 173
(A) Duty of Advocates 174
(B) Propriety of Judges 212

6. PROFESSIONAL AND OTHER MISCONDUCTS OF ADVOCATES **225**

I. Professional Misconduct : Meaning and Scope 226
(A) Professional Misconduct Committed by Advocates 231
(B) Other Misconducts Committed by Advocates 277
(i) Obscene Behaviour 278
(ii) Criminal Conduct 279
(iii) Sexual Misbehaviour 282
(iv) Physical Assault 283
(v) Abuse of Privileges 284
(vi) Political Activities and Civil Disobedience 285
(C) Contempt of Court Committed by Advocates 287
(i) Imputation of Partiality 290
(ii) Allegation of Corruption 292
(iii) Unsavory Language 296
(iv) Threatening 299
(v) Unbecoming Behaviour 303

(vi) Criticism of Judges and Judicial Conduct 306

(vii) Contempt During Conducting Cases 318

(viii) Strike and Boycott of Court 321

(ix) Disturbing the Court Proceedings 326

(x) Influence by Private Communication 328

7. ILL HEALTH OF THE JUDICIARY AND UNBECOMING BEHAVIOUR OF JUDGES 331

I. Corrupting the Administration of Justice 332

II. Unbecoming Behaviour of Judges and Contempt of Court 347

(A) Conduct of Subordinate Court Judges Amounting to the Contempt of Court 349

(B) Conduct of the Superior Court Judges and Contempt of Court—An Unresolved Issue 370

8. MECHANISM FOR MAINTAINING ACCOUNTABILITY OF BENCH AND BAR IN INDIA 379

I. Mechanism Provided for Maintaining Accountability of Advocates 380

(A) Disciplinary Proceedings by the Bar Councils and its Committees 381

(B) Disciplinary Proceedings by the Bar Council of India and its Committee 392

(C) Disciplinary Powers of the Bar Council of India and its Committees 393

(D) Award of Punishments 398

(E) Nature of Disciplinary Proceedings and Standard of Proof 401

(F) Quantum of Punishment Under Advocates Act 405

II. Appellate Jurisdiction of the Supreme Court 412

(A) Persons Who May Preferred Appeal 413

(B) Procedural Aspect of Appeal Before the Supreme Court 414

(C) Exercise of Appellate Jurisdiction 416
III. Contempt Proceedings 417
IV. Critical Appraisal of the Mechanism Provided for Disciplining Advocate 425
V. Mechanism for Maintaining the Accountability of Judges 429
(A) Impeachment Process 431
(B) In-house Procedure 434
(C) Recent Attempt Towards Ensuring Judicial Accountability 443
VI. Proposal for New Law on Existing Judges (Inquiry) Act and Formation of National Judicial Council 445
(A) Object and Reason of the Bill of 2006 446
(B) Changes Proposed by the Bill 447
(C) Procedure Under Proposed Bill 449
(D) Findings of the Council 452
VII. Critical Apprisal of the Proposed Mechanism for Disciplining Judges 454

9. CONCLUSIONS **458**

Bibliography 477

Index 481

Foreword

Administration of justice is the first and foremost task of any legal system in an ordered society. A good and upto mark justice is the result of the co-operation of able advocates and noble judges. Ability of advocates and nobility of judges makes the legal profession learned, grand and noble. Like medicine and divinity, law is a noble profession with distinguishing mark of service to the mankind quite unconcerned with money-making and profit-oriented business.

Lawyers and Justices are the two pillars of the administration of justice. Both pillars are equally important. Rather lawyers are to be more informed, imaginative, legally trained and futuristic than the justices because a judge has to listen patiently and discern truth out of briefs of the advocates. Learned and bigger the stature of a lawyer, everlasting is the judgment. The backbone of legal justice system, *Marbury v. Madison*[1] came out from the pen of Marshal C.J. because that case was argued by the great advocate Daniel Webster, who was great orator of nationalistic outlook and always remindful: "remember the trust, the sacred trust, attaching to the rich inheritance which we have received from our fathers. Let us feel our personal responsibility to the full extent of our power and influence, for the preservation of the principles of civil and religious liberty. Let us hold fast the great truth that communities are responsible, as well an individual, that no

1. 2 law ed. 60.

government is respectable, which is not just that without unspotted purity of public faith, without sacred public, public principles, fidelity and honours no mere form government, no machinery of law, can give dignity to political society." In our system the most realized and celebrated doctrine of enforcing constitutional discipline on parliamentary amending power came into existence in the form of the 'Basic-structure' because Nani A. Palkhivala argued the case in famous and historic judgment of *Keshavananda Bharati* v. *State of Kerala*.[2] The great advocates are torch bearer of the principle that advocacy is a branch of administration of justice (and not a mere money-making occupation).[3] Above all, an advocate must be socio-economic conscience keeper with factual briefs like 'brandies-brief.'[4] An advocate must be of unquestioned and unquestionable honesty; courageous and bold along with sincerity, because the power of clear statement is the great power at Bar (D. Webster); hard working, witty, eloquent, amicability with brethren and tactful. Lawyers must work to win. The other wheel of the Chariot of Justice is the Judge who sits in the court of Justice in the image of Lord or the Goddess of Justice. Quranic message is that a Judge on the bench acts not only in the image of justice but in the image of God too. Quran says, 'O' ye who believe; be ye staunch in justice, witness for Allah, even though it be against yourselves or your parents or your kindred, whether rich or poor, for Allah is nearer to akin to you than either.'[5] A Judge imbibes fairness

2. (1973) 4 SCC 225.
3. Sajjan Raj Surana *v.* Jaipur Vidyut Nigam Ltd., AIR 2002 Raj. 109 (Arun Madan J.), M.P. Electricity Board *v.* Shiv Narain (2005) 7 SCC 283.
4. Brandies brief is used for the imitative brief submitted by Louis, D. Brandeis in Muller *v.* Oregon (U.S. 412 (1908). The brief was prepared in defense of Oregon ten-hour law for women and in brief only two scant pages were devoted to the conventional legal arguments and over one hundred pages were devoted to the new kind of evidence drawn from hundreds of reports, both domestic and foreign of committees, statistical bureau, commissioners of hygiene and factor all providing that long hours are as a matter of fact dangerous to women's health, safety and morals and short hours result in social and economic benefits.
5. Quran IV, 135 (Fliige ed.) IV, p. 134.

keeping himself aloof. His life is serene, pure and self-disciplined. Chief Justice of Canada, Bora Laskin very aptly said: "when you become a judge, you loose half of your freedom and when you become a chief justice you almost loose the other half". A judge like Lady Macbeth must be above—suspicion, searching truth and seeker of justice and sense of civility. He should be bold enough to assert the majesty of law like Lord Coke who may not fail to remind the Crown that *"the King is under no man, but under God and the law"*. He should imbibe the courage of Chief Justice Ramaswami who ensured the authority of law against Peshwa King Raghunath Rao who had plotted murder of his nephew Narayan Rao. That he did at the cost of his service and ultimately Raghunath Rao was dethroned. A historian of Marathas observed: "thus once is a way both Raghunath Rao and the public realized what power the silent judiciary possessed in a well governed state and what support it has to its preservation."[6] An honest judge does not care about his personal interest. The strong, convincing, freedom loving and bold judgment of H.R. Khanna J. made him immortal. He knew the result of his judgment—more suppression. He knew the cost of his free and fair judgment: "it was plain to me that my colleagues were going to accept the contention of the Attorney-General. It was also plain that if I gave the judgment as I was contemplating, I would have to lose the office of Chief Justice of India as the then incumbent of office was due to retire in some months' time and I was next to him in seniority."[7] On April 12, 1976 Khanna, J. had told his younger sister, "Santosh, I have prepared a judgment which is going to cost me the Chief Justiceship of India."[8] As a great judge he scarified Chief Justiceship for the sake of rule of law. In famous *Habeas Corpus case* he delivered the Judgment with note: "What is at stake is the rule of law. If it could be the boast of a great English judge that the air of England is too pure for a slave to breathe, can not we say with justifiable pride that this sacred land shall not suffer eclipse of the rule of law and that the Constitution and

6. Sir Desai, New History of Marathas, Vol. II, pp. 30-33.
7. H.R. Khanna, Neither Roses Nor Thorns, p. 79.
8. *Ibid.*, p. 80.

laws of India do not permit life and liberty to be at the mercy of absolute power of the Executive, a power against which there can be no redress in Courts of law, even if it chooses to act contrary to law or in an arbitrary and capricious manner."[9]

Justice Khanna lost Chief Justiceship of India. But, what he got many Chief Justiceships will not be equated. His portrait in American Bar and above all the praise of even opposite litigants' advocates could not check themselves from expressing great admiration of Justice Khanna. For example, Mr. Niren De, Attorney General, who had won *Habeas Corpus case*, expressed words of great appreciation: "Judge, may I express my admiration and congratulations to you for that great Judgment."[10] The importance of a Judge Quality in Judges is always required: ONCE A JUDGE ALWAYS AND EVERYWHERE A JUDGE. The Law Commission of India, headed by the first Attorney General 'Mr. Law'—M.C. Setalvad said: "If the public is to give profound respect to the judges, the judges should, by their conduct try and deserve it—not only in the performance of his duties but outside the court as well, a judge has to maintain an aloofness amounting almost, to self-imposed isolation". The considered opinion of the Commission was that:

> "It has to be realized that if the public is to believe that justice is being impartially administered judges can rub shoulders with and all in a manner which any other person may do. Their public activities and even their pronouncements outside the court have to be consistent with the isolation which their office demands."[11]

The Commission's Report has echo of what the great Judge Holmes on his elevation to the Supreme Court did. On his appointment Mr. Owen Wister, his friend expressed his desire to entertain him in Bar of quality. for a drink. He tactfully but firmly refused by saying that "I do not some how

9. A.D.M. Jabalpur *v.* Shiva Kant Shukla, AIR 1976 S.C. 1207.
10. Neither Roses Nor Thorn, p. 82.
11. The Law Commission of India, 14th report, 1958, Vol. I, pp. 101-02.

agree to the notion of judge hobnobbing in hotel bars and saloons."[12] Reinforcing the idea of once a judge, always a judge and everywhere a judge, Justice Jagannatha Shetty upholding the removal of a judicial officer who was caught in copying at LL.M Examinations, observed:

> "Judicial officers can not have two standards, one in the court and another outside the court. They must have only one standard of rectitude, honesty and integrity. They can not even remotely be unworthy of the office they occupy."[13]

Not only this, judges are ideal of the social inspirational conduct and their conduct is expected to be exemplary and superb. High tradition and higher standard than the others is essential. To quote K. Ramaswami J. in *Ravichandra Iyer v. A.M. Bhattacharjee*,[14] "the standard of conduct is higher than that expected of a layman and also higher than that expected of an advocate. In fact, even in his private life must he adhere to high standard of probity and propriety, higher than those deemed acceptable for other."[15] The reason behind the expectation of high standard is due to obvious reasons: (1) Judicial office is essentially an office of public trust and therefore, high integrity, honesty, moral vigor, ethical firmness and imperviousness to corruption or venial influences is requirement of society from the judge, and (2) to keep the stream of justice clean and pure, the judge must be endowed with sterling character, impeccable integrity and upright behaviour.[16]

A note of caution was issued by the Supreme Court of

---

12. The Mind and Faith of Justice Holmes, 1974 XXIX.
13. Daya Shanker *v.* High Court of Allahabad, AIR 1978 S.C. 1469.
14. (1955) 5 SCC 457.
15. *Ibid.*, p. 473, see also Krishnaswami *v.* Union of India (1992) 4 SCC 605.
16. Anirudh Prasad, Principles of the Ethics of Legal Profession in India, 2006 p. 14.
17. (2005) 1 SCC 1.

India in *Tarak Singh* v. *Jyoti Basu*.[17] The court reminded of its place in society as repository of public faith, trustee of the people and last hope of the people. It observed:

> "It is high time the judiciary must take utmost care to see that the temple of justice does not crack of inside, which will lead to a catastrophe in the justice delivery system resulting in the failure of the public confidence in the system. We must remember that woodpeckers inside pose a larger threat than the storm outside."

Judiciousness, circumspection, self-discipline and eternal vigilance are needed lest the judiciary suffers from self-inflicted moral wounds.[18]

The ideal of justice—blindfoldness—the silent speaker of impartiality, aloofness, equality, prejudicelessness, ignorance and fairness, sword in one hand—authorityful enforcement of law and vindication of the majesty of law and balance with lifted scales—an utter sense of impartial justice what judge RUFUS CHOATE elaborates, "if on the one side, the executive power and the legislature and the people, the sources of his honor, that givers of his daily bread and on the other individual nameless and odious, his eye is shut to see neither great nor small, all ending only to the "trepidation of the balance", can be achieved only if the courts have the co-operation of able advocates and noble justices.

In backdrop of such high ideals but cracks both from inside and outside courts, the book authored by Mr. Rajneesh Kumar Patel under caption *"Administration of Justice in India: Ethics and Accountability"* is most timely, lively, thought provoking and suggestive of all round introspections—from people, people at the helm of affairs, advocates and justices themselves. The author has narrated well the history of the tradition of bar in India and abroad, urge of bar autonomy and integratedness on All-India basis, the high tradition of judicial impartiality and uprightedness. The main thrust of the book is cracks in legal profession of advocacy, recalcitrant behaviour of advocates heading towards professional and other misconducts under section 35 of the Advocates Act, 1961 as well as

18. State of Rajasthan *v*. Prakash Chand (1998) 1 SCC 1.

contempt of court under Articles 129 and 215 of the Constitution of India dealing respectively with the contempt of the Supreme Court and contempt of the High Courts, strike, boycott and putting hurdle in functioning of the court is becoming the culture of the Bar—unwieldy bar.

The author has extensively dealt with and given the critical account of the advocates' duties towards client, court, opposite party's advocate and the litigants and has established well the advocates' duties to fairness, respectfulness and service mindedness towards the society. But the author has exposed the not upto mark conduct of advocates in courts, i.e. to say imputation of partiality, allegation of corruption, unsavory language, threatening, instances of misleading the court, corrupting administration of justice, disrespectful behaviour towards the court, etc. The author has also exposed the corruption and unbecoming behaviour of the judges like unseemly behaviour of the judge, abusing the decorum of the court, insubordination by attributing bias on superior judge, etc. The author has lamented the unruly behaviour of the advocates and has come with a number of suggestions to deal with the deteriorating condition of bar. The author has also lamented the loosing of confidence in the judiciary and has critically examined the unsatisfactory working of in-house procedure in a number of cases. He has also pointed out the impractibility of the impeachment process given under Article 124 of the Constitution of India. The author has very well evaluated the suggestibility and effectiveness of the Judges' Inquiry Bill, 2006.

The overall situation of the court and the bar is not satisfactory. Neither the advocates have stood upto the mark nor have the judges proved to be above board. Both for the judges and the advocates the first and foremost quality is that they should be gentlemen, they enjoy respectability and prestigious position in the society. People take lessons from them. As former President of India, A.P.J. Abdul Kalam had pointed out about the judges, they are role model. To quote Dr. Kalam : "You are twenty-six (now thirty-one) judges of the Supreme Court, you are twenty-six role models of the judiciary for this nation of more than one billion people. People look up at you for indicating their grievances and for removal of injustice. You must come, upto their expectation."[19]

The melody is that there are so many allegations of corruption against the judges. Once upon a time the judges were conscious of their dignity and honour and would resign the post even on slightest allegation, but now there are judges who are ready to face impeachment (what to say of in-house procedure) in the belief that even they are corrupt, in peculiar political set-up of the country the removal motion would not be carried on in Parliament. The horrible condition of the judiciary was very much exposed by the former Chief Justice of India, Mr. Justice S.P. Bharucha, who stated that more than eighty percent of judges in the country were honest and smaller percentage was bringing the entire judiciary into disrepute. It means that in the eye of the former Chief Justice of India at least twenty percent of judges were not honest and were corruptible.

The author has very well exposed the recalcitrant attitude of the judges by citing Mr. Justice J.S. Verma, former Chief Justice of India who passed remark "today however, if after making a reasonable inquiry you find that there is something wrong and you tell the judge concerned, he will say... who are you to ask me to resign. . . . I have taken oath. That is the attitude."

The author has come with a number of suggestions. It is highly appreciable that many a suggestion made by the author two years earlier in his research work have found place in serious thinking for cleansing the court.

The present book authored by Dr. Rajneesh Kumar Patel will be very much helpful in giving serious thinking to the appointment procedure in relation to the superior courts (including rethinking about the role of the collegium) and will persuade to think afresh. Whether the time has not come to think over the present appointment process and switchover to the system of appointments through Judicial Appointments Commission on the pattern of the South Africa?

19. Quoted from Lahoti, R.C. (J.), "The Culture of Judges", available at www.judicialacademy.ac.in..

The book authored by Mr. Rajneesh Kumar Patel will be helpful to the law students, teachers of law, advocates and judges on the bench. It will be of utmost importance to the policy-makers and the persons at the helm of affairs who are concerned with making the process of administration of justice pure and just. I wish all success to the book and congratulate the author for such candid presentation of the national problem.

Anirudh Prasad

ANIRUDH PRASAD
Visiting Professor and Dean, Academic
Hidayatullah National Law University
Raipur, Chhattisgarh

Acknowledgements

Administration of justice is the foremost virtue of a civilized society. The author has given a serious thought to the present affaire of administration of justice and the two wheels of it. The time is both challenging and threatening as well as coming forward for changes at a time when the winds of change are blowing on the world plane.

The enterprise of such a justice seeking could not have been completed without the active co-operation and suggestion given by different legal persons. The author is indicated to all his colleagues and friends for proffering valuable suggestions and extending helping hands in completion of the book. This book is an outcome of the author's research work submitted by him for the award of Ph.D. in the Department of Law, D.D.U. Gorakhpur University, Gorakhpur. The author is very much thankful to his supervisor Prof. Anirudh Prasad who had been kind enough and co-operative in completion of the Ph.D. thesis as well as giving present shape to the present book. He has been kind enough to extend his blessings through writing a Foreword to the book with learned insight into the matter and upto date tendencies. The author owes a debt to him which a mere words of expressing the gratitude will not be sufficient.

The author is very much thankful to the library staff of B.H.U. and D.D.U. Gorakhpur University, Gorakhpur which have been co-operating in providing relevant materials. The author is thankful to his parent Shri Brahmachari Prasad,and

Smt. Yashoda Devi, brothers Shri L.B. Patel and Shri S.B. Patel and Bhabhis Smt. Usha Devi and Smt. Abha Shyam, and nephews Abhishek, Abhinav, Adamya, Aviral and Apurva without whose care and blessings it would not have been possible for the author to accomplish the work. I am also thankful to my better half Smt. Purnima and daughter Somil at whose cost of comfort and with active co-operation it has been possible for me to complete the present work.

The author is also thankful to his students Shri K.M. Gupta, S.K. Gupta and Sanjay Kumar for their active co-operation.

The author is also thankful to Sunil Kumar for his painstaking typing without blemish. At last the author is thankful to M/s. Deep and Deep Publications (P) Ltd. for publishing the book with attractive getup and promising publication. Every care has been taken to keep the book without blemish and upto date, however healthy comments are welcome.

R.K. Patel

RAJNEESH KUMAR PATEL

1

Introduction

GENERAL OBSERVATIONS

Since the dawn of civilization unending efforts have been made to establish order and security with a view to establish an ordered society for the betterment and welfare of the people. The very existence of the state came out of the feeling of insecurity prevailing in the early society and disorder resulting into chaotic situations. Contractarian theory of the State Justifies that people surrendered their right only for the sake of order and security in life. Order means some measure of uniformity, continuity and consistency in the operation of social process. Security relates to the contents of norms concerned with the protection of human beings against acts of aggression, spoliation and depredation with mitigating effects of certain hardships, vicissitudes and hazardous incidents to human existence.[1]

Security provides material value which justice in social relations must seek to promote. Safety of the people is said to

1. Edgar, Bodenheimer, *Jurisprudence,* 1974 (Indian reprint, 1997), p. 172.

be the supreme law.[2] In order to secure safety, security is to be ensured. Security ensures and makes possible the enjoyment of life, property, liberty and equality. It has been very aptly pointed out that "Human welfare demands at a minimum efficient order to ensure that such basic needs as food production, shelter and child rearing be satisfied, not in a state of constant chaos and conflict, but on a peaceful, orderly basis with a reasonable level of day to day security".[3]

Thus, security is one of the major components of justice which makes the justice a reality. Alongwith freedom and equality, justice is the prime value which is to be secured and maintained in all ordered and civilized societies. Since justice is an important motto of all governments, securing of justice is the prime concern of the State. With a view to ensure justice there is no better test of the excellence of a government than efficiency of its judicial system. In this way administration of justice is the firmest pillar of the government.

Administration of justice becomes the foremost job of the state as Salmond views 'the administration of justice implies the maintenance of right within a political community by means of the physical force of the state.[4] Without effective administration of justice one cannot think of the welfare, well-being and order in society. Justice is administered through the judicial organ of the government. Justice is administered according to law. As Chief Justice Coke pointed out, "*The wisdom of law is wiser than any man's wisdom*".[5] Legal profession represents the collective wisdom of the community.

Since justice is to be administered objectively and fairly in the modern state, the administration of justice according to law is commonly taken to imply recognition of fixed rules. But in some cases justice requires to be done even without law, i.e., fixed rules. Discretion plays vital role but even in such cases

---

2. Hobbes, Thomas, De Cive, ed. S.P. Lamprecht (New York, 1949), pt. II xiii 2.
3. Law and Order Re-consider: Report of the Tast Force on Law and Law Enforcement of the National Commission on the Cause and Prevention of Violence (Washington, 1970).
4. *Supra, note*, 1, p. 179.
5. Quoted from Lord Denning, *What Next in the Law*, 1982, p. 311.

discretion does not mean arbitrary use of one's own inclination. It means judicious exercise of fair wisdom to find out what is right and what is wrong.

In administration of justice the Courts of Justice play vital role. The administration of justice through courts involves the active, positive, constructive and meaningful cooperation between the advocates and the judges. In addition to them litigants also have to play their role. But, the two segments of the administration of justice—the courts and the counsels have to play dominant role. The real purpose of administration of justice can be achieved only through the well informed professional advocates and learned, efficient and independent judges. The traditions of legal profession also play very significant role in administration of impartial justice. It necessitates the imbibing of good qualities among the lawyers and the judges. In other words, Bench and Bar both have to maintain certain decorum and possess certain good qualities, so as to attract public confidence in the administration of justice.

Thus, judges have to maintain the image of goddess of justice, i.e., discarding party, friendship and kindred ensuring innocence, impartiality and fairness, keeping the sword of righteousness and balance with lifted scales, imbibe fairness, stand above suspicions, maintained decorum and civility. On the other hand, the advocate has to be reminded of the nobility of the profession and should maintain honesty, integrity, respect, cooperation, etc. justifying the gentleman of the long robe. The element of gentlemanship is essential, because the legal profession required confidence and well mannerism. It is said that a lawyer can be deferential without being abject; and independent and fearless without being disrespectful. The greatest amount of firmness can co-exist with an equal amount of grace and politeness. Neither truckle nor the truculent expresses the duty and the right.[6] In the similar vein Judges are always to be reminded that *"Justices come and go, but Justice itself should endure.*[7] It goes without saying that legal profession

6. Ayar, K.V. Krishnaswami, As quoted (in) Prasad, Anirudh, Principles of the Ethics of Legal Profession in India, 2006 ed., p. 101.
7. *Marsland v. Taggart* (1928) 2 K.B. 447 (Shearman J.).

is a noble, dignified and learned profession. As justice *Brandeis* of the Supreme Court of the United States pointed out it possesses three qualities, *first*, a profession is an occupation for which necessary preliminary training is essential in character involving knowledge and to some extent learning, as distinguished from mere skill. *Secondly*, it is an occupation which is pursued largely for others and not merely for one-self. *Thirdly*, it is an occupation in which the amount of financial return is not accepted measure of success.[8] The nobility of profession is maintained by the adherence and observance of professional norms by those who adopt the legal profession. It is termed as legal ethics or the ethics of the Legal Professions. As Chief Justice *Marshall* pointed out the fundamental aim of legal ethics is to maintain the honour and dignity of law profession, to secure a sprit of friendly cooperation between the Bench and the Bar in the promotion of highest standards of justice, to establish honourable and fair dealings of the counsel with his client, opponent and witness, to establish a sprit of brotherhood with the Bar itself and to secure that lawyers discharge their responsibilities to the community generally.[9] The status and responsibility of an advocate is very delicate as what is morally wrong cannot be professionally right, however it may be sanctioned by time and custom. The honourable position of the profession is very much dependent upon the observance of professional ethics. As is the case with the lawyers so is the case of justices because they are equally important segment of the legal profession. The Judges are expected to search the truth and be reminded of their duties on the high seat of justice. Depicting the image of a Judge *Mr. Baker,* a very famous lawyer of America and Secretary of War during the First World War pointed out:

> "A man of learning who spends tirelessly the weary hours after midnight acquainting himself with the great body of traditions and the learning of law. A man who bears

8. Quoted from Iyer, V.R. Krishna, "Profession for the People: A Third World Perspective (in) XV (1998) I.B.R., pp. 221-22.
9. *Id.*, p. 222.

himself in his community with friends but without familiarities, almost lonely, devoting himself exclusively to the most exacting mistress that man ever had, the law as a profession in its highest reaches where he not only interprets the law, but applies fearing neither friend nor foe, fearing only one thing in the world, that in a moment of abstraction, or due to human weakness he may in fact commit some error and fail to do justice. *That is the Judge*".[10]

The honourable justices have to be reminded of the guiding principles that an independent and honourable judiciary is indispensable for justice in our society and there can be nothing of great consequence than to keep the stream of justice clean and pure. A very correct idea behind the honourable justices of the highest court, is expressed in the words of the U.S. Supreme Court Judge, Mr. Justice *Jackson* "we are final, not because we are infallible, we are infilliable because we are final",[11] or what Mr. Justice *Gajendragadkar*, a honourable Judge of the Supreme Court of India (as he then was) once expressed in a speech delivered at Allahabad that "the only correct Judgement is one from which no appeal lies".[12]

Thus, with a view to ensure confidence of masses in the administration of justice maintaining the dignity and majesty of law as well as requirement of a civilized welfare state, the proper cooperation between the Bench and the Bar with high quality of integrity, honesty, fairness and sense of justice is essential. As the advocates have to maintain more decorum and etiquette than what is expected of a common man, so the Judges have to be vigilant and remember that—"*once a Judge always and everywhere a Judge*".[13]

The necessity of the maintaining of decorum and ethics and thereby requiring accountability of lawyers as well as

10. Quoted from Prasad, Anirudh, Principles of the Ethics of Legal Profession in India, 2006 ed., p. 7.
11. Sarkar, Modern Advocacy, p. 129.
12. Speech Delivered at the Gathering of Allahabad High Court Bar.
13. *Supra* note 10, p. 13.

Judges is more desirable in Anglo-Saxon system of Common Law countries like United Kingdom, United State of America and India than the continental or Civil Law countries. The reason being that in continental legal system Cannon Law prevails. In Civil Law tradition the Statutory Law or codification plays vital role. Though even in countries like France the high traditions of Bench and Bar is required but the magnitude of such requirement increases in common Law countries because of the supremacy of common law in which the courts play very important role. The precedent finds due importance. Therefore, the high expectation of decorum from the Bench and Bar in India is more needed because it fallows the common law traditions of United Kingdom and United States of America.

History is witness that advocacy has played very important role and has provided justice to many persons saving the life from wicked, crook and evil persons.

We may very well be reminded of the role of advocacy in the famous Shakespearean drama *"The Merchant of Venice"*. One shylock had lent money three thousand ducats for three months free of interest. But on default he had a bond from Antonio to give a pound of flesh. He pressed the case too far on default and death of Antonio appeared to be imminent, if the band of a pound of flesh was executed. The lawyer's mind of Portia made all efforts to resolve the issue by a very emotive appeal to mercy as an attribute to God himself. Having failed from all corners of appeal for merciful justice, she searched flaw by noting difference between 'flesh' and 'blood'. She went on to consider the letter of the bond and held it was contrary to public policy that it should be enforced, because it could not be achieved without the spilling of blood. Then came her celebrated argument—

> "Tarry a little; there is something else. This bond doth give thee here no jot of blood; the words expressly are a pound of flesh; Take then thy bond, take thou thy pound of flesh. But, in cutting it if thou dost shed one drop of Christian blood, thy lands and goods are, by the law of Venice, confiscate unto to State of Venice".

The lawyer's mind of Portia saved the life of Antonio and thereby set a milestone in the field of administration of Justice. She also brought counter charge against Shylock on the ground that he had been guilty of a criminal offence.[14]

History is also witness that the lawyers and the judges have played vital role in liberation of countries and doing service to the people. In England the Bench and Bar personnel had played very important role in struggle of power and assertion of sovereignty of the people through Parliament. Similar was the case in United States of America. In our country too the role of great lawyers like Motilal Nehru, Madan Mohan Malviya, Ballabhbhai Patel, C.R. Das and Mahatma Gandhi himself alongwith some of the Judges like, Sir Ashutosh Mukherjee, Ranade, etc. is always to be remembered.

Thus, the role of Bench and Bar in administration of Justice, nation creation and building has always to be recognized. It is the high position of the legal profession which inspired Edmond Burk to observe that: "The law is one of the first and noblest human sciences, a science which does more quicken and invigorate the understanding than all the other parts of learning put together".[15] In the same vein Edward Coke remarked, "there is no Jewell in the world comparable to learning; no learning excellent, both for prince and subject as the knowledge of law".[16] Such compliments represent the very high idea about the law and the men of law adorning the Bench and the Bar.

Nothing inspires respect, dignity and confidence than the introspection, sense of commitment towards the profession and accountability of the persons who are involved in the profession. The accountability of persons belonging to bar is envisaged through adherence of the code of conduct evolved and reduced in writing by the Bar Associations themselves. The accountability of the Judges is envisaged through (i) the requirement of giving decisions with reasons, and (ii) removal of judges for judicial misconduct.

14. *Id.*, p. 55.
15. *Supra* note 10, p. 56.
16. *Ibid.*

STATEMENT OF PROBLEMS

The upto mark functioning of the courts with proper cooperation of the Bench and the Bar ensures the seat of justice as the seat of God. But the 21st century phenomena of administration of justice compels to remark that God is not in his Heaven and everything is not right with the world. The high tradition of Bar is getting eroded day-by-day. More than often the incidents of delinquent behaviour on the part of advocates are reported in news papers. Honesty, courage, industry, wit, eloquence, judgement, fellowship, tact and other qualities of a good lawyer are withering away and misuses of professional status are increasing day-by-day. A tendency of converting legal profession into a trade or business is increasing very fast. Lord *Bolingbroke* once remarked of legal profession that "it is in the nature of noblest and most beneficial to mankind, and in its abuse the most sordid and most pernicious".[17] Similar feelings were expressed by the great American lawyer *Daniel Webester* when he said, "our profession is good if practised in the sprit of it; it is a damnable fraud and inequity when its true sprit is supplemented by mischief-making and money-making".[18] Commercialization has over-shadowed professionalisation. There is prevalence of misuse within the profession bringing disrepute and decay in the professional attitude. There are instances of using trick or deceiving the court or attempting to gain for client by dishonest means. There are also number of cases of unfair dealing of lawyers with the clients' money. In 1971 Gujarat Legal Aid Committee very aptly depicted the situation: "Today, we find that the law of supply and demand operates in all its naked form in the legal profession. There is practically no limit to the fees which a lawyer may charge to his client. If a litigant wants to engage one of the top most lawyers, he would have to pay the most exorbitant fees which may be demanded by the lawyer. This directly leads to

17. *Supra* note 10, p. 70.
18. *Ibid.*

inequality in the quality of legal representation as between the rich and the poor".[19]

There was a time when the word from a lawyer was treated by Judges as the last word, but the trust fading, the indulgence in falsehood, concealment, trickeries and fabrication to satisfy the clients and snatching more and more money is becoming order of the day and resulting into loss of respect and inviting scorn. The incidents of misappropriation of client's money and neglect of duty on the part of lawyers are not the only cases bringing disrepute to the lawyers in society, there are incidents of committing contempt of court, showing disrespect to the court, etc. and sometimes even attacking on the presiding officer of the court. Such incidents are adding bad name to the lawyers and the legal profession. The professional or other misconducts are committed by the advocates and autonomy of the Bar to discipline the recalcitrant advocates is not proving efficient and effective.

The problem of corruption and misbehaviour in relation to the honourable bench has remained no more a hidden fact. More than often the incidents of misbehaviour of the Judges are reported in the press and the corruption is rampant. The high expectation from the Judges that "Judges as trustees must give and account for their conduct" is getting belied. Judicial accountability is not properly enforced. Even some of the Judges themselves have exposed the situation of rampant corruption in Judiciary. In 2002 in his address to Bar, the then Chief Justice of India Mr. Justice S.P. Bharucha stated that more than 80% of the Judges in the country were honest and smaller percentage was bringing the entire Judiciary into disrepute.[20] It means that in the eye of the Chief Justice of India at least about 20% Judges were not honest and were corruptible. The other Chief Justice of the Supreme Court of India Mr. Justice J.S. Verma after his retirement admitted that there is no point in saying that there is no corruption in the Judiciary. No one is going to say it, much less accept it. One cannot go on sweeping it under the carpet and not expect to show. It is showing now. The moral sanctions are belied. There was a

19. Madhav Menon, N.R., Editorial X(4) I.B.R. IV.
20. (2002) 2 S.C.A.L.E. J-1.

time when Judges had sense of propriety, dignity and self-respect. To quote the former Chief Justice, J.S. Verma, Mr. Shiv Prasad Sinha, a Judge of the Allahabad High Court faced certain allegation that some of his Judgements appeared to be made for extraneous consideration. The self-respecting Judge resigned. It is also said of another High Court Judge who faced the charge of forging his date of birth and having won the case on technical point in the Supreme Court, resigned on the advice of the then Chief Justice of India.[21] But time is over and such incidents have become rare. A very alive, correct and informing situation has been depicted by Mr. Justice J.S. Verma, the former Chief Justice of India, when he remarks, "today however, it after making a reasonable inquiry you find that there is something wrong and you tell the Judge concerned, he will say ... *who are you to ask me to resign ... I have taken the oath*. That is the attitude".[22] Honestly speaking social sanction does not work.

The problem of recalcitrant behaviour and erosion of ethics is becoming more and more acute. The necessity of research is imminent both in the field of professional behaviour of the Bar and the Bench. With respect to the professional and other misconduct of advocates it is desirable to narrate the high tradition of Bar, to discuss the mechanism evolved for disciplining recalcitrant and delinquent advocates through the Bar Council of States and Bar Council of India, i.e. self-regulating procedure, to critically examine whether the control mechanism has worked well or has proved to be unsuccessful and if so what suggestion can be put forward in this direction. With respect to the Judicial corruption and misbehaviour it becomes imperative to deal with the problem whether the Constitutional control mechanism envisaged to discipline the cases of misbehaviour of the superior court

21. *Jyoti Prakash Mittar v. Union of India*, A.I.R. 1963 S.C. 735.
22. Shivani, "There's Corruption in Judiciary it's Showing Now: J.S. Verma", available at www.expressindia.com., visited on 05.06.06.
23. Sonawala, R.K., Advocacy; its Principles and Practices, Tripathi Publication, 1960.
24. Goswami, B.K., *Legal Profession and its Ethics*, 1995, Gururajachari, *Advocacy and Professional Ethics*, Wadhwa & Company, ed. 2000.

Judges has worked well, if not what can be done in this respect? Whether the proposed Judicial (Inquiry) Bill, 2006 will fulfil the need of the efficacy of the self-control mechanism? As regard the incidence of corruption and conduct short of misbehaviour of the superior court Judges envisaged to be controlled through judicially evolved in-house procedure has worked well or not is the most alive issue. The imminent problem with respect to the decline of both Bench and Bar is to enquire into and make a thorough study with a guideline "when moral sanctions have not worked, the legal sanctions are imperatively required". It also needs to be studied whether alongwith the amendment of the Judges Inquiry Act, 1968, Article 124 of the Constitution itself needs amendment, because it provides for impeachment which is very difficult. But what is needed is to make the Judges accountable so that in cases of aberrations there should be some solution to remove that aberration. At present we have none.

Paradoxes in Administration of Justice: Breaking Wheels

1. The legal profession has always been kept in high esteem but the individual advocates have earned nick name.
2. The major factors deteriorating the condition of the sense of accountability of Bench and Bar has been the uncontrollable mushroom growth of Law colleges and lack of proper legal education resulting into flood of advocates without tradition of judicial decorum and commercialization of the profession.
3. There is tendency towards the need of inclusion of superior court Judges too in the definition of 'Judge' as defined under the Contempt of Courts Act, so as to bring the conduct of the judges of High Courts and the Supreme Court also within the purview of the contempt of court.
4. The self-disciplinary control mechanism ensuring discipline among advocates through the State Bar Council and the Bar Council of India has not worked satisfactorily and well.

5. The in-house procedure evolved by the judiciary itself as a self-regulatory measure to deal with the blamed Judges has not worked effectively.
6. The constitutionally envisaged impeachment procedure to deal with Judges' misbehaviour has proved to be impracticable and therefore, a total failure.
7. The judicial accountability has been underscored in view of the overriding value of the independence of the judiciary and unwritten norms appear to prevail over the norms written under the Constitution or the Statues.

THE OBJECTIVE OF THE BOOK

The object of the book is limited to the inquiry and study of the professional ethics and their observance or defiance on the part of the honourable members of the Bench and Bar. Therefore, the study will not cover the area of the organization and independence of judiciary. The book veers around and will be connected with the issue relating to the conduct of the members of Bench and Bar, control mechanism to discipline them, their efficacy or otherwise, so on so forth. In view of the importance of the subject, paucity of any systematic work on the topic and too much incidents of professional or other misconducts relating to the bar as well as bench and mount of decisions on the point, the length of study cannot be avoided and the book is bound to become lengthy. The main objectives of the book are:

1. To spell out the code of conduct, written or unwritten, for the members of Bench and Bar.
2. To study the cases of the breach of professional or other conducts amounting to the violation of professional ethics.
3. To present the study of the conduct of errant Judges necessitating action against them.
4. To spell out control mechanism and its efficacy and desirability.

5. To suggest remedies with a view to check the cases of errant behaviour on part of justices and ensure accountability.

SCHEME OF THE BOOK

The book has been divided into nine chapters. Chapter I will introduce the essentiality of the role of the Bench and Bar in administration of justice with its high traditions.

Chapter II will deal with the historical account of legal profession and traditions of impartial administration of justice in different common law countries based on Anglo-American jurisprudence including the countries like England, United States of America and India. It will present a detailed account of legal profession in different era alongwith steps towards the meaningful autonomy and unification of Bar in light of such provisions under Advocates Act, 1961.

Since traditions play vital role in governing the conduct of people in all walks of life. Chapter III of the book will be devoted to the study of high tradition and nature of legal profession.

As is the case with Bar so is the case of Bench, therefore, Chapter IV will be devoted the High tradition and image of judiciary alongwith the factor deteriorating the image of judiciary and recent issue regarding transparency in view of the *Right to Information Act.*

With a view to keep the stream of justice pure and clean professional ethics of Bench and Bar will form the subject of the book in Chapter V. A brief sketch of professional ethics, necessity of codification and professional norms for the members of Bench and Bar will be analysed in this chapter. It will also cover the discussion of certain unresolved and controversial issues like acceptance or refusal of brief of accused whom the advocate knows to be guilty and acceptance of brief or refusal of accused of anti-national and terrorist activities.

Chapter VI will be devoted to study of professional and other misconducts envisaged as means of imposing discipline on the members of Bar under Section 35 of the Advocates Act, 1961. It will cover the wide range of misconducts of advocates in relation to clients and courts alongwith contempt of courts.

As corollary to the professional misconduct of advocates Chapter VII will cover the study of deteriorating health of the judiciary and increasing incidents of unbecoming behaviour of the judges. A very alive and topical issue is emerging in view of the unbecoming conduct of superior courts judges in relation to the courts themselves; whether the superior courts judges still need to be left out of the preview of the contempt of courts. The book will devote space for the inquiry on this issue.

Since the contempt of court is essential for ensuring the dignity of the court it will be dealt at length at different places with relation the advocates and judges. Thus it will form part of Chapters VI and VII and proceedings there for in Chapter VIII. But study will be limited to contempt of court committed by advocates and judges only and not by the general public.

Chapter VIII of the book will cover the study and critical evaluation of the mechanism provided for maintaining accountability of advocates through disciplinary proceedings of the State Bar Councils and the Bar Council of India, alongwith the appellate jurisdiction of the Apex Court. It will also cover the contempt cases in relation to advocates and providing procedure to deal with them. It will also include study of the efficacy of the self-regulating measures disciplining the advocates. It will further cover the different mechanism like in-house procedure and impeachment to deal with the misbehaviour of Judges for ensuring their accountability. In this connection a detailed discussion on judges (Inquiry) Bill, 2006 is proposed to be taken up.

Chapter IX will conclude the book will try to give suggestions in this regard.

2

Historical Account of Legal Profession and the Tradition of Impartial Administration of Justice

As a social and rational creature man can live only in association with fellowmen of the society. The ordered society needs disciplined behaviour of all. It has been aptly said that the restraining influence is essential to growth, to security and to character. Without the limit of law, the ownership of property would cease and men would contend for their share as the wolves divide their substance. Without the restraint of law the trees might grow and reach above the sky, and without the limit of law, the ambition of man, with his present environment would never cease, till he managed the earth and stood above the sun.

Thus, the law makes us, keeps us, rules us, gives us hope for effort and reward. 'It leaves man within its limits to work out mighty plans and accomplish result'.[1] However, in the primitive ages when society had not developed its formulated strength, the necessity of law had little importance. In those times might was right and physical power was the foundations for all claims—claim to food, to shelter and to pleasing possession of women. As society developed, need to curb the mighty with his greed, his lust and his ambition arose. The conflict between man to man was the natural outcome of this ambition. Thus there was an urgent need for the regulation of those conflicting interests with the help of law and the law knowing persons. In absence of it, it would have never been possible to protect the weaker persons of the society.

The concept of protection of the weak, the helpless, the unprotected, from the subjection of the strong and powerful came into existence. A class arose which lacked in physical prowess, but excelled in intellectual capacities, and this class gradually evolved moral codes to subdue the mighty and to protect the weak against acts of the former, prompted by greed, lust and selfishness.[2]

With a view to extend helping hands to needy and oppressed persons some great men emerged who pursued advocacy as a profession. The institution of trained lawyers who might be engaged by the litigants to appear on their behalf in the law courts is of ancient origin in Europe as well as in the East. But, before it took proper shape it had to over a long way. For centuries together legal knowledge was the monopoly of priests, who only had the right to appear on behalf of the clients.

Though Advocacy in this form was known in Europe and East but it was unknown in Greece, where only relatives were allowed to speak on behalf of litigants. Later on friends and relatives were allowed to speak on behalf of litigants who were ill or were prevented by other means to appear in the court for any reason.[3] In Rome the legal profession took its earliest form

1. An address of Nageshwar Prasad, former Judge of Patna High Court, to the Annual General Meeting of the Patna Law College, held at Patna on 6th October, 1961.
2. Jenks, Edward, *Short History of English Law*, 1912, p. 198.
3. Cohen Herman, *History of the English Bar and Attornatus to 1450*, (1929), pp. 38-40.

in the relationship between the *patron* and his client. Originally *patrons* were appearing in court to expound the law in court for his client, when his liberty or property was threatened and before that court addresses were prepared for clients by legal experts.

In the course of time when transactions became more complicated, there arose two new classes of persons conversant with law who were known as *jurisconsults* and *agents*. The *jurisconsults* were supposed to give legal advice out of court and the *Agent* was permitted to appear for the parties in the courts. Originally money was not the consideration for giving legal advice or assistance and in most of the cases it was a means of influence or to get popularity.

Against this background an attempt is made here to discuss and examine the short history of legal profession in common law countries like U.K. and U.S.A. which have influenced to a large extent the development of legal profession in India.

I. HISTORY OF THE LEGAL PROFESSION IN ENGLAND

In England the early history of the legal profession is still a little vague. At the time of Norman Conquest[4] there was no class of professional advocates and no organization of entitlement body of bar in England. Even before this time it was common for a party to have assistance in the conduct of his case but the help was given by a friend and not by professional expert. During the two hundred years of succeeding the *Conquest emerged.* This practice developed a class of legal advisors increasingly experienced and competent in legal technicalities.[5]

It was really in the reign of Henry II[6] that the first foundations of the common law were truly laid. This reign was

4. The Norman Conquest is a catastrophe which determined the whole future of English law. We can make but the vaguest guesses as the kind law that would have prevailed in England of 13th century. For detail, see Pollock and Maitland, p. 179.
5. *Supra* note 3, p. 49.
6. Before the year of 1272.

remarkable in legal development for two things. Here the first book of English law was produced. The book is known as 'Glanvil' and is entitled *'de legibus Angliae'*. Secondly, Henry II took steps both to administer the criminal law under royal auspices and to provide for the determination of disputes in civil matters by royal judges.

During that period, however, a different type of assistance became necessary. The growing complexity of common law and the procedure developed in common law courts called for more expert help and consequently the unpaid friend[7] came to be replaced by the professional pleader or narrator, who conducted the oral pleadings and argued question of law on behalf of his client. When the defendant appeared to the writ the next stage was for the plaintiff to expound in greater detail the nature of his claim and defend it against various objections made by the defendant. This was known as "counting" or "narrating" and it became usual for both parties to civil litigation to employ counters or narrators to conduct this technical part of the case. In criminal trials the development was different and the prisoner in trials for felony had no right to the advice of an advocate for some centuries.[8]

In 1181, certain persons having clerical training were appointed as Attorneys, but their functions were not defined. After some year in England a new class of legal practitioners emerged. It may be noted in this regard that the actual history is not very clear and authentic. In the period about 1300 A.D. we find the term Serjeant-at-law, applied to pleaders. But whether it was used for all or to some only, is not certain. It became clear some how in the reign of Edward Ist when the order of Serjeants was created who could appear in courts to represent litigants. For several centuries in England this privilege of being represented by Serjeants did not extend to prisoners charged with felony. This position of anomaly could

7. While they would not sue for fee for help in the litigation, but expected and received a reward in the form of honorarium.
8. *Supra* note 3, pp. 18-34. In 1158-63, the counsel were not, however allowed to plead for the accused, in the gravest cases. The party went to trial *cum amicis et a uxillis meis,* the consilium.

be removed only in 1836 when the Serjeants were allowed to defend the accused of felony too.

The Serjeants had the sole right of audience in the common bench. For a long time the judges remained members of sergeants. The serjeants, who were usually chosen from the Benchers and Readers, and had a rank equal to a Knight, had their own Inn, called the Serjeant's Inn, to which the judges, who had been Serjeants, also belonged, and hence addressed the Serjeants as brother.[9]

By the end of the 14th century the Serjeants-at-law formed a close body or guild selected by the crown, generally upon the nomination of the judges, from which the ranks of the bench were recruited. Candidates having practised at least sixteen years could be elevated to the Bench. Until 1834 Serjeants had a monopoly of practice in the common pleas but were not retracted to it. They could appear in the court of common pleas and the judges were appointed exclusively from their order and remained members of it even after appointment. The Serjeants sat in court within the bar (a barrier of iron or wood) they were addressed by another (even the eldest by the youngest) by their surnames without Mr. They earned large fees, but some barristers were reluctant to become Serjeants and had to be forced to do so or pay fines.[10] The order of Serjeants was finally abolished in 1877 and thereafter the senior barristers are named as Queen's counsels.

The origins of the Inns of courts are also not very clear. In the reign of Edward Ist it were established in proximity of courts for the training of apprentice in law. There were incorporated societies and private teaching foundations of residential character. Though they were subject to the visitorial jurisdiction of judges, they were in all other respects autonomous societies. It finally coalesced into the four Inns of Court-Gray's Inn, Lincoln's Inn, Inner Temple and Middle temple.

9. Holdsworth, *History of English Law,* IInd ed., p. 261.
10. In addition to the Serjeant there were other pleaders, who might be considerable, but who nevertheless were ranked merely as apprentices alongwith those were skill at stage of student.

In each Inns of Court there was a governing body of leading members called "Benchers". They acted as judges in the moot or mock courts which constituted one of the main methods of instructing students. The governing body of each Inn were conferred the power of calling persons to the Bar and of disbarring or inflicting any other punishment on them for breaches of rules of professional etiquette.[11] The Inns of Court bore close analogies to the old Oxford and Cambridge colleges. Although some lawyers studied classics or Roman law at the universities the training at the Inns of Court in English law was very practical and was antagonistic to Roman influence.

Thus, the forgoing discussion reveals that, with the developments of the Inns of Court, the judges gave up direct control of admission to the rank of pleaders. The benchers of the Inn still have sole right in England of admitting to the bar and of disbarring those admitted, though the power is said to be delegated to them by the judges. The judges did not, however, abandon all control of legal education and particularly in the 16th century, they issued numerous general orders regulating the education, conduct and qualification of members of the Inns of Court.

It is to be noted in this regard that in 1292 Edward Ist ordered the judges to take steps to ensure that adequate numbers of skilled "apprentices" were available to argue cases in court. Some authors see in this the origin of the requirement of legal teaching for the novice barristers, who was known as an apprentice in medieval times and the origin of the ultimate disciplinary authority of the High Court Judges over barristers (on appeals from the Benchers of their Inns).[12]

The barrister remained a member of his Inn for life and used its library and dining-hall and social facilities while practising from his chambers in London or the larger provincial cities. Barristers often joined one of the seven circuit messes and practised at assizes or quarter sessions in the provinces. In the middle ages barristers were in direct professional contact with clients in many cases but the growing

11. Clive, Richard, *The Law and Conduct of the Legal Profession*, 2nd ed., 1963, p. 7.
12. *Id.*, p. 9.

separation of barristers from solicitors led to the development in different way. Since the 17th century, a barrister could not sue for his fees, and it had become etiquette that a barrister should not be consulted for reward by a lay client, but should be reached through a solicitor.

The attorney originated as a friend or advisor who undertook various steps such as the service of writs which were inconvenient for the client. Many litigants were monasteries or brought corporations who necessarily appeared through attorney as they were not natural persons. The crown also so appeared. The practice spread and by 1235 the power of attorney entitled the attorney to take steps in litigation binding on his client and to make admission of fact and statements of evidence to the barristers. From 1292 attorneys acting for reward had to be approved by the judges and in 1402 and 1605 new laws were passed for the examination of attorneys and their entry on court rolls.[13]

Thus, in the later middle ages the two branches of the profession were not so completely separated as they became apparent in following days. Attorney could remain members of the Inn of Court and until the end of the 17th century could be called to the bar of an Inn. Similarly, the court allowed them to plead their clients and preparatory sides of legal work as distinct from advocacy, came to be regarded as proper for attorneys, and this was reflected in the judges orders as to their training. Gradually the Inns of Court gave effect to the distinctions of function by excluding practising attorneys from a call to the Bar. The general result was that if a man intended to be an attorney he did not enter in Inn of court.

In addition to the barristers and attorneys there were also the Solicitors,[14] a distinct class who in the middle ages were not members of the legal profession. Solicitors began to appear as professional class in about 1450, but did not secure a recognized status until about fifty years later. Solicitors conducted legal business on behalf of another, but were neither

13. Maitland, W. Fredric, *English Legal History*, (1915), p. 95.
14. The term Solicitors were first used in dealing with the Chancery clerks in equity proceedings, but by 1605 they were on the same footing as the Attorneys in the Common Law Courts.

an attorney nor a barrister. They were associated mainly with the Court of Chancery and had their own Inns of Chancery. Early in the 18th century the solicitors substantially amalgamated with the attorneys.

It is interesting to note that the Barristers derived their authority to practice from the Inns of Court, while the roll of solicitors was kept by the incorporated Law Society. The requirement of articles of clerkship or apprenticeship dates from 1729 and since 1739 there is a fairly continuous record of professional organization, culminating in the Modern Law Society since 1903. The Law Society, under the Act of Parliament, examines for admission to the roll of solicitors, supervises their accounts and activities and strikes from the roll those guilty of unprofessional conduct.

The solicitors had little direct influence on case of law because County Courts and Magistrates Court decisions seldom created important precedents. His drafting of documents indirectly gave him influence, though difficult drafting problems might be referred to counsel. Barristers and Solicitors also exercised functions formerly belonging to another legal profession. This profession was the outcome of the claims of the Church to maintain its own courts, which in England at least were known distinctively as the Court of Christian. The judges and practitioners in those courts were not drawn from the ranks of the ordinary profession and they were called Advocates[15] and Proctors.[16] The Advocates and Proctors also practiced before the Court of Admiralty, whose rules of maritime law were based on Roman law.

To be an advocate it was necessary to be a Doctor of Law of the University of Oxford or Cambridge. On the other hand, Proctors like attorneys get qualified by a term of apprenticeship. Their small number and the specialized nature of their work on the whole made them a rather more exclusive body of practitioners than the attorneys who were their principal clients. Proctors had the right of audience in the

15. Equivalent to the Barristers.
16. Equivalent to the Solicitors.

provinces. Solicitors now performed many the duties formerly belonging to the Proctors.[17]

In the 18th century their branch of the profession was placed on its modern basis. A comprehensive Act was passed in 1729 which required service under articles for five years, provided for examination by the Judges, and also made some detailed provision as to costs.

It is important to note that in England till 1833 there was no organization of the entire body of the English Bar. In 1883 a representative "Bar Committee" was set-up. It was to express opinions of members affected by the profession. But that Bar committee was General Council of the Bar. However, supplementing the Inns of Court were two other organizations of barristers, viz. the General Council of the Bar and the Circuits. The General Council of the Bar formed in 1895, is a body elected from the Bar. It considers all matters affecting the profession including those of professional conduct, but in disciplinary matters while it may investigate complaints it has to refer cases to the Benchers of the Inn for appropriate action.[18]

Each circuit mess is a society consisting of barristers practising on the circuit. It lays down rules of professional etiquette for the members and supervises their professional conduct.

At present the legal profession in England is divided into two branches-solicitor and barrister. The solicitors are directly consulted by the client for advice on legal matters. He drafts wills and contracts, conducts the sale and purchase of land and advises on business matters with legal implications, e.g., the formation of companies. He has the "right of audience" in the lower courts. If litigation is in prospect in the superior courts the solicitor confers with a barrister of his choice and the barrister advises on the preparation of the case, draws up the pleadings and conducts the client's case in court. The solicitors as "professional client" instructs counsel on the facts expected to be proved and arranges the attendance of parties and

---

17. Boulton, W.W., *Conduct And Etiquette at The Bar,* 2nd ed., p. 19.
18. *Id.* p. 68.

witnesses.[19] He also conducts the machinery of issuing writs, exchanging pleadings, entering judgements and suing out execution of judgements. He is present if the barrister confers with the lay client.

The foregoing study shows that in England the legal profession is a developed and dignified profession. In the course of time and in view of experiences the work between the solicitors and barristers has got clearly divided. It is more similar to our system dividing works between senior advocates and others.

II. HISTORY OF THE LEGAL PROFESSION IN UNITED STATES

The American legal profession is the largest in the world. It is an integral, important and significant segment of the Administration of Justice that, in the United States over 6,500,000 lawyers[20] are practicing in the courts.

In order to understand the particular condition of the legal profession in the American colonies two things must be born in mind; *first*, a class of professional, and *second*, the social environment in which the lawyers work, because several American colonies were founded separately and were operated independently of one another, often on greatly different principles and for vastly different purposes. They did not pursue a common policy or follow a parallel development. Each colony had its own government, its own system of courts and in fact its own laws. The above reason and complex situation the history of legal profession in the United States is very complex and not as straight as it is in the United Kingdom.

However, the history of legal profession in U.S.A. may start with the 11th and 12th centuries. The legal profession in America, is viewed historically as a part of the family of western legal systems. Its main institutional and doctrinal foundations were laid in the late 11th and 12th centuries in the monasteries and universities and in the ecclesiastical and royal

19. *Supra* note 3, p. 56.
20. Most of the Chamber Practising lawyers.

households of western Christiandom. The Jurist of that era transformed the primitive Germanic and Frankish legal systems through the inspiration of Roman law of Greek philosophy, and of Hebrew and Christian ethics. Ultimately, diverse type of legal systems were built on these common foundations, but it is important to recognize that, as the English Statesman Edmund Burke said two hundred years ago "the law of every country of Europe is derived from the same sources".[21]

Thus the immediate parent of American legal system is English law, which the English colonists brought with them to the new world in the 17th and 18th centuries and which was formally received after the American Revolution by the various states of the union as foundation for their own law. Through this reception of English law the continuity of American law with the common western legal heritage was served. However, the paramount question whether or not the common law of England was binding upon the colonial courts was hotly debated for some time in every colony. In 1776 when the early 13 English Colonies on the Atlantic Coast declared their independence, they had become impatient of the British concepts of English common law, the system of judiciary in which as the expression *Aula Regis* indicated, the king dispensed justice and first hand which in later times become the king in council, which so far as the colonies were concerned, was represented by a standing committee of the Privy Council.[22]

This committee was more or less the same thing as the Court of Star Chamber, but since 1640 without the extraordinary penal jurisdiction which gave that body so evil a reputation for Americans. The attitude of the English Rulers was that there should be no departure in the colonies from the common law of England. This much, however, seems to be certain; with the possible exception of New Jersey, Virginia, Georgia and perhaps New York, where the common law of England was received at fairly early date and in a relatively

21. Pound, *A Hundred Years of American Law* (8), 1837, p. 17.
22. Goebel, *"Kings Law and Local Custum in England"*, 31, *Columbia Law Review*, 41 6ff. (1931).

complete manner. The colonists, as a rule, did not recognize the common law as *ipsofacto* binding upon their courts. Because of this general attitude each colony gradually developed a sort of common law of its own which often differed greatly from that of England as well as from that of any other colony.[23]

Moreover, the American legal profession, although its historical roots are in the English Inns of Court which trained some of the lending American lawyers of colonial times, has developed its own characteristic. However, that was not an one-day process and it has taken at least one hundred and fifty years of American legal profession. After the Revolution of 1688, the quality of colonial bar started improving with the advent of professionally trained English lawyers.[24] Barristers called to the Bar by the Inns of Court in England were in the main regarded as persons properly qualified to practise law in the American colonies. The English-trained lawyer usually had a considerable advantage over his American-trained brethren. As a rule, he had studied in the chambers of an experienced English barristers; he had attended the Readings and participated in the moots which were part of the educational programme provided by the Inns of Court; he had access to far better law libraries than those existing in America; and he had the opportunity of attending and taking notes in the courts in Westminster, which must be considered to have been the very heart of the common law.

About the year 1700 a number of competent professional lawyers began to arrive from England to the United States. Some of these men settled permanently in the colonies. Also, at approximately the same time a small native-born (though perhaps English-trained) bar began to make its wholesome influence felt. In 1725 there were to be found on the bench, at the bar, or in public office lawyers of prominence and real professional competence. Thus, it was the professional lawyer himself who improved the general situation and thereby improved his own condition.[25]

23. Haskins, *Law and Autority in Early Massachusetts*, 69, 163ff. (1960).
24. Goebel, *The Courts and the Law in Colonial*, New York, Ist ed., p. 3.
25. *Id.* p. 19.

However, the problems were to be faced by the American lawyers in the ways of developing a strong and healthy legal profession authoritative and competent, as well as accessible and understandable, legal materials—an important if not decisive factor not only for the unification and stabilization of the administration of justice but also for the development of a true legal profession—were solely lacking in the early American colonies. Although in the course of the eighteenth century this calamitous state of affairs improved somewhat, it remained one of the crucial problems in American legal history until the Revolution and beyond.

The early colonial era lawyers and courts were handicapped not only by the serious dearth of English law books and law reports but also by the absence or unavailability of printed copies of colonial statues. With the exception of Massachusetts and Connecticut, the colonies were late in printing their statutes: New York, in 1710; Rhode Island, in 1730; New Jersey, in 1732; Virginia, in 1733; South Carination, in 1736; Pennsylvania, in 1742; and Maryland, in 1765. And even where the statutes has been printed, it was unusual for the practitioner, except for the very rich lawyer, to possess a complete set of the statutes of his own colony, not to mention those of the other colonies.[26]

The emergence of a class of professional lawyers in colonial America was also hampered for a long time by the lack of proper training facilities for the native-born American. In America there were no collegiate lectures on law before 1780. In addition, the study of law was seriously handicapped by the dearth of competent law books and reports. During the seventeenth and eighteenth centuries there existed in England not only a number of treatises dealing with the study of the law as such but also several "outlines" showing how one should go about these studies. But it is well-nigh impossible to ascertain with any degree of certainly what law books or "study aids", if any, were used by law students in colonial America before the middle of the eighteenth century. It must be assumed, however, that some of the English lawyers, who, beginning with the latter part of the seventeenth century,

26. *Ibid.*

arrived in America in ever greater numbers to become judges, law officers of the Crown, or simply to engage in the private practice of law, either brought with them some law books, including some didactic law treatises which were at that time in use in England or ordered them to be sent from England. Until the very end of the 18th century, for reasons of expediency as well as the serious dearth of trained lawyers, it was simply necessary and, in some places even advisable to report to judges not familiar with the law. This was especially true in the lower courts, but the higher courts, including the Supreme Court of colony, also had their share of incompetent and often ill-tempered laymen.[27] It took a considerable time before sound legal training and experience was considered an essential prerequisite for colonial judges. As late as 1764 it was said that the gentlemen sitting on the benches of court of law in colonies, are not to be expected to be lawyers or learned in law.[28] Between 1691 and 1778 only seven of thirteen Chief Justices of New York had any degree of legal learning. Obviously, such a situation could not and in fact did not produce or support a strong and effective class of professional lawyers.

The position of Judges itself speaks of the lack of proper training and knowledge on the part of lawyers. When, in the course of the late 17th and early 18th centuries, trained lawyers became more numerous and more influential, the common law of England assumed a novel importance and with the increase in trained lawyers the courts began to display a greater inclination to turn to the traditional common law. It has been estimated that down to the American Revolution only about forty-eight legal treatises were printed in the Colonies, but none of these could be called a treatise intended for the use of the professional lawyer. They were in fact, meant for the use of laymen and designed to assist them in the everyday incidents of business and other affairs. Conversely, the few copies of Coke's Institutes,[29] which found their way to America

27. Pownall, *The Administration of the American Colonies* (1764) as quoted by Warren, *History of The American Bar* (1911), p. 15.
28. *Ibid.*
29. Published between 1628-44.

contained little useful information for the average Colonist or Colonial lawyer.

During the 18th century, lawyers through their professional and political activities brought about closer relations among the several Colonies, a factor which contributed greatly to the ultimate success of the revolution. The young men who, in Colonial times, went to study law at the Inns of Court, on their return became leaders in their respective communities. Due to their influence and competition, high standards of education, craftsmanship and conduct-established and maintained in the period immediately following the revolution. Many of the important features of American legal system were established prior to the great industrial expansion which followed the civil war. Of course, the enormous economic, political and social changes of the past one hundred years have been accompanied by corresponding changes in legal system of America.[30]

Thus, in the American Colonies in 18th century, the absolute distinction prevailing in England between Barristers and Solicitors broke down, because of a shortage of any kind of qualified lawyers. Yet a functional difference does exist today in American legal practice. Being a litigator is in practice a special branch of the American bar, and 80 percent of American lawyers never appear in court of trial. Another major difference between English barristers and American litigators is that barristers do not work out of corporate law firms. There are indeed no English firms of barristers in the American sense of a number of lawyers, who are corporate partners sharing annual yields or profits from the firms practice as a whole.

In the formative era of American laws, prior to the civil war of 1861-65, courts, lawyers and legal scholars reshaped and modernized basic legal concepts. Thus, it would be wrong to suggest that the rules of law worked out in that era were "modern" in the sense that they correspond to modern needs. The apprenticeship system gradually gave way in the 19th century to university education in law. At the same time, the

30. Howard Judith Chirlin, "Judicial Appointments In America", *J.I.L.I.*, Vol. 9(3), pp. 521-30.

faculty of American Universities constituted professional school maintaining close connections with the practising legal professionals. The great majority of 19th century American lawyers learned law by interning in a lawyer's office or were self-taught. The sprit of Jacksonian democracy militated against an academic training for lawyers. It was widely held that the profession should be open to any literate male.[31]

The upgrading in the quality of Harvard Law School under deans Christopher Columbus Langdell and Roscoe Pound between 1885 and 1925, and their insistence on the case method in which law was learned by close reading of Appeals Court ruling as well as greater attention to relationship between legal study and cognate university disciplines such as history and philosophy was a major turning point in the development of the American legal profession. Harvard was taken as the Model and other University-based law school rushed to imitate the "Langdell-Pound" System. By 1930 the majority of American lawyers were law graduates and by 1960 all had become law graduates.

Efforts made at Yale and Columbia University in the 1930 and 1940 to integrate legal study with the leading edges of the social and behavioural sciences had a modest and mostly epheral impact.

Thus, in America today there are 175 accredited law schools. They graduate around fifty thousand new lawyers a year, which is close to the size of the whole existing legal professionals in England.

It is clear from the foregoing discussion that the legal system of American is largely derived from England, but it has not followed the English practice in the organization of the legal profession. In America there is no formal division of the profession. They do not have barristers, or court room lawyers on the one hand and solicitors or office lawyers on the other. The lawyers of America are free to engage in any sort of legal activity and they may be in court one day and engaged in drafting legal papers the next.

31. In America, Women were not Admitted to the Bar until 1880 and Remained a Small Minority of the Profession Until 1960.

Indeed, the notion of the separation of the legal profession into different branches is so unknown in the United States, that most American lawyers have difficulty in understanding the English or French systems. Of course, there is a certain amount of specialization in the actual activities of many American lawyers but they are accustomed to doing whatever they feel their client needs and they feel qualified to do, and they find it hard to see how any other arrangement can be entirely satisfactory either to the lawyer or to his client.[32]

The foregoing discussion also reveals that, with relatively few exceptions, colonial America did not produce lawyers who were deeply learned in the law by the exacting English standard. The large majority of the colonial attorneys were little more than smatters and, perhaps admirers of the law. With the establishment of tradition of legal expertise a group of significant men developed in the form of lawyers claim special privileges in the society. This created another problem.

During the second third of the nineteenth century, however, there developed a growing hostility against special privileges granted by the government to the lawyers. Professions, and particularly bar associations, were deemed undemocratic and un-American. This manifested itself ever—were in a lowering of the required qualifications of character, education, and training. In a number of states statutes and even constitutional provisions were passed upholding the inherent and "natural" right of every voter of good moral character to practise law. In others the right of admission was assured after a brief period of study. There was also widespread objection to the organized bar as a "secret trade union" or a privileged class not open equally to all citizens. Even bar meetings, which had been primarily social gatherings of the legal fraternity, or to honour a distinguished judge or lawyer, usually decreased and were generally discontinued. In the period immediately after the Civil War, the bar reached its lowest ebb.[33]

About 1875 the leaders of the bar, realizing the deplorable condition into which their profession was falling, as well as the

---

32. Tulsi, K.T.S., "Legal Systems in India and America—A Comparative view", *A.I.R.(J)* 199, pp 81-85.
33. *Supra* note 30, p. 525.

imperative necessity of taking a firm stand against the rising tide of commercialism and the growing influence of those who would turn the profession from a "branch of the administration of justice" into a "more money making trade", began the movement for the reestablishment at the bar of standards of character, education, and training, and also for the organization of bar associations all over the country. This movement has grown and prospered until now in every state. It is recognized that for the protection of the public no one may practise law whose character has not been subjected to examination and found worthy, and who has not passed a prescribed test as to his education and legal training. These are not merely fraternal societies, holding annual dinners and memorial meetings, or trade associations for the material advancement of their members, but organizations devoted to the pursuit of a learned profession in the spirit of public service.

In twenty-five states the bar is "integrated", whether by statute or by authorized Rule of Court, whereby every practising lawyer must be a supporting member of the bar association and subject to its Canons and to discipline by it. In all the other states there are voluntary associations.

An Unified Bar Association also Came Into Existence

In United States of America, an Association, namely the American Bar Association was founded on 21-8-1878 in Saratoga springs, New York by hundred lawyers from 21 states, which has, now, Membership of more than 400,000. It is the world's largest voluntary professional Association. The influence of A.B.A., does not stem only from the large number of membership or its size, but its multi-dimensional activities and diversity and the quality of its membership. A.B.A.'s members represent approximately half of all lawyers in the whole of the United States.

There is one interesting feature in the membership of A.B.A. and it is individuals who are not allowed to practises law in any jurisdiction but who have an interest in the work of A.B.A. are, also, entitled to join A.B.A. as associates. The members of legal fraternity in other countries, who have not been admitted to practise law in the United States can, also become International Associates. Any law Student is, also, eligible to become a Law Student Member of the Association under such conditions and with such rights, privileges and limitations, as the bye-laws may provide. The professed mission of A.B.A. is to be the national representative of the legal profession serving the public and the profession, by promoting Justice, professional excellence and respect for law and justice.[34]

Through various organs and divisions, the A.B.A. undertakes study of variety of issues and formulates responses ranging from policy position to clearing house efforts. The members, who are involved in such activities are primarily, but not exclusively, lawyers who volunteer their services for the Association. A.B.A. has commenced hundreds of programmers involving and addressing diverse disciplines and various facets and faculties of life, including legal-aid, child abuse, problem of senior citizens, high cost of Justice, law practice management, Juvenile crime, information technology, environmental issues, free press, domestic violence, clinical education law teaching, and so on and so forth. While new programmers and initiatives are consistently increasing, an overview of current and recent activities undertaken by A.B.A. offers crashing profile, of the Association. The A.B.A. consist of more than 2200 individual entities and medium through which active work is done. There are 23 Sections, 5 Divisions, more than 80 commissions, committees and 6 Forums in the existing set up of the Association. The main object of such forums and entities is to addressing professional development improvement of laws and continuing education through the work of more than 1700 Committees, and issue publication of outstanding quality. Interestingly, A.B.A. is involved in publishing 30 Magazines and Journals, over and above 40 news letters. Division of A.B.A. differ from sections and so far as internal structure is concerned. There is a Law student Division. It is governed by the Board of Governance and has an Assembly consisting of law school representatives and Student Bar Association representatives.

34. Bhatt, Jitendra (J.), "The American Bar Association" (2001) 1, *S.C.C. (J)*, pp. 18-22, p. 19.

The membership of Law practice management section is open to lawyers, legal assistants, law libraries, marketing professionals, counsels, consultants, co-coordinators and anyone interested in development and publications, covering wide variety of aspects of cultivating clients to managing and building a practice and long range planning.[35]

The brief sketch of the history of legal profession the United States of America shows that though legal profession is broadly based on the pattern of English system with necessary modifications, it has surpassed in some respects due to the important role played by A.B.A. in relation to the legal profession.

III. HISTORY OF THE LEGAL PROFESSION IN INDIA

In the Vedic age and in the subsequent Hindu period law was generally combined with morality and religion in the subsequent period. In Muslim rule the Shariat law was based strictly on Islamic injections but Modern Indian legal system which peacefully and still effectively functions throughout India to-day is essentially a contribution of the British.[36] In India the administration of justice was the foremost function of the State and the State and the king was the fountain of Justice. There has also been the narration of the Judges being helped by the learned persons well versed in law. Advocacy for others was allowed in limited way and that too was great odiously. Thus, the development of legal Profession can be studied as a development from gratuitous to litigants to the service for the gain as a Profession.

(A) Position in Ancient India

The redeeming feature of the indigenous legal system prevalent since the ancient times was that the village society was controlled to some extent by the participation of elected people. Vedic Indian Society did not have complex Justice

35. *Id.*, p. 21.
36. Roy, Mantosh, "Evaluation of The Indian Legal System And The Administration of Rule of Law In India", *A.I.R.(J)*, 1970, p. 21.

System and therefore, there did not arise any necessity of expert legal interpreters to help the litigants.

An issue always arises whether there was any legal profession in existence in Ancient India, if yes to what extant? There are two contradictory views on this point. The first view denies existence of such any legal Profession in existence in ancient India, while the other view supports the idea of the existence of legal profession in ancient India.

According to the first view Vedic Indian Society did not have complex Justice System. In early period, the plaintiff or the defendant was himself allowed to present or defend his cause. *P. Varadachariar* expresses the opinion that it is not possible to say anything as to the existence of legal Profession in ancient India.

Varadachariar disputes *K.P. Jaiswal's* interpretation of vipra used in Manu VIII.169 as 'lawyer Brahmin'. Advocate General of Madras *Mr. Varadachariar* while addressing a *vakil's* gathering held in Madras on April 17, 1909 said, "the origin of English Bar is shrouded in the remotest antiquity. It has been traced as far as Edward I. Turing to the history of India, whether ancient or medieval, you find no glimpses of the existence of the legal profession".[37]

The above view of the *P. Varadachariar* found strong support in the argument of *Ludo Rocher.*[38] *Ludo Rocher* accepts only the idea of legal representative and the person represented by him linked by personal tie of blood relationship. The commentator on Arthasastra, *R.P. Kangle* does not find the existence of legal profession in Ancient India and draws conclusion that "there is no reference in the text to the professional lawyers. Most probably such a class did not exist".[39] However, it is submitted that the views of *Varadachariar, Rocher* and *Kangle* does not appear to go undisputed. There are supporters of the view that the institution of men, learned in the law, who as private agents, plea for others in Courts is of ancient origin in India. Mention is made of such lawyers by Narada, Virihaspati, Katayana,

37. Varadachariar, V., *The Hindu Judicial System* (1946) 156.
38. A Scholar from the University of Pennsylvania.
39. Kautilya's *Arthasastra*, Part III, p. 220.

Manu and Shukra. It appears; however, from their writings that before persons could plead and argue for another in Court he had established either that he was a relative or the appointed agent of the party. For instance, Narada says.

> "He deserves punishment who speaks on behalf of another, without being either the brother, the father, the son or the appointed agent, and so does he who contradicts himself at the trial".[40]

Jullius Jolly is also of the opinion that institution of legal profession existed in ancient India. Though in his classical treatise on Hindu Law and Custom, jolly does not refer to lawyer explicitly but these are translations from text which suggest that Jolly firmly believed in the existence of a legal profession of ancient India.[41]

Similar view has been taken by the *Dr. K.P. Jaiswal* in this regard. Citing Manusmriti, *Dr. K.P. Jaiswal* clarifies that the professional lawyers were already in existence in the time of Manava Code.[42] There appears to be much force in saying that king administered justice with the help of Sabhyas and Brahmans. The distinction between the two was that Sabhyas were appointed by the king as judges while "Brahmans were persons who were well versed in Dharmashastra, who could attend the court though not appointed (aniyukta), and whose opinions on difficult points of law were respectfully received by the judges". As Dr. Kane observes such learned Brahmans were in the position of *Amicus Curiae*.[43]

It is also true that there is vast literature in Smritis which related to the qualities of the judges and even prohibition of hot temper, greed, threats, enmity and hearing disputes in privates, but nothing is said about the code of the conduct or etiquette of the lawyers. There appears to be much force in the

40. *Naradasmriti*, int. 2.23.
41. Jolly, Julius, *The Minor Law Books*, 29 (Sacred Book of the East, 33, 1889).
42. Jaiswal, K.P., *Manu and Yajnavalkya: A Compassion and Contrast, A treatise on the Basic Hindu Law*, 288-89 (1890).
43. Kane, P.V., *History of Dharmasastra*, Vol. III, p. 288.

opinions of *Dr. U.C. Sarkar,* when he summarises: "There is no sufficient indication that at the time of the Smrities there was any legal profession in the modern sense of the term persons versed in the science of law could give their opinion for the consideration of the king and his counsellors.

But, it is to be noted that *Dr. P.V. Kane,* though initially doubted the existence of legal procession as such in ancient India, yet he admitted that "this does not preclude the idea that persons well-versed in the law of the Smritis and the procedure of the courts were appointed (niyukta) to represent the party and place his case before the court.[44] "There appears to be three reasons to support Kane on this point. *First,* he concludes from a story narrated in 'Asahaya' commentary on the Naradasmriti it appears that persons who has studied the Smrits helped parties in return for a monetary consideration to raise the contention before the court".

Second, Kane's views are based on fee structure for lawyers given in Sukranitisara. It speaks as follow:

1. The lawyer's fee is one-sixteenth of the interest involved (i.e. value defended or realized).
2. Or fees are one-twentieth or one-fortieth, or one-eightieths or one-hundred and sixtieth portions, etc.
3. Fees ought to be small in proportion as the amount of value or interest under trial increases.
4. If there be many men who are appointed as pleaders in combination they are to be paid according to some other way.
5. Only the men who know the Dharma should be appointed as pleaser.

Dr. Kane Comment's that:

"The rulers of Sukra made a clear approach to the modern institution of the Bar and the fees prescribed by Sukra are similar to those allowed by the Bombay Regulation II of 1827 and by Schedule II to the Bombay Pleader's Act.[45]

44. *Id.,* p. 290.
45. Act of XVIII of 1920.

Third, the necessity of the Lawyer's help is said to have been realized due to the technicalities involved in the court process. It was concluded. The procedure prescribed by Narada, Brahaspati and Katyayana reaches a very high level of technicalities and skilled help must often have been required in litigation.

Relying on Asahaya's commentary on the Institution of Narada, *Sir Ashutosh Mukhorjee*, Judge Calcutta High Court draws the conclusion that "as regards Hindu court, it is clear that the legal profession existed in the Seventh Century of the Christian era".[46] It is also concluded from Buddhist books that the profession of lawyer existed in the first Century before the Christian era. They were known as "sellers of law" or "traders of law" who explained and re-explained, and argued and reargued.

The strongest argument in favour of the existence of legal profession in ancient India is Sukranitisara. But, Lucas Rocher repudiates it on the ground that it has been so far overlooked that at least part of these verses although reproduced in Opprets edition, actually occurred in one manuscript only, they were missing in all other manuscripts and in the printed version used by Oppret. They appear to be very recent edition to the original text—Rocher rules steering clear of the controversy whether lawyers as professional are there is Ancient India, the texts of Narada, Brahaspati, Katyayana, Vyasa and even Kautilya's Arthasastra relying on the translation by P.V. Kane, Jullius Jolly and K.P. Jaiswal shows that although the institution of lawyer was not there as we have understand today, there was in existence some mechanism very close to the same, which clearly lays down that a representative could be engaged and that he should be well versed in law and procedure. He should also not charge an unreasonable fee and if he is not knowledgeable in law or procedure which he claims to be, or charges unreasonable he is liable to be punished. Though, in view of the two conflicting versions as to the existence of legal profession in Ancient India, nothing definite can be concluded. But one thing is clear

46. *In the Matter of Regina Guha* (1916) 21, C.W.N. 74.

that there existed legal experts in one form or the other who assisted courts is administration of justice.

(B) Position in Muslim Period

In the Muslim period the legal profession was matchless and excellent but nothing like modern legislation or a written code of laws existed. However, the one main notable exception to this was the twelve ordinances of Jahangir and the fatwa-a-Alamgiri, a digest of Muslim law prepared under Aurangzeb supervision. The judges chiefly followed the Quranic Injunctions or precepts, the fatwas or previous interpretations of the holy law by eminent Jurists and the ordinances of the Emperors.

The Sultanate period and Mughal period witnessed prominence of administration of justice. Under Sikander Lodi, the Wazir presided over the Muzalim Court. The Qudi pronounced final verdict with the assistance of 12 learned lawyers. Some Sultans like Balban and Mohd. Bin Tuglaq set a high example of justice. But it did not show symptom of legal profession in the present sense, of course, the help of learned jurists was enlarged but it was not made necessary.

Mughal emperors held a Court of Muzalim which was attended by the officers of the court the quadi-i-asker, jurists and other learned in law.[47] Court of muzalim was to contain men well versed in inquiry and assessment of evidence as well as learned lawyers for a proper application of law.

The Qazi-ul-Qazat or the chief qazi was the principal judicial officer in the realm. He appointed qazis in every provincial capital. The qazis made investigation into and tried civil as well as criminal cases of both the Hindu and the Muslims. The muftis expounded Muslim law and the Mir drew up and prounced judgement.

The above discussion reveals that during the Muslim period administration of justice was given the prominence and court systems existed but lawyers were not employed in the local and informal courts. Thus, the question of the role of lawyers during Muslim period is relevant primarily for the administration of justice within the relatively circumscribed

---

47. Hamid, Abdul I., p. 150.

upper level of a complex system and rural area could not be benefited by it.

W.H. Moreland once maintained that there were no group of professional lawyers during the mughal period and that plaintiff and defendants had to plead their own causes in the mughal court.[48] But modern investigation reveals the presence of persons performing some functions of the modern lawyers. However, activities of these persons were not so well defined as they become clear during the British rule.

There were certain persons known as vakil but there was lack of precise legal definition of the term. *H.H. Wilson* defined vakil as "A person invested with authority to act for another, an ambassador, a representative as agent, an attorney". Thus a vakil was a representative. He was not necessarily a legal representative. He was a negotiator.[49] Most of them were specialists in the arts of bargaining, negotiation, and pleading cases, but usually they did not work in law courts, and they were not even concerned with legal matters. Some of them were courtroom lawyers. A French traveler, Francious Bernier, describing mid-17th century India remarked that "they have fewer lawyers and fewer law suits and those laws are more speedily decided. The offshoot of such a situation was the prevalence of corruption and bribery of both judges and witness was common". Bernier remarked: "In Asia, if justice be ever administered, it is among the lower classes, among persons who being equally poor, have no means of corrupting the judges and of buying false witnesses".[50]

Thus, it is clear from the above discussion that the entire judicial system during the Muslim period was unscientific, uncodified and somehow it was a face saving device to the king emperors, the noticeable feature is to be found that in Muslim period the legal system was relatively undeveloped in

48. Moreland, W.H., *India at The Death of Akbar*, 33 (1962).
49. Wilson, H.H., (in) *A Glossary of Judicial Revenue Terms*, 884 (A.C. Ganguly and N.D. Basu, ed. 1940), pp. 119-30.
50. Bernier, Francois, (in) *Travels in the Mughal Empire*, 236 (A Consitable ed. 1968), p. 237.

the rural areas because mughal possessed neither manpower nor the means of communication that would enable them to staff and operate such a system of court extensive enough to provide convenient access to the villages. Those whose approach to the palace was easy and accessible administration for justice was balanced and truth speaking. Obviously those who were residents of cities and towns always obtained benefit and asked for justice and maintained that balance of administration but those who were resident of villages they always suffered and they never obtained relief. But this is a fact that emperor always tried to dispense justice and to keep strict discipline in the administration as far as possible by him. Particularly the names of the Akbar and Jahangir cannot be forgotten in this respect. In the legal profession during the Muslim period there were *vakils* to argue the case before the court but there was no well defined legal profession as could be found later on during the British regime.

(C) Position in British India

It is widely acknowledged that the legal profession as it exists in India today is highly professionalized and product of the legal system which came into existence with the advent of British rule in India. The very organization and growth of a system of court with the superior courts of record at the apex and the trial and district courts at the base were introduced with the growth of British Power in India.

The provisions regarding the legal profession as they have existed for some years past and as they are today are the natural outcome of the legal profession introduced by the Britishers and therefore, it would be necessary to begin with the history of the profession from the time when the Britishers came to the country.

After the mercantile success of some of the European power in 15th and 16th centuries inspired a group of London merchants to form into a company to trade with the east. On December 31, 1600 queen Elizabeth I granted charter empowering the Governor and the company to make laws, order, ordinances for good governance of the company and for the better advancement.[51] James I renewed the same power by his charter granted in 1609. In 1618 Sir Thomas Roe, Ambassador of James I of England in court of Jahangir obtained a treaty from the Mughal authorities which gave to the company a privilege to decide dispute between the English within their factory at Surat. After that in 1661 by the charter of Charles II judicial power was vested in the executive government which dispensed justice by the law then in force in England.

Again in 1668 and 1669 Charles II obtained the Island of Bombay that the present Bombay harbours and it environs from the Portuguese as his marriage dowry and English king leased out the city and harbour to the East India Company at an annual rent of ten pound.

However, the actual story of the legal profession in India; begins with establishment of first British court in Bombay in 1672 by the Governor Gerald Aungier. The first attorney general appointed by the Governor was George Wilcox, who was acquainted with legal business and particularly in administration of estates on deceased persons on granting probate. Wilcox made provisions for parties to be represented by attorneys and at the inaugural procession of the court of judicature there were four attorneys and fixed the Councillor's fee at a little more than Rs. One. In early times solicitors and barristers were not liked. In this context it is important to note that East India Company discouraged the growth of profession because the directors believed that more lawyers would bring an increase in law suits and ferment more disputes in colonies. Company instructed the Bombay council to encourage litigants to manage their own cases. The charters and rules of the court of judicature and later Mayor Court did not mention the profession. This led Samuel Schmitheener to draw the conclusion that for a hundred years the profession developed haphazardly with direction, regulation or proper recognition.

(i) Position of Legal Profession during King's Court System

By a charter granted by King George I on 24 September 1726 a court of record in the name of Mayor Court and a court

51. Veera Raghvan, A.N., "Legal Profession and the Advocates Act", *J.I.L.I.*, Vol. 94, p. 231.

of record in nature of a Court or Oyer and terminer and goal delivery was established in Madras, Bombay and Fort William. They were authorized to frame such rules of practice and nominate and appoint such clerks and officer and to do such other thing as could be found necessary for administration of justice and the due execution of any of the power given to them. But there was no provision as to who could act or plead before those courts. The language of the courts appeared to have been English. Prior to the establishments of the king's court at Madras and Fort William there were no legal practitioners. It is said that in Madras there were four attorneys at the mayor court in 1764 and the same number at Fort William in 1769.[52]

Over the year the Mayor's Court improved the quality of justice and gave importance to the pleading of case because they were crown courts with a right of appeal first to the Governor in Council and if necessary over him to the Privy Council.

During the era of the Mayor's Court two important professional principles were established, first the right of an attorney to protect the rights of his client in spite of opposition from the Governor or the council members and second the power of Mayor's Court to dismiss an attorney for guilty of misconduct. But in this connection it is interesting to note that, the charter of 1726, introduced uniform judicial system in all the three Presidency Towns and Royal Courts in India, but it did not make provisions for the regulation of legal practioners.[53] There was no provision for legal training and the legal profession was not organized. Many persons having no knowledge of law were practising because the charter establishing the Mayor's Court did not lay down qualification for person who would act and plead as legal practitioners in those courts.

Thus, in the era of Mayor's Court the legal profession was not paid due attention. For this reason, despite the two

52. Misra, B.B., *The Judicial Administration of the East India Company in Bengal,* 1765-1782 (1961), p. 62.
53. Prasad, Anirudh, *Principles of The Ethics of Legal Profession In India,* 2nd ed. (2006), p. 30.

professional principles legal profession could not be regulated or organized and for this reason the profession did not enjoy high order of prestige. Even after this charter the judicial administration remained in the hands of non-professional persons. In 1753 new charter was issued to modify the charter of 1726, but even this charter could not introduce any thing more. The Charter of 1753 did not contain significant provisions for legal training and legal education of legal practitioners. Thus the legal profession was also not organized in this time.

After the passing of 20 years the Mayor's courts were succeeded by the Supreme Courts. This was the time when the legal profession went to a new height. Thus, the Regulating Act of 1773 ultimately abolished the Mayor's court and provided for the establishment of Supreme Court for three Presidency towns in India. In actual fact the Supreme Court at Fort William was established in 1774 that of Madras in 1801 and Bombay in 1823. These Supreme Courts were very similar the king bench division courts of England administering both the law and equity.

Clause II of the charter establishing the Supreme Court at Calcutta provides: "we do hereby further authorize and empower the said Supreme Court of judicature, at Fort William in Bengal, to approve, admit and enroll such and so many advocates and attorney at-law as to the said Supreme Court of judicature at Fort William in Bengal deem fit who shall be attorney on record and shall be and are hereby authorized to appear and plead and act for the suitors off the said Supreme Court of judicature at the said Supreme Court at Fort William in Bengal and the said advocates and attorneys on reasonable cause to remove and no other person or persons whatsoever but such advocates or attorneys so admitted and enrolled shall be allowed to appear and plead or act in the said Supreme Court of judicature at Fort William in Bengal for or on the behalf of such suitors or any of them".

The above clause of charter reveals that the establishment of the Supreme Court brought a new shine in the legal profession. The main advantages of this era were:

1. For the first time the qualification of Chief Justice and puisne judges was prescribed.
2. The•charter brought recognition, wealth and prestige to the legal profession.
3. The charter brought a steady flow of well trained barrister and solicitor.[54]
4. The charter empowered the Court to approve, admit and enroll advocates and Attorney to plead and act on behalf of suitors.
5. The charter gave the Court authority to remove lawyers from the roll of the Court.
6. The Charter prohibited those practitioners who were not properly admitted and enrolled.
7. Charter employed the Supreme Court to settle the table of fees to be allowed to such sheriff and other officers, clerks and attorneys for all or every parts of the business to be done by them.

Thus, it is clear from the above discussion that the Supreme Court era opened new vista in the legal profession and for the first time the legal profession was recognized in a systematic way.

(ii) Position of Legal Profession during Company Courts System

Prior to the rise of British power in India, in northern India, Justice was administered by the courts established by the Moghul Emperors and ruling chiefs. The services of persons called vakils were available to litigants in those native courts but subsequent to the battles of Plessey and Buxer when Lord Clive acquired from the Moghul Emperor the Dewani of Bengal, Bihar and Orissa, the East India Company established Civil and Criminal Courts for the administration of justice in the mofussil areas outside the town of Calcutta. For Civil matter Sadder Dewani Adalat and for criminal matter sadder Nizamat Adalat were set-up. The vakils practising before the Moghul courts appeared in the company's Courts also till the

54. *Ibid.*

insertion of Bengal Regulation but there was no law relating to their qualifications, relationship to court, mode of procedure or ethics of practice. Legal practice by vakils or agents was neither recognized nor controlled by Dewanee Court. There was little order, vakil pleaded cases by simultaneous exchange of question and answer. As Mr. B.B. Mishra points out "clients would sometimes silence vakil in the midst of pleading and act themselves or have another agent to take up the argument. There were two kinds of legal agent—untrained relatives or servant of the parties in the court and professional pleaders claiming training either in Hindu or Muslim law. Pleaders demanded exorbitant money and situation was very deplorable".[55]

There was urgent necessity of the organization and control of law as a public profession. Bengal Regulation VII of 1793 brought reform. It brought order and some measure of quality to pleading and endeavoured to establish it as a respectable profession.

The Bengal Regulation regulated the appointment of vakils or native pleaders in the courts of Civil Judicature in the Provinces of Bengal, Bihar and Orissa and gave powers to the Sadder Dewani Adalat to enroll pleaders for all company's courts to fix the retaining fee for pleaders and to fix a scale based on a percentage of the value of the property. Only Hindus and Muslims could be enrolled as pleaders.

Thus, the Bengal Regulation was to control both recruitment and conduct of Legal practitioners in the Company's Courts by prescribing qualifications in the first case and rules of dealings in the second. Main advantages of this regulation were, the Sadder Dewani Adalat could appoint as many persons provided them being a Mohammedan or Hindu and who were also men of good character with liberal education. They were also required to be acquainted with regulation.

The Sudder Dewani Adalat was empowered to appoint as many pleaders of Muslim and Hindu religion as necessary. Before getting his sanad the pleader was to take an oath of

55. Mishra, B.B., *The Indian Middle Classes, their Growth in Modern Times* (1961), 164.

faithful discharge of professional responsibilities and in the cases of a Muslim pleader oath had to be renewed every month.

There was separate bar far each court. Pleaders had to show their presence daily in respective courts. The attendance was compulsory except in cases of indisposition when a written application for leave had to be submitted.

To regulate the profession a number of rules were laid down concerning receiving of retainers, execution of Vakalatnama and amount of fees. Regulation VII also provided for punishment of the legal practitioner by fine, suspension and dismissal for disrespect of court, promoting and encouraging litigious suits, fraud, wilful delaying of suits, accepting gifts of more than the authorized amount of fees from the client, or dropping a client after receiving a retainer.[56]

However, in cases concerning suspension or dismissal Sudder Dewani Adalat was to take action only after the charge had been proved. Clients could also prosecute their legal agents for malpractice.

Thus, the Bengal Regulation, which created for the first time a regular legal profession for the Company's Courts permitted only Hindus and Muslim to be enrolled as pleaders.

IV. THE IMPACT OF LEGAL PRACTITIONERS ACTS ON LEGAL PROFESSION

For the purpose to regulate the legal profession a new great step taken in evolution of the Indian Bar, was the legal Practitioners Act. This Act was enacted three times in India. That was All India Legislations for amending law regarding the appointment and remuneration of pleaders in the Court of East India Company.

Firstly, the Legal Practitioners Act was enacted in 1846 which made three important changes, namely:[57]

1. The office of pleaders was thrown open to all persons of whatever nationality or religion duly

56. *Supra* note 53, p. 31.
57. Firstly in 1846 and thereafter in 1853 and 1879.

certified by the Sadder Court to be of good character and duly qualified for the office.

2. Attorneys and Barristers of any of Her Majesty's Court in India were eligible to plead in any of the Sadder Courts subject to the rules of those Courts as regards language or otherwise.
3. The pleaders were permitted to enter into agreements with their clients to settle the professional fees by private agreement.

Thus, the above Act gave the right to the Barrister to practise in any court of India and gave full liberty to pleader and their clients to settle the fees by private agreement. It is important to note that in this regard whenever a pleader conducted himself in such manner which was not worthy of his office, the court was competent to fine him.

The second Legal Practioners Act was passed in 1853. This Act permitted also Barristers and Attorneys of the Supreme Court not entitled till then, to be admitted as pleaders in the Court of Company subject to all the rules in force in the Court relating to language and other matters connected with pleadings. It was also provided that a pleader was not bound to attend the court except at the hearing of a case in which he was employed.

By virtue of the Act the Barristers and Attorneys were empowered to practice in the company courts while the Indian Legal Practitioners could not appear before the Supreme Court.

The third Legal Practitioners Act, 1879 showed enough improvement. But it can be appreciated only in light of certain measures adopted by the Government of India Act, 1858 with a view to appreciate the improvement brought by the third Legal Practitioners Act, a brief sketch of changes brought by the Act of 1858 are being discussed hereunder.

The Crown took over the charge from East India Company in 1858. The Government of India Act, 1858 consolidated into a unified Judicial system in each of the three presidency by doing away with the separate systems of the Companies Court in Mofussil and the Royal's Court in the presidency town.

In historical perspective the two separate systems of the King's Courts and the Company's Court came to end after 1857. The year of 1857 brought the career of the East India Company to end and Government of India was placed under direct control of the Crown in 1858. The position clearly underwent a change after British Crown took over the administration of the country from the Company and the Government of India Act, 1858 was passed.

One of the major impacts of this change over was that the separate systems of the Company's Courts in the Mofussil and Royal Courts in the Presidency towns were consolidated into a Unified Judicial system in each of the Presidencies. The Supreme Court of 1774 was replaced by the High Court. At the apex of the new judicial system were High Courts, chartered by the Crown established at Calcutta, Bombay and Madras in 1862.

At the termination of the rule of the East India Company in 1858, there existed two categories of legal practitioners, namely: (a) English barristers and solicitors who had the monopoly of practice in the Supreme Court and who could also practise in the Company's Courts, and (b) pleaders enrolled under the Indian Regulations who could practise only the Company's Courts.

It is submitted that, by virtue of this Act, the major change came in outlook towards Indian lawyers. As the High Court was aimed to give a combined look of the Supreme Court and Sadder Court traditions by uniting the "legal learning and Judicial experience of English barristers" with the intimate experience of Indian custom, usages and laws possessed by the civil servants. With the establishment of High Courts a combined look of the Supreme Court and the Sadder Court tradition came into existence by uniting the legal learning and judicial experience of English Barristers. The High Court bench was envisaged to represent different segments including the Indian lawyers . . . "At least one-third of the judges, including the Chief Justice, were to be Barristers of the United Kingdom, another one-third to be recruited from the Judicial branch of the Indian Civil Service and the remaining places were made available to members of the subordinate Judiciary, and Indian lawyers practicing in the High Court".

The Indian High Courts Act, 1862 was enacted by the British Parliament authorizing the setting up by Letters Patent of High Courts in the several presidencies in place of the respective Supreme Courts and the Sudder Diwanni Adalats and Sudder Nizamat Adalats.[58]

Clause 9 of the Letters Patent of 1856 which replaced the earlier Letters Patent creating a High Court in Calcutta authorized it to approve, admit and enroll advocates, vakils and attorneys.

Each of the chartered High Courts framed rules under the relevant clause of their respective letters patent. In the High Court there were, apart from the attorneys, two classes of lawyers. One class called advocates were mainly Barristers, though High Courts other than the Calcutta High Court also permitted non-barristers, to be enrolled as Advocates. The other class of lawyers in the high Courts was called vakils, for whom different kinds of qualifications were laid down by different High Courts.

Thus, in Calcutta, the qualification required for admission as a vakil were a degree of Bachelor of Arts or Science followed by a degree of Laws and two years service as an articled clerk to an approved practicing vakil of five years standing.

The holder of a law degree of an Indian University was also admitted after four years practice as a pleader in a Superior Court. Three years practice as an attorney of the High Court would also entitled the Attorney to be enrolled as vakil, subject to his passing an examination.

On the other hand, in Bombay, a matriculate of the Bombay University or an Attorney could be admitted as vakil on passing an examination prescribed by the High Court. But a Bachelor or Master of Law was eligible without further qualification. Similarly, the High Courts of Calcutta, Bombay, Madras, Allahabad and Patna prescribed qualifications for enrolment of attorneys, though the attorneys, now more commonly known as Solicitors, existed in prominent numbers only in the commercial cities of Bombay and Calcutta.

58. Jain, M.P., *Outlines of Indian Legal History*, 2007 ed., pp. 92-105.

While the High Courts had those three different classes of legal practitioners, namely Advocates, Attorneys and vakils, there were different classes of legal practitioners practicing in the district and other subordinate courts. The setting up of a regular hierarchy of Civil and Criminal Courts and the shortage of law graduates necessitated grant of permission to non-graduate lawyers to practice in these courts.

Those were pleaders who did not quality for enrolment as vakils of the High Courts. In some provinces, they were pleaders of different grades; example, first, second and third grade. Besides the pleaders there was another class of legal practitioners in the subordinate courts called mukhtars, who after passing the matriculation examination were required to pass the mukhtarship examination held by the High Courts.

In 1879 the third Legal Practitioners Act was passed, which consolidated and amended to law relating to legal practitioners in certain provinces and empowered the Government of every other province to extend thereto such provinces of the Act as it considered fit. It regulated the functions of legal practitioners and made provision regarding their discipline and control.[59]

Prior to enactment of this Act, there were two sets of person engaged to practise before the High Courts and Lower Courts.

The Act defined the term legal practitioner to mean an advocate, vakil or attorney of any High Court, a pleader, mukhtar or revenue agent. By virtue of this Act, all the six classes of legal practitioners were brought under the disciplinary jurisdiction of the High Court.

The disciplinary authority, in respect of pleaders and mukhtar was vested in High Court. The High Court could suspend or dismiss any pleader or mukhtar holding a certificate, issued under Section 7 who was convicted of any criminal offence employing a defect of character which unfitted him to be a pleader or mukhtar, as the case might be. The High Court could also after such inquiry as it thought fit,

59. Singh, M.P., *Outlines of Indian Legal & Constitutional History*, VIIIth ed., p. 173.

suspend or dismiss any pleader or mukhtar, holding a certificate, issued under session 7 of the Act.

However, the Act was not a complete code of law on the subject of professional conduct and it did not apply to pleaders in the presidency of Bombay for whom the law was contained in the Bombay Pleaders Act, 1920. Similarly, it did not apply in the case of advocates in whose case control was vested in the several High Courts by their Letters of Patent. But the Act enlarged the rights of advocates, vakils and attorneys of High Courts by enabling them the exercise their practise in all subordinate courts in British India as well as in any revenue courts. Besides, an advocate or vakil on the rolls of any High Court was empowered to practise with the permission of the Court in any High Court on whose roll, he was not entered. However, these provisions did not extend to the criminal jurisdiction of the High Courts in a presidency town.

Sufficient improvement had been done over the years, yet the legal profession was not without blemishes. The arbitrary differention between advocates and vakils unmerited precedence of even the most junior advocate over the most senior vakil, the compulsion imposed on a vakil to file vakalatnama which was not required of an advocate, baseless distinction between Barristers and vakils, special privileges enjoyed by the British barristers and solicitors, their distinct professional robes and the requirement of having to submit to an examination test for enrolment as an advocate on the original side of Bombay High Court; was the main problematic features of this regime.

It is submitted that, this dual system was wholly repugnant to the idea of a unified Bar with a common roll of advocates entitled to practise in courts. The said system divided legal practitioners into two distinct classes of lawyers which was a vestige and legacy of the foreign Rule. Even its staunch protagonists were not able to advance any cogent or convincing argument for its retention beyond that it resulted in efficient preparation of the brief and presentation of the case. Thus, the system of legal profession during British was at any rate a needless luxury and it was hard on litigants to insist upon employing two sets of lawyers working in water tight compartments. It could not also be said that the system worked properly and suitably in India as it worked in England. A need of unified bar became the need of the time.

V. STEP TOWARDS AUTONOMY AND UNIFIED INDIAN BAR

With the passage of time the demand for the removal of arbitrary distinctions between barristers and vakils and the special privileges enjoyed by the British barristers and solicitors got ground. This position of legal profession led to a strong agitation in support of a uniform Bar abolishing all such distinctions. In response to these demand the Government of India set-up the Indian Bar Committee in November, 1923 under the Chairmanship of Sir Edward Chamier to examine and report on:

(A) The proposal for constituting an Indian Bar, whether on all India or provincial basis, with particular reference to the constitution, statutory recognition, functions and authority of Bar Council or Bar Councils, and their positions, *vis-à-vis* High Courts.

(B) The extent to which it might be possible to remove the existing distinction enforced by statute or practice between barristers and vakils.

(A) Report of the Chamier Committee

The Chamier Committee gave its report in the year 1924. The committee agreed in principle with disappearance of the different categories of legal practitioners, but on the question of the continuance of the dual system in Calcutta and Bombay, the Chamier Committee was sharply divided and hence it did not consider it practicable to have the Bar organized on an All India basis and to form an All India Bar Council. For this reason it did not make any recommendation about the All India Bar Council.

The significant recommendation of the Committee was with regard the establishment of Bar Council for the High Courts. However, the Committee recommended that in all High Courts, a single grade of practitioners, to be called

Advocates, should be enrolled and that the grade of High Courts Vakils or pleaders should be abolished. It recommended that attorneys should continue to be enrolled as such in three presidency towns.[60]

The Committee also suggested the creation of Statutory Bar Councils at Calcutta, Madras, Bombay, Allahabad, Patna and Rangoon. It further recommended that provisions should be made permitting the constitution of councils at Lahore, Nagpur, Karachi and Lucknow later on. It felt that the existing disciplinary jurisdiction of the High Courts should remain, but before taking any action the High Court would refer any case of the misconduct except contempt to the Bar Council for enquiring into and making report.

Though the Committee made many valuable suggestion but many issues were left untouched. The pleaders, mukhtars and revenue agents practicing in the mofussil courts and revenue offices were left out of consideration and the main drawback of this committee was that a unified Indian Bar remained a distant dream.

(B) The Indian Bar Council Act, 1926

With a view to implement some of the recommendations of the Chamier Committee and to consolidate and amend the law relating to the legal practitioners, the Indian Bar Council Act, 1926 was enacted. It received the assent of the Governor-General on 9th September. This Act was passed with two-fold desire of the legal practitioners to have a unified Bar, abolishing the distinction of vakalatnama and to give legal profession some measure of autonomy in the management of its own affairs.

The Act introduced, *interalia*, two main changes. Firstly, it made separate provisions for advocates, while the Legal Practitioners Act of 1879 continued to be applicable to other legal practitioners, and in so far as it was related to touts also. Secondly, it provided for the constitution of a separate Bar Council as a corporate body for every High Court.

Every Bar Council was to comprise of fifteen members, with the Advocate General as an ex-officio member. Out of

60. *Suptra* note 53, p. 41.

those 15 members four members were to be nominated by the High Court and ten members were to be elected amongst advocates of the High Court.[61] With reference to the High Courts of Fort William in Bengal and Bombay, a certain proportion of the members had to be advocates entitled to practise on the original side, and out of them a number fixed by the High Court had to be barristers of England and Scotland. The Advocate-Generals in the Bar Councils of Madras, Bombay and Calcutta were to be Ex-Officio Chairmen. The term of the Bar Council was for a period of three years.

The High Court had to prepare and maintain a roll of advocates, vakils, and pleaders entitled as of right to practise immediately before the date when section 8 of the Act was brought into force like all other admitted thereafter as advocates. While with reference to advocates seniority was to be decided on the basis of the date of admission as advocates with regards and as barristers it was decided on the basis of earlier standing.

While the roll was maintained by the High Courts, section 9 authorized the Bar Council, with the previous sanction of the High Court, to make rules to regulate the admission of any person, and the fee payable to the Bar Council. On the line of the Legal Practitioners (Women) Act, 1923, Act of 1926 specifically declared that a woman shall not be disqualified for admission as an advocate by reason only of her sex.

The Act also reserved the rights of the High Courts of Fort William in Bengal and at Bombay to prescribe the qualifications of persons applying to practise in the original jurisdiction of the High Court, or refuse, as they think fit, any such application or to prescribe the condition under which such persons shall be entitled to practise or plead.

The qualifications for admission as laid down under the rules permitted, *interalia,* those who had taken a degree in law and barristers and attorneys to be enrolled. The rules in some Bar Councils provided for a period of training as a pupil for a year by way of compulsory attendance at the chambers of the master (an advocate of certain years standing), maintenance of diaries, attendance at lectures and passing of examinations

61. Section 3(2) of the Indian Bar Councils Act, 1926.

conducted by the Bar Councils. The rules in this regard varied in the different Bar Councils.

An applicant for enrolments had to pay a stamp duty for the entry in the rolls as provided for under the Indian Stamp Act. While the papers of the applicants for enrolment had to be presented to be Bar Councils, the enrolment was actually moved before the High Courts after the certificates were issued by the Bar Councils.

Section 14 of the Act empowered an advocate to practise:

(i) In the High Court where he was enrolled, subject to the rules or conditions to be made by the High Courts of Fort Williams in Bengal and Bombay regarding persons practising in the High Courts, and in the exercise of their original jurisdiction.
(ii) In all subordinate courts and tribunals in India (whether in the High Court, where he was enrolled or not).

Where rules had been made by any High Court under the General Clauses Act or by a Bar Council under section 15 of the Act regulating the conditions subject to which such advocates of other High Courts could practise, they were permitted to practise subject to such conditions.

The rules so made were generally to the effect that an advocate on the roll of any other High Court could be specifically permitted by the Chief Justice or the Bench hearing a case to appear and plead in that case. The Power of the High Courts of West Bengal at Fort William and at Bombay to make rules as to persons who were entitled respectively to plead and act in the High Court in the exercise of its original jurisdiction was preserved.

The High Court was empowered under section 10 of the Act to reprimand, suspend or remove from practice any advocate of the High Court for professional or other misconduct after following the procedure described below.[62]

62. The Bar Council was not given sufficient power to discipline its member.

Complaints against advocates for professional or other misconduct had to be made to the High Court. If on receipt of a complaint, the High Court did not summarily reject it, it had to refer the case for enquiry to the Bar Council, or after consultation with the Bar Council, to a district judge. The High Court had power to make such a reference *suo motu* even if there was no complaint. Cases referred to a Bar Council had to be enquired into by a committee of the Bar Council (called tribunal) comprising not less than three and not more than five members appointed by the Chief Justice of the High Court.

The High Court was required to make rules for the conduct of the disciplinary enquiries. The finding of the tribunal after enquiry was to be forwarded to the High Court through the Bar Council. Finding of a district court was to be forwarded directly to the High Court which required sending a copy to the Bar Council. Notice was to be given of the date fixed for hearing to the advocate concerned and to the Bar Council and to the Advocate-General and after giving them an opportunity of being heard, final orders were passed by the High Court. A record of the punishment of suspension or reprimand was made in the rolls of the High Court. If the advocate was to be removed from practice, his name was removed from the roll and the certificate of any advocate so suspended or removed was to be recalled. The tribunals and the district judge conducting the enquiries were vested with powers of a court under the Code of Civil Procedure examining him on oath, compelling the production of documents and issuing commissions for the examination of witness.[63]

However, it may be pointed out that under the Act, the power of enrolment of advocate virtually continued to remain in the High Court and the function of the Bar Council was advisory in nature. The Act did not affect the original side of the Calcutta and Bombay High Courts. Further, the attorneys of Calcutta and Bombay were not affected by the Act and the enrolment of and the disciplinary jurisdiction over the attorneys continued to be in the hands of the High Courts under their respective Letters Patents. The right of the

63. Section 10 of the Indian Bar Councils Act, 1926.

advocates of one High Court to practise in another High Court was made subject to the rules made by the advocates of other High Courts only with the permission of the Chief Justice provided an advocate enrolled in that High Court appeared with him.

It is submitted that though there is no doubt, this Act took an important step towards unification of the bar by removing some of the distinctions in the privileges of vakils and barristers, but the provisions of the Indian Bar Council's Act were unsatisfactory, because it was not only a half-hearted measure but also it did not establish an All India Bar Council for reason that the Indian Bar Committee Report considered such a proposal as impracticable at that time. It also excluded attorneys from the scope of its provisions. Pleaders and mukhtars were also left out of consideration.

Thus, the Bar Council Act, 1926 did not satisfy the legal profession. During the next 25 years, before the constitution of Republic of India came into force in 1950 several attempts were made by means of private bills in the Legislature to promote reform but they remained unsuccessful. The Supreme Court advocate (practise in High Court) Act was passed in which 1951, gave a right to every advocate of the Supreme Court to practise in any High Court. Even it did not solve the problem as that was not enough. Members of legal profession, wanted on unified autonomous bar with no class distinctions among lawyers.

However, the political independence gave fresh stimulus to the demand and eventually the Government of India appointed a fresh committee to examine and report on the unified and Autonomous Bar for the whole India with a view to undertake the necessary reforms and binding about comprehensive legislation.

(C) The Recommendations of the All India Bar Committee and the Law Commission

As has been discussed earlier, the Bar was not satisfied with passing of the Bar Council's Act, 1926. Since the Act had not covered the pleaders, mukhtars and Revenue agents practising in the mofussil courts and revenue offices and it did not set-up a unified Indian Bar. Further the powers conferred on the Bar Councils constituted under the Act were limited and the Bar Councils were neither autonomous nor had any substantial authority. Therefore, several non-official members' bills had been introduced, from time to time to amend the law relating to the legal profession. Since, such bills had lapsed and nothing concrete emerged. With coming into force of the Constitution in 1950 and the establishment of a Supreme Court for India the need for an All India Bar was stressed by the legal fraternity with new vigor. In this situation, the Union government set-up a committee known as the *All India Bar Committee* under Chairmanship of Justice S.R. Das Hon'ble judge of the Supreme Court. In 1953, the committee recommended, *inter alia,* an All India Bar Council and the maintenance of a common roll of advocates by the All India Bar Council. The committee had considered at length the questions of the constitution and powers of the state Bar Councils and the All India Bar Council and made detailed recommendations.[64] It proceeded on the principle that the Bar should be autonomous in matters relating to the profession.[65] But the government did not take any steps in pursuance of the committee's recommendations.

Subsequently in 1955, the Law Commission, presided over by M.C. Setalvad, then Attorney-General of India, in its fourteenth report on the Reform of Judicial Administration endorsed the recommendations of the All India Bar Committee, as regards the creation of a unified all India Bar as well as the establishment, composition and functions of the state and all India Bar Councils.[66] The Law Commission further recommended *inter alia* that the requirements of a certain number of years' practise in the High Court for enrolment as a Supreme Court advocate should be dispensed with, the advocates on the common roll should have the right to practise in all the courts in India.[67] The commission also recommended that the dual system should continue on the original side of

---

64. Report of All India Bar Committee, 1954, p. 25.
65. *Id.*, Para 65-66.
66. Law Commission of India, XIVth Report VI.I 581-83.
67. *Id.*, p. 576.

the Calcutta and Bombay High Courts[68] and the Bar should be divided into senior advocates and advocates.[69]

(D) Advocates Act, 1961: A Great Step Towards Unification and Autonomy of the Bar in India

To implement the recommendations of the All India Bar Committee and of the Law Commission in its fourteenth Report, the Legal Practitioners Bill, 1959 was introduced in the Lok Sabha on the 19th November, 1959. The Bill was to amend and consolidate the law relating to legal practitioners and to provide for the constitution of State Bar Councils and an All India Bar Council. It was referred to a Joint Select Committee of Parliament of which Shri C.R. Pattabi Raman was the Chairman.

It is necessary to refer to a few of the clauses, particularly in the bill as introduced, since after the recommendations and report of the Joint Selected Committee, there were certain changes made before the bill was finally passed. It included:

(a) The composition of the State Bar Councils consisting of two Judges of High Court nominated by the Chief Justice of the High Court. In the case of the Assam and Orissa Bar Councils, only one such Judge was to be nominated.

(b) Membership of the All India Bar Council including, *inter alia,* two judges of the Supreme Court "who have been advocates" nominated by the Chief Justice of India, and three members elected by the Supreme Court Bar Association from amongst its members.

When the Bill came to be passed, the name Legal Practitioners Bill was changed into The Advocates Act and amongst the other changes made, the above referred provisions as to the nomination was dropped, and a separate Bar Council known as the Bar Council of Delhi was to be constituted.[70] This Act was enacted for the purpose of

---

68. *Ibid.*
69. *Ibid.*
70. Sction 3(1)(f) of the Advocates Act, 1961.

amending and consolidating the law relating to legal practitioners and also for providing the constitution of Bar Councils and an All India Bar. The Advocates Act made provision for the establishment of State Bar Councils[71] and Bar Council of India.[72] The Advocates Act recognized only one category of advocates which could be classified into senior advocates and advocates.[73]

The main feature of the Act is two-fold: unification of the Bar and autonomy of the Bar[74] with respect disciplining[75] its own members.

(i) Unification of the Bar

The Advocates Act, 1961 was the great step to lay down the unified Bar for the first time in India. This Act has united and organized the legal profession. Following provisions of this Act may be advanced to support the attempt to unify the bar.

(a) Class of Advocates

The Advocates Act, 1961 ended the legacy of Six Classes[76] of legal practitioners which was created by the Legal Practitioners Act, 1879 and left unaffected by the Indian Bar Council Act, 1926. It has limited advocacy to only one class of persons. Section 29 of the Act provides that:

> "Subject to the provisions of this Act and any rules made thereunder, there shall, as from the appointed day, be only one class or persons entitled to practice the profession of law, namely, advocates".

The above section is the first example, which is intended to strengthening a unified Bar on all India basis, because the

---

71. *Ibid.*
72. *Id.* Section 4.
73. *Id.* Section 16.
74. *Ibid.*
75. Section 35 of the Advocates Act, 1961.
76. Pleaders, Vakils, Mukhtars, Attorney, Agent and Solicitors.

Act limiting the legal professions into one class of persons, namely, 'advocates'.

Now the question is whether the existing class of legal professionals, i.e. Vakils, Mukhtars, etc. can have right to practice after the commencement of the Advocates Act? The answer of this question is given by the section itself, because the Section 29 is subject to the other provisions of the Act and rules made thereunder. In this regard Section 55 of the Advocates Act, 1961 specifically saved the right to practice of existing legal professional.[77]

By virtue of section 33 read with Section 55 they have been allowed to continue practice even after the enforcement of the Act. The commission was conceded only to old practiotioners.

In *Janilabai Abdul Kar* v. *Shankarlal Gulabchand*[78] Mr. Justice Krishna Iyer pointed out in this regard that :

> "By the Advocates Act, national integration in the profession of lawyers was statutorily achieved whereby the Indian Bar, with a classes orientation, came into existence. Even though a vakil or a pleader might not have chosen to get himself enrolled as an advocate, but all these categories of legal practitioners substantially had the same power *vis-à-vis* client and court".

However, it should be noted that though they have equal right to practice but after the commencement of the Act no fresh vakils, pleaders attorneys, mukhtars and agent shall be enrolled.

The Act divides advocates into the categories 'senior advocate' and advocates other than senior advocates. A person who was senior advocate immediately before commencement of the Act was deemed to be senior advocates for the purposes of the Act. Besides, section 16 of the Act confers power on Supreme Court and High Courts to designate any person as senior advocate if the Supreme Court or a High Court is of

77. Section 55 of the Advocates Act, 1961 has preserved the power of the High Court to reinstate an advocate dismissed earlier.
78. A.I.R. 1975 S.C. 2202.

opinion that by virtue of his ability, standing at the Bar or special knowledge or experience in law, he is deserving of such distinction. Some doubts have been raised as to designation of some of advocates as senior advocates. If such categorization attracts Article 14 and render it discriminatory? Such a distinction between senior advocates and advocates was appreciated by the Law Commission in its Fourteenth Report. Firstly, large number of junior experienced considerable difficulty in making their living. Secondly, large volume of work was concentrated in the hands of a few senior lawyers. The division was desirable due to two reasons, first from the angle of junior advocate and second from the point of view of common litigants. It should result in putting works in hand the junior members of the Bar resulting in heartening them and raising their morals. The distribution of works among larger number might also help to prevent delays caused by adjournments due to over-work on the shoulders of few senior spreading over many courts.[79]

By virtue of the Rules framed under the Act, senior advocates are debarred from drafting and pleading. In fact they can only argue in Court. They are not to 'act' for the client and not to have direct contact with him. He can only settle what has been prepared by the advocates. Senior Advocates wear a different type of gown. In the case of *J.R. Parashan* v. *Bar Council of India*[80] a questions arose before the Delhi High Court whether this amounts to discrimination and violate the Article 14 of the constitution of India? Rejecting the above contention, the single judge of the Delhi High Court held that it is not at all discriminatory. The High Court expressed the basis of distinction that, where a distinction between a Senior Advocate and other advocate is statutorily recognized, the wearing of a distinct gown, which is different from the one worn by other advocate cannot be termed as discriminatory.

79. See, Rule (1)(a) of Chapter Ist of the Bar Council of India Rules, 1975 and Order IV, Rule 2(b) of Supreme Courts Rules, 1966.
80. A.I.R. 2002, Del. 482.

Thus, the conferment of designation is based on the collective wisdom of the court and it cannot be graded as arbitrary.

(b) Right to Practise

The provisions relating to the right to practise, is another example which are intended to strengthen the unification of the bar on all India basis. The Advocates Act, 1961 gave the right to practise for every such advocate, whose name is entered on the state roll. Though section 30 of the Advocates Act, 1961 has not been brought into effect by the Central Government, till now, but it may become a unique peace of enactment.

By virtue of section 30 the enrolled advocates will be entitled to practise in all courts including the Supreme Court and before all authorities and persons throughout the territories to which the Advocates Act extends.[81] Therefore, the first and foremost objective of enacting this section was to unify the bar on all India level. The true effect of section 30 is that, an advocate who obtained his degree from one state may be enrolled as advocate in another State. It means Section 30 treated the entire legal profession on all India level and not only the state-wise. But, it is unfortunate that, inspite of fact, that section 30 was enacted way back in 1961, it has not been brought into effect by the Central Government. Because of it, the advocates are being debarred from appearance before many tribunals, namely, Industrial Tribunals, Family Courts, Juvenile Courts, etc., as under these Acts a specific bar is provided against the appearance of the Advocates in the Acts itself.

In India, since most of the litigants are not aware of their legal rights and quite a large population of the country, specially those living in the village are illiterate, the litigants do not have the requisite skill to defend themselves in a court of law which could seriously prejudice the conduct of their case. In the present day of human rights activism, environmental consciousness, right to information, intellectual property right, consumer's rights there is pressing demand

81. Every such Advocate is entitled to practise in whole India.

that there should be the representation by professional lawyers, everywhere in cases requiring redressal. Therefore, at present there is an imperative and urgent need to implement section 30 of the Advocates Act, 1961.

However, on the point of implementation of Section 30 of the Advocates Act, the judiciary has taken two contradictory approaches. In some cases it observed that Section 30 of the Advocates Act was not implemented rightly. Thus, in *Pardeep Port Trust* v. *Their workers*[82] rejecting the argument that under Section 30 of the Advocates Act an advocate has the right to appear before the tribunal, the Supreme Court took the view that the right of advocate under Section 30 is subject to other laws. Section 36(4) of the Industrial Disputes Act, 1947 for bids parties to industrial dispute, to be represented by a legal practitioner, except with the consent of the other parties and with the approval of the Labour Court, Tribunal, etc.

The Supreme Court held that Industrial Disputes Act, 1947 is legislation with avowed object of labour welfare, and representation before adjudicatory authorities has been specifically provided. The court further held that a special Act would prevail over Advocates Act, which is a general piece of legislation.

Likewise the Madhya Pradesh High Court in *Tikam Chand Sunlanji Agarwal* v. *Joint Registrar Co-operative Societies, Bhopal,*[83] held that Section 67(2) of the Co-operative Societies Act, which is restricting the right of a litigant to be represented by a legal practitioner is not repugnant to Section 30 of the Advocates Act.

Thus, the above decisions reveal that Section 30 of the Advocates Act, 1961 which has not been enforced so far does not confer an absolute right to practice, and is subject to other provision of Act, and other laws.

A quite different stand has been taken by certain High Court and the Supreme Court of India. Thus, in *Jaswant Kaur* v. *State of Haryana*[84] a full bench of Punjab and Haryana High Court held that any provision debarring an advocate from

82. A.I.R. 1977, S.C. 36.
83. A.I.R. 1971 M.P. 86.
84. A.I.R. 1977 P&H. 221.

appearing before any authority except Financial Commissioner, were unconstitutional as they placed restrictions on an advocate's right to practice.

The court held that, this argument must not be accepted that Section 30 had not been brought into force, because Section 14 of the Bar Councils Act, 1926 is *parimateria* and should be treated to continue in force. This approach of Punjab and Haryana High Court found support from the Apex Court's decision in *Lingappa Pochanna Appelwar* v. *State of Maharastra,*[85] the Supreme Court observed that Section 30 had not been brought into force, so far and a person enrolled as an advocate is not *ipsofacto* entitled to a right of audience, unless this section is first brought into force. The extent of right to practice and appear in court is still regulated by different statute including Section 14(1)(a)(b) and (c) of the Bar Council's Act, 1926. However, the Supreme Court emphasized the need for implementation of Section 30 of the Advocates Act, and stated that it is unfortunate that Section 30 has not been brought into force though the Act has been in force for the last 22 years (now more than 47 years). The spirit of the above judgment found strong support in *H.S. Srinivasa* v. *State of Karnataka,*[86] wherein the Supreme Court of India held that Section 48(8) of the Korapaka Land Reform Act, which prohibits the appearance of a lawyer before the tribunal is illegal and unconstitutional.

Though there is difference of opinion as to the effect of non-enforcement of Section 30 of the Advocates Act, 1961, the judicial inclination appears to favour the early enforcement of that section. Thus, in *Altemesh Rein* v. *Union of India,*[87] the Supreme Court of India emphasized the need of implementation of Section 30 of the Advocates Act, 1961 and directed the government to spell out its own views on the point. It is submitted that much will depend on the situational assessment in future if section 30 of Advocates Act is brought in force. The courts will have still discretion to allow or disallow specific prohibition of lawyer's appearance before

85. A.I.R. 1985 S.C. 389.
86. A.I.R. 1987 S.C. 1578.
87. A.I.R. 1985 S.C. 389.

specific tribunals on the principle that general provision gives way to specific provisions. Any way it is in the interest of the lawyers and broadening the scope of legal practice that Section 30 of the Advocates Act, 1961 should be given effect to Advocates Act, 1961 prescribes procedure for entitling an advocate to practice.

Every State Bar Council is under an obligation to prepare and maintain a roll of advocates[88] and no person shall be enrolled as an advocate of more than one State Bar Council though transfer of the name from one state roll to another is allowable with the sanction of the Bar Council of India.[89] The State Bar Councils are also required to send copies of their rolls of advocates to the Bar Council of India.

In this regard Section 24 prescribes the certain qualifications for persons who may be admitted as advocates on state roll. Under Sub-section (1), the requirements are, that the person seeking enrollment should be a citizen of India, however foreigners, on a reciprocal basis, can also be admitted as advocates; should have completed the age of 21 years, has obtained a degree in law or is a barrister, etc.

Every person whose name is entered in the roll of advocates is issued a certificate of enrollment which shall be recalled when the advocate is suspended or removed from practice. Any person who practise in any court, to which he is not entitled, is punishable under Section 45 of the Act with imprisonment for a term which may extend to six months.[90]

It appears that, a person who has not been enrolled as an advocate, cannot practise law. This is also true in the regard of United States of America and England. Both American and English Courts have adopted the doctrine that a non-lawyer may not appear in court to represent another person. Though, the history of these countries shows that, outside the court

88. Section 17 of the Advocates Act, 1961.
89. *Id.*, Section 19.
90. Prior to this Act, under Section 32 of the Legal Practitioners Act the deliquent was liable to a fine not exceeding ten times of the stamp required for a certificate authorizing him to practice. In default he was liable to imprisonment in Civil Jail for a period of not exceeding six months.

house non-lawyer freely performed tasks that today would be called the unauthorized practice of law. The general pattern still remains in England and other countries in Europe, where there has been never a prohibition against non-lawyers performing such legal functions out of the court room, that is to say, legal advice or preparing some kind of legal document.[91]

After First World War, Bar Associations waged a campaign to eradicate unauthorized practice. The American Bar Association formed a Committee in 1930 for this purpose. About the same time, the courts began to announce sweeping common law doctrines of exclusive lawyer competence and helped the Bar's newly kindled concern for protecting potential clients against incompetence and unscrupulous charlatans.

The underlying idea before this type of restriction was based upon various principles viz. to avoid harm to the client in hands of a person, who are not legally qualified, preventing harm to the legal system as a whole and for assuring a basis for profession discipline and for protecting lawyers against competition.

Likewise, the Indian legal system bears also the same feeling that a poor litigant may not be thrown in the hands of professionally unqualified persons. Sections 29 and 33 read with Section 45 of the Advocates Act, clearly lay down that a person duly enrolled as an advocate, can only appear, plead and conduct cases in court of law and if not so, he will be liable to punishment.

However, it should be noted that this general rule does not prevent any one from appearing in a court of law in particular case with the permission of court. Many Legislations not only exclude the appearance of lawyers but also permit the appearance of agents and other professionals such as, chartered accountants, company secretaries, office[92] leaders of Trade Unions[93] etc. Though, any professional or representative, other than a lawyer, appearing on behalf of a party, before any

91. Charles, W. Welform, *Modern Legal Ethics*, 1985, p. 825.
92. The Companies Act, 1956.
93. The Industrial Disputes Act, 1947.

tribunal or forum, when permitted to do so have to rely on legislations, refer to case law and argue and this would virtually amount to practicing law, which is the prerogative of advocates.

But it should be noted carefully that Section 33 of the Advocates Act, uses the word 'practice' and while section 32 uses the word 'to appear' in the court. The special significance of the above word came up for consideration before a full Bench of Madras High Court, in *Thaamammal* v. *Kuppuswami Naidu*.[94] In the instant case, a lady who was not able to stay in Madras for conducting the case, appoint a power of attorney against to do several things on her behalf including 'appearing and pleading' in court. The agent claimed a right to plead in court just as advocate.

Chief Justice Beasley of the Madras High Court held that the "right to appear in court for principal under order 3, rules 1 and 2 of Civil Procedure Code, did not include a right to plead and that it meant only a power to take proceedings to submit oneself to jurisdiction. Therefore, an agent cannot claim the right as advocate".

The word 'any appearance application or act' in rule 1 of order III, Code of Civil Procedure, 1908 could not include pleading or arguing. Therefore, Rajasthan High Court in *Samdu Khan* v. *Mohan Lal*[95] held that a recognized agent holding a general power of attorney, could not be allowed to plead and argue for his principal. Likewise, in *Surendra Raj Jaiswal* v. *Chlaritty Commissioner*.[96] Andhra Pradesh High Court held that there are difference between 'right to practice' and 'to appear' in particular case. Therefore, the court cannot allow a person to appear in all matters, because that is the right of duly enrolled advocates.

The judicial pronouncements in the above decisions reveals that under Section 32 of the Advocates Act, a non-lawyer cannot claim to act as an advocate. But some flexibility is attached in view of special situation. Thus in *T.K. Kodandaram* v. *E. Manohar*,[97] the Madras High Court held that,

94. A.I.R. 1997 Mad. 752.
95. A.I.R. 1959 Raj. 35.
96. A.I.R. 2003 A.P. 317.
97. 1985 Cr.L.J. 124 (Mad.).

where no advocate was available to appear for the petitioner, permission given to petitioner's brother to represent him is just and proper. The judiciary is always conscious about the circumstances in which a person may be granted permission to appear in the particular case. An elaborate observation on the point was made by the Apex Court in *Harishankar Rastogi* v. *Girdhari Sharma*[98] speaking for the Supreme Court Mr. Justice Krishna Iyer said that a person who is not an advocate, has no right to barge into a court and argue for a party. He must get prior permission from the court. For which the motion must come from the person himself. It is the discretion of the court to grant or withhold permission. The court may even if it grants permission withdraw it half-way through, if the representative proves himself to be reprehensible. The court observed that a plurality of considerations should weigh with the court in granting permission. The judicial approach favours disallowing a non-advocates arguing before the Court. But in certain circumstances, when it becomes pressing demand of justice, courts allow non-advocate to argue before them.

In *Nimbaram Bora* v. *Union of India*,[99] an issue was raised before the Assam High Court whether a person could habitually represent parties in public interest litigations and conduct cases. It was argued that it would be a violation of Section 32 of the Advocates Act, 1961. Rejecting this contention the High Court observed that practice means repeated action or habitual performance or succession of acts of a similar kind. A person who is not an advocate have no absolute and blanket right to appear before the court or tribunals.

The learned Judge considered the scope of Sections 29 and 32 of the Advocates Act and observed that Section 32 contains a specific provision, which is both in negative and positive form and further referred to Section 45 to make it clear that a person who practice without any authority is liable for prosecution.

Likewise in *L.M. Manukar* v. *Bar Council of Maharashtra*,[100] the apex court dealing with a case of sales tax practitioner,

98. A.I.R. 1978 S.C. 1019.
99. A.I.R. 1992 Goa, 54.
100. A.I.R. 1996 S.C. 1602.

observed that a sales tax practitioner, although was allowed to practice under Section 24 of the Advocates Act, however an appearance before the Sales Tax authorities would not entitle him to practice law by virtue of the provisions of the Bombay Sales Tax Act.

It may be summed up that a right given to a person other than a lawyer is only permissive in nature and cannot be claimed of as a matter of right. The decisions discussed earlier also clarify that a mere right to appear in any matter, does not empower a person, either to be enrolled as an advocate or to argue matters of law as of right, because these right are only prerogative of duly enrolled advocates. In a nutshell right practice granted only to enrolled advocates is a rule and granting permission to no advocates in certain special cases is exception.

(ii) Autonomy of the Bar

The history of the autonomous bar in India shows that prior to the Advocates Act, there was lack of autonomy of bar in matters relating to the professional matters. In those days each High Court had a Bar Council of its own. The All India Bar Committee and the Law Commission recommended that a body to be called the 'All India Bar Council' should be established. Indeed, the All India Bar Committee had accepted the principle, while making recommendation that the Bar should be autonomous in the matter relating to the profession. While recommending that the state and All India Bar Council should, *interalia* consist of two judges nominated by the Chief Justice of High Court or Chief Justice of India, respectively, care was taken to ensure that the two judges nominated would be persons who had been advocates, so that notwithstanding judges being members, the council still retained their domestic character and were composed exclusively of advocates.[101]

Seeking to implement the recommendation of the All India Bar Committee and the Law Commission of India, the Advocates Act, 1961 was enacted. The Advocates Act made a drastic change in the field of legal profession, by not only

101. See XIVth Report of Law Commission of India, 1958, p. 576.

making the unification of the bar on all India basis, but also making the bar autonomous too.[102]

Therefore, true to the spirit of the recommendations made by the All India bar committee and Law Commission of India, the Act constituted Bar Council of India and 20 Bar Councils for the different States, at present, which are completely autonomous. Each council consists beside the Advocate General of State, of member elected in accordance with the system of proportional representation by means of single transferable vote from among the advocates on all of the State Bar Council. On the other hand Bar Council of India consists, beside the Attorney-General of India and the Solicitor General of India, of one member elected by each State Bar Council from among its members.

Section 3(3) of the Advocates Act, 1961 also provides that the State Bar Councils had to elect their Chairman and Vice-Chairman to be elected by Councils itself. Likewise Section 4(2) gave the same power to the Bar Council of India too.

In this regard it is relevant to note that during emergency an attempt was made to disturb the autonomy of the Bar, by the Parliamentary amendment[103] to the above sections of the Act. The said amendment affected the autonomy of the bar in the sense that, Attorney General of India became *ex-officio* Chairman and Solicitor General of India became *ex-officio* Vice-Chairman of the Bar Council of India and Advocate General of the States became *ex-officio* Chairman of the Bar Council of the States. In the case of Delhi Bar Council an advocate nominated by the Central Government, become the Chairman. The Central Government was also empowered to nominate one officer as a member of the Bar Council of India.

It may be submitted that the above amendment in Section 3 of the Advocates Act was most objectionable and inconsistent with the views and recommendation of the All India Bar Committee and the Law Commission of India. It was so retrograde and injurious to the autonomy and smooth functioning of the Bar Council that it invited vehement opposition and reactions from several Bar Council members'

102. *Supra* note 67-75.
103. Act No. 107 of 1976 (w.e.f. 15.10.1976).

and legal profession. The reaction was such that it could survive for land and in 1977, with the Change of Central Government, amendment which was created during emergency was called off by a fresh amendment.[104] It restored the pre-1976 position and once again established the democratic principle of elected Chairman and Vice-Chairman of the Bar Council of India and State Bar Councils. The provision relating to the nomination of an officer on the Bar Council of India was also omitted.

The above discussion reveals that the Advocates Act provided a autonomous Bar in India by ensuring the membership of the Bar Council only to advocates and no judge is nominated to it. Attorney General and Solicitor General or in the case of States Advocate General, who themselves are advocates simply are ex-officio members of the Bar.

It is also be noted that, the Act has not only ensured the Structural Autonomy of the Bar Councils of India and State Bar Councils, it has also created an autonomous bar in the sense of power too.

By virtue of the Advocates Act, every Bar Council is a body corporate, having perpetual succession and a common seal with power to acquire and hold property and to contract and may by its own name sue and be sued.[105] Section 6 of the Advocates Act, enumerates the various functions of the State Bar Councils.[106] While Section 7 provides, the functions of the Bar Council of India.[107]

The Advocates Act, 1961 made Bar Councils the master of their houses by authorising them to handle the matter of admission, enrolment and the cases of misconducts by advocates on its roll. In *Baldeo Raj Sharma* v. *Bar Council of India*,[108] the Apex Court of India upheld the power of the Bar Council to allow only regular law student to be enrolled as an advocate. Likewise in *Ratan Singh* v. *Bar Council of India*,[109]

104. Act No. 38 of 1977 (w.e.f. 31.10.1977).
105. Section 5 of Advocates Act, 1961.
106. *Ibid.*
107. *Ibid.*
108. A.I.R. 1989 S.C. 1541.
109. (1994) 2 S.C.C. 102.

Supreme Court upheld the power of the Bar Council of India to recognize only degrees in law of those who had attended lectures, tutorials and moot court.

The Bar Council can also frame rule for the above purpose, but the rules framed by the Bar Council have to be tested upon the touch stone of the constitutionality. Thus, in *V. Sudeer* v. *Bar Council of India,*[110] the Apex Court held that, the power of the Bar Council of India to frame rules regarding enrolment is not absolute and without limitations. It is subject to Part IIIrd of the constitutions, therefore, the rule providing for pre-enrolment training and apprenticeship is *ultravires*. Likewise, in *Indian Council of Legal Aid and Advice* v. *Bar Council of India,*[111] the Supreme Court made it clear that the rule debarring a person who has completed the age of forty-five year is beyond the rule making power of the Bar Council of India. The decisions of the Supreme Court appear to be too technical in view of under training of new entrants and their conducts not upto mark. However, in matters of discipline the Bar councils have full say. Prior to the Advocates Act, 1961, the Bar did not have autonomy in Matters of disciplinary actions against its members. Earlier the courts had disciplinary power over the advocates. Even under Bar Council of India Act, 1926 the State Bar Councils had been given power to initiate an inquiry and then to recommend the High Court to punish the advocates committing professional misconduct. The Act for the first time made the legal profession autonomous in respect of the management of its own affairs and claiming right to set its house on right path. Under the Act, the Court's jurisdiction in disciplinary matters was completely ousted. The Supreme Court has been given only appellate jurisdiction under Section 38 of the Act and no jurisdiction in the ordinary course of the things.

Thus, it is clear from the above discussion that with the complete control and jurisdiction regarding enrolment of advocates, their discipline and other powers, the Bar Councils have become completely autonomous bodies with elected representatives of Bar. The Advocates Act, 1961 by unifying

110. A.I.R. 1995 S.C. 1167.
111. A.I.R. 1995 S.C. 691.

and organizing the independent Bar in India has stimulated a new sense of unity, dignity and pride among the members of the Bar, and brought a fresh hope to the legal practitioners about their profession. It is hoped that the conferment of privileges and opportunity will also result in a new sense of responsibility and service, lawyers will acquire fresh prestige in society and free and sovereign State of India will get a Bar worthy of new status among the nations of the world.

Since bench and bar are two wheels of the chariot of justice both wheels have to be in right condition and therefore, two ensuing chapter will be devoted to the study of the nature and high tradition of Bar with a view to give the clear message for future course of conduct to be observed by those by whom the profession is manned and the high tradition and image of judiciary.

3

High Traditions and Present Status of the Legal Profession

The field of law has not remained static nor a mere social science, but, it has developed into a veritable science touching various aspects of life and challenges of various other social sciences. The legal profession has to accept these realities to enhance itself to meet these modern challenges. There is no doubt that medicine, education, journalism and accountancy among others, are liberal, dignified and noble profession, however, there is no other profession in which a high tradition of morality is more imperatively necessary than that of the law.

There is certainly without any exception, no profession in which so many temptations beset the path to swerve from the line of strict integrity. "The legal profession is marked by prevalent high character and deserved reputation for learning and honesty. It has not only set itself high standards of professional conducts but has also been strenuous in following and maintaining them".[1]

1. Gururajachari, K., *Advocacy and Professional Ethics*, Ist ed. (2000), p. 4.

The legal profession is the presentation of logical facts of any disputes in a right perspective, dealing with the criterion of differentiating between right and wrong, just and unjust, equitable and inequitable by applying the knowledge of law acquired by extensive and intensive learning; and in doing so, it employs the noblest faculties of the human mind and soul in order to discover the true motives of his action. The highest compliment paid to the legal profession is that lawyers run civilization for us and the institution of advocates promotes confidence in the administration of justice.

For the above reasons the legal profession is graded the highly esteemed profession. Some paradox however is attached to this high profile profession. Though, the legal profession has always been regarded as noble, honourable and the profession of high tradition throughout the world "the members of the profession are not always held in high esteems".

Thus, there was a time when lawyers were regarded as a society friend. "They commanded awe and respect, but at present the public image of legal profession is far from Flattering. They are seen as fortune seekers rather than seeking to serve, a selfish class who on account of their special knowledge and expertise, provide services on such terms as they please.[2] Bentham, himself a lawyer described his uncle as "one of the gentlest of all human being though a lawyer by profession". Even a well known legal scholar Maitland passed the remark that "Englishman do not love lawyers and the law they have loved they did not think of as lawyer's law. Lord Brougham defined a lawyer as a "learns gentleman who rescues your estate from your enemies and keeps it himself".[3]

In short, the legal profession is no longer noble profession and at present it is regarded as a money making private company.

An attempt will be made in this chapter to discuss and examine the nature and present status of the legal profession under the following heads—

---

2. Sorabji, J. Soli, "Lawyers as professionals", A.I.R.(J) 2002, p. 4.
3. As quoted Prasad, Anirudh, *Principles of the Ethics of Legal Profession in India*, 2nd ed. (2006), p. 53.

I. NECESSITY OF THE LEGAL PROFESSION

From the very inception of human civilization, law exist in various forms. In ancient era law could be found in the form of the principles of morality, which imposed obligations upon mankind. If it in this sense that Manusmriti, Arthashastra and the Quran refer to law, judges, courts and advocates. The law has played an important role in the history of the development of human being and moral principles of society. The nature of law has been changing according to time, place and the requirements of the people, though justice as its goal remains unchanged. As dispenser of justice the profession of law has been and still is essential in all societies whether ancient or modern. It is essential to move machine of civilization. As justice Mc Cardie says:

> "the alternative to the reign of law is the chaos of the jungle. Imagine what would be the state of things, if every litigant were to plead his own case. Conceive a court without a Bar. Conceive the situation of a judge set to try causes and administered legal rights between party and party without the aid of professional advocates".[4]

A lawyer represents facts for his clients and assists the judges to arrive at correct, rather fairest judgment. This is the arch-duty of an advocate. Moreover, he can play and has to play an active and vital role in other fields of national and social service. Thus, the legal profession is essential to provide a rational balance in order to arrive at just decisions. Employment of advocates by the litigants has ceased to be a thing merely of convenience and has become a matter of necessity. In this regard 'Forsyth' has rightly said that the advocates are the organs whereby the complicated wants of mankind reach the ear of Themis".[5]

It is important to note that, the need of members of the public for legal services arises as they recognize their legal

4. Ramchandran Raju, *Legal Ethics*, 2006 edition, Butterworth Publication, p. 233.
5. As quoted Anand, C.L., Principles of Legal Ethics, p. 49.

problems, appreciate the importance of seeking assistance, and are able to obtain the service of acceptable legal counsel.[6] Hence, it is important function of the legal profession to educate people, to recognize their problems, to facilitate the process of intelligent selection of lawyer and to assist in making legal services. To quote Forsyth again, "as the relation of society continue to grow more varied and complex, so will the lawyers' profession become corresponding more essential in the adjustment of any difference that may arise; because there can be no civilization without order; and there can be no order without law and no law without lawyers to interpret it.[7]

Thus, in a law courts effective representation of litigants is not possible without a specialized and impartial professional to plead for them, because the proliferation of enactments is so technical that a common man cannot argue his own case successfully.

The above view has also been subscribed by judiciary. As justice Sutherland pointed out in *Powell* v. *Albama*":[8]

> "Even the intelligent and educated layman has small and sometimes no skill in the science of law. If charged with crime, he is incapable, of determining for himself whether the indictment is good or bad. He is unfamiliar with the rules of evidence. Left without the aid of counsel he be put on trail without a proper charge and convicted upon incompetent evidence or evidence irrelevant to the issue or otherwise inadmissible. He lacks both the skill and knowledge adequately to prepare his defence, even though he has a perfect one. He requires the guiding hand of counsel at every step in the proceedings against him. Without it, though he be not guilty, he faces the danger of conviction because he does not know how to establish his innocence. If that be true of men of intelligence how much more true is it of the ignorance and illiterate, or those of feeble intellect".

6. Canon 2.1 of the New York Bar Association.
7. *Supra* note 5.
8. 1898, All E.R., 72.

Likewise the apex court of India also recognized the necessity of advocates. In the case of *Sukh Das* v. *Union Territory of Arunachal Pradesh*[9] the Supreme Court of India observed:

> "Even literate people do not know what are their rights and entitlements under the law. It is this absence of legal awareness which is responsible for the deception, exploitation and deprivation of rights and benefits from which the poor suffer in this land. Their legal needs always stand to become crisis-oriented because their ignorance prevents them from anticipating legal troubles and approaching a lawyer for consultation and advice in time their poverty magnifies the impact of the legal troubles and difficulties when they come. Moreover, because of their ignorance and illiteracy, they cannot become self-reliant; they cannot even help themselves. The law ceases to be their protector because they do not know that they are entitled to the protection of the law and they can avail of the legal service programme for putting and end to their exploitation and winning the rights".

However, not only the litigants but the judges also need the help of the advocates to aid them in coming to just conclusion. Thus, the beneficial effect of the employment of advocates in the administration of justice is unbounded. Judicial administration functions and duties assigned to judges under the democratic government would be inoperative or would operatic in vacuum if the Advocates were absent. The existence of the members of the legal profession is imperative to the fulfilment of the duty imposed upon the judiciary by the laws of a democracy and the rule of law. Another field, wherein the necessity of legal profession is mostly recognized, is the legislation.

By reason of the experience gained in the daily application and interpretation of laws, the lawyers become best aware of the imperfections of the legal system and constitute

9. A.I.R. 1986 S.C. 991.

the most competent class of man to advise on law reform and to promote popular enthusiasm and support for it. The most difficult part of the process of legislation is the drafting of its provisions and no one is better fitted to give guidance on this, than the lawyers. In the discharge of their functions in the law courts lawyers develop such habits and training which eminently qualify them to play their part successfully in the legislative debates. Their broad general education and daily close contacts with all sections of society make them most fitted for leadership in the political affairs of the community. Thus, it is not therefore, surprising that in the democratic states, where political institution rest on the electoral principles; lawyers generally dominate the legislative bodies; because people choose them as their representatives. It is common knowledge that in Nehru Cabinet there were 62 percent, in Lal Bahadur Shastri's Cabinet 65 percent and in Indira Gandhi's first three Cabinets on an average 63 percent ministers who had law degree. More than one fourth M.Ps. in Lok Sabha has been the law degree holders. In crisis situation lawyers have led the people. Advocates led the freedom movement,[10] framing of the constitution[11] and raised voice against 1975 internal emergency.[12]

Hence, it will be relevant to take into account the remarkable contribution of advocates in securing and maintaining independence of the nation. Indian history of independence shows that the movement was led and guided by prominent advocates. "It can be unhesitatingly said that

---

10. During the struggle for the independence country was benefited by the service of the top rank lawyers like Mahatma Gandhi, Pandit Motilal Nehru, Lala Lajpat Rai, C.R. Das, Pandit J.L. Nehru, Sardar Ballabh Bhai Patel, B. Desai, etc.
11. The Constituent Assembly was dominated by Lawyers and/or men with law. G. Austin identified "inner circle" of eleven senior persons who guided the work of Assembly, viz. Rajendra Prasad, Azad, Patel, Nehru, Pant, Sitaramaya Sinha, B.R. Ambedkar, A.K. Ayer, N.G. Ayyangar and K.M. Munsi were lawyers or had taken law degree.
12. During emergency country was benefited by the service of top rank Lawyers. For detail, see, H.R. Khanna: *Neither Roses nor Thorn*, Eastern Book Company, pp. 74-75.

their jurisprudential and legal thinking accompanied by their morality might have helped them in achieving these credits".[13]

It should be noted carefully, that Mahatma Gandhi showed the way of non-violence and truth. Vallabh Bhai Patel guided against injustice and suppression, and Jawaharlal Nehru put the foundation stone of non-alignment and world peace. They had insight of the minds and hearts of masses.

Thus, it is clear from the foregoing discussion, that legal profession is an essential necessity of the society. It holds a unique place in the life of the community. Sir John Duoys has rightly said that "for neither do all men at any time, nor any one man at all times, stand in need of the physician for they that are in the health the great physician of our souls and our only advocate which is in heaven. That all men at all times and all places, do stand in need of justice; and of law which is the goal of justice and of the interpreters and Ministers of Law, which gave life and motion unto justice".[14]

It is submitted that the soul of legal profession is not making large income but delivery of effective justice to the community. However, it will be possible only when, if the true nature of accountability to the people, to the court and to the justice itself, is realized and the profession make themselves accountable to the people that the professions become relevant to society.

II. STATUS AND NATURE OF THE LEGAL PROFESSION

The state of any profession is closely linked with its members and their physical, mental, intellectual, moral, ethical and spiritual values, that is attached to life. A question always arises, that what is profession and what's difference between profession and business? Webester Dictionary defines profession as calling requiring specialized knowledge and often long and intensive preparation including instruction in skills and methods and committing its members to continued

13. Austin Granville: *Indian Constitution: A Cornerstone of A Nation* (1966) 164.
14. Quoted from Gurarajachari, K., *Advocacy and Professional Ethics*, Ist ed. 2000, p. 79.

study and to a kind of work which has for its prime purpose the rendering of a public service".

Thus, the term refers to a group of men pursuing a learned art as a common calling in the sprit of public service. No less would amount to a public service because it may incidentally be a means of livelihood. Pursuit of the learned art in the sprit of a public service is the prime purpose. However, a profession implies something more than specialist knowledge and the ability to apply it for the benefits of clients. It implies also a desire among the members of the calling to serve the public. Dean Roscoe Pound summed up the matter with admirable aptness when he said, "Historically there are three ideas involved in a profession, i.e. Gainistation, Learning and Sprit of public service".[15]

These are essential and the remaining idea that of gaining a livelihood is incidental. Theoretically, public service motivation and intellectualized expertise for community good are dominant, with a discipline and high ethics to guide their exercise and income for the practitioner and material success for one's client being lesser values in the scale.

In fact the essence of a profession lies in three things, viz.

(i) Organization of its members for the performance of their function;
(ii) Maintenance of certain standards, intellectual and ethical, for the dignity of the profession; and
(iii) Subordination of pecuniary gain to efficient service.

Thus, in any profession organization is first thing. Unlike a trade or business a profession is not simply a collection of individuals who get a living for themselves by some kind of work. It is however, possible that a group of persons engaged in some trade may also organize themselves for the economic protection of its members. Organization therefore, is not the distinguishing feature of a profession. The second normal characteristic of a profession is the maintenance of certain standards, intellectual and ethical, on the part of the members, both of dignity of the vocation and for better quality of service

15. Pound, *A Hundred Years of American Law,* 8 (1937), p. 39.

of the public. It assumes certain responsibilities for the competence of its members, and deliberately prohibits certain kinds of conduct on the ground that, though they may be profitable to the individual, they are calculated to bring into disrepute the organization to which he belongs. The third characteristic which is the distinguishing feature of a profession is the subordination of pecuniary gains to the efficient service.

Thus, in business the only criterion of success is the financial return which it offers to its shareholders. The essence of a profession is that though men enter it for the sake of livelihood, the measure of their success is the service which they perform to promote health, safety and good of the society and not the gains which they amass. While in business any kind of conduct is allowable which increases the income, in a profession there are certain kinds of conduct which be practiced, however.[16]

Justice Brandeis of the U.S. Supreme Court also applied three criteria to a profession, *first*, a profession is an occupation for which the necessary preliminary training is intellectual in character, involving knowledge and to some extent learning, as distinguished from mere skill. *Second*, it is an occupation which is pursued largely for others and not merely for one's self; and *third*, it is an occupation in which the amount financial return is not the accepted measure of success.[17]

Thus, it is forgotten that, the essential difference between business and a profession is that while the chief end of business is personal gain, the main goal of a profession is public service. The legal profession is marked as noble profession. It is also marked by prevalent high character and a deserved reputation for learning and honesty. It has not only set itself high tradition of professional conduct, but it has also been strenuous in following and maintaining them. "The members of legal profession deserve to be highly esteemed because, with such large members at the Bar, with such varied activities in which he is called upon to take a responsible part, and with such opportunities and temptation to misconduct

16. Shetree Shimon, *Judges on Trial*, 1976, p. 279.
17. *Supra* note 14 p. 284.

himself, he has not fallen from his high estate with any frequency".[18]

The profession of law is a great calling, and to discharge the responsibility, the members of this profession must make themselves equal to the task. It is a great profession of talents and talent is bound to make headway through many vicissitudes of circumstances and through many reversible of fortune.

For the above reasons the legal profession calls for great knowledge, high mental capacity and wide culture. Such qualities of the legal profession are being discussed hereafter.

(A) Profession of High Traditions

High tradition is the first and foremost essential nature of the legal profession, because lawyers are the inheritors of tradition of scholarship, wisdom, dignity, courage and service. The spirit amongst lawyers is one of generous emulation and not of embittered and petty rivalry. The high traditions of the legal profession are springs of strength and sustenance in its days of trial. Thus, the profession of the lawyer is perhaps the single most powerful instrument for the protection of the liberty of man and decencies of the civilized living.

As the lawyer is an officer of the court, it is his duty to assist the court in administration of justice. He must, therefore, strictly and scrupulously abide by the code of conduct behaving the profession and must not indulge in any activity which may tend to lower the image of the profession in the society. A basic tenet of the professional responsibility of lawyer is that every person in our society has ready access to the independent professional service of a lawyer of integrity and competence.[19] Maintaining the integrity and improving the competence of the Bar to meet the highest standards is the ethical responsibility of every lawyer.

The profession of advocate is monopolistic in character and this monopoly itself has certain high traditions which its

18. Aiyer Krishna Swamy, *Professional Conduct and Advocacy*, IIIrd ed., Oxfrord University, p. 92.
19. See, also Canon 1.1 of New York Bar Association on Professional Ethics.

members are expected to upkeep and uphold. In *Bar Council of Maharastra* v. *M.V. Dabholkar,*[20] Mr. Justice V.R. Krishna Iyer very aptly observed:

> "The Bar is not private guild, like that of barbers, butchers and candlestick makers, but by bold contrast, a public institution committeed to public justice and *'pro pono publico service'*. The grant of a monopoly licence to practice law is based on three assumptions. *First,* there is a socially useful function for the lawyer to perform; *Second,* the lawyer is a professional person who will perform that function and *Third,* his performance as a professional person is regulated by himself and more formally, by the profession as a whole. The central function that the legal profession must perform is nothing less than the administration of justice".

Since the duty of an advocate is to assist the court in the administration of justice, the practice of law has also morals flavour. Consequently, an advocate is required to be absolutely fair with moral excellence. He should not betray the confidence and the interest of his client of which he is trustee.

Money is not needed as much as the maintenance of honesty and character. "There are pitfalls of temptations at every step in the legal profession but it is only one's moral excellence which acts like a torch in darkness".[21]

It is, Therefore, necessary for a lawyer from the commencement of his career as lawyer to cultivate truth, honesty and moral excellence above all the other things in the society. However, morality does not pay in the beginning for his substance, but ultimately it bring reputation which is highly paying to the profession.

With these expectations the legal profession is known as high tradition's profession. It is a profession of faith and a profession of trust. Ryan poignantly articulates the extremity of expectation with lawyers, when he says—

20. A.I.R. 1987 S.C. 242.
21. *Id.*, p. 245.

"The world may from, friend falls off, children rebel, wife desert or betray; but the client has an adherent whose faith never fails; whose loyalty never wavers; truth to death and to the memory which survives death. It is the wise policy of the law that lawyer should be the legal alter ego of his client".[22]

The foregoing discussion reveals that the legal profession expects from the lawyer not only for his better legal opinions and professional conduct, but the correctness of his moral attitude also. Every lawyer owes a solemn duty to uphold the integrity and honour of the profession, because in the recent era of globalization the imminent change of unpredictable dimensions, there are certain basic values and immutable varieties that are at the core of the tradition of legal profession which continue to sustain and inspire it. Thus, the members of the legal profession, both as a man and as a professional, must cherish these values. The advocates to be respected in society shall continue to be a scholar, a fearless warrior, a compassionate field and above all a great gentleman.

(B) Learned Profession

The profession of law is regarded as learned profession, because learning is supposed to be part of the equipment of legal professionals. The component[23] of legal profession have always to engage them in the process of learning. They spend tirelessly the weary hours after mid-night accounting themselves with the great body of tradition and learning the law, because they know Bacon's version of reading that "reading must be chewed and digested".

It must be the aim of an advocate to be person of varied accomplishment because there is hardly any subject with which a lawyer may not have to deal in his professional work. However, "it is not necessary that the advocate must have the knowledge of each and every subject on the earth, but an advocate should be jack of all trades but master on none

22. Quoted from Boorstin: *The Americans: The Colonial Experience,* 199 (1958), p. 7.
23. The Judges and Advocates.

except the case which he is pleading in the court of law". He should possess the knowledge of humanities, social and technological science. For instance, when he is pleading a case relating to building construction, he must know about the architecture and be able to form an opinion as to the requirements of materials needed for the construction of a structure; when he is pleading a case relating grievous hurt, he must know something about the medicine and surgery; and in a case relating to dissemination he has to depict himself as a poet, a novelist and an author. In this regard Lord Brougham has rightly said that "a lawyer must know everything about something and something about everything".[24]

Thus, it is therefore, necessary for lawyers to know the law and other subject to some extent and to know the source from where to find them out. Learning begets courage and wise self-confidence can only be founded on knowledge. It is only possible through learning which an advocate has to do in his every day life. They should be learned not only in law but also in fact. They should know how to apply laws in set of certain facts. An advocate should never go to the court without thorough preparation.

These are the expectations from this highly great profession, and these expectations are also the reason, why the legal profession is called a learned profession. It is important to note that, in the legal profession there is no such thing as knowledge which is useless. A man may not be better engineer because he is a good classic or a more successful merchant because he is a good linguist, but at the Bar the wider the field of knowledge the better.[25] It will be useful to quote what Sharaswoods said of the legal profession:

> "A lawyer without the most sterling integrity, may shine for a while with meteoric splendour, but his light will soon go to out in blackness of dark. It is not in every man's power to rise to eminence by distinguished abilities. It is not in every man's power, to attain respectability, competence and usefulness. The

24. *Supra* note 1, p. 5.
25. Clark, *Great Saying By Great Lawyers*, IVth ed., p. 67.

temptations which beset a young man in the outset of his professional life, especially if he is in absolute dependence upon profession for his subsistence, are very great. The strictest, principles of integrity and honour are his only safety".[26]

Again, pointing out of the advantage of learned profession Sharaswood said "It is one of the most striking advantages of having learned profession, who engage as a business in representing in courts of justice, that men are Thus, brought nearer to a condition of equality that causes and tried and decided upon their merits and do not depend upon the personal character and qualification of immediate parties".[27]

Thus, the foregoing discussion reveals that the profession of law is known as learned profession. It is a nature of this profession, that it has not satisfied with the bones of law and their knowledge, but it has always to search the truth beyond that in light of the knowledge of other allied and necessary subjects required for its interpretation. The importance of education and learning the law and other social sciences is the necessary equipment of the legal profession, which is universally recognized today. Therefore, in England members of the legal profession have always controlled the training of persons for admission to the Bar. The Inns of courts, now-a-days are some of the best colleges of law in the world. It act jointly for the purpose of determining rules for the admission of student, conduct examinations and call to the Bar. The Benches of each Inn may refuse to admit a student or refuse to call him to the Bar on the ground of unfitness. For the practice he has to previously serve as an apprentice for at least one year. However, in Germany, France and Austria the standard of legal education are much higher, wherein for the practice of law it is necessary that a person has law graduate degree and thereafter to get graining for a couple of years and finally, he must pass a state examination which will qualify him for admission to the rank of advocates. In the United States the minimum standards prescribed for a law degree is

26. *Ibid.*
27. *Id.*, p. 71.

of three years whole time course after not less than two years course is an Arts or Science college of University.[28]

However, in India for the practice of law only the LL.B. degree is required. The necessity of apprenticeship was called off in the year about 1999-2000.

(C) A Noble Profession

The profession of law is regarded also, as a noble profession. It includes as one of the five intellectual professions[29] and not only this, the profession of law is regarded to "excel all other professions due to its element of enforcement of justice".[30]

Legal profession derives its nobility necessarily from its moral, social and national duties cast upon the advocates. So it would be absurd to talk of an advocate as a noble profession if he doesn't observe these necessary professional ethics and moral duties. Therefore, in this context, it would be interesting to quote view of Mahatma Gandhi.

> "I had learnt the true practice of law. I had learnt to find out the better side of human nature and to enter man's heart". I realized that the true function of a lawyer was to unite parties given as under. The lesson was so deeply burnt into me that a large part of my time during the twenty years of my practice as a lawyer was occupied in bringing about private compromises of hundreds of cases. I lost nothing thereby not even money; certainly not by soul".[31]

The nobility of this profession calls for settling the disputes and avoiding furtherance of these disputes by every possible means. The apex court of the India in the case of *In re Sanjiv Bitta, Deputy Secretary, Ministry of Information and*

28. Bhatt Jitendra (J), "The American Bar Association" (2001) 1 S.C.C., pp. 18-22.
29. That is, Theology, Medicine, Education and Accountancy.
30. Ruskin (J.), Unto the Last, Ist ed., 47.
31. Gandhi M.K., *My Experiments with Truth*, p. 100.

Broadcasting,[32] held that "It is in the hands of the members of the legal profession to improve the quality of the service, they render both the litigant public and to the courts, and to brighten their image in the society. The legal profession is a solemn and serious occupation. It is noble calling and all of those who belong to it are its honourable member. The legal profession is different from other profession in that what the lawyers do, affects not only an individual but also the administration of justice, which is the foundation of the civilized society. It must not be forgotten that the legal profession has always been held in high esteem and its members have played an enviable role in public life".

The above view of the honourable Supreme Court shows that the legal profession is a noble profession not merely in the sense that learning and knowledge is displayed in the practice of it but that it calls for the high noble conduct which is a corollary and consequence of all true knowledge.

Again, in *Shambhu Ram Yadav* v. *Hanuman Das Khatri*[33] the Supreme Court held that, "The credibility and reputation of the profession depends upon the manner in which the members of the profession conduct themselves. There is a heavy responsibility on those in whom duty has been vested under the Advocates Act, 1961 to take disciplinary action when the credibility and reputation of the profession comes under a clout on account of acts of omission and commission by any member of the profession.

In this regard, it is submitted that no doubt if an advocate does anything which is against the credibility or nobility of the profession, the provisions of Advocates Act are available to punish the lawyer, but it should be noted that the nobility of the legal profession is also based on its self-regulatory or in house correction norms. The proceeding from a conception of law as a noble and nearly spiritual profession is a foregrounding of its massive influence. It lies on the codes of ethics governing relationship between Bench and Bar and the people at large which is self-regulatory and cases of

32. (1995)3 S.C.C. 619.
33. *Roman Service Private Limited* v. *Subhas Kapoor and Others*, A.I.R. 2001 S.C. 207, p. 212.

professional or other misconduct are tackled by the bar itself and not by any external agency.

(D) Profession of Great Honour and Dignity

The profession of law is also regarded as dignified profession. It is a profession of great honour, because no other person carrying on any other profession has to shoulder greater responsibilities than persons engaged in this profession. Members of the legal profession are concededly the elite of the society. They have always been in the vanguard of the progress and development of not only law, but the polity as a whole.

Citizenary looks at them with hope and expectations for traversing on the new paths and virgin fields to be marched on by the society. "The profession by and large, till date has undoubtedly performed its duties and obligations and has never hesitated to shoulder its responsibilities in larger interests of the men. The lawyers, who have been acknowledged being sober, task-oriented, professionally responsible stratum of the population, are further obliged to utilize their skills for socio-political modernization of the country".[34]

Thus, by these reasons the legal profession is composed by a body of persons with a high sense of honour. In England the place of the training of Barristers, i.e. Inns of the court, were older law colleges and were described as honourable societies.

Now the question is why the legal profession is regarded as honourable and dignified profession in the society? Is the legal profession dignified and honourable merely because lawyers wish to practise their vocation? If not wherein lays the greatness and honour of the legal profession?

The honourable and dignified position of the legal profession is largely due to the tradition of Bar stood against the tyranny. It lies in the first place in the codes of its ethics governing the relations of lawyer between themselves and with others in their professional capacities. Advocates gave to the society, the idea of a professional ethics existing over and above the ordinary rule of morality which governs the

34. *Ibid.*, p. 213.

relations of men in general. Thus, the rules of ethics are the most glorious heritage of the legal profession. With these rules the legal profession constitutes the badges of honour and dignity.

It may be submitted that these rules of conduct and ethics gave this position to legal profession because in the absence of these rules, the legal profession will degenerate into a trade or mere sordid pursuit for livelihood and accumulation of wealth.

The honourable and dignified position of legal profession lies in the second place in the high function of advocates in society, because they are the guardians of three of the greatest gifts of modern civilization, namely order, justice and liberty. Justice Nageshwar Prasad has rightly said that "It is no wonder, that lawyers through the ages in all countries have enjoyed esteemed respect as pillars of justice, a preserve of the weak and poor against oppressor or tyrants as upholders of the freedom and liberty of human being, as a sword for the guilty and a shield for innocent".[35]

Similarly, the dignity of the legal profession lies in third place in its appearance and symbolization. Advocates like judges wear in court the 'Robes' of their office which is a mark of dignity.[36] Band is an essential part of Advocate's official costume like the gown.[37] Provided that the wearing of advocates' gowns shall be optional except when appearing of the Supreme Court or High Court.[38] In court other than High Court and Supreme Court a black tie may be worn instead of bands.[39]

Beside being a profession of dignity and responsibility, it is the noblest of profession and the most honourable of all secular profession. The practice of law is elevated, clothed with so lofty a mission that its practitioners are to be exhorted to loftier path and higher destinies than those of others. The legal profession is a profession which is exercised in all free

35. Prasad, Nageshwar, "Professional Ethics", A.I.R. (J) 1962, p. 42.
36. The dress is worn only when they appear in court.
37. Chapter IV of the Bar Councils of India Rule, 1975 as on 31st July, 1995.
38. *Ibid.*
39. *Ibid.*

governments, a controlling influence and which is more intimately connected with acts more powerfully with reference to the interest of the society.

After independence the concept of social justice has become a part of our legal system. This concept gives meaning and significance to the democratic ways of life and of making the life dynamic. The concept of welfare state would remain an oblivion unless social justice in dispensed with. The prevailing willing socio-economic-political system is the country needs treatment which can immediately be provided by judicial decisions.[40]

Such a surgery is impossible to be performed unless, the Bench and the Bar make concerted effort. Thus, the role of the members of legal profession assumed great importance in the society.

But today the legal profession does not enjoy the same degree of public confidence as it did two decades ago. Now the legal profession is going on political and business line. It is more commercialized and there is steep fall in professional ethics. Therefore, it will be relevant to discuss the causes of deterioration in the image of legal profession at present.

III. FALLING STANDARDS AND DEGRADATION OF THE LEGAL PROFESSION

The earlier discussion under this chapter reveals that the legal profession is a highly ethical and noble profession and a profession of great honour and dignity. "Lawyers run our civilization for us". The profession dominated the public life of the country and played prominent role in the social, economic and political life of the common persons.

However, some paradox is attached with this noble profession. At present the image of legal profession is not far from faltering. Though the legal profession has always been regarded as a noble and honourable profession throughout the world but the members of this profession are not always held in high esteem. In fact the criticism is as old as the profession itself. Plato said that "it was a sign of intemperate and corrupt

40. *Supra* note 33, p. 623.

Commonwealth where lawyers abounded". Bentham, himself a lawyer described his uncle as 'one of the gentlest of all human being though a lawyer by profession'.

Likewise, a famous Attorney General of India, Soli, J. Sorabjee comments that "Lawyers are seen as fortune seekers rather than seeking to serve, a selfish class who on account of their special knowledge and expertise, provide services on such terms they please".[41] Lawyers have been called both unavoidable scoundrels and necessary evil. "They are said to be unsocial robots whose duty is to lie, conceal and distort everything and slander everybody, and to fortify their position the lawyers resort to writing and speaking in a language that is hardly understandable to non-lawyers. Often it is said that the minute you read something you cannot understand, you can almost be sure it was drawn up by a lawyer".

Thus, the members of legal profession are addressed as "learned for learning is supposed to be part of their equipment. Some remark that gone are the days when learning as such had its own value. But today when the economic barons rule the roost, lawyers are not far behind. The profession has, thus, been turned into a bread and butter supply industry or into a commercial organization, devaluing learning as such in its process.[42]

It has dehumanized the human depriving him of the finer sensitivities and more especially of the moral and ethical values.[43]

Moreover, it is relevant to note that the Law Commission of India was also worried about the general loss of moral prestige of the legal profession. In its 14th report[44] the commission noted that—

> "The evidence given before us reveals a general consensus that there is a fall in efficiency and standards at the Bar. The recent recruit to the profession is said to be interior in

41. *Supra* note 2.
42. Crally Bimal, "A Minusule Profile of Lawyers And His Profession", A.I.R. (J) 2000, p. 205.
43. *Id.*, p. 206.
44. See the Report of 1958, p. 170.

his legal equipment, less painstaking and in a hurry to find work".

Thus, the legal profession has lost its leadership in public life. These days the legal profession is being criticized from different quarters. There seem to a vital gap between expectations, high moral ideals and the hard reality. Today people are apt to agree with Dean Swift's description of lawyers as a society of men bread up from their youth in the art of proving by words multiplied for the purpose, that white is black and black is white, according as they are paid "no longer is the profession of law regarded as noble one".[45]

Now the question is what are the reasons for this said decline? What are aliments? Why legal profession is loosing fast its credibility? Some of the reasons may be advanced for the said deterioration in the image of the legal profession.

(A) System of Legal Education

Legal education is the foundation of sound legal profession and therefore, the quality of legal profession will depend on the quality of legal education. The discussion about the degradation of legal profession may be started with the condition of education in law colleges and the universities. If we start with legal education from our law colleges and the universities, it can be found that by and large the condition of our educational institutions is in very deportable position.

. It is undoubtedly accepted that in India the legal education, which is the basis of an efficient legal profession and a well organized and sound judicial system, was not paid due attention during the British period. In pre-independence era condition of legal education was more neglected. As early as 1948, the *Radha Krishanan Commission on University Education*[46] in its report lamented "our colleges of law do not hold a place of high esteem either at home or abroad, nor law has become an area of profound scholarship and enlightened research".

45. *Supra* note 2.
46. *Supra* note 3 p. 68.

Similarly, after ten year of Radha Krishnan Commission, the Law Commission of India[47] was also of the view that the condition of our law colleges was very ill. The Law Commission reiterated the same feelings, when it stated that—

> "It is unfortunate that we should have to present to dismal a picture of the character of legal education imparted in the majority of institutions named by part-time teachers and accessible to any graduate of mediocre ability and indifferent merit".

While deploring the deterioration of the standards of legal education the Law Commission of India suggested that the All India Bar Council should be given certain powers for improving such standards. Accordingly, the Advocates Act, 1961 was enacted and All India Bar Council has been empowered with several powers[48] to deal with the legal education. With these powers in hand, the Bar Council of India is trying, regularly to regulate and update the legal education as well as the entire legal profession.

The position of legal education in post-independence era is marked by the involvement of the Bar Council of India, statutory body empowered to lay down to standards for improvement of legal education. Such a body was not available in pre-independence era. The Bar Council of India has been trying its best to raise the standard of legal education. But due to numerous factors the condition of legal education, barring at few institutions, is not satisfactory.

Before coming to the causes of degradation of legal profession it is relevant to give in brief the steps taken by the Bar Council for improving the conditions of legal education.

---

47. Law Commission of India XIVth Report, 1958.
48. Section 49(1)(c) of the Advocates Act, 1961, provides "The Bar Council of India may make rules for discharging its functions under the Act and in particular such rules may prescribe the standards of legal education to be observed by the Universities in India and inspection of Universities for the purpose". The Bar Council of India has full autonomy for regulating the legal education. Its' powers are independent from U.G.C. or Central Government or the State Government.

Following steps of the Bar Council of India are intended to regulate the legal education in India.

Earlier, the LL.B. degree course was of two years duration. This period was not sufficient to cover the important branches of law. Subsequently, the period of two years was extended to three years by the Bar Council of India.[49] The Council found that even this period was not sufficient for covering the subjects newly introduced by the council itself and then the Bar Council of India started a separate LL.B. degree course for five years.

Now, by virtue of the Bar Council of India Rules, the two years degree course has been done away and both the three years and five years degree course may be run jointly or separately by the law colleges and the universities in the same institutions.[50] After recognizing the two separate periods of LL.B. degree course the Bar Council of India found that the extension of the period would not be sufficient for improving the legal education unless its syllabus is prepared taking into account the relevant and practical importance of law.

Keeping the above object in mind the Bar Council has introduces 28 compulsory papers for teaching including four papers exclusively of practical training, requiring knowledge of English and now legal language, revising courses from time to time, requiring whole time law colleges/universities, minimum 66 percent attendance, fixing the ratio of part-time teachers upto maximum of 25 percent of the full strength of

49. Menon Madhav, N.R., "Restructuring the Legal Profession for Strengthening Administration of Justice" (in) Vol. 15(1). I.B.R., p. 82.
50. Rule 1 (Sections A and B) of Part IVth of the Bar Council of India Rules, 1975. It provides that, for enrolment under three year course it is necessary for the candidate that he has obtained a graduate degree or equivalent to a graduate degree. However, for the five years course he must passed 10+2 or 11+1 examination recognized by the educational authority of Central or State Governments or possesses such academic qualifications which are considered equivalent to 10+2 or 11+1 courses by the Bar Council of India. The five years degree course shall comprise two parts viz., part I which will be a two year course programme of pre-law study as necessary qualifications for entering to next three years course of study in law to be commenced thereafter. The last six months of three years of the law course shall include a regular course of practical training.

the full time teaching staff. Introducing semester system of imparting legal education along with seminars and tutorials and another several steps,[51] which are the great measures in improving the conditions of legal education.

Though some improvement came about through these steps taken by the Bar Council, the greed of some college managements and the indiscipline among the law students generally soon brought about a situation in which the Bar Council norms[52] came to be violated with impunity at several places. Correspondence courses in law were started in many Universities, though the Bar Council refused to recognize it as a professional degree for the purpose of enrolment.

However, a trend is whereby the Bar Council's spirit of improving the legal education got set back. The decision of Calcutta High Court in *Aparna Basu Mallik* v. *Bar Council of India*[53] marked the in effectuation of the Bar Council's efforts. In that case Aparna Basu had passed the law examination as a non-collegiate student and the University had in the case of female candidates allowed an exemption from regular attendance for LL.B. examination. The Bar Council refused to enrolled her.

The High Court held that the function of Bar Council was to recognize the Universities and not the degree in law and

---

51. Part IV of the Bar Council of India, Rules 1975 makes elaborate provisions for ensuring the standards of legal education either through three years degree course or five year degree course. It requires:
    (a) Location of Law College only at a place where there is a District Court or a Circuit District Court.
    (b) Professional law education to be imparted only through whole time/day College or University department.
    (c) Fulltime college has to engage students for at least $5^1/_2$ hours a day—4 lecture periods of one hour and $1^1/_2$ hours for contact with teachers, library work, tutorial work or extra curricular activities.
    (d) Library to be opened for eight hours on every working day.
    (e) Principal of the college is to be a full time teacher.
52. Sub-rule 4 provides that the student shall be required to put in minimum attendance of 66 percent of the lectures on each of the 28 papers.
53. A.I.R. 1983 Cal. 461.

rule debarring the *ad-hoc* student was consequently held invalid.

It is submitted that the above decision of Calcutta High Court is contrary to the objects of Advocates Act, 1961 and it unduly restricts the scope of the expression to lay down standards of such education. In the instant case the candidate admittedly did not pursue any regular course of study at any college recognized by the University by attending classes, therefore, they could not be said to have complied with the requirements for enrolment as an advocate. It is matter of great satisfaction that the Supreme Court did not approved of the views of the Calcutta High Court in appeal which will be discussed a later. The Supreme Court's approval of the Bar Council of India's regulations may be seen in a number of cases. Thus, in *Baldevraj Sharma* v. *Bar Council of India,*[54] the Apex Court of India held that a person who has obtained a degree of law in two years as a private candidate and did only the third year course as a regular student is not entitled to enrolment.

In this case the petitioner was denied admission for three years law course, by the Registrar of Madras University, as the Bar Council of India had issued a communication that candidates who had completed B.L.G. course, through correspondence are not eligible for admission to three year law course and if any one had been awarded degree in law, contrary to this direction, he would not be entitled to be enrolled as an advocate.

The petitioner questioned the constitutionality of those rules. The Supreme Court held that the expression 'to lay down standard of such education' is capable of taking in every ingredient which will go to constitute the end of ultimate level of education that is expected of a candidate who applied for enrolment as an advocate under the Advocates Act. The court further observed that the "rule was not discriminatory under Article 14 of the Constitution as the degree obtained after pursuing correspondence course cannot be equated with a degree obtained after attending regular classes".[55]

54. A.I.R. 1989 S.C. 1541.
55. *Id.*, p. 1543.

Again, in *Bar Council of India* v. *Aparna Basu Mallik,*[56] the Apex Court held that the regular attendance in a college imparting legal education is a mandatory requirement and part IV, rules 1(c) of the rules framed by the Bar Council of India is valid.

This appears to be a good decision, which may help in promoting an efficient legal education system. It will also help to fulfil the aim and objects of Advocates Act, 1961.

The above discussion reveals that, with a very sharp power in its hand, the Bar Council of India is trying to regulate the legal education as well as entire legal profession. It is accepted very wisely that some improvement came about through the Bar Council of India Rules.

At some places the law colleges and University departments are doing very well in the field of legal education. The ideal example which may be advanced for the above contention is National Law School of India University, Bangalore, which is admitting 80 students from all over the country, with highly qualified teachers, a rich library and a lot of computers with internet facilities. According to the rankings given by the outlook magazine in its Hindi edition in a recent issued the other premier institutions in the field of legal education, are—NALSAR, Hyderabad, NLIU; Bhopal; Faculty of Law, DU; ILS, Pune; NUJS, Kolkata; Symbiosis Law College, Pune; Government Law College, Mumbai; NLU, Jodhpur; Centre for Study of Law, JNU; Faculty of Law, AMU, Aligarh; Faculty of Law, B.H.U. Varanasi; Haldia Law College, Haldia; Dr. Ambedkar Law University, Chennai; Faculty of Law, JMI, Delhi. These institutions are performing remarkably well.

There are also some faculties in the Indian Universities which are maintaining standard of legal education. Being inspired by the Bangalore experience the various states are proposing, to establish law Universities some of the states have already established such institutions. However, some of the earlier institutions founded on Bangalore pattern have not been able to maintain the same standard. Thus, barring a few exceptions, the general condition of legal education in the country is not very much inspiring and satisfactory. The

56. A.I.R. 1994 S.C. 1334.

reasons for overall deterioration of standards in legal education are many:

1. In our country the best young brain prefers medical, engineering, information technology, etc. to legal education.
2. Lack of proper facilities in most of the government aided institutions such as, libraries and quality teaching staff.
3. Till now, the courses in law have not become fully professional.

Thus, it is clear from the above discussion that fallen standard of legal education is the first cause which is affecting the image of legal profession. Unlimited number of admission in law colleges, part time students and part time teachers, mass copying in law examinations, evening classes, lack of infrastructure, etc. led things to deteriorate while the Bar Council of India with all statutory authority remained a helpless spectator.

Even the few faltering attempts made in some educational institutions to improve the quality of law teaching were not sufficiently supported by the profession at large or by the government in the State and at the Centre. The contradictory decisions of various High Courts also create problems in this regard. However, it is true that the Bar Council is trying to regulate the legal education but with few exceptions improvement does not appear to be a reality and the position of legal education in mass is deteriorating day-by-day.

It should be noted that success of any educational institutions depends mainly on devoted teaching staff/ students, infrastructure, and rule of discipline of the institutions. It is therefore, high time to consider the importance of legal education keeping in view the present state of affairs which we are facing in our day-to-day life. Thus, it is essential to introduce a real reform in the present system of education so that the best brains could be produced.

(B) Mushroom Growth of Law Institutions

The Mushroom growth of law institutions is the second

cause which is very much affecting the image and integrity of legal profession. The sudden growth of law colleges and Universities after 1990 has not been on the basis of any rational plan or control. Vested interests in the educational business and a section of private individuals exploited the increasing demand for law degrees and started law colleges without proper building, teaching staff, library and any kind of infrastructure or even the formal sanction of the Bar Council of India.

The numbers of law institutions are increasing day-by-day and the quality of law teaching therein is affecting the image of legal profession. The Table 1 given below shows the real picture in this regard.[57]

TABLE 1

Name of the States	*No. of the Universities Law Department*			*No. of Affiliated Colleges*		
	1950	*1985*	*2007*	*1950*	*1985*	*2007*
(1)	*(2)*	*(3)*	*(4)*	*(5)*	*(6)*	*(7)*
Andhra Pradesh	—	6	8	2	16	45
Bihar	1	6	9	2	17	27
Gujarat	1	6	8	—	28	33
Karnataka	1	5	7	2	35	73
Kerala	—	3	5	2	5	9
Manipur	—	1	1	1	4	4
Assam	—	2	3	2	11	18
West Bengal	—	3	7	1	10	13
Madhya Pradesh	—	9	7	3	80	88
Maharashtra	1	6	10	4	45	84
Orissa	—	3	5	1	12	7
Rajasthan	—	3	7	5	33	63

(*Contd.*)

57. The data of 1950 and 1985 is taken from Bar Review 1988, Vol. 15 (132), p. 90 and the data of 2007 is taken from www.barcouncilofindia.com; visited on 16.2.2008.

TABLE 1 (*Contd.*)

(1)	(2)	(3)	(4)	(5)	(6)	(7)
Tamil Nadu	—	5	7	—	7	7
Uttar Pradesh	2	14	19	9	41	112
Jammu & Kashmir	—	1	2	—	2	10
Punjab	—	2	6	—	3	14
Haryana	—	2	3	—	2	6
Chandigarh	—	2	3	—	2	3
Delhi	1	1	2	1	3	6
Meghalaya	—	1	1	—	3	3
Himachal Pradesh	—	1	1	—	1	5
Chhattisgarh	—	—	3	—	14	16
Goa	—	—	1	—	2	2
Mizoram	—	—	1	—	1	2
Nagaland	—	—	1	—	1	2
Pondicherry	—	—	1	—	1	1
Sikkim	—	—	1	—	1	1
Tripura	—	—	1	—	1	1
Uttaranchal	—	—	3	1	5	12
Total	7	82	119	36	386	687

Aforementioned table reveals that at the time of independence there were only seven Universities law departments and only 36 law colleges in the country. But in post-independence-era the number of law colleges is raising very fastly. The close scrutiny of the table shows that in 1985 the number of university law departments raised to 82 and number of law colleges reached to 386. Even that position was not very bad, but after that the law colleges were opened just like a mushroom. At present there are 119 university law departments and 687 law college in whole country.

It will be interesting to note that the State of Uttar Pradesh enjoys the top position with 19 University Law Departments and 112 Law Colleges. However, the State of Sikkim, Tripura and Pondicherry at the lowest position which have only one University Law Department and only one Law College. It is so because they are small States with lesser population.

In this regard a fact also be noted that in the years between 1985 to 2000 the total 134 new Law Colleges were opened and year between 2001 to 2006 only these five year is the eye witness of 279 new Law Colleges.

That was the period in which the University of Jammu started its all (except University Law Department) Law Colleges. Again in this period the Rajasthan University, Jaipur opened the 22 Law Colleges against the total number of 27 Law Colleges of that University.

Likewise Chaudhri Charan Singh University of Meerut, Uttar Pradesh has started 29 New Colleges in the period of 2001 to 2006, however the total number of Law Colleges of this University is 35. Dr. Bhim Rao Ambedkar University, Agra has started 10 Colleges, against total 14, in the period between the years 2001 to 2006.

Obviously quantity and quality cannot go together. Most of the new colleges are self-financing colleges. For them finance has top priority and teaching is relegated to periphery. They collect all sorts of students, collect money from them and adhere to the policy of less investment all profit.

(C) Lack of Service Spirit

The legal profession is a service-oriented profession. It is by its ethics a career of service to the community. It has never been equated with business or trade. Lord Bolingbroke remarked of legal profession that is "in its nature the noblest and most beneficial to mankind, and in its abuse the most sordid and most pernicious". Similar were the feelings of Daniel Webster, when he said "our profession is good if practised in the spirit of it, it is a damnable fraud and inequity whom its true spirit is supplanted by mischief-making and money-making".[58] In the recent time unfortunately there has been a growing tendency to measure success at the Bar by the commercial standards or the amount of money which the

58. *Supre* note 3, p. 75.

lawyer collects and not be the quality and efficiency of service rendered to the community.

Thus, the lawyers seem to operate on the rule of demand and supply and the forces of commercialism have overtaken the profession by and large. For this reasons the legal profession is converted into a trade or business. Today the fees charged by some lawyers are staggering. Apparently lawyers have forgotten that they are the guardians of noble ideals and traditions and not mere traders in market place, whose sole aim is the amassing of vast fortunes. Thus, the high cost of fighting a case is the important factor which is affecting the image of legal profession. In recent time the case does not make progress unless the demand is met. For this reason the civil litigation has become costly by requiring the litigants not only to incur legal costs, but also illegal costs. Furthermore, the advocates do not desire about the speedy disposal of case, because if this happens the fees of the next date may not be recovered. However, it is true about the lower courts. But in High Courts the advocates demand fees in four figures and while in the Supreme Court lawyers do not talk except in five figures.

It is submitted with due respect to the legal professionals that, this is unfortunate part of the legal profession. Addressing the Allahabad High Court Bar Council Sir Iqbal Ahmad, Chief Justice of Allahabad High Court has rightly observed:

> "The legal profession which used to be the glory and pride of the country has fallen from its grace. Many evil practices, such as toutism, canvassing, in fact evils for many to mention have so disfigured it that it has ceased to be a profession. It has been reduced to a trade".[59]

Similarly, *John F. Fillon* remarks that:

> There is I fear, some decadence in the lofty ideals that have characterized the profession in former times. There

59. As quoted Sharma, K.L., Sociology of Law and Legal Profession, 1984 ed., p. 154.

is in our modern life a tendency—I have thought at times very strongly marked—to assimilate the practice of the law to the conduct of commercial business. In great law firms with their separate departments and heads and subordinate bureaus and clerks with their staff of assistants there is much resemblance to the business method of the great mercantile and business establishments situated closely. The true lawyer is one who grudges no time and toil, however great, needful to the thorough mastery of his case in its facts and legal principles, who takes the time and gives the labour necessary to go to its very bottom and who will not cease his study until every detail stands district and luminous in the intellectual light with which he has surrounded it".[60]

This attitude of commercialization towards legal profession, general ignorance of legal ethics, lack of service spirit and chronic unemployment in this profession are certain important factors which are damaging the real concept of Advocacy. It is important to note that in India, the relation between lawyer and client is contractual. His fee is not an honorarium but a debt for which he may sue his client. For this reason a lawyer holds the dominating position and they sell their skill for the maximum price which they can obtain.

However, it is not suggested that the lawyers should not charge for their services, because a lawyer also needs to make money like any other person, but it should be noted carefully that his main purpose and desire should be of rendering service to those who seek his aid and also to the community of which he is a necessary part.

A question always arise that what are the causes responsible for this commercial attitude towards law. Prof. C.L. Anand explained the three causes for this viz.:

(a) The natural temptation to accumulate wealth;
(b) Reluctance of persons to discriminate between the

60. Processual Justice to people (1973).

various callings as means of livelihood and making many; and

(c) Intimate relations of lawyers as advisers of business concerns.[61]

In most of the countries the lawyers employed by the big business houses is proving a testing ground in practice for the boundaries of the professional ethics. The attitude of the legal profession from learning to earning has turned the profession into a bread and butter supply private company. But this attitude helps "only in developing selfish attitudes and even unsocial activities resulting in the violation of the fundamental principles of peace, truth, eternal law, vow of service, austerity, faith and sacrifice.

Thus, a question remains unanswered if a doctor can have free medical clinics why should lawyers not run free legal clinics. The urgent need for the legal profession is to become service-oriented. The lawyers must show recognition of what is meant by the spirit of service, because lawyers must serve as healers not a money-making company.

View of honourable Justices V.R. Krisna Iyer and P.N. Shinghal expressed in *M.P. Sinha* v. *State of Bihar*[62] is noteworthy:

> "The time has come to examine the quality of the product or service, control of price, enforce commitment to the people and practice internal distributive justice so that the profession may flourish without wholly hitching the calling to the star of material amassment immunized by law from the liabilities of other occupations—law reform includes lawyers reform".[63]

By this way the dignity and image of legal profession may be maintained. It is submitted that it is the legal, moral and ethical duty of the legal professional which preserve the traditions of the Bar by his serviced ideals.

61. *Supra* note 5, p. 25.
62. Special Leave petition No. 6056 of 1979 decided on 13.9.79.
63. A.I.R. 1980 N.O.C. 2.

(D) Problem of Over-Crowding

The overcrowded bar is the other cause which is very much responsible for the degradation of the image of legal profession. The Bar is over-crowded everywhere but in absolute term India has a very large legal professionals second only to the United States of America[64] comprising over 8,47,015 advocates on the rolls. It is increasing 50,000 more advocates every year. Of course, all advocates were get enrolled with State Bar Councils do not necessarily continue practising on a regular basis.

"Though retiring from the profession because of old age is not a normal phenomenon, a substantial number of advocates do join services in the public and private sectors of the economy as well as in government including judicial services".[65] It is difficult to determine exactly the actual number of active legal practioners on the rolls at any given time.

Therefore, the Table 2 shows the pattern of distribution of lawyers in various States in India and increasing rate with the relative figures of enrolment in successive years.[66]

Table 2 reveals that in the year of 1985 the total number of enrolled Advocates to the Bar was 2,90,673, out of which 280,183 were men Advocates and 10,493 were women advocates. In 1985 the State of Uttar Pradesh was on Top position with approximately 72,000 advocates on States Roll, however, State of Himachal Pradesh was on lowest position with only one thousand, three hundred and fifty nine advocates on roll. However, it is may be due to size of the small State like Himachal Pradesh. A rough study by an author shows that in 2000 the total number of advocates in India was above 5,00,000, but as table shows that presently it is on 8,47,015.

Table 2 shows that in the year between 2000 and 2007 the number of advocates increased above three lacs and five thousand. Therefore, our country is producing approximately

64. In America there are most of Chamber practicing lawyers.
65. *The Times of India* dated 15.7.2006, p. 7.
66. The data is taken from www.barcouncilofindia.com. Visited on 16.2.2008.

TABLE 2

Name of the States	1985			2007		
	Men	Women	Total	Men	Women	Total
(1)	(2)	(3)	(4)	(5)	(6)	(7)
Andhra Pradesh	12918	403	13321	46620	6553	53173
Bihar	23898	230	24128	—	—	86462
Gujarat	12204	1111	13315	—	—	41820
Karnataka	11841	398	12239	—	—	48265
Kerala	8426	600	10214	—	—	33894
Manipur	—	—	—	—	—	—
Assam	3345	139	3484	7255	1183	8438
West Bengal	27364	1358	28722	—	—	52261
Madhya Pradesh	18879	760	19639	—	—	51323
Goa/Maharashtra	27499	2569	30069	—	—	75152
Orissa	7161	129	7290	—	—	33341
Rajasthan	12246	359	12605	—	—	34485
Tamil Nadu	17284	618	17902	—	—	41670
Uttar Pradesh	71500	500	72000	—	—	201780
Himachal Pradesh	1299	60	1359	—	—	4197
Jammu & Kashmir	—	—	—	—	—	2516
Punjab/Haryana	15497	445	15942	—	—	38652
Delhi	8822	815	9637	22500	3650	26150
Chhattisgarh	—	—	—	—	—	11403
Jharkhand	—	—	—	—	—	

50,000 advocates every year. Once again the State of Uttar Pradesh is enjoying the top position with 2,01,780 advocates on roll, however the State of Himachal Pradesh which was the lowest position in 1985, now on third position and newly born State of Jharkhand is now on the lowest position with only 2033 advocates on roll.

In this regard a fact may also be noted that the legal profession is till overwhelmingly male dominated and females constitute less than three percent of advocates throughout the country.

Now the question is what are the reasons of overcrowded Bar in India? It may be contended in this regard that the sudden growth of law colleges and Universities department during 2000 to 2007 has not been on the basis of any rational plane or control. When the number of law colleges fastly increases, there is bound to corresponding decline in the standards of law teaching, and flood of law graduates too.

It is submitted that if the established traditions are eroded gradually, there is a real risk of the legal education and legal profession metamorphosing into a business. We are already seeing its sign. Advocates accustomed to making a living in such an atmosphere can clearly be visualised. Immediate reforms at the law college level are, therefore, imperative.

However, these reasons may be advanced for increasing the number of advocates which is over-crowding the bar. Mushroom growing of the law colleges is the first and foremost cause of over-crowding the Bar. *Secondly*, entry of the legal professionals are totally unrestricted, and a man simply pass the LL.B. three years or five years degree course may join the Bar. *Thirdly*, the retirement on account of age is practically unknown by the legal profession.

(E) Lack of Training

As noted earlier in this chapter, that the profession of law is a learned profession. The very word "learned" relates not only the knowledge of law but a proper training also, because the legal profession embraces the whole range of human relations and the study of law requires a mature mind which can only result from a high standard of professional training, which is totally lacking in the bar in recent days.

It should be noted carefully that, the two marks of a truly educated man, whose understanding has been enlightened, are the capacity to think clearly and his intellectual curiosity. If an advocate imbibed the ability to think clearly, he will adopt an attitude of reserve towards ideologies that are popular and be critical of the nostrums that are fashionable, enabling to advocate finding the truth.

Thus, in the complexity of the legal system one needs a long course of training to practise at the Bar. In this regard, as has been noted in the first chapter of this research work that in England the Inns of court are voluntary unincorporated societies, which are giving the training to the members of legal profession. The Inns of Court in recent time are some of the best institutions in the world, wherein the provision is made for lectures and moots. Examinations are compulsory and discourses are also held, occasionally in the ethics of the legal profession. The Inns act jointly for the purpose of determining rules for the administration of student, conduct of examination and call to the Bar. It should be noted that no one takes to practise at the Bar unless he has previously served as an apprentice for at least one year in a senior barrister's chamber.

Likewise in the United States of America the American Bar Association is running the special training programme to not only for the new entrants but also for the already trained senior advocates.[67] But in India there is no worthwhile scheme of training for junior advocates is existed at present. It may be said that the above position is not healthy situation for the image of legal profession. The Law Commission of India has stated the two reasons for this situation; First, with very large increase in the number of new entrant to the Bar, it becomes difficult for many to obtain admission to the chamber of senior and Second, even if admitted, junior due to pressure of their needs to make immediate living, do not show much inclination to plod this weary way of equipping themselves for the profession.[68] While between 1963 to 1974, pre-enrolment training and examination was prescribed as a condition by the State Bar Councils,[69] but in 1974 the legislature withdrew the same. Again, in 1995, a training rule was framed by the Bar Council of India, which made necessary that a new comer take apparentiship of at least one year in the senior chamber. The said training rules, provided for certain pre-conditions to be complied with by an applicant to be enrolled on roll of State

67. It is regulated also by American Bar Association.
68. Law Commission of India XIV Report, 1958, pp. 57-58.
69. As per the then existing conaition, Section 24(1)(d) of the Advocates Act, 1961.

Bar Council. That rules had been promulgated in exercise of the Rule-making power of the Bar Council of India.[70] However, the Judiciary did not appreciate that above rules and declared invalid and illegal on very technical ground. In *V. Sudeer* v. *Bar Council of India*,[71] the Supreme Court observed that "the impugned rules were said to have been framed by the Bar Council in exercise of its statutory powers under section 24(3)(d) of the Act. This enabling provision available to the Bar Council of India by rules to extend the scope of eligibility in favour of those who were ineligible under section 24(1) to be enrolled as Advocate did not touch upon the question of eligibility in connection with pre-enrolment training or to put it differently, the enabling power available to the Bar Council of India to make eligible otherwise ineligible persons for enrolment as advocates under section 24(1) did not cover the question of pre-enrolment training and examination at all. It must, therefore, be held on express language of section 24, sub-section 3(d) that the rule-making power of the Bar Council of India proceeded only in one direction, namely, for bringing into the sweep of section 24(1). It was a power given to the Bar Council of India to extend the coverage of section 24(1) and not to whittle it down. It is therefore, difficult to appreciate the contention that by exercise of the said rule it could impose a further condition of disability of otherwise eligible candidate to be enrolled even if he had satisfied all the statutory condition laid down by Section 24(1).

The Apex Court further clarified that the provision of Section 49(1) (ah) cannot be of any help to the Bar Council for sustaining the impugned rules for two obvious reasons; *first*, provision for pre-enrolment training of prospective advocate is not entrusted by the legislature to the Bar Council of India

70. Rule 2 of the impugned rule has provided that no person shall be entitled to be enrolled as an advocate unless he is eligible to be enrolled as such under Section 24 of the Act and has undergone training as prescribed these Rules. During the period of training such candidate has to maintain two type of diaries as approved by the State Bar Council—one for the work done in chambers and the other the work in Court".
71. A.I.R. 1999 S.C. 1167.

while laying down its statutory functions under Section 7. Therefore, the very first part of Section 49 will hit the said rule as it would not be rule for discharging the statutory function of the Bar Council of India. But there is still a *second*, cogent reason for showing that clause (ah) of Section 49(1) cannot support the impugned rules, because right to practise as available to an advocate duly enrolled under the Act is a full-fledged right to practise, which would include not only seeking adjournment but also to plead and argue".[72]

Thus, any truncating of the very right to practice itself in exercise of rule-making power under Section 49(1) (ah) by creating a new class of trainee advocates cannot be sustained by the said provision.

After giving the above reasons the Supreme Court held that the impugned Training Rules, 1995 are invalid and illegal and quashed it. It was made clear that because of the quashing of the impugned rules, only applicants who apply for the first time for enrolment after the date of the present judgment, will not have to undergo pre-enrolment training.

It may be contended that the above decision of honourable Supreme Court is contrary not only to the very object and aim of the Advocates Act, but it will also affect the quality of profession. The main effect of the above decision is that the most useful system devilling with seniors which gave rich training and experience and real opportunities to the junior advocates has called off its function in India.

Therefore, at present we have lost the system to give proper training either to pre-enrolment or the past, which is no doubt affecting the justice delivery system rather badly. If without any proper training a person carries a licence to process the legal profession, the result is obvious that not only there would be degradation in this profession but also to give wrong advice to the client for which poor litigants could miserably.

Thus, it is humbly submitted that, there is a need for special training to the legal professionals not only pre-enrolment but after enrolment too. The newly enrolled advocates must satisfy that they are fit to adopt a career in law

72. *Id.*, p. 1169.

and thus, enrolment at first instance be made provisional for atleast one year and only thereafter permanent licences be granted after an successful completion of rigorous training.

It is also submitted that senior advocates are under an obligation not only to train the juniors but also to encourage them. They should not deny entry into their chambers to those who are keen to learn and have a commitment to practise law. The role of a Senior Advocate is not merely to familiarize the junior with case law and the relevant statutes, but the habit of independent thinking and questioning should be inculcated, and above all, the junior must be exposed to and imbibe the noble traditions of the Bar, the tradition of truthfulness, the tradition of fearlessness, the tradition of fairness and the tradition of service to the indigent and the disadvantaged.

The study in this chapter has given account of the high tradition of the legal profession as a learned, noble and dignified profession and also the account of falling standards and degradation at present.

4

High Traditions and the Image of Judiciary

The rule of law is the foundation of any democratic society and the Judiciary is the guardian of the rule of Law. It is the very heart of republic and the bulwark of democracy. Therefore, it is undoubtedly accepted that the success of a democracy, especially one based on a federal system, depends largely upon an impartial, strong and independent Judiciary endowed with sufficient power to administer justice.

If this bastion is broken or undermined, democracy is bound to crumble, but "if the Judiciary is to perform its duties and functions effectively and remain true to the spirit, with which they are sacredly entrusted, the dignity and authority of the judiciary has to be respected and protected at all costs.[1] However, it is absolutely essential to remember that such dignity and authority of judiciary is not based on the power of contempt of court, but it rests on public confidence only.

It is the trust and confidence of people in this great institution to deliver true, fearless and impartial justice, which

1. *In Re Ajay Kumar Pandey,* A.I.R. 1998 S.C. 3299. per A.S. Anand, J.

is the foundation of democracy and the bedrock of every civilized society.

It is a matter of great pleasure that, in our country, the judiciary has by and large enjoyed immense public confidence. One of the chief reasons for this has been the fact that judiciary has generally been manned by persons who were devoted to the cause of justice and performed their duties without fear and favour. The people have always considered the judiciary as the ultimate guardian of their rights and liberties and this institution has amply stood the test of times.

However, in recent era this great institution of justice has been under constant attacks and the judiciary appears now to be at a crossroad. Therefore, it comes to be generally felt that the health of our judiciary is steadily deteriorating. This is a symbol of danger, because if people loose faith in the justice dispensed to them, the entire democratic set-up may crumble down.

In the above background an attempt is made in this chapter to discuss and examine the status and image of the judiciary in present day context, under the following heads.

I. NECESSITY AND ROLE OF THE JUDICIARY

'Peace' is word of wide import, which is required not only by an individuals, but by the entire society, because in the absence of peace no one can live peacefully. Necessity, therefore, arose for having an agency to decide the issues cropped up at all levels impartially and authoritatively.

It is accepted, however, by everyone that, it is in the nature of things that in every society and in every country, there are bound to be disputes and grievances among the people and therefore there has to be a forum for peaceful resolution of the disputes and peaceful ventilation of these grievances. Otherwise, the disputes will be resolved and grievances will be ventilated with bombs, bullets and sticks in a violent manner.[2]

2. Speech delivered by Mr. Justice Markandey Katju at the Judicial Officer's Meet on 11.12.2004 at the Madurai Bench of Madras High Court.

Similarly, when people have some grievances, they come to court, they are heard through their lawyers and the opposite parties are also heard through their lawyers and then a decision is arrived.

Even if the decision goes against that person, he has the feeling that he was given a hearing and this pacifies him. Otherwise if the judiciary does not hear him, then the feeling of injustice may turn into violence.

Therefore, the primal function of Judiciary throughout the world is to help keep peace, which is a great safety value, because it prevents violence. "The judiciary ensures peace and tranquility in society and that is the most important purpose".[3]

Initially, the necessity of judiciary was to settle disputes mostly of civil nature between private citizens. The judiciary also determined the question about the guilt of the persons charged with offences and punishment to be inflicted upon them.

With the emergence of socio-economic and political rights and with the emergence of 'Welfare State' the role of Judiciary is not confined only to the above two purposes. Now the Indian Constitution has provided for a federal constitutional democracy. In such a polity, there will be conflicts between the center and the States, between the two or more States, between the Parliament and Judiciary, between the State and citizens, between majority and minority interests and between those parties who believe in democracy and those who do not believe in it. Therefore, in recent times the function of judiciary as arbitrator of disputes between the different parties points out the necessity and importance of the impartial and independent judiciary in view of the changing scenario of the society.

In *Delhi Judicial Service Association* v. *State of Gujrat*[4] the Supreme Court of India highlighted the position in the following words:

> "Advent of freedom, and promulgation of Constitution have made drastic changes in the administration of justice

3. *Ibid.*
4. A.I.R. 1991 S.C. 2176.

necessitating new judicial approach. The Constitution has assigned a new role to the Constitutional Courts to ensure rule of law in the country. These changes have brought new perceptions. In interpreting the Constitution, regard must be had to the social, economic and political changes, need of the community and the independence of the judiciary".[5]

Judiciary is also required in the field of human rights and fundamental rights. Universal Declaration of Human Rights, 1948, declares that men avoid resorting to rebellion against tyranny and oppression. While enumerating as many as twenty-seven human rights, it declares that "everyone charged with a penal offence shall have guarantees necessary for his defence and that everyone has right to an effective remedy by the competent courts and Tribunals".[6] Likewise, Part IIIrd of the Indian Constitution guarantees several fundamental rights to the person as well as to the citizens of India.

Can the Declarations and fundamental rights come to be true without the active role of Judiciary? The answer shall always be negative. Indeed, the judiciary is the ultimate protector of our human rights as well as fundamental rights. The Supreme Court and various High Courts have not only protected the rights but have also declared the various rights as a fundamental right.

Through innovative use of its powers under Article 226, Article 32, Article 136, Article 142, Article 144, etc. the higher Judiciary in India have made significant contribution in upholding the Constitutionalism, rule of law, personal liberty, human rights, secularism, gender justice, democratic values, rights of minorities and industrial peace. Though the India Judiciary is based on British legal system over the years it has evolved an indigenous jurisprudence to suit the needs of the people of the country. It has determinedly endeavored to ensure that men are ruled by law and not by caprice and that 'rule of law' becomes the imposing and effective inhibition upon arbitrary power, thereby ensuring to the citizens the

5. *Id.*, p. 2179.
6. Universal Declaration of Human Rights, 1948.

enjoyment of their guaranteed rights consistent with the rights of society and the State.

However, in *A.K. Gopalan* v. *State of Madras*,[7] the Supreme Court had adopted a positivistic approach of interpretation and propounded the theory of exclusivity of Article 21 from Article 19 of the Constitution, but this theory was overturned in *R.C. Copper* v. *Union of India*.[8] Finally, in *Maneka Gandhi* v. *Union of India*[9] the Apex Court in effect introduced the concept of due process in Indian Jurisprudence. The court pronounced that the procedure contemplated by Article 21 of the Constitution must be right, just and fair and not arbitrary and must also pass the test of reasonableness.

At the same time, the Apex Court enlarged the concept of life and liberty in Article 21 to include the dignity of the individual and the worth of human person.[10] The Court has said that life does not mean merely animal existence or continued drudgery through life but the finer graces of human civilization which makes life worth living.[11] The right to life has been held to include right to privacy,[12] to development of urban areas,[13] to fresh water and air,[14] to protection against environmental degradation,[15] to food and clothing and shelter,[16] to health,[17] to education,[18] and even a right to roads in hilly regions—because access to road are said to have access to life itself,[19] right to the conservation of the physical

7. A.I.R. 1950 S.C. 27.
8. (1970)1 S.C.C. 248.
9. (1978)1 S.C.C. 248.
10. *Francis Coralie Mullin* v. *Administrator*, U.T. of Delhi (1981) 1 S.C.C. 608.
11. *Board of Trustees of the Port of Bombay* v. *D.R. Nadkarni* (1983) 1 S.C.C. 124.
12. *Kharak Singh* v. *State of U.P.* (1964) 1 S.C.R. 332.
13. *Municipal Council Ratlam* v. *Virdichand* (1980) 4 S.C.C. 162.
14. *M.C. Mehta* v. *Kamal Nath* (2000) 6 S.C.C. 213.
15. *ARC Cement Ltd.* v. *State of U.P.*, 1993 Supp. (1) S.C.C. 426.
16. *Shantistar Builders* v. *N.K. Totam* (1990) 1 S.C.C. 520.
17. *Shantistar Builders* v. *N.K. Totam* (1990) 2 S.C.C. 165.
18. *Mohini Jain* v. *State of Karnataka* (1992) 2 S.C.C. 666.
19. *State of H.P.* v. *Umed Ram Sharma* (1986) 2 S.C.C. 68.

environment[20] and protection against import of injurious insecticides,[21] environment protection[22] and protection against sexual harassment of women.[23]

Indeed, there is no aspect of protection or advancement of human life which cannot be brought into the ambit of Article 21. The Judicial outlook leads to the common feeling that when gross violation of human rights are brought before the Judiciary it cannot be passive on looker.

Another area, where the necessity of the Judiciary may not be overlooked, is its power of Judicial review. The task of the Judiciary is to interpret the laws and to adjudicate about their validity. It is more valuable need of the society. However, the courts do not act as super legislatures to suppress what they deem to be unwise legislation for. If they were to do so the court will divert criticism from the legislative door where it belong and will thus dilute the responsibility of elected representatives of the people.

This onerous duty is entrusted to the Judiciary, because it is by knowledge, experience, training, tradition and free from political and emotional pressures best suited to discharge it. The necessity of active Judicial role may be summarized as follow :

I. It is the balancing wheel of the federation.
II. It keeps equilibrium between fundamental rights and principles of social justice.
III. It keeps all the authorities functioning in India within their bounds.
IV. It controls the administrative tribunals.
V. It decides disputes between people and between State and the people.
VI. And last but not least, it plays an active role of guardian among all the people of India.

---

20. *M.C. Mehta* v. *Kamal Nath* (1997) 1 S.C.C. 388.
21. *Ashok (Dr.)* v. *Union of India* (1997) 5 S.C.C. 10.
22. *Vineet Kumar Matur* v. *Union of India* (1996) 1 S.C.C. 10.
23. *Vishaka* v. *State of Rajasthan* (1997) 6 S.C.C. 241.

II. STATUS AND IMAGE OF THE JUDICIARY

As discussed earlier an efficient, independent and impartial Judiciary is the very backbone of our democracy. Judiciary according to the Indian concept is not a citadel of bricks and mortar, but it is a temple of Justice and a seat of the Divinity. It should, therefore, be as perfect as it can and as ideal as it is humanly possible. This is the reason why, the Indian Judiciary is held in very high esteem of culture and tradition in all the developing as well as the developed countries of the world.

Indeed, every judicial system consists of two components—*first* a framework provided by the law, and *secondly,* the judges who work within the system. The status and image of a system usually depends, in a substantial measure, on devotion, truthfulness, fairness and effectiveness of the men who belong to and operate the whole system. It should be noted that the Judicial system, even if it is perfectly structured, may yet not be an effective-justice-delivery system, if the persons working as Judicial Officers, discharging Judicial functions, do not have the requisite operational skill or are not enthused to deliver robust substantial Justice. Thus the image of the Judiciary depends more on the persons who administer the laws than on the law they administer.

For the above reason, the society and the law demands a very high standard of conduct, ethics, temper, courtesy, humility, integrity and fairness towards the members of the Judiciary, because they are the trend setter of the values in society. They are worshipped, honoured and looked as ideal of the social norms. Thus, like the members of the Bar, the Judges' functions are another phase of the profession of law.

With a view to give the clear picture of and expectations from the Judiciary the discussion on the point is proposed to be carried on under the following heads:

(A) Seat of High Tradition

Judges hold a unique position in the life of community. The seat which judges hold is not a seat of simple dispute resolution but it is a seat of Justice, which owe a great sense of duty and high traditions. A Judge on the bench acts not only in the image of justice, but in the image of God too. In words of Koranic message, "O ye who believe; Be ye staunch in justice, witness for Allah, even though it be against yourselves or your parents or your kindred whether rich or poor, for Allah is nearer to akin to you than either".[24]

The high esteem in which Judges are held is not based on a codified law or a set of principles laid down in text books. It is rather based on a reputation, a prestige built by tradition gradually and slowly. It is not the work of one Judge or of tradition built in one day. The edifice on which this sound and solid construction has been developed is integration of honesty, integrity, character, fairness and impartiality. It has matchless record in this aspect.

The history indicates that in primitive society also, the law seems to have insisted upon the Judge and maintaining decorum and adherence to the code of Judicial conduct requisite for keeping administration of justice unsullied.

To quote Kautilya:

> "when a judge threatens, browbeats, sends out or unjustly silences any one of the disputants in his court, he first of all, be punished with the first embracement, if he defames any of them, punishment shall be double".[25]

Centuries ago, the great Indian Jurist Sukra said in his NITI, that the King should decide cause according to shastras and added—

> "where the King cannot personally attend to administration of justice, he should appoint Brahmanas, who are versed in the Vedas, self-controlled, high born, impartial, unagitated and calm, who fear next life, are religious minded, active and devoid of anger".[26]

24. Koran, IV 135 (ed. Fligel, IV 134)
25. Asim, Pandiya, "How is a Judge expected to conduct himself in Temple of Justice", A.I.R. 2001 (Jour-sect.) 154-55.
26. Prasad, Anirudh, *Principles of the Ethics of Legal Profession in India* 2nd ed. 2006, p. 25.

Manu too observed:

> "Let the Judge observe the eternal law of Justice and decide all cases of disputes among men justly, that is without partiality. Where justice having been wounded by injustice approaches the court and no one extracts the dart, shot by injustice, from the wound, all the judges who constitute the bench shall be considered as wounded. Either a just and virtuous man should not enter a court or justice, or when he does enter it, should invariably speak the truth. He who looks on injustice perpetrated before his very eyes and still remains mute or says what is false or unjust is the greatest sinner. Where Justice is destroyed by injustice and truth by untruth under the very nose of the judges whilst they simple look on, all the judges in the court are as if dead, not one of them is alive".[27]

Likewise, in the 4th Century B.C. the wise Greek philosopher Socrates said that there are four qualities required in a Judge—"to hear courteously, the answer wisely, to consider soberly and to decide impartially.[28]

Thus, the judges should be conversant with actions, character and attributes of people, impartial to both enemies and friends, to be truthful and know the high traditions of this great Institution. That is why the holder of a judicial office is not permitted to deviate from these virtues even in his dream. The Judiciary itself is of the view that, the purity, dignity and high standard of tradition of this great institution should be maintained at any cost by its own members. In a series of cases the Judiciary has warned the Judges for the same, to cite some of them. In *State of Rajasthan* v. *Prakash Chand*,[29] the Supreme Court of India observed that "Judges must be circumspect and self-disciplined in the discharge of their judicial function. It needed no emphasis to say that all actions of a Judge must be judicious in character. Erosion of credibility of the judiciary, in the public mind, for whatever reasons, is

27. *Manu*, VIII 3-8, 12 and 19.
28. Visit hptt:/www.Judicialaccademy.nic.in
29. (1998)1 S.C.C. 1.

greatest threat to the independence of judiciary. Eternal vigilance by the Judge to guard against any such latent danger is, therefore, necessary lest we suffer from self-inflicted mortal wounds".

In *Baba Abdul Khan* v. *A.D. Savant, JMFC, Nagpur*[30] the Bombay High Court observed that—

> "Court of justice are called as temple of justice. Temple denotes sanctity, purity and reality. So in the temple of justice these things are observed while administering justice. As the temple is a holy place, so is the Court where justice is made impartial and aggrieved parties are put to happiness with dignity and justice. Judges have remained the moral guardian of Indian polity preserving high ideals of law and liberty enshrined in the constitution".

In every case, a Judge's conduct should be above reproach. He should be conscientious, studious, thorough, courteous, patient, punctual, just, impartial fearless of public calmour, regardless of public praise and indifferent to private, political or partisan influences. A Judge is expected to administer justice according to law and deal with his/her appointment as a public trust; he should not allow other affairs of his private interest to interfere with the prompt and proper performance of judicial duties; nor should be administer the office for the purpose of advancing his personal aims or increasing popularity.

In *Harischandra* v. *Justice A. Ali Ahmed,*[31] the full Bench of Patna High Court observed that—

> "There cannot be two opinions that judges of the Supreme Court and High Courts are expected conduct the proceedings of the court in dignified, objective and courteous manner and without fear of contradiction. It can be said that by and large the proceedings of the higher courts have been in accordance with well settled norms."

30. 1994 *Cr.L.J.* 2836 (Bom.).
31. A.I.R. 1986 Pat. 65.

Likewise, in *Tarak Singh* v. *Joyti Basu*,[32] the Apex Court of India noted that Judiciary's function is divine. It is repository of public faith, trustee of the people and last hope of the people. The court said—

> "It is only temple worshipped by every citizen of this nation, regardless of religion, caste, sex or place of birth. Because of the power he wields, a judge is being judged with more strictness than others. Integrity is the half mark of the judicial discipline, apart from others. The Court warned—It is high time the judiciary must take utmost care to see that the temple of justice does not crack from inside, which will lead to a catastrophe in the justice delivery system resulting in the failure of public confidence in the system. We must remember that word peckers inside pose a larger threat that the storm outside".

Thus, the above decisions reveal that judges are envisaged to maintain high tradition of impartial judiciary. If his robes are coloured with any extraneous influences including his own predilections, knowingly or unknowingly he should be deemed to have fallen low from the high standard of traditions, that are set for him by the Divine. Judges are public officers and therefore they serve not the government, who might have pushed them into that high office, but the public whose cause must always be dear to them and whose estimation and good wishes he must attempt to earn, not by pampering to the gallery, but being honest, upright, truthful and God fearing.

(B) Seat of Great Respect and Dignity

The seats of Judges enjoy the great respect and dignity in comparison with any other services on this earth. About the high seat of Judges Mr. Justice R.C. Lahoti, in first foundation training programme[33] has rightly said that—

32. (2005)1 S.C.C. 1.
33. Conducted by Judicial Academy, Delhi at 2.07.2006.

> "Dispensation of Justice is an attribute of God. Blessed are those on when that Godly assigned has be fallen. Still blessed are those who acquit themselves of such assignment with pride, dignity and honour. Even God, who has created the human being, does not sit in judgment over his deeds until the human's death, whence only he determines whether he deserves to be sent to hell or heaven. You have been given the authority to sit in judgment over the deeds of a man in his life time. Your pen has power to grant the freedom of living or the sentence of death to an accused. You can take away his liberty for a number of days, months or years (subject to the limitations of law). Your mighty pen can turn riches into rags and a pauper into a millionaire. The more power you have, the more humility, rationality and balance must be among your possessions".[34]

Likewise a famous Moughal emperor Muhammad Bin Tuglak is said to have instructed the Quadi not to rise when the Sultan entered the court. He is said to enter the Court in cases against him, without arm and salute the Judge with great respect.[35]

The above instances clearly indicate that the judiciary holds a respectable and dignified status in the society. However, the gravity and dignity of this great institution does not depends upon its power as it does not have it. To quote Mr. Justice Frankfurter *'the Judiciary has neither the purse not the sword'*. The Judiciary has only its moral authority. So it is not the power of contempt of the court which enforces the order of Judiciary, rather it is the moral authority and public confidence, which makes the order of judiciary enforceable.

Therefore, it is essential for the members of the Judiciary to maintain the highest standards of integrity and rectitude and function with impartiality to maintain its respectable and dignified status in the society. The Judges should always remember that there is yet another Judge who is the Judge of

34. *Supra* note 28.
35. Qureshi, I.H., *The Administration of Sutanate of Delhi*, p. 163.

Judges. The remains confined within the precincts of the temple and carry home everyday the weight of his good deeds he had done and also the burden of his sins he had knowingly or unknowingly committed.

The honourable Judges of the superior Courts are known as Justices. In England Judges of the Court of Queen's Bench and Common Pleas are called Justices and the heads of the two courts are called Chief Justices.[36] In United State the title of Justice is given to Judges of United States and State Supreme Courts and as well as to Judges of appellate courts.

The United States Supreme Court and most States' Supreme Courts are composed of a Chief Justice and several associate Justices. Trial Judges are known as Judges and not Justices.[37]

In India all the Judges of the Supreme Court and High Courts are known as Justices. On the other hand, Judges of the City Civil and Session Courts or Small Causes Courts are known as Judges.

One of important consequences of the Judges termed as Justice and Judge is that the former do not commit contempt of their own court whereas the latter may commit. Therefore, under section 16 of the contempt of Courts Act, 1971 a Judge, Magistrate or persons acting Judicially are liable for contempt of their own court or of any other courts in the same manner as any other individual is liable, the High Courts and the Supreme Court are excluded from the purview of this section by the Judicial pronouncements[38] by interpreting the said section. In view of the exclusion of the High Courts and Supreme Court from the purview of Section 16 of the Contempt of Courts Act, 1971, it becomes more important for these courts to adhere to the Code of Conduct as indicated above.

Thus, the provision of Contempt of Courts Act gives the extra privileges to the higher Judiciary with keeping in view,

36. Since the Judicature Act, 1873, the ordinary Judges of all the divisions of the High Court have been called justices.
37. Tulsi, K.T.S., "Legal System in India and America: A Comparative View", A.I.R. (J) 1987, p. 81.
38. *Spencer & Company* v. *Vishwadarshan Distributors Private Limited* (1995) 1 S.C.C. 259.

the special status of the Supreme Court and High Courts' Judges, but it does not mean that the Judges of the Higher Judiciary are free for doing anything. There has been always a standard of outlook and conduct on the part of those judges who are the member of High Judiciary.

While deciding the case of *Krishnaswami* v. *Union of India,*[39] Mr. Justice K. Ramaswami has rightly said that the holder of the office of the Judge of the Supreme Court and High Courts should be above the conduct of ordinary mortals in the society. The standards of Judicial behavior, both on the Bench and off the Bench are normally high.

The foregoing discussion reveals that the Judiciary as a guardian of the constitutional goal and protector of our interest and rights enjoy the great respect and Highly dignified status in the society. Like the common member of the society and legal profession, the member of the Judiciary is also expected to maintain such dignity of the Judiciary, because if the Judges become too inhuman, loose their temper or do anything against the dignity of their own seat, then the impersonal concept of the seat of Justice is offended against, even by its occupant in bringing into disrepute the administration of Justice and in interrupting an even, unfitted and clean flow of the stream of justice.

(C) Life of Judges and Expectations

Man is basically a social being and is called a social animal and has to live in society. As the great philosopher Aristotle used to say that we are basically gregarious creatures, we like to mix with each other so it is natural among human being to socialise and mix. But it has certain demerits too. Too much socialization is not expected of Judge. The delicate nature of a Judge's duties requires certain degree of aloofness to be maintained by the Judges, be they members of Higher Judiciary or the Lower Judiciary. Chief Justice of Canada, Bora Laskin very aptly remarked: "*when you become a Judge, you loose half of your freedom and when you become a Chief Justice you almost loose the other half*".[40] That is the reason why Justice Holmes

39. (1992)4 S.C.C. 605.
40. *Supra* note 26, p. 5.

firmly refused to accompany Owen Wister to a bar for a drink, after his appointment as a Supreme Court Judge.[41] He said, "*I do not somehow cotton to the motion of our Judge hobgoblin in hotel bars and Saloons*".[42]

It depicts that, a Judge has no personal and social life. It is said that the life of a Judge is like Hindu widow. The axioms may be erring on side of extremity as the Judges are not superman but simply human beings, but one thing is certain that the members who adore this office must command respect from society. This needs not only talent but also restraint. As Sir Winston Churchill, the great statesman observed, "A form of life and conduct for more severe by a restricted than that of ordinary man is required from the Judges and though unwritten has been most strictly observed. They are at once privileged and restricted".

In 1945, when the Second World War ended, the conditions in England were very bad, because due to the war, there were shortages of coal and electricity; shortage of food and so on. People were shivering in the cold. There was shortage of food. At that time, Prime Minister Winston Churchill doubled the salary of the judges throughout England and there was a big hue and cry about this in the House of Commons. Some people said what is this? Are the judges' superior beings or a privileged class? Everybody is suffering, shivering and hungry; so let the judges also shiver, and be hungry and suffer. Why are they being treated like this and their salaries being doubled when the whole country is facing a terrible time? In reply to this criticism, Prime Minister Winston Churchill gave a historic speech in the House of Commons. He said that you people must understand that the life of a judge is a very difficult life. You will not see an English Judge anywhere, except in court. He never goes to any social functions or parties anywhere, and even his wife has to lead a very restricted social life. So, you have to compensate him for that, for the very difficult life he has to lead, if you want high-quality justice, because without high-quality justice,

41. *The Mind and Faith of Justice Holmes*, 1974, p. xxix.
42. *Ibid*.

there will not be any peace and law and order in society. This is why we have doubled the salaries of the judges.[43]

It seems that, there is requirement of fairness in administration of Justice which is expressed in dictum 'justice should not only be done, but it should also appear to have been done'. There should not be any semblance of partiality on the part of judges and it is maintained by their character of not mixing with others and self-curtailment of their freedoms.

In *Ravi Chandra Iyer v. Justice A.M. Bhattacharjee,*[44] the Supreme Court observed that Judges should maintain high standard of conduct both in public and private life based on high traditions. Speaking for the court Mr. Justice K. Ramaswamy ruled that—

> "The standard of conduct is higher than that expected of a layman and also higher than that expected of an advocate. In fact, even in his private life he must adhere to high standard of probity and propriety, higher than those deemed acceptable for other".

Thus, it is clear from the above discussion that, the seat of Judges demands the highest quality of conduct, learning, dignity and character. A form of life, conduct for more severe and restricted than that of any other persons on the earth. The law and society expect from the holder of the high seat of justice to maintain high conduct as a rule a tradition of isolation and aloofness.

The society expects from Judges to hold a bundle of virtues:

(1) The first quality of a Judge is to be a gentleman. Judges are bound by the moral code for 24 hours of the days. It is expected from the Judge that his every action should be transparent, because he is watched by the society. His personal actions, his family life and his behaviour with every living creature, with whom he deals must all be judicious, upright, above

43. *Infra* note 45.
44. (1995)5 S.C.C. 457.

board and set an example to the society. His Excellency Dr. A.P.J. Abdul Kalam, the former President of India wished to communicate the same expectations when he addressed to the Supreme Court Judges. Dr. Kalam said:

"You are 26 Judges of the Supreme Court. You are 26 role models of Judiciary for this nation of more than one billion people. People look up at you for vindicating their grievances and for removal of injustice. You must come, upto their expectations".[45]

(2) Judges should in all activities must avoid any appearance of impropriety.

(3) Judges should be aware of the value of time because the time of a Judge is public time of which he is trustee. Punctuality, therefore, should be a part of his personality. As Justice Hidayatullah said, who does not believe in punctuality of time does not have faith in the rule of law.[46]

(4) Judges are expected to be very cautious and choosy in selecting his company, because their seat holds not only power but a higher degree of dignity, therefore, a sensible line of distinction has to be drawn while accepting invitation for participation in functions or mixing with any one.

(5) Judges are also expected to develop a temperament of deriving pleasure out of reading, because the knowledge of a Judge is said to be capital of a Judge.

(6) Independence and impartiality of Judges who are the keepers of conscience of the Constitution has become proverbial, therefore, the fearlessness of the judge is not a privilege but an attribute necessary for the proper discharge of the function of the Judiciary.

(7) And last but not the least, Judges are expected to perform their duty very wisely, because the seat of administration of Justice can be performed only by a Judge legally and professionally trained and

45. Quoted from Lahoti, R.C. (J.), "The Culture of a Judge" available at *www.judicialacademy.acc.in*, visited on 2.07.2006.

46. *Ibid.*

acquainted with the tradition of learning and applying the law. Mr. Baker, a famous lawyer of America has summed these expectations in following words—

"A man of learning who spends tirelessly the weary hours after midnight acquainting himself with the great body of traditions and the learning of law. A man who bears himself in his community with friends but without familiarities, almost lonely, devoting himself exclusively to the most exacting mistress that man ever had, the law as a profession in its highest reaches where he not only interprets the law but applies fearing neither had friend nor foe, fearing only one thing in the world, that in a moment of abstraction, or due to human weakness he may in fact commit some error and fail to do Justice—'That is the Judge".[48]

The foregoing discussion reveal that society as well as the nature of service rendered by Judges to the mankind have very high expectations from the Judiciary. But, everything is not right with the functioning of the Courts. Occasionally expectations get frustrated when bad news spread about the conduct of some judges.[49] Such incidence may be few, but they are enough to demolish the image of the high tradition of the judicial functioning. The moot question is: Has the judiciary always stood well on the touchstone of high expectations from the judge? The coming discussion will be devoted to this challenging issue.

III. DETERIORATION IN IMAGE OF THE JUDICIARY

As noted earlier in this chapter, the act of administering justice is considered to be a divine function and judiciary is designed to a service of great honour and dignity, but realism demands that we must acknowledge and not remain unaware

47. *Ibid.*
48. *Supra* note 26, p. 7.
49. See, Chapter VI.

of the fact that there has been a slow and gradual shrinkage of the image of the judiciary.

The image of the judiciary in the ultimate analysis depends upon the way the cases are handled, upon the extent of confidence the courts inspire in the parties to the cases before them, upon the promptness or absence of delay in the disposal of cases, upon the approximation of the judicial findings of fact with the realities of the matter and finally, upon the conduct of the members of the bench.

Therefore, when we tried to analyse the causes which are deteriorating the image of the judiciary, we found that there is difficulty in putting one's finger on a particular cause and say that, this thing is responsible for loss of faith and respect, being suffered by the judiciary.

It is really a conglomeration of a great many numbers of factors. It may be due to degeneration of the Bar and the Bench, of the society in general, or it may be due to some defect in the entire judicial system, or it may be due to the pressure of the present day society coupled with desire or continuing something at the shortest possible time, or it may be due to the increased tendency in everybody to be materialistic, or it may be due to corruption in judiciary and so on and so forth. We find it difficult to pin point any one cause and say "correct this and judiciary will have respect and enjoy faith".[50]

The reasons causing degradation in the image of judiciary may be summarized as follows :

(A) Delay in Justice

Delay in justice is a perennial problem of Indian legal system, which is foremost responsible for affecting the image of the judicial wing of the Indian Government. With the rapid increase in legislation targeted to fulfil the constitutional objectives, the pendency in courts has increased enormously. Attempts made in the past to reduce law delays, have not succeeded in expected measure. Even the Supreme Court of India is not immune from delays. It should be interesting to

50. Iyer, Krishna V.R., "Accountability of Professions", *I.B.R.*, Vol. 14(4), 1987, pp. 651-70.

note that its much acclaimed judgement in the *D.K. Basu case*[51] in 1997 well known for its directives aimed at to prevent custodial torture, took ten years to be reached. If a judgement takes this long in the Supreme Court, what can be expected from court of lesser authorities?

The denial of justice, through delay is the biggest mockery of law, but in India it is not limited to mere mockery, the delay in fact is killing the entire justice dispensation system of the country. This has led to people setting scores on their own reflecting the loss of people's confidence in the judiciary. The problem has now almost reached unmanageable levels. In the words of Mr. Justice Krishna Iyer, *"Litigation is now a terror and horror. It is never final and is ever perennial. It bankrupts both sides, shocks and shames socio-economic egalite"*.[52] Sharing the same sentiments, the former Chief Justice of India Mr. Justice Bhagwati said in his speech on Law Day[53]:—

> "I am pained to observe that the judicial system in the country is almost on the verge of collapse. These are strong words I am using but it is with considerable anguish that I say so. Our judicial system is creaking under the weight of arrears".

Thus, arrears cause delay and delay means negating the accessibility of Justice in true terms to the common man. In this regard Chief Justice K.G. Balakrishnan stated that 2.59 crore cases were pending disposal. Of this 98 lakh are in High Courts and 43,000 in the Supreme Court. There are several thousand cases where judgments have not been delivered long years after arguments are over. Judicial officers adopt cover-up devices to wide this truth from the people.[54]

One of the apparent reasons for delay in justice is the readiness with which adjournments are granted by courts and the determination with which advocates drag on cases for long

51. *D.K. Basu* v. *State of West Bengal*, A.I.R. 1997 S.C. 610.
52. Iyer, Krishna V.R., "The Patchy India Judicial Record", *The Hindu*, dated 6.9.2007, p. 5.
53. *The Hindu*, 26 November.
54. *The Hindu*, dated 26.5. 2008, p. 7.

years, sometimes even decades. Sometimes Judges of Superior Courts retire or secure transfer without pronouncing pending judgments. Thus, the backlog may be partly blamed on the judges themselves who listlessly listen to hours of arguments, allow months and years of adjournments, on matters that would be disposed of in a fraction of that time period in the U.S. and the U.K.[55] There are subordinate courts where adjournments are liberal and there are no cases to hear in the afternoons. It is a wrong notion that if cases are dragged on too long, the advocate's practice would increase, because, when litigants show disinclination to approach courts for redressal due to delay in justice, how can the advocate hope to build up their practice?

Competence of judicial officers is another reason which is liable for delay in justice. In some matters where complicated questions arise, judicial officers avoid deciding them partly because of the strain involved and partly because of their incapacity to come to grips with the questions of fact and law involved.

That was the reason, why Parliament delegated judicial power to other agencies and the judges without reluctance upheld such legislative attempts and approvingly recognized their lack of expertise.[56] The result is that Parliament is becoming, in part, a "Super Court of appeal" and even the Supreme Court's decisions are "reviewable" by it as has been proved by the enacted Muslim Wife (Protection of Rights on Divorce) Act, 1986. Broadly speaking, lack of a set of standards to enable judges to guide their behaviours *vis-à-vis* the other shortcomings of the system affect the people's belief in the fairness and impartiality of the judiciary. Such legislative reactions as Administrative Tribunals Act, 1985 and Legal Service Authorities Act, 1987 evidence that lack of confidence in the judiciary. The former removed service matters from the

55. *Supra* note 37, p. 83.
56. See *Sampath Kumar* v. *Union of India* (1987) 2 S.C.C. 124, where the Apex Court of India upheld the constitutional validity of the Act setting up administrative tribunals and accepted these agencies as a substitute for the jurisdiction exercised by the High Court in service matter.

courts and placed jurisdiction over them in the administrative tribunals and the latter sharply curtailed judicial power over matters within the jurisdiction of Lok Adalats.[57]

Besides, this fact can also be proved by a series of battle fought between the Court and the Parliament in the first half century of the working of our Constitution which resulted in a number of Constitutional amendments. All these showed a lack of expertise on the part of judges to handle complex socio-economic matters dealing with agrarian reform.

The cumbrous procedure laid down in Civil Procedure Code and Criminal Procedure Code is also responsible to some extent for the delay in justice. Therefore, delay becomes identification mark of not only the cases of civil nature but also for the criminal cases. In civil cases one such delay is primarily caused by technical snags in delaying tactic by the lawyers. The attitude of the judges, once the case has finally been heard, resulting in the reservation of any open pronouncement of the judgment for years, are another contributing factor. In criminal cases the delay starts from the very inability and often refusal of the investigating agency to submit a charge sheet in time after the proper completion of and investigation. It is shocking to note that when the backlog of cases increases, judges connive with police officers and force people to plead guilty on charges so that cases can be summarily tried.

The lack of basic infrastructure within the entire justice system is another crucial issue that causes delay and inefficiency. When a prosecutor's office wants to communicate with a particular Police Station, there is no mechanism available other than the initiative of the prosecutor to spend from his own pocket or to make the interested party pay for this communication if the entire proceedings were not to be settled. It may be submitted that this lacks of basic infrastructure not only result in the delay of proceedings but is also a root cause for corruption. In this regard it is relevant to

57. The first Lok Adalat in India was held on 14th March, 1982 at Junagarh in Gujarat, in the matter of the land of Mahatma Gandhi.
58. Quoted from *"Envisioning Justice in the 21st Century, Lahoti,* R.C.(J) available at www.ebcindia.com., visited on 02.07.2006.

note that the Government of India intended to improve the infrastructure of the Judiciary.[58] During the Eighth Plan (1992-97), the Centre spent Rs. 110 crores on improving infrastructure, such as constructing courtrooms, etc. In the Ninth Plan (1997-2002) the Centre released Rs. 385 crores for fulfilling priority demands of the judiciary. This was 0.071% of the Centre's Ninth Plan expenditure of Rs. 5,41,207 crores. During the Tenth Plan (2002-07), the allocation is Rs. 700 crores which is 0.078% of the total plan outlay of Rs. 8,93,183 crores.[59]

But, the experience shows that these meagre allocation of 0.071% and 0.078% by the Planning Commission in the Ninth and Tenth Plans respectively are totally inadequate and coupled with the formulation of a centrally sponsored scheme with a condition that the utilization of the central grant is permissible only if a matching grant is provided by the states makes it also unfortunate. The Central Government had represented before the Supreme Court in the year 1993 that it had included the judiciary in the plan expenditure.

The Planning Commission is then expected to make not such meagre allocation and that too by way of the formulation of centrally sponsored scheme, which makes the utilization of the central grant conditioned and dependent upon a matching grant being provided by the states, in the context of the grave need to established more courts and appoint more judges ignoring immense pressure on courts and general criticism as to the heavy backlog. The sanctioned strength of judges in 21 High Courts of the country is 719 out of which 228 remain to be filled up. In the subordinate courts the sanctioned strength of the judges is 13,204 out of which 2010 posts are lying vacant and are yet to be filled.

Special judges are appointed at the request of the Central or State Governments. But, that is done from out of the existing strength without increasing the number of the judges and without providing additional infrastructure. Therefore, far from delivering speedier justice, this has an adverse impact on the justice delivery system.[60]

59. *Ibid.*
60. *Ibid.*

According to recent statistics, acknowledged by the former Chief Justice of India, Mr. Justice Bharucha, the judge population ratio is 12-13 judges per million which is the lowest in the world. A study conducted by the Ministry of Finance reveals that at the current rate it will take 324 years to dispose of the backlogs of case in Indian Court.[61] The Law Commission of India in its 189th report,[62] acknowledged that over two million cases are pending in about 13,000 district subordinate courts. The Chief Justice of India, Mr. Justice K.G. Balakrishnan recently pointed out that there should be substantial increase in the number of judges to avoid this critism, but a mere increase in their number will be of no use unless these Judicial Officers are able and efficient.[63] Therefore, these appointments should be based on merit alone with no role for considerations of region, caste, community and gender. Further, much of the delay could be avoided by cutting short-long arguments. In this regard the U.S. experiment of having a two-hour limit for argument may be adopted. But the most important steps to reduce delay is to see that the hierarchy of appeals and the jurisdiction of the appellate courts are curtailed. Because in India three, four or more appeals, revisions, reviews and special leave petitions make litigation a horrendous gamble.

It should, however, be noted that litigation does not always lead to a satisfactory result. It is expensive in terms of time and money. It is also true in India that a case won or lost in a court of law does not change the mindset of the litigants, who continue to be adversaries and go on fighting in appeals after appeals.

The plurality of appeals, the frequency and dilatory revisions and reviews, can be avoided if the system is slimmed down. A.P. Herbert, a literary celebrity, in a lovely blend of wit and wisdom, observed: "The institution of one Court of appeal may be considered a reasonable precaution; but two suggest panic people can be taught to believe in one court of appeal,

61. *The Hindu,* dated 06.09.2007, p. 5.
62. Published in February 2004.
63. The Role of Judiciary: available at http/law.indiainfo.com., visited on 08.06.2005.

but when there are two they cannot be blamed if they believe in neither".[64]

The causes for accumulation of arrears in the High Courts and Supreme Court are numerous. Analysing the problems of arrears Dr. Rajiv Dhavan, a noted advocate in the Supreme Court feels that "the Judiciary itself can control the system to a very limited extent because it has been denationalized to private market forces. The private market force have handed the system over to lawyer and thus judicial process is systematically used for the oppression of the poor".[65]

The best way to lessen the burden of the Supreme Court is to vest in it jurisdiction of only cases involving a substantial question of constitutional law, cases involving differences among High Court on questions of law applicable to the whole of India; original jurisdiction between the States or between the States and the Union; jurisdiction under Article 32 which should be invoked only after exhausting the remedy before the High Court and in cases involving death sentence and of public importance. In all other cases, the decision of the High Courts should be final. As appeal is said to be a vested right, the existing appeals before the Supreme Court should be transferred to a special court which should be wound up after such appeals are disposed of.

Similarly, the jurisdiction of the High Courts should be curtailed to deal only with cases involving a substantial question of law; the death sentence; cases coming under Article 226 and cases where there is difference of opinion between two judges of the subordinate judiciary who will have jurisdiction to hear civil cases above a certain value and criminal cases involving imprisonment above a certain limit.

(B) Illusory System of Trial Proceedings

The illusory system of trial proceedings is the another factor which is deteriorating the image of the judiciary. It is generally accepted that the trial proceeding in India is a

64. Quoted from, Ramchandran Raju, *Legal Ethics*, Lexis nexis, Butterworth Publication, 2006, p. 456
65. Dhavan, Rajiv, "*Litigation Explosion in India*" (1986), *Cr.L.J.*, Vol. 4:6, p. 387.

system of justice, wherein truth becomes secondary to the skill and connections of advocates. Therefore, the question arises: how far the judicial findings of fact accord with the realties of the situation? Judges of course, have to give their findings upon the evidence adduced in the case. Sometimes witnesses do not tell the truth. On other occasions, persons who could give true version are not willing to come forward and give evidence which might have the effect of antagonizing one of the parties. Whatever might be the reason, the result is that judicial finding of fact is sometimes entirely divorced from the realities of the situation. It is one thing if this incongruity between the realities of the situation and the judicial finding of fact is confined to a small number of cases. If, however, the incongruity between the realities of the situation and the judicial finding of fact becomes extensive and widespread, it is bound to shake the confidence of the people in the ability of the courts to find the truth of the matter and thus create a credibility gap for them.

Although it is not possible in any judicial system to prevent such incongruities in a marginal number of cases, our efforts should be to ensure that our judicial system functions in such a manner that consistently with a fair procedure, such incongruities are reduced to the minimum.

Every incongruity between those realities and the judicial findings is bound to bring down the judicial system in the estimation of the people and undermine their confidence in the capacity of the courts to arrive at the truth.

In the course of devastating criticism of the adversary element in trail and the difficulty of ascertaining true facts, Frank observes, "the lawyer aims at winning in the fight, not at aiding the court to discover the facts. He does not want the trial court to reach a sound educated guess if it is likely to be contrary to his client's interests. Our present trial method thus the equivalent to throwing pepper in the eyes of a surgeon when he is performing an operation".[66]

The above observations indicate the difficulty experienced in arriving at true finding of fact. The adversary and accusatorial system has become a part of our judicial tradition

66. *Supra* note 64, p. 322.

and both the members of the Bench and Bar not their heads approvingly. Therefore, the system has factually rendered the judges to play the part of silent witnesses by allowing the parties to fight and test their might. In other words, the judges have not been able to play a much creative role in their search for truth.[67]

Another thing which is shaking the confidence of the people in the judicial system is the high incidence of acquittals and the increasing failure of the system to bring major culprits to book. Judges, of course have to give their verdict on the material on record and no one can and should expect the courts to hold a person guilty unless there be credible evidence to substantiate the charge against him. One major reason for the high percentage of acquittals is the decline in the quality of Police investigation and its consequent inability to procure and produce credible evidence as many to establish the guilt of the accused.[68]

It is shocking to note that, investigation of crime occupies comparatively lower priority in the functioning of the Police. The result as such is deterioration in the quality of investigation and the increasing inability of the police force to adduce credible evidence at the trial. Be that it may, whatever may be the reason for the high incidence of acquittals the inevitable effect of that would necessarily be the loss of confidence of the people in the court to bring the major culprits to book. Thus, the foregoing discussion reveals that, the lack of judicial expertise, unpredictability of judicial approach and intellectual adherence to the theory of judicial decision-making has become the part of our judicial system.

The high cost of fighting a case is another cause which is contributing in the deterioration in the image of the judiciary. The felling there is that the amounts required for pursuing a legal remedy or defending a claim is too much exorbitant which most citizen can ill afford to pay, whatever might be the justice of the matter. The concept of "*Nyay Chala Nirdhan Se Milane*" is not doing well in this regard, and has become only the pious declaration of providing justice to the poor people.

67. *Id.*, p. 298.
68. Gururajachari, K., *Advocacy and Professional Ethics*, Ist ed. 2000.

Therefore, it is high time to improve the illusory system of trial proceedings.

(C) Behaviour of the Judicial Officers

It is undisputed fact that, the seat of Judges is like a seat of God. Therefore, the persons who discharge this divine function are expected to conduct themselves in a manner which befits to their function and position. Under the Indian Constitution, the position of a judge is exalted and various privileges and protections[69] have been conferred on him. The Judges of High Courts and Supreme Court, secure guaranteed tenure except removal by impeachment procedure in exceptional cases of proved misbehaviour or incapacity.[70]

Because of the position which a Judge holds in the society and the judicial system, and because of the wide power available to a Judge, it is quite possible that a Judge may start, developing "God Complex", resulting into the misuse of their power and position and may involved in such type of activities which may deteriorate the image of entire judicial system.

However, in India the history shows that the judiciary was acknowledged as the 'least corruptible' of all departments of the Indian Government. "It is a matter of pride and satisfaction that the Indian Judiciary enjoys credibility far greater as enjoyed by the other two wings of the State". That was what Chief Justice (Dr.) A.S. Anand speaking on the occasion of the Golden Jubilee celebration of the Supreme Court in January 2000[71] expressed, but a year later this self-satisfaction was shocked, when Chief Justice S.P. Bharucha, publically lamented that "Eighty percent of Judges in the country are honest and incorruptible and the smaller percentage was bringing the entire Judiciary into collapse".[72] Now corruption a term which includes in the large sense nepotism and favoritism is becoming more prevalent in the

69. Article 129 of the Constitution of India.
70. Article 124 of the Constitution of India.
71. At New Delhi.
72. *India Today*, (Hindi ed.), Dec. 1-15, p. 12.

subordinate judiciary and to some extent in the higher judiciary too.

It should be noted that the corruption in judiciary has not come in a day soon. For long, many knew of corruption in the most hallowed in this divine institution and many more suspected it. But the former Chief Justice Bharucha had the courage to talk about it openly during his tenure of Chief Justice of India. A very bad feeling about the judiciary, is expressed in the observation of Mr. Justice Bharucha, when he estimates that "20 percent of Judges are corrupt".[73] He added that "the corruption has spread in judiciary particularly in the Lower Courts. But, in the light of many cases of corruption of judicial members, having come into light, the situation appears to be more terrible".[74]

However, the present Chief Justice of India, Mr. Justice K.G. Balakrishnan is of the view that "against only a handful of Judges are there allegation.[75] Answering the question of reporter of the Hindu Newspaper Mr. Justice K.G. Balakrishnan observed:

> "If people perceive the Judiciary as whole system consisting of the Judges, the members of the supporting staff, members of the High Courts and Supreme Court, the advocates, clerks all those involved in the system, in that way there may be some corruption, but I do not agree that there is so much percentage of corruption amongst the sitting Judges of the Superior Court. Therefore, I feel that against only a handful of Judges are there allegation of corruption".[76]

About the problem of corruption in Judiciary, Mr. Justice K.T. Thomas, a retired Judge of the Apex Court is also of the view that "only a small section of Judges are corrupt". Addressing a talk series "Maarunna Malayali" organized by

73. Das Crus, *Judge and Judicial Accountability*, 2005 edition, p. 45.
74. *Ibid.*
75. *The Hindu* dated 27.09.2007.
76. *Id.*, dated 18.10.2007, p. 11.

the press club at Kallam,[77] Mr. Justice Thomas said that a totally honest Judiciary will be a utopian notion, therefore it may be accepted that a small section of Judges are found involved in corruption, but when it comes to international statistic on judicial corruption, India rank IX, that is some relief.

The above referred observations of the Mr. Justice K.G. Balakrishnan and Mr. Justice K.T. Thomas, clearly indicate that our Judicial Officers of today have to realize that, Indian Judiciary is suffering from corruption today. It is submitted with all due regard that it is not a matter of any relief that we are standing on the IX position about the judicial corruption. Similarly, it may be accepted that, (as opinion of Mr. Justice K.G. Balakrishnan) all the staff of the courts and all the advocates are the part of the any judicial system, and they may be the contributors of such corruption, but it should not be forgotten that the position of a Judge is very much different with a clerical staff or advocates of any Courts.

It should always be kept in mind that in one way or the other, judicial corruption is far more dangerous than plunder elsewhere. Our judiciary has been a beacon of hope and conscience—keeper of the nation for long. The Indian philosophy, heritage and even Indian constitution lays a great emphasis on the impartiality, integrity and good moral behaviour of the members of the Judiciary.[78]

Justice M.N. Rao has rightly said in this regard that—

> "I must mention with all vehemence at my command that corruption in judiciary is conceptually different from the corruption in other spheres. The theory of deterrence must apply with all its rigour to case of judicial corruption. There is no question of consideration of principle of proportionality with all its nuances in punishing a Judge. The context compels me to mention that the prevailing view among knowledgeable circles that the level of the Bench will not be higher than the

77. *Id.*, dated 6.09.2007, p. 14.
78. *Supra* note 70.

level of the Bar is very realistic one. Generally, judicial corruption is not possible without the collusion of Advocates. To uproot the evil completely, total cooperation of the Bar is absolutely necessary. It is to the enduring fame of British Justice that there has been no case of judicial corruption there for over a century".[79]

Thus, it will be better for the image of the judiciary, if we try to obey the way of British example. However, it may be true that the position regarding the lower judiciary is more worse, but we never ignore this very fact that the position of the Higher Judiciary in India are not at all happy. At least, last decade of the Indian Judiciary is the eyewitness of the cases of corruption even in Higher Judiciary. There have been the series of cases which have tarnished the image of the judicial system. For example, in 1995, a Judge of the Rajasthan High Court had to resign on the charge of misconduct.[80] We are also aware of the resignation of few Judges of the Bombay High Court.[81] The very other day, the three Judges of the Karnataka High Court were alleged to be involved in sex exploitation in a hotel.[82]

It was hardly forgotten that Justice Mukherji was arrested by the C.B.I. team, on the alleged charges of giving judgment in collusion with a property dealer fetching a handsome amount. He was sent to jail. This incident was related with a High Court of Delhi. However, he had been granted bail for one month to enable him to serve his ailing mother and wife. He was arrested on 30 April, 2003 on charge of corruption, bribery and forgery. This has undoubtedly brought a blot on the image of the Higher Judiciary.[83]

The history of corruption did not end here. Justice Veeraswamy, former Chief Justice of the Madras High Court was also proceeded against for alleged acts of corruption.[84]

79. Rao, M.N. (J), 'The Judges' (1993) 2 A.L.T. (Journal section), p. 1.
80. Raghavan, V., "History of Corruption in Judiciary", available at www.ebcindia.com., visited on 22.10.2007.
81. *Ibid.*
82. *Ibid.*
83. *Ibid.*
84. *Ibid.*

Numereous allegation was made against the Chief Justice of Madhya Pradesh High Court which presented a very deplorable state of affairs of the judicial institutions.[85]

We have not forgotten that proceedings for impeachment of his son-in-law, Justice V. Ramaswami were initiated in the Parliament for his alleged acts of corruption when he was Chief Justice of Punjab and Haryana High Court.[86] Though it did not succeed but message is obvious.

The story above are about the Higher Judiciary, then we can imagine what will be the position of the Lower Judiciary. These are some of the examples only. The cases of corruption are coming one after another and there is a series of them. Thus, really it is matter of great thinking, that the judiciary, our ideal protector is involved in disputes, only due to the malpractice and misconduct of few of its members. It conveys very bad signal. This sort of habit and behaviour degrades the dignity of judiciary and brings a bad name as such things cannot be kept secret. Thus the question arises, that what are the reasons for corruption in the judicial system?

Answer of this particular question is not a easy task. However, on this point we are able to say that the corruption in judiciary is basically due to the deterioration in our character, humanity and moral value. The result being that the Gods we worshipped yesterday have been slowly and gradually dethroned.

Now-a-day good behaviour is not rewarded and indeed is penalized at times; bad behaviour is not only left unpunished, but is rewarded consistently and extravagantly. Therefore, it is time for the heart searching. The processes of appointment of the judicial officers are also responsible for the said decline in the judiciary. Therefore, it is submitted that there should be no place for any corrupt in the judicial system. There is need to take effective steps to ensure rigorous and impartial scrutiny before recruitment into the higher judiciary and there should not be any hesitation in removing the corrupt judges.

Only best talent and a man of character and integrity should be appointed as Judicial Officer. The Supreme Court

---

85. *Ibid.*
86. For details see Chapter VIIth.

must recognize that the Malaise is not limited to one corrupt judge exposed; it should direct all the High Courts to act in a similar manner to weed out corruption in subordinate judiciary. "Institutional Checks could be evolved to guard against arbitrariness and injustice".[87] One more step need to be taken to promote integrity, impartiality and competence in judiciary at all levels. We need to create an Indian Judicial Service and recruit judges through a nation wide competitive examination. A good proportion of the judges in our High Courts consist of erstwhile practising Advocates, though brilliant Advocates who may have built up sizeable practice would hardly be attracted to sit on the Bench. These ex-Advocates cannot suddenly be expected to be shorn of their past connections and equations in local society and the traditional effects of the environment in which they had been practising merely due to their elevation to the Bench. It take them time and effort to develop the requisite detachment of a judge. Many of them as such are apt to develop cold feet and shut their eyes when called upon to deal with malpractices in society and the judicial system, in due course of their duties. They find themselves suddenly called upon to pronounce judgment on the morals of others and feel it irksome to be forthright. It is desirable in the overall public interest that such Advocate-Judge should be posted to other High Courts away from their previous areas of practice. The problem of their kith and kin practising before them will also be avoided thereby.

It must be remembered that, we are today passing through an age of social questioning. There is all round a spirit of iconoclasm. No institution can take for granted the reverence of the community. The community demands from every institution the justification of its existence and the proof of its utility. There was at one time, an aurora about the judiciary that is a temple of Justice, but such a time is now past and no more.

Thus, the legal institution and the courts have to earn reverence through the test of truth, test of promptness, test of utility, test of credibility and finally test of a good moral behaviour. Because justice is not a cloistered virtue it must be

87. *Supra* note 80.

allowed to suffer the scrutiny and respectful, even through outspoken comments of ordinary man.

The judges should function in such a way as to deserve the praise and respect of all those who are connected to the judiciary in one way or the other. "Only Justice should not be done, but it should appear to have been done". This is possible only when, if the judiciary functions without fear and favour or any kind of bias, official, pecuniary or the other. Lastly, one should keep always in the mind that name, fame, service and dignity attached to it is more valuable as compared to the immediate gain of any things or any kind.

Therefore, a judge should be learned not only in law, but also in the great traditions and heritage of this great India, its philosophy, its sacred and secular literature also.

(D) Should Judges be Left Out of the Information Act

Now new issues has arises as to requirement of transparency with judges some doubts have also been raised as to their assets which erodes faith in judiciary. The Right to Information Act, 2005 was enacted to give Indian citizens access to information held by any authority. The said Act is a step forward towards opening a closed and secretive judicial system also. The preamble of the Act specially states that India is a democratic republic and in a democracy an "informed citizenry and transparency of information are vital to its functioning and also to contain corruption and to hold Governments and their instrumentalities accountable.

However, a controversy arose recently with the statement of the Chief Justice of India, Mr. Justice K.G. Balakrishnan during a conference of Chief Ministers and Chief Justices at *Vigyan Bhavan* in New Delhi,[88] that "the office of the Chief Justice of India should be out of the ambit of Right to Information Act, 2005, as the Chief Justice is not a public servant. He is a constitutional authority, therefore, the Act does not cover constitutional authorities".

It is interesting to note that, it is not the first time the Chief Justice of India has expressed his preference for secrecy over transparency in refusing to divulge information

88. Held on 20-21 April, 2008.

pertaining to judges' assets. In 2007 in an interview to a television news channel the Chief Justice of India said that "no self-respecting judge would accept the idea of a compulsory declaration of assets".[89]

As noted earlier, in the said conference in response to the application of the Information Act, once again refused to reveal details of judge' assets stating that the information was not available with the Supreme Court registry.

It is respectfully submitted that section 2(h) of the said Act defines a public authority as "any authority or body or institution of self-government established or constituted under the Constitution". Therefore, it may be true that Chief Justice of India is not ordinary authority but how can we forget that every judge is oath bound to dispense public justice without fear and favour. As Mr. Justice V.R. Krishna Iyer wrote:[90]

> "Public justice is public service, and obviously judges are public servants. The Right to Information Act, therefore, does cover constitutional authorities too".

Thus, the statement of the Chief Justice is respectfully not supported by the law and intent of Parliament. The denial of Mr. Justice K.G. Balakrishnan is also contrary to the resolution adopted in a full court meeting in 1997.

It is humbly submitted that, in a democracy all institutions, including the judiciary must be transparent and accountable and Chief Justice of the Supreme Court and High Court should not be left out of the ambit of the Right to Information Act, 2005.

---

89. Pandey, Suchi, "Judiciary should go for Transparency not Secrecy", *The Hindu*, dated 07.05.2008, p. 11.
90. Iyer, V.R.K., "Judges are Public Servants, not Bosses", *The Hindu*, dated 20.05.2008, p. 11.

5

State of Professional Ethics in Administration of Justice and Bench-Bar Relations

After having had the study of high tradition and image of judiciary and its deterioration at present in the preceding chapter, the present chapter will be devoted to the examination of the state of professional ethics and bench-bar relations in the administration of justice. The greatness of the profession of law, which is the basis of the survival of democracy, depends not only upon the high office or not only upon the strict statutory rules, but also on the value, ethics and wide culture of the members, who are involved in the dispensation of justice system. Therefore, one can say that the greatness and honour of the system of administration of justice is due to the ethics and canons of conduct governing the relations of judges and Advocates' interest and with others in their professional and personal capacity. The theory underlying the administration of justice is that the best means of finding out the truth out of the contentions of parties is to listen the best that can be said for each side by a skilful and honest advocate and entrust the decision to an impartial judge capable of weighing the arguments on both sides.

The legal system of any country necessarily involves a division of function between the members of Bench and the Bar. "There are the two arms of the same machinery and unless they work honestly and harmoniously, justice cannot be properly administered through the court of law.[1] It is the business and duty of the advocate to make out the best of his client's case and it is the province of the court to weigh the contention, to balance and determine without fear and favour, on which side, the right lies.

How these two conflicting interests will be harmonized? The rules of professional ethics strike a judicious and harmonious balance between the members of Bench and the Bar by requiring to follow certain basic norms of decency and decorum. The rules of professional ethics cast two-fold obligations on the members of the Bench and the Bar. On the one hand, it requires that any acts and behaviour of the members of Bench and the Bar should not be disgraceful and dishonourable and on the other hand, it says that mutual confidence and cooperation between the Bench and the Bar is essential for the smooth functioning of the administration of justice.

Thus, the rules of professional ethics are very much helpful in achieving the goal of the administration of justice. For this reason the profession of law requires a code of conduct, like other professions. It shows that a person by becoming an advocate or judge does not cease to be governed by the general rules of law and morality. As Hoffman has stated, "what is morally wrong cannot be professionally right".[2]

Ethics regulates the conduct of the members with the help of a set of binding norms. The entry into the profession regulated by internal discipline is ensured and every conduct of its members is regulated by sets of rules called professional or legal ethics.

---

1. Observation of Din Mohammad, J., quoted by Gururajachari, K. (in) Advocacy and Professional Ethics, 2000 p. 126.
2. See, 'Resolution 33', by Hoffman for the guidance of Advocates.

In India we have an organized Bar and disciplinary authorities to regulate the conduct of the advocates. Likewise to regulate the conduct of judges also we have certain norms and rules. But unfortunately the position of justice delivery system is not appreciable and we cannot run away from the reality that the reputation of the entire justice dispensation system is today at its lowest ebb. There is general feeling that the standards of the legal profession are on the decline. Though, there are many reasons[3] for the same, but the main reason is the deviant behaviour from the accepted standards of the professional ethics.

As D.A. Desai, former judge of the Supreme Court of India observed that "It cannot be gainsaid that the profession has fallen in the estimate of the society. It is in the cherished compliancy closing its eyes to regrettable realities. The present none-too-respectable position arises from the mala-adjustment of the profession to the needs of the legal service and deprivation to consumers of such service any public accountability in a fast changing society".[4]

It should be remembered that only through the adherence of highest standards of professional ethics, the stature of the Bench and the Bar can be enhanced. Unless the judges and lawyers observe the highest standard of professional ethics, they cannot earn the respect of the society, nor do their peers in the profession accept them as an outstanding and truthful judge and advocate, because the professional ethics is the only tools, which helps to preserve the stream of justice "pure and clean".

In the context of above background the natural question arises as to what is the professional ethics. An attempt will be made in this chapter to discuss and examine the meaning and nature of the term professional ethics. We will also discuss the duties which are imposed by the law and traditions on the judges and advocates as a rule of professional ethics and the relationship between the Bench and the Bar.

3. For details, see Chapter VI.
4. Desai, D.A., "Role and Structure of Legal Profession", 7, J.B.C.I., 1981, p. 117.

I. PROFESSIONAL ETHICS

We have already analysed that under the legal system of any country, the two wings of the administration of justice, namely, the Bench and the Bar have to work according to certain norms. In their dealings, they should always bear in mind that every member of the Bench and the Bar is a trustee for the honour and prestige of the profession as a whole. In *Jamphier* v. *Phipos*[5] Chief Justice Tindal of England has said that "Every person who enters into a learned profession undertakes to bring to the exercise of it reasonable degree of care and skill. There may be persons who have higher education and greater advantages than he has; but to undertake to bring a fair, reasonable and competent degree of skill".[6]

Though professional ethics is normally concerned with the conduct of judges and advocates in their professional capacity only, but it does not mean that they are free to do anything outside the court campus. Therefore, the members of the Bench and the Bar are required both inside the court and outside to conform to high moral standards, which are collectively called professional or legal ethics.

In order to examine the canons of professional ethics for judges and lawyers it will be relevant to discuss the meaning and nature of the term professional ethics.

(A) Meaning and Nature

In its general sense ethics of a profession is a code of conduct by which it regulates actions and sets standards for its members and assures high standard of skill and worthiness in a given field. It strengthens the relationship among its members and promotes the welfare of the whole community. Therefore, it is the rules of conduct pertaining to particular class of human action. When we talk of ethics of legal profession, we refer to the action of the members of the Bench and the Bar in discharge of their duties and obligations and in the exercise of their rights and privileges. It deals with the duties of the professionals which they owe to the public, to

5. All E.R., Vol. 173, p. 581.
6. *Ibid.*, p. 587.

courts, to other professional brethren and to the clients. It demands the members of the Bench and the Bar from the very beginning of their stepping into the profession to cultivate truth, simplicity, condour and fairness. which are the virtues of a judge or advocate.

The term professional ethics connotes two words, the profession and the ethics. The term profession connotes and aims at predominantly intellectual task as opposed to mental, mechanical or physical work. It is an employment or calling, which is not mechanical but an activity which requires some degree of learning, special skill and personal ability.[7] It depends on personal qualification and ability derived from training and experience.

On the other hand, the word ethics means norms, usage and custom among members of any profession involving their moral and professional duties towards one-another. "It is only concerned with human character and conduct, and so it is branch of moral science".[8] It is that branch of moral science which treats such duties which a member of the justice dispensation system owes to the public, the court and to his professional brethren.

The term professional ethics is not defined in any statue book. It may be taken to mean general principles of conduct which are not confined only to a corpus of specific rules. It is more an expression of self-fulfilment and self control.[9] It is a code by which it regulates actions and sets standards for its members and it assumes high tone of skill and worthiness in a given field.

7. According to Justice Brandies of the U.S. Supreme Court three criteria can be applied to a profession :

   First—A profession is an occupation for which the necessary preliminary-training is intellectual in character, involving knowledge and to some extent learning as distinguished from mere skill.

   Second—It is an occupation which is pursued largely for others and not merely for one's self.

   Third—It is an occupation in which the amount of financial return is not the accepted measure of success.

8. For details visit www.ebcindia.com.
9. Geoffery, Hazards, *Ethics in the Practice of Law*", 5th ed. 1978, p. 135.

The Oxford Companion to Law explains professional ethics as the "standards of right and honourable conducts which should be observed by members of learned profession in their dealing one with another and in protecting the interests and handling the affairs of their clients".[10]

The Canadian Law Dictionary defined the term ethics as the basic principles of right action. It says that "Ethics of a profession "means the general body of rules, written or unwritten relative to the conduct of the members of the profession intended to guide them in maintaining certain basic standards of behaviour".[11]

Black Law Dictionary[12] explains professional ethics as an act or behaviour relating to moral action, conduct, motive or character; as ethical emotion; also treating of moral feeling, duties or conduct; containing precepts of morality; morals professionally right or befitting; conforming to professional of conduct.

There is also another term used in relation to professional ethics and that is etiquette. Black's Law Dictionary explains etiquette of the profession as the code of honour agreed on mutual understanding and tacitly accepted by members of legal profession, especially by the Bar.[13] Like-wise David M. Walker in Oxford Companion to Law explains the legal etiquette as a "code of honours and customary rules of behaviour within the legal profession. To a large extent this is unwritten, customary and assimilated by entrants to the profession and inculcated by the example of their senior as much as by precept".[14]

In the field of law collectively it is also known as "legal ethics". It is the study of the meaning and application of judgement of good, bad, right, wrong etc. and every evaluation of law involves an ethical judgement.[15]

---

10. *Oxford Companion to Law*, 1987 ed., p. 929.
11. *Canadian Law Dictionary*, 1970 ed., p. 225.
12. Henry Campbell Black (ed.) Black's Law Dictionary, West Publishing Co., 6th ed. 1990, p. 894.
13. Quoted from, Prasad, Anirudh, Principles of the Ethics of Legal Profession in India, 2006 ed., p. 53.
14. *Supra* note 10.
15. *Legal Ethics*; New York, Columbia University Press (1953), p. XI.

The above definitions of the term professional or legal ethics clarify that it is a branch of moral science. Ethymological origin of the word moral and ethics appear to be the same. The word moral comes from the Latin word *Mos*, which means "customs or way of life". The related term ethics is derived from the Greek word *ethos* which also means custom or character.[16]

Thus, both the term moral and ethics are essentially synonymous and refer to a type of behaviour which tends to become customary because of the approval or practice of the group.

The above discussion shows that the term ethics and morality are closely related. In the earlier usage, the term referred to morality itself, but to the field of study, or branch of inquiry that has morality as its subject matter. In this sense ethics is equivalent to moral philosophy: but it does not mean that professional ethics and morality are the same thing. Ethics is distinguishable from morality or law as a command of sovereign. In this connection it is important to note that the term ethics is slightly different from the Greek word *ethos* also, because ethics is a part of moral science and consists of a set of moral principles, but the term *ethos* is the characteristic spirit and beliefs of a community, people, system or person.[17]

Ethics is also distinguishable from morality which involves mystery and has divine origin. It appears to be that, morality ordinarily refers to the conduct itself, while ethics ordinarily suggests the study of moral conduct or the system or the code which is followed.[18]

It is worth-mentioning that because of divine origin of morality the priesthood become the ultimate interpreter of morality. It, thereby acquired power for itself, which could not be readily relinquished. Consequently, the link between morality and religion has been so firmly forged that during the course of time it has become very difficult to assume the existence of morality without religion. On the other hand ethics appears to be the branch of theology.

16. *Supra* note 13, p. 83.
17. Brangan A. Granee, *"A Dictionary of Morden Legal Usage"*, 1987, p. 224.
18. Titus, Harold H., *Ethics for Today*, p. 3.

In the field of law the term professional ethics are also not exclusively rule-based. The customs and cultures of the judges and advocates to the extent that they have some effect on the delivery of justice, should also be included within the wider definition of the term professional ethics.[19]

Ethics may be called science also, in the sense, science means any body of facts in a particular sphere classified and systematized. However, it is distinguishable from natural science in so far as it is concerned with the value of an activity in the form of ends or ideals of certain forms of activities. Therefore, ethics is the science of what is morally right. In other words while natural science deals with "what exists", the ethics deals with what matters.

Harold J. Titus has explained the position of professional ethics very succinctly. To quote him—

> "Professional ethics, as distinct from morals and from law, gives attention to certain additional ideals and practices which grow out of a man's professional privileges and responsibilities. Professional ethics applies to certain functional groups and is the expression of the attempt to define situations, which otherwise would remain indefinite or uncertain. The ethical codes are the result of the attempt to direct the moral consciousness of the members of the profession to its peculiar problems, they crystallize moral opinion and define behaviour in these specialized field".[20]

The definition-*cum*-explanation of Harold J. Titus is very elaborate and appealing. It depicts that ethics is not an independent phenomena or the independent field of study. Although ethics has always been viewed as a branch of philosophy and it is also applied to any system of moral values or moral principles, its all-embracing practical nature

19. Stepn Parker and Charles, *Sampford Legal Ethics and Legal Practice*; Contemporary Issue, Clarendon Press, Oxford (1995), p. 11.
20. *Id.*, p. 15.

links it with many other areas of study, including anthropology, biology, economics, history, politics, sociology and theology.

Yet ethics remains distinct from such disciplines because it is not a matter of factual knowledge in the way that the science and other branches of inquiry are, rather, it has to do with determining the nature of normative theories and applying these sets of principles to practical moral problems.

Ethics deals with a variety of questions how should we live? Shall we choose happiness or knowledge, virtue or the creation of beautiful objects? If we choose happiness, will it be our own or happiness of all? The more particular questions we face, is: Is there right to be dishonest in a good cause? What are our obligations if any, to the generations of humans, who will come after us and to the non-human animals with whom we share the planet?

Ethics deals with such questions at all levels. Its subject consists of the fundamental issues of practical decisions making and its major concerns include the nature of ultimate value and the standards by which human actions can be judged as being right or wrong.[21] The members of the Bench and the Bar owe allegiance to these ethical values and canons of conduct which have been shaped through ages. The ethics of the profession developed as the profession grew in the stature and assumed its dignified status as a strong arm of our judicial system. Such canons of conduct serve as guide to understand the social as well as professional responsibility of lawyers and judges.

Thus, the standards of morals which are applied to an ordinary citizen in any other walk of life, shall be the standards of morals for the members of the Bench and the Bar also.

(B) Sources of Professional Ethics

Our earlier analysis depicts that the rules of professional ethics cannot always be discovered by institutions. In fact good number of them rest on the ordinary ethical ideas, which

21. "History of Ethics", available at www.ind.law.com., visited on 13.12.2007.

regulate the conduct of men in general. The first and foremost question arises that when ethics did begin and how did it originate? Although there is no historical record of the origin of the term ethics; history cannot reveal; nor is anthropology of any help, because all human societies that have been studied so far had their own forms of morality and ethics. Our 'Shastras' enjoin that, success in life is measured not by the riches one is able to collect money or the power wielded but by the faithful and efficient performance of duties according to one's capacities and there is no greater virtue than living up to one's 'Dharma'.

In the oldest of the Indian writings—the Vedas; ethics is an integral aspect of philosophy and religious speculation about the nature of reality. It is interesting to note that Vedas have been described as the oldest philosophical literature in the world[22] and what they say about how people ought to live may, therefore, be the first philosophical ethics. The 'Vedas' are, in a sense, hymns, however, the Gods to which they refer are not persons but manifestations of ultimate truth and reality. Ethics could have come into existence, only when human beings started to reflect on the best way of life. This reflective stage emerged long after human societies had developed some kind of morality, usually in the form of customary standards of right and wrong. The process of reflection tended to arise from such customs, even if in the end it may have found them wanting.

In the Vedic philosophy the basic principles of the universe, the ultimate reality on which the cosmos exists, is the 'principles of Ritam' and this principle is closely related with the term ethics.[23]

In view of the ancient origin of the idea of ethics in Vedas, India may be regarded as the originator of the term ethics and thus the concept of ethical values were first given to the world by our Vedas and Shastras. But if we try to search the sources of professional or legal ethics in India we find that no attempt has yet been made in India to codify the rules of professional ethics in authoritative form. Therefore, as to the

22. *Ibid.*
23. *Ibid.*

crystallized form of the ethics we have to look at the British history. The ethics of the Bar are the necessary outcome of the system of administration of justice in England and all the other countries have borrowed it from England.

Professional ethics has a wide range and covers ethics of bar as well as the bench. As Mr. Justice J.S. Verma clarifies that the word 'Bar' in this context means not merely the lawyers but also the judges, because administration of justice is a joint venture in which the lawyers and judges are equal participants and so both should obey the rules of professional or legal ethics.[24] Out of the rules of professional ethics, there are some which rest on the peculiar conventions and usage of profession itself, and are not the result of application of general normal philosophy.[25] Some rules of professional ethics are directly related to judicial decisions and legislative enactments of the various countries.

Speaking generally there are four sources of professional ethics; viz.—

I. The tradition and usage or practice of legal professionals;
II. The Judicial decisions;[26]
III. Legislations of Central and State Legislature;[27] and
IV. The Canons of Bar Associations for the regulation of Bench-Bar relations.

Above all four sources of the professional ethics may be traced out primarily in the legal system of England. Although the country in which codification has been attempted in most systematic manner, is United State of America, wherein the canons of professional ethics is example for other civilized countries. Therefore, it is worth to discuss the sources of professional ethics in England and United States of America before we make any attempt to analyse it in our country.

---

24. Verma, J.S. (J), "The Role of The Bar In The Preservation of the Rule of Law" (1995) 1 S.C.J. 11.
25. As in the case with Prohibition against Touting and Advertising.
26. See, *D.P. Chadha* v. *Triyugi Narayan Mishra* (2001) 2 S.C.C. 221.
27. The Advocates Act, 1961.

In England professional conduct and etiquette were supervised by the Inns of the court of which barristers were member. In the beginning, the rules of professional ethics were contained in the regulation of the Inns of court.[28] It covered a long history and till more recent times it was not in written form. It was understood that any gross misconduct or serious breach of professional etiquette might result in censure and even expulsion. Since the unwritten norms worked well no attempt was made to define the rules and practice in black and white for guidance of the members of the Bar. In England the influence of tradition has been so strong that the Parliament may be said to have not cared to look into the matter. The only exception to this complete absence of legislative interference is an old state which was passed in the year of 1275 and which is still unrepealed.

In 1895 a body entitled 'The General Council of the Bar' has been constituted to look after the question of etiquette, and on many such questions the Council has already expressed its views. Ruling given by the General Council of the Bar on questions referred to are published each year in the Annual Statement and rules laid down by each of circuit message composed of barrister. In 1895, when the General Council was constituted it was given only investigative power and it had no disciplinary powers. The disciplinary action for professional misconduct had been controlled by the Benchers of the Inns and it was not subject to ordinary court also. The decisions of the Benchers were applicable before the Lord Chancellor and the judges of High Court.

Appeal lies to the judges as visitors but as a rule they follow the Bencher's decision. In the year of 1957, with the introduction of Solicitors Act the disciplinary power of the Inns of the court extended to suspension from practice, disbarment and even expulsion from the Bar. However, such power was limited to the actions against solicitors and did not extend to barristers.

In most of the States[29] there is a grievance committee of the State or the local Bar Association which makes the

28. Anand, C.L., Principles of Legal Ethics, 2nd ed., p. 179.
29. Now all the States.

preliminary investigation of the complaint and its findings are referred to the court which may have power to decide. The lawyer has thereafter, the right of appeal to the highest court of the state. When disciplinary jurisdiction is invoked, the question for consideration is of the fitness of the person to remain a member of the honourable profession of law. In case of English barristers, as has been pointed out earlier, the power is vested in the Benchers of the Inn, but for the solicitors there is a disciplinary committee of Solicitors under the Solicitors Act, 1957 with power to suspend or strike off the roll.

Thus, in England the sources of professional ethics depends mostly on the traditions, with solitary exception of the Act of 1215 which is the another source dealing with the issue in statutory form.

In United States of America the sources of professional ethics for lawyers and judges mostly depend on canons of Bar Associations. They resemble to English system. It is submitted that these canons are also the example of traditions. However, in United States it is in a very authoritative form and it is running as effectively as statutory rules.

In United States of America an earlier attempt to make such rules was made in the *thirty-three resolutions,*[30] written by 'Daniel Hoffman' of the 'Baltimore Bar' as guides for young legal practitioners. But systematic attempt was made in 1887. Firstly, the Alabama State Bar Association formulated and adopted its code in 1887. Its adoption was the outcome of a desire among the leaders of the Bar to counteract the growing spirit of commercialism in the profession. At the time when American Bar Association formulated its code in 1908, twelve out of forty-four States Bar Associations had adopted formal codes of legal ethics and there were two States in which attempt had been made by statues to define the professional obligations.

By 1914 thirty one States adopted canons of the American Bar Association and at present all the States have done so. The American Bar Association has from the two time amended and made addition to its canons.[31]

30. Now it is known as *Fifty Resolutions*.
31. The first amendment was made in 1928, effected from 1933.

In the United States of America court of superior jurisdiction has inherent power to discipline an attorney for his misconduct as attorneys are officers of the court in which they are admitted to practise, because Bar Associations are not legislative bodies and their canons, therefore do not as such create obligations which have inherently the force of law. It is other thing that, in the States in which they have been adopted by Statute or Statutory rules or rules made by the court, they have the force of law. Besides the Bench and the Bar have recognized that the canons contain wholesome rules of professional conduct in United States.

Coming to India, before the Advocates Act, 1961, breaches of rules of professional etiquette were subject to disciplinary jurisdiction of the High Courts. The primary reason for which the courts were armed with this power was the conception that advocates were officers of the court. That being so, the court, in maintenance of its purity and dignity of the administration of justice must enjoy the authority to remove its unfit officers.

In India statutory provision regulating professional conduct of lawyers were made also in the Legal Practitioners Act, 1879, the Bar Council Act, 1926, the Letter's Patent of several High Courts order XXI, Rule 73 of the Civil Procedure Code, 1908, Section 136 of the Transfer of Property Act, 1882 and Section 126 of the Indian Evidence Act, 1872. The provisions made in the Legal Practitioners Act, Bar Councils Act and Letters Patent have been repealed by the Advocates Act, 1961.

It is submitted in this regard that although in India the above referred statutory provisions are available to regulate the conduct of advocates, but these Acts are only the power giver statutes and do not fix any norms of conduct. After the enactment of the Advocates Act, 1961, the Bar Council of India has been authorized to lay down the standards of professional conduct and etiquette for advocates, but still in the absence of fixed rules and expert guidance in India, the solution is left to the sense of fairness of each individual advocates and inevitable result is that self-interest often becomes the chief determining factor.

Likewise, at present there is no such legal machinery or set of norms to regulate the conduct of judges also. Farmers of the Constitution provided only for the removal from office of Supreme Court and High Courts judges for proven misbehavior/incapacity through Parliamentary impeachment. The cumbersome procedure, prescribed under Arts. 124 and 217 of the Constitution read with Judges (Inquiries) Act, 1968 dealing with removal of judges for which support of the two third majority in Parliament is necessary, does not work well.[32]

Thus, it is clear from the above discussion that, in India, there are lack of proper, fixed and codified rules of conduct for the members of Bench and the Bar.

The absence of fixed rules of the ethical ideals has led to deterioration of professional observance and entire judicial system. Therefore, it is humbly submitted that mere self-regulation and judicial control is not enough to secure respect for professional observance by the members of the Bench and the Bar. Judicial supervision and self-regulation may be effective only when, the proper codified rules of professional conduct and etiquette will be made by the legislative agencies.

The coming discussion will be focussed on the necessity of the codified rules and problem in framing such codified rules and norms of the etiquette.

II. NECESSITY OF CODIFICATION

Professional ethics cannot be conditioned, controlled or regulated merely by allusive guidelines like self-conscience and self-controlled or even pious declaration of the judicial agencies, unless there is a body of specific rules for that purpose. Codification of professional ethics makes it clear and certain the rules which are to be followed and also reconciled with divergent and conflicting views.

It brings uniformity and minimise the confusion on important aspects. It increases the efficacy of the professional ethics by its binding forces. It is to apply and enforce the codified law. From time to time the rules of code of conduct lay down are to be amended or revised to suit the changing circumstances of social values. In short-codification of rules of conduct makes them certain, single, intelligible and accessible

32. See the discussion under Chapter VIII.

to all the codified rules. It preserves and promotes the dignity and prestige of the profession and also the interests of the general public.

Regarding the necessity of codification of the professional ethics Mr. Sundaram Iyer in preface to his book on professional ethics wrote that—

> "Rules are necessary even for the best self-interest in misleading factor when you have to decide on the spur of the moment what is test to be done in the circumstances".[33]

Likewise Mr. Justice R.P. Sethi of the Supreme Court is also of the view that codification is necessary for the members of the Bar. In *R.D. Sexena* v. *Balram Prasad*,[34] recognising the importance of code of conduct, he opined that—

> "It is high time for the legal profession to join hands and evolve a code for themselves in addition to mandate of the Advocates Act, Rules made there under and the Rules made by various High Courts and this court, for strengthening the belief of the common man in the institution of the judiciary in general and in their profession in particular. Creation of such a faith and confidence would not only strengthen the rule of law but also result in reaching excellence in the profession".[35]

Before making the plea for the necessity of a code of professional ethics, one may have to look at the advisability and practicability of the adoption of such a code. A code of legal ethics is not only advisable, but under existing conditions, it is of great importance for several reasons. Some of such reasons are presented hereunder:

33. Iyer and Iyer, *The Duties of the Advocate to this Client and Legal Ethics*, 2001 ed., p. XI.
34. (2007) 7 S.C.C. 264.
35. *Ibid.*, p. 269.

1. Legal profession is necessarily the keystone of the arch of Government. So if this key stone is weakened by increasingly subjecting it to corroding and demoralizing influence of those who are controlled by greed, gain or other unworthy motive, then the arch will definitely fall. The maintenance of the Shrine of justice pure and unsullied is possible only if the conduct, and motives of members of legal profession are what they ought to be. For this, a code of ethics, adopted after due deliberation, with the Bar of the country, is necessary.

   With the change of time, the situation of legal service also changed and professional assistance ceased to be gratuitous. With the multiplicity of the proceedings, increase in litigation and complications of law, the legal assistance could not be in the nature of a mere social obligation and the service rendered as honorary because a great deal of time was needed by a lawyer to equip himself with the laws, which prevented him from earning his livelihood from other sources. The ancient tradition having ceased to exist, the profession of law could have flourished only if those who pursued it were allowed remuneration for the service rendered. The other reason for no necessity of code of conduct for lawyers and judges was that early advocates were generally persons in holy order who rendered their services to weak and afflicted without charge as an act of pity.[36]

   But, with the emergence of commercialised view of profession, the old concept of advocacy is no longer practicable. Existence of a code, based on ancient traditions are suitable no more. The guidance of lawyers in statutory form will be of great help in checking the growing tendency in the direction of commercializing the vocation of the Bar.

(3) Members of the Bar, like judges, are officers of the court. like judges, they should hold office only

36. *Supra* note 3.

> during good behaviour. As in the *Matter of "G" Senior Advocate of the Supreme Court,*[37] the Apex court was of the view that an advocate is liable to disciplinary action if he departs from the high standards which the profession has set for itself and conducts himself in a manner which is not fair, reasonable and according to law.

Such standards should be crystallized into a written code of professional ethics.

If we compare the situation prevailing in India with England, we will come to conclusion that the necessity for codification of professional ethics is even greater in India than in England. The traditional rules of conduct in such countries are quite at variance.

Following reasons may be advanced for the same. In the first place, the Bar in this country has no traditions which can serve as guide and inspiration. Secondly, whereas, in England the Attorney-General is the final authority upon all questions of professional conduct and can readily be consulted, in India there is no such guidance available. Thirdly, the English practices in the matter do not always afford correct guidance to us. Though the traditions of English Bar are well known and definite, their application in the case of legal practitioners in India will create a lot of difficulty; and lastly, in England, there are two classes of legal practitioners and their rules of etiquette are not the same for both. On the other hand, in India our advocates usually combine the functions both of attorney and barristers.

The above comparative reasons make it clear that there is urgent need of codification of professional ethics in India. Therefore, it is submitted that the codification of rules of professional conduct is required not only for—

(1) Attaining high standards of competence in law.
(2) Strengthening mutual relationship amongst the members of the Bar.

37. A.I.R. 1954 S.C. 557.

(3) Promoting the welfare of the community as a whole but also for—
   (a) Providing guidelines to the advocate with regard to the problems to be dealt with by him.
   (b) For reminding them of their rights and duties towards the profession, public, clients, the courts and to the country.
   (c) Making provisions for dealing with the members of the Bar who violate the rules of ethics.
   (d) Making provisions for dealing with the members of the Bench who violate the rules of ethics and for reminding them of their duties towards a very high seat of justice.

If law demands them to act on their rules of etiquette, professional ethics should not be a vague, meaningless or shadowy; but it must be specifically defined in written form. Therefore, the codification of rules of professional ethics may help in this situation and provide certain advantages. The main advantage of codified rules is that, it will furnish an authoritative statement of ideals by which every judge and lawyer, when in doubt, may safely be guided.

Likewise character is nothing but a bundle of habits, which cannot be built in a day. Only a proper and well defined code of conduct can help the new comer advocate and judge to establish their etiquette according to the prescribed manner.

The codification may also help in the autonomy of the profession, because if a degree of standardization is needed and that is done by the profession itself, it will keep outside interference away.

As Harold H. Titus says in his book that—

> "Governmental regulations through law tend to be negative, while ethics points to the goal desires".[38]

It is clear from the foregoing discussion that the codification will tend to raise and strengthen the standard of

38. *Supra* note 18, p. 284.

professional honour. It is submitted that in this regard that if the rules of conduct is expressed and codified, any members of the Bench and the Bar will hesitate before violating or disregarding the rules; and any departure from the prescribed standard will tend to a loss of professional reputation and no member in the ordinary circumstances will be likely to risk it.

III. PROBLEMS IN FRAMING THE RULES OF PROFESSIONAL ETHICS

It is no denying fact that in the field of legal profession, there is an urgent need to codify the rules of professional ethics, but it is also fact that codification of professional ethics is not an easy task. It is a big question how to frame the abstract ethical proposition, which may be readily understood by every member of the Bench and the Bar. Obviously such propositions should be in general to cover the judge's and lawyer's responsibilities in the great variety of relations and problems, with which they will have to deal.

The first and foremost problem in framing the code of professional ethics is that, the term professional ethics is different from law and it is concerned with social relations and external conduct, which condemns any sort of life. On the other hand, the area of law is very much limited, and confined only to those acts which are prohibited under any rules or judicial decisions. For this reason the formulation of the ethical code or convert the ethics into the rules of law is very difficult.

The problem in framing a comprehensive code of professional ethics has been very well summarized by *Dr. Radha Vinod Paul*, in these words—

> "The difficulty in framing a comprehensive code of professional ethics lies specially in the fact that the question involved is ultimately one of means to the ideal and for individual and community, and indeed there is no conceivable branch of knowledge which may not, at this or that point, have bearing upon the questions that may crop up in the field. I would again emphasize that in our present effort we are in the field of conscience, we are in the field which should be one of morality. Unless we feel

stimulated by this idea we may be compelled to resort only to provisional suppositions and crude explanations and may ultimately content, ourselves with what scientifically viewed, would be only practical result".[39]

He also pointed out the difficulties relating to the question of sustaining sanction for the rules remembering that these are to function as ethical one.[40]

The above difficulties highlighted by Dr. Paul, is also accepted by the honourable Supreme Court of India. In *Bar Council of Maharashtra* v. *M.V. Dabholker*,[41] Mr. Justice Krishna Iyer, is of the view that, canons of conduct for an advocate or judges cannot be crystallized into rigid rules, but felt by the collective conscience of the legal professionals as right.

Speaking for the Supreme Court, the learned judge said:

"One of the objections to a code is the danger of it being regarded as exhaustive; anything not coming within its express prohibition is allowable. However, it is not possible to formulate a code of legal ethics, which will provide the lawyer with specific rules to be followed in all the varied relation of his professional life. The maximum that can be done is to state with as much particularity as possible and with due regard to custom and tradition those general principle which experience has taught us to be observed, so that the profession occupied its high place in social structure".

He also added that—

"It would be a folly to assume that these canons of ethics are sufficient enough in laying down rules of conduct, which will be sufficient for all purposes and under all circumstances. This is because many duties quite as important and equally imperative though not specified

39. Paul, Radha Binod, "Professional Ethics", *A.I.R. (J)*, 1961, p. 67.
40. *Id.*, p. 68.
41. A.I.R. 1976 S.C. 242.

will arise in the course of almost every lawyer's practice".[42]

The problem in framing code of ethics is taken from another angle by Prof. Dr. Anirudh Prasad. In his book, he wrote that—

> "The problem of the codification of law relating to professional ethics may be viewed from the angle of Justice. Justice provides the area of common concern to their jurisprudence and ethics. The problem of enforcement of professional ethics may be viewed on a similar plane as it has been with respect to the enforcement of morals through legislation".[43]

First, even the great liberitarians like John Stuart Mill and H.L.A. Hart agree that restraints can be imposed on personal liberty with a view to deter any person from inflicting harm on others. Since the conduct of a lawyer is likely to affect others court, client and brethren at the Bar, code of conduct may be permissible. *Secondly,* since society can regulate the conduct of individuals for self-protection, a code of conduct for lawyers may be desirable for maintaining the confidence in the administration of justice and not allowing it decay. *Thirdly,* as conduct having tendency to corrupt public morals are to be regulated through criminal law, the conducts of lawyers with tendency to corrupt and bring disrepute to the administration of justice may also be regulated. *Fourthly,* as the morality reaching a point to cause a Jury intolerance, indignation and disgust is to be enforced likewise the conduct of an advocate causing a Jury or a judge intolerance, indignation and disgust must be enforced. *Lastly,* even a positivist thinker, like H.L.A. Hart "approves minimum content of natural law or existence of some shared morality for the survival of the society. Some shared ethics is essential for the retention and survival of the effective and appreciable administration of Justice".[44]

42. *Id.*, p. 244.
43. *Supra* note 13, p. 85.
44. *Id.*, p. 97.

Thus, the foregoing discussion reveals that here is not only the problem of the codification of professional ethics, but the problems may arise about its enforcement too. But though there are difficulties in the codification as arises in the case of codification relating to any branch of law determining the social relation, there is nothing impracticable about it. That is possible to codify these rules is evident from the successful attempts made by the American Bar Association providing code of conduct although not in the form of statutory rules but are working very well.

Thus, it may be difficult to formulate the code of ethical value, but it is not impossible by any angle. So in India, there is an urgent need to codify rules of professional ethics by the legislative agency which will provide an advocate and judges with specific rules to be followed in all the varied relations of their personal and professional capacity of life.

IV. PROFESSIONAL ETHICS FOR THE MEMBERS OF BENCH AND BAR

Ethics are the most precious heritage of the Bench and the Bar. It is due to the norms of ethics governing the relation between judges and advocate, *interse* and *vis-à-vis* others. It is that code of conduct, which imposes duty upon the members of Bench and the Bar to maintain the high standards of probity, propriety, honesty and good moral behaviour; not only in their personal and individual capacity but also in their professional and collective capacity.

The code of professional ethics is necessary for maintaining the dignity of the profession as well as for development of cordial relationship among all the persons who are the member of entire judicial system or who come to that system. These obligations of advocates and judges have different aspects. First aspect expresses the duties towards the system of justice, towards the court of law, towards the clients and towards others. Since, the Bench and the Bar are the two arms of the same machinery, the second obligation, therefore are related with themselves or duty to each others, which is properly known as Bench-Bar relationship.

The norms of professional ethics deal with both of them. In order to analyze these norms, it is necessary to discuss the duties of the members of Bench and the Bar under following heads:

At present, the discussion given below is in brief and enumerates the duties only. The rules of punishment relating to breach of these duties will be discussed in the coming two chapters of the study.

(A) Duty of Advocates

Advocacy is a profession, not a trade or business, and as a profession certain standards, intellectual and ethical must be maintained both for dignity of profession and for better quality of service to the public. The moral quality of this work makes the profession most honourable. Its root lies in the code of ethics, which create a proper balance between relation to his client and court of law.

As Sir Asutosh Mookerjee, J. in case of *Emperor* v. *Rajani Kanta Bose*,[45] observed: "a lawyer is more than a mere agent or servant of his client; he is also an officer of the court and as such he owes the duty of good faith and honourable dealing to the court, before which he practises. His high vacation is to inform the court as to the law and facts of case and to aid it to justice by arriving at correct conclusion".

In this connection another relevant observation of His Lordship is worth quoting:

> "The pleader by his obligation is bound to discharge his duties to his clients with the strictest fidelity and is answerable to the disciplinary jurisdiction of the court for dereliction of duty.[46]

The above observation of Sir Asutosh Mookerjee, J. has been quoted with approval by the Apex court of India in *E.S. Reddi* v. *Chief Secretary, Government of Andhra Pradesh*.[47]

In the instant case Supreme Court held that—

45. A.I.R. 1922 Cal. 515.
46. *Id.*, p. 519.
47. A.I.R. 1987 S.C. 1550.

> "An advocate is required to maintain a high standard of ethics, probity and integrity. As an agent of his client he is not merely a mouthpiece of his client, but he plays a much more important role by rendering assistance to the court in the administration of justice and consequently he has also a duty to the court itself as an officer of the court and also to the society at large as the legal profession is a public utility service:
>
> Likewise, in *Onkar Singh* v. *Angez Singh,*[48] a learned single judge of the Punjab and Haryana High Court, following a division Bench decision in *Soudager Singh* v. *Executive Officer,*[49] held that, the advocates have dual obligation in the matter of conducting cases; firstly, the obligation towards their client who engage them. Such obligation is subject to terms and conditions to the contract or authority given to the counsel. The other obligation of advocate is towards the court as an officer of the court to assist the court in the matter of dispensation of justice".

It appears from the above decisions that access to justice is one of the most important social right and the lawyers taking part and actively being also associated with the administration of justice in all courts play an absolutely vital role in the society. The above decisions also clarify that the advocate is under dual obligation as to duty to his clients and duty to court and others.

Such a vital and important duties of advocate as laid down in different judicial decisions has also been recognized by the Bar Council of India itself, by framing rules under the Advocates Act, 1961, relating to the standards of conduct and etiquette; which are as under:

(i) ***Advocate's Duty to the Client***

In many countries including India, the relationship between an advocate and his client mainly rests on the

48. A.I.R. 1993 P & H, 134.
49. (1989) 96 Punj. L.R. 693.

principle of contract. This aspect brings a direct relationship between an advocate and his client. On the other hand, in England where the relationship of counsel and client does not originate in contract, a barrister does not come into direct relationship with his client at all, because of practice of appointing solicitors.[50] Unlike England, an advocate in India not only presents his client's case in court of Law but also prepares it. Therefore, the relationship between advocate and client is much more strong, express and virtual in India than England.

The closeness of this relation, imposes a lot of duties upon the shoulder of an advocate, which he is expected to obey in relation to his client. In a series of judicial pronouncements these duties have been announced by the different High Courts as well as supreme judicial body of the land. With a view to ensure the proper relationship between the advocate and his client so as to enable smooth administration of justice, the Bar Council of India has framed certain norms of professional ethics for regulating the same. Section II of Chapter 11 of Part VI of the Bar Council of India Rules, frames rules 11 to 33 relating to duties of an advocate to his client, which are as follows:

1. An Advocate is bound to accept any brief in the courts or Tribunals or before any other authority in or before which he professes to practise at a fee consistent with his standing at the bar and the nature of the case. Special circumstances may justify his refusal to accept a particular brief.
2 An Advocate shall not ordinarily withdraw from engagements once accepted, without sufficient cause and unless reasonable and sufficient notice is given to the client. Upon his withdrawal from a case, he shall refund such part of the free as has not been earned.
3. An Advocate should not accept a brief or appear in a case in which he has reason to believe that he will

50. In England, it is the duty of Solicitors to prepared the case and barrister, who present the case in court.

be witness and if being engaged in a case, it becomes apparent that he is a witness on a material question of fact, he should not continue to appear as an Advocate if he can retire without jeopardizing his client's interests.

4. An Advocate shall at the commencement of his engagement and during the continuance thereof make all such full and frank disclosures to his client relating to his connection with the parties and any interest in or about the controversy as are likely to affect his client's judgement in either engaging him or continuing the engagement.
5. It shall be the duty of an Advocate fearlessly to uphold the interests of his client by all fair and honourable means without regard to any unpleasant consequences to himself or any other. He shall defend a person accused of a crime regardless of his personal opinion as to the guilt of the accused, bearing in mind that his loyalty is to the law which requires that no man should be convicted without adequate evidence.
6. An Advocate appearing for the prosecution in a criminal trial shall so conduct the prosecution that it does not lead to conviction of the innocent. The suppression of material capable of establishing the innocence of the accused shall be scrupulously avoided.
7. An Advocate shall not directly or indirectly, commit a breach of the obligations imposed by Section 126 of the Indian Evidence Act.
8. An Advocate shall not at any time, be a party to fomenting of litigation.
9. An Advocate shall not act on the instructions of any person other than his client or his authorized agent.
10. An Advocate shall not stipulate for a fee contingent on the results of litigation or agree to share the proceeds thereof.
11. An Advocate shall not buy or traffic in or stipulate for or agree to receive any share or interest in any actionable claim. Nothing in this Rule shall apply to

stock, shares and debentures or Government securities, or to any instruments which are, for the time being, by law or custom negotiable, or to any mercantile document of title to goods.

12. An Advocate shall not, directly or indirectly, bid for or purchase, either in his own name or in any other name, for his own benefit or for the benefit of any other person, any property sold in the execution of a decree or order in any suit, appeal or other proceeding in which he was in any way professionally engaged. This prohibition, however, does not prevent an Advocate from bidding for or purchasing for his client any property which his client may himself legally bid for or purchase, provided the Advocate is expressly authorized in writing in this behalf.
13. An Advocate shall not directly or indirectly bid in court auction or acquire by way of sale, gift, exchange or any other mode of transfer either in his own name or in any other name for his own benefit or for the benefit of any other person, any property which is subject matter of any suit, appeal or other proceedings in which he is in any way professionally engaged.
14. An Advocate shall not adjust free payable to him by his client against his own personal liability to the client, which liability does not arise in the course of his employment as an Advocate.
15. An Advocate shall not do anything whereby he abuses or takes advantage of the confidence reposed in him by his client.
16. An Advocate should keep accounts of the client's money entrusted to him, and the accounts should show the amounts received from the client or on his behalf, the expenses incurred for him and the debits made on account of fees with respective dates and all other necessary particulars.
17. Where moneys are received from or on account of a client, the entries in the accounts should contain a reference as to whether the amounts have been

received for fees or expenses, and during the course of the proceedings, no Advocate shall, except with the consent in writing of the client concerned, be at liberty to divert any portion of the expenses towards fees.

18. After the termination of the proceeding the Advocate shall be at liberty to appropriate towards the settled fee due to him any sum remaining unexpended out of the amount paid or sent to him for expenses, or any amount that has come into his hands in that proceeding.
19. Where the fee has been left unsettled, the Advocate shall be entitled to deduct, out of any moneys of the client remaining in his hands, at the termination of the proceeding for which he had been engaged, the fee payable under the rules of the court, in force for the time being, or by then settled and the balance, if any, shall be refunded to the client.
20. A copy of the client's account shall be furnished to him on demand provided the necessary copying charges is paid.
21. An Advocate shall not enter into arrangements whereby funds in his hands are converted into loans.
22. An Advocate shall not lend money to his client for the purpose of any action or legal proceedings in which he is engaged by such client.
23. An Advocate who has, at any time, advised in connection with the institution of a suit, appeal or other matter or has drawn pleadings, or acted for a party shall not act, appear of plead for the opposite party.

A close reading of the above referred rules, appears that, in relation to his client he is not only in the position of an agent, and bound with the principles of contract but his is also bound with the rules of trust and confidences as a trustee of his client.

(a) Contractual Nature of Duty of an Advocate

An advocate owes duties to his client in his personal and

contractual relation in several ways. After the acceptance of his employment he is duty bound to give a patent pursuance in the court of law and protect his interest with all legal means and proper skill. Although the contractual relation between an Advocate and his clients results into a number of duties, some of them are elaborated below.

(1) Duty to Brief

The relation of Advocate and client is established by the fact of agreements between them in which the client appoints his Advocate for the pursuance of the case. It is not necessary that a retaining fee should have been paid for it, or that there should have been an agreement for compensation, though that is usual evidence of employment.[51]

Before accepting the client's case, the Advocate is under the prime duty to give his candid opinion regarding the merits of the case.[52] On this point Sharaswood says in his Legal Ethics:

> "It is nothing, but selfishness that can operate upon a lawyer when consulted, to conceal from the party his candid opinion of the merits and the probable result. It is fair that he should know it; for he may not choose to employ a man whose views may operate to check his resorting to all lawful means to effect success. Besides, most men, when they consult on attorney, wish a candid opinion; it is what they ask and pay for".[53]

After giving his candid opinion, once the Advocate has accepted the case, the etiquette requires that he should bear no grudge as to time or toil, however great, needful to the thorough mastery of his case in its fact and legal rules irrespective of the amount of fee paid to him. After the completion of agreement he comes under the duty to prepare all necessary brief and give all helps related with that cues. It is the prime duty of an advocate to keep himself constantly in

51. *Supra* note 28, p. 105.
52. See, In the matter of 'S', a vakil, A.I.R. 1928 Cal. 820 (F.B.).
53. Quoted from Thoughtson, Pandia, 'Professional concept', p. 106.

touch with his client and inform him to every step that is being taken with respect to the case. In all matters connected with his client's case the Advocate is expected to attend the work personally.[54] There can be no dwelling or delegation of his duties by the advocate to other counsel except with the assent of the client as well as the extraordinary situations.[55]

The canons of the American Bar Association on this point are very clear, wherein, it is said that "It is not permissible or in accordance with professional etiquette for a counsel to hand over his brief to another counsel to represent him in court and conduct the case as if the latter counsel had himself been briefed unless the client consents to this course being taken".[56]

The above canon of the American Bar Association and duty not to delegate the brief to another Advocate is also affirmed by the Supreme Court of India. In *V.C. Rangadurai* v. *D. Gopalan*[57] the client instructed his Advocate to file two suits on the basis of promissory note. He also gave some amount for court fee and expenses. The Advocate filed suit on one of the promissory note but did not represent. He did not file suit on other promissory note and misrepresented the client that suits were pending. Not only had this he also handed over brief to another Advocate.

A three judge bench unanimously agreed to the committing of professional misconduct. Speaking for the court Mr. Justice A.P. Sen observed:

> "Nothing should be done by any member of the legal fraternity which might tend to lessen in any degree the confidence of the public in the fidelity, honesty and integrity of the profession".[58]

54. *Supra* note 28, p. 123.
55. Where the delegate is appointed without consent, the person originally appointed continues to be liable for any want of reasonable skill or gross negligence of delegates. For detail see, in the matter of 'S', a vakil, A.I.R. 1928 Cal. 820.
56. See Canon 37 of the American Bar Association.
57. (1979)1 S.C.C. 308.
58. *Id.*, p. 319.

In this connection a controversial question arises; if a client comes to an Advocate with proper instructions and is prepared to pay a fair and proper fee and invites him to undertake a case of a kind which he is accustomed to do and he refuses, will such refusal amount to professional misconduct? Will the Advocate be punished for it?

Rule 11 of the Bar Council of India is most pertinent on this point. It says that, an Advocate is bound to accept the brief, but special circumstances may justify his refusal to accept a particular brief. Even though the Bar Council of India Rules says that an Advocate may refuse to accept a particular brief in special circumstances, it does not state what those special circumstances are? Therefore, the duty as well as the right to refuse particular brief, arises the controversy about extent of his right and provision of the Bar Council of India Rules are not very much clear. However, honourable exceptions are available everywhere.

In England, a barrister is under an obligation to accept brief in the courts in which he proposes to practice, offered to him at proper fee. He need not accept a brief if it is beyond his capacity or experience or for any other justifiable circumstances. But, it is unlawful to discriminate on ground of colour, race, etc. It is the paramount duty of defending counsel to ensure that an accused person is never left unrepresented at any stage of his trial and so also the prosecuting counsel has a duty to be present throughout the trial.[60]

In India, the judicial pronouncements have taken a clear stand on the point. Judiciary is of firm view that the counsel should not refuse the brief. The rationales of the cases in *Lalta* v. *Zahoor,*[61] *Ram Dular Lal* v. *Chhangamal*[62] and in the *Matter of Shyamapada Bhattacharji,*[63] are clear. An Advocate by his very calling is duty bound to act for anybody who fulfils, certain conditions. In such circumstances the advocate cannot refuse.

59. *Id.*, p. 316.
60. H.L.E. 4th ed., Vol. 3, Para 1138.
61. A.I.R. 1925 Oudh. 67.
62. A.I.R. 1930 All. 309.
63. A.I.R. 1932 Cal. 370.

If he does so, such refusal amounts to professional misconduct and should be punished as such.

In *Muhammad Inayet Ali* v. *Fazal-ul-Rahman,*[64] Chief Justice (as he was then) Gimwood Meags pointed out that 'There is a definite and well recognized rule, which, however, does not seem to be understood in this country, that a lawyer must take up a case for any member of the public if a fair and proper fee is tendered to him, if adequate instructions are given to him and the case of a class which the lawyer is accustomed to do".

It is submitted that the above decision of the Allahabad High Court enumerates only one side of the coin, i.e. the duty of Advocate for accepting the brief but it does not explain the question that in what circumstances an Advocate may refuse to accept the brief.

In *Muraleedharan Nair* v. *N.J. Antoney,*[65] Mr. Justice Bhaskaran Nambiar of the Kerala High Court, enumerated certain circumstances in which an Advocate may refuse to accept the particular brief, as:

1. When he is physically disabled from appearing for the client;
2. When he may not be available to present the case in court;
3. Where his training in a special branch limits his usefulness in other branches;
4. Where the client is not prepared and able to pay him his reasonable fees;
5. Whether he confines his practice in some courts and in some places only;
6. When he is likely to be called as a witness in the same case; and
7. When he has been already consulted by the other side.

However, these circumstances are not exhaustive and need proper analysis. This controversial issue becomes more

64. A.I.R. 1936 Cal. 603.
65. (1985) 2 S.C.C. 515.

complicated, if the advocate is to deal with a client whom he knows to be guilty.

It is not an easy question, because here not only the question of right and duties arises but it arises the question of ethics too.

Rules of Bar Council of India do not provide any help on the point because it is self-contradictory and not clear. Rule 1, requires from an Advocate to conduct the proceedings in the court with dignity and self-respect; and second part of the Rule 15 requires that "He shall defend a person accused of a crime regardless of his personal opinion as to the guilt of the accused; bearing in mind that his loyalty is to the law which requires that no man should be convicted without adequate evidence".

It indicates that Lawyer's duty towards his client is overriding over his duty towards court itself. On this point canons of American Bar Association are much clear and unambiguous. It is said that "The office of attorney does not permit much less does it demand of him for any client, violation of law or any manner of fraud. He must obey his conscience and not that of his client".[66]

It seems that the United State's Lawyers are free to accept or refuse the case of known guilty clients, depending upon their own conscience.

Likewise in England, the General Council of the Bar has said that "where the confession has been made, before the proceedings have been commenced, it is most undesirable that an advocate to when the confession has been made should undertake the defence, as he would most certainly be seriously embarrassed in the conduct of the case, and no harm can be done to the accused by requesting him to retain another advocate".[67]

But in India, our accusatorial system demands that 'no one can be said to be guilty, unless the case has decided to beyond reasonable doubt'. Therefore, several arguments have been proffered to support the idea of an Advocate supporting

66. *Supra* note 13, p. 197.
67. The Annual Practice, 1917, pp. 2434-39.

a known guilty client or the accused of Anti-National activities:

1. Case is still not decided.
2. The client may claim "I need your argument not your judgment".
3. The prisoner makes a statement to his counsel for the purpose of his defence, and not to manufacture a witness against him.
4. An advocate is only an agent of his client.
5. Pre-judgment by lawyer may amount to lynching without trial.
6. Advocate's choice of retire from arguing such a case may amount to usurpation the power of the judge by the Advocate.

It is well recognized principle of the criminal law, that an accused is to be tried according to the evidence and there is nothing unprofessional or morally improper in an Advocate's ensuring that the prosecution discharges its onus of proof, what ever his personal knowledge or opinion may be. It is said that his personal knowledge is wholly irrelevant to the case which he represents.

Mr. Justice Sundara Aiyar is also of the view that, an Advocate has no right to refuse a brief even if he is convinced that the client is guilty of particular offence".[68]

A very complicated issue may arise. It is true that no one be punished unless the guilt is proved. But the question is, if an Advocate has produced any document which he knew or even he did not knew, to be false, then he became an offender of contempt of court, and is accordingly punished? Then what would be the demands of law, if he represents a client about him he knew that he is guilty?

It is also true that the court of India is called to be court of Law, not the court of Justice, even another question arises, what is the ultimate goal of our court of law? To search the truth or prove the guilty as innocent? On this point the opinion of Mahatma Gandhi is worth mentioning that—

68. Aiyar Sundara, "Professional Ethics", p. 154.

> "My principle was put to the test many a time in South Africa. Often I knew that my opponents had tutored their witnesses, and if I only encouraged my client or his witness to lie, we could win the case. But I always resisted the temptation. . . . It may heart of hearts I always wished that I should win only if my client's case was right . . . I warned every new client at the outset that he should not expect me to take up a false case or to coach the witnesses, with the result that I built up such a reputation that no false cases used to come to me. Indeed some of my clients would keep their clean cases for me, and take the doubtful one elsewhere.[69]

He had the reputation, among both professional colleagues and his clients, of being a very sound lawyer and was held in the highest esteem by the courts. To quote, Gandhiji again:

> "there is another thing I would like to warn you against. In England, in South Africa, almost everywhere I have found that in the practice of their profession lawyers are consciously led into untruth for the sake of their clients. An eminent English lawyer has gone so far as to say that it may even be the duty of a lawyer to defend a client whom he knows to be guilty. There I disagree. The duty of a lawyer is always to place before the judges, and to help them to arrive at, the truth, never to prove the guilty as innocent".[70]

It is submitted that no clear conclusion can be arrived in such situations and two divergent views are possible—the Gandhian and conscientious conclusion will be that in special circumstances it. The other view is that the advocate is to take brief and not refuse it without valid reasons. He should do his best to defend his client and leave decision with the court.

69. As, quoted, (in) Krishna V.R. Iyer, "The Indian Lawyer: His Social Responsibility And Legal Immunities", Vol. 15, I.L.R., 1 & 2 (1988) p. 125.
70. *Ibid.*, 127.

Another and more controversial issue relates to the acceptance brief of accused of anti-national and terrorist activities. The high tradition of bar requires that an advocate should accept their brief. In India such issue has arisen more than often. *First,* the issue arose in the case relating to the attack on Parliament on December 13, 2001. In this case seven persons including Syed Abdul Rahman Geelani, Lecturer in Arabic at the Zakir Hussain College of Delhi University, were accused of conspiracy of waging war against the state. The accused were defended by different lawyers, namely Mr. Ram Jethmalani, Mr. N.D. Panchali and Miss Seema Gulati. On the date of judgement the motives of the counsel appearing for accused were questioned, their effigy were burnt and they were accused of being anti-national. Likewise, when Mr. Ramjethmalani declared that he would defend Syed Abdul Rahman Geelani against his death sentence, Shiv Sena workers furiously reacted.

An unfortunate incidence took place in Varanasi, wherein the advocates of District Bar not only refused to accept brief of suspected terrorist of explosion at Sankat Mochan Mandir on March 6, 2006, but on the date of trial they beaten *black and blue* to accused. An advocate appearing for accused of attack on Ram Janambhoomi at Ayodhya was expelled from the bar by the Bar Association. The advocate of Raja Raghu Raj Pratap Singh, a detenue under POTA was detained by D.M. of Pratapgarh.

What is the requirement of professional ethics? Should the accused have been left undefended? Whether lawyer's profession require defense all persons even a terrorist who come to the court for seeking justice? Our accusatorial system provides two guidelines in this regard. *First,* every body is presumed to be innocent unless the prosecution proves his guilt beyond reasonable doubt, and *secondly,* no man could be punished without a proper and reasonable hearing.

In this respect the answer of the counsel of Mr. Geelani, Sima Gulati's is more convincing when she said, "it is not that we want to protect terrorist. If found guilty the accused should be given the severest of punishment. But one cannot bypass the rule of law and facts when fighting against terrorism".

(2) Duty to Protect Client's Interest

Under the contractual relation of an advocate with his client, another duty imposed by the rules of ethics is, to conduct a case with all sense of responsibility for the protection of his client's interest. It includes not only the pursuance of client's case in court of Law, but also a proper case and skill to be exercised by the advocate.

In accordance with the agreement the client has right to get service of his Advocate at relevant time in the court. As in *Sriniwas Prasad Singh* v. *Keshva Prasad Singh*,[71] Lord Thankerton said: "every litigant has right to have his case heard and disposed of. It makes obligatory on an Advocate to be present in the court at the time of hearing of the case and party should not be made to suffer for the negligence or default of his advocate".

The aforesaid observation of the Privy Council found strong support in the case of *S.J. Chaudhary* v. *State*,[72] wherein the Apex court of India held that, "It is the duty of every Advocate who accepts the brief in a criminal case to attend the trial from day to day. It would be negligence and breach of his professional duty, if he fails to attend the case of his client".

Thus, every advocate should be present at the time when a case is called on for hearing. However, in England, a barrister cannot be sued for negligence or loss sustained through his ignorance, but it does not mean that, he has right to negligence.

The law on the subject of advocate's liability for negligence in the discharge of his duties was clearly laid down by Chief Justice Tindal in the case of *Godefroy* v. *Dalton*.[73] In the instant case the learned Chief Justice observed that—

> "It would be extremely difficult to define the exact limit by which the skill and diligence which an attorney undertakes to furnish in the conduct of a cause are bounded. The cases however, which have been cited and commented upon at the Bar, appear to establish, in

71. 63, *I.A.* 12 (P.C.).
72. A.I.R. 1984 S.C. 618.
73. 6, Bing. 460.

general that he is liable for the consequences of ignorance, or non-observance of the rules of practice of the court in which he practices, for want of care in the preparation of the cause for trial; or for his attendance in court with his witness and for the mismanagement of so much of the conduct of a cause as, is usually and ordinarily allotted his deportment of the profession".

Likewise in India, the advocate is liable for the loss sustained by the client due to his negligence, that is to say, want of ordinary care and skill. This duty has been also applied by the Supreme Court in the case of strike by the advocates in *Roman Services Private Limited* v. *Subhash Kapoor*.[74] In the instant case, the trial court had passed *ex-party* decree in consequence of non-appearance of the counsel on a day fixed for hearing. In special circumstances of the case, the Supreme Court set aside the *ex-party* decree subject to payment of Rs. 5000 as to the costs to the respondent. The court passed order for future that Advocates would be answerable for the consequence, at least for the monetary loss, suffered by their clients due to non-appearance of advocates on the ground solely of a strike call. Speaking for the Supreme Court Mr. Justice K.T. Thomas observed that—"So when advocate opts to strike work or boycott the court he must as well be prepared to bear at least the pecuniary loss suffered by the litigant who entrusted his brief to the Advocate with all confidence that his cause would be safe in the hands of that advocate".[75]

The other issue on non-availability of an Advocate may arise when he is busy in other court for the pursuance of any other matter. This situation is slightly different from the case of strike as the Advocate appears to be absent under pressure of work. In *Bansilal* v. *Mukund Das*,[76] the Hyderabad High Court held that, when an advocate is busy in other court, he should submit a memo intimating about the Advocate's being busy in another Bench and pray for the case being put by; it will not

74. (2001)1 S.C.C. 18.
75. *Id.*, p. 24.
76. A.I.R. 1952 Hyder 121.

do for an advocate to get the case dismissed for the default with impunity and then file an application for restoration stating that his absence was accidental.

Again a case of absence of an advocate may arise due to unwillingness of the advocate to appear in a particular case for certain reasons. Dealing with such a situation in *Mahabir Prasad Singh* v. *Jacks Aviation Association Private Limited,*[77] Mr. Justice K.T. Thomas of the Supreme Court observed that, if any counsel does not want to appear in a particular court, that too for justifiable reasons, professional decorum and etiquette requires him to give up his engagement in that court, so that the party can engage another counsel. But the permanent feature obtaining from appearing in court is unprofessional and also unbecoming of the status of an advocate.

It is advisable in this connection that, having regard to the personal relation, it should be his duty that, advocate must not accept other employment, if any interest of a former client is affecting. The advocate must remember that though it may be one of the many engagements for him it may be important matter for his client; therefore, he will realize in their full import many of his duties, to his client. A counsel ought to bear in mind that he should not appear for two clients, whose interest may conflict.[78] Being an officer of the court he should represent only one or other than of litigant.

When an advocate has once started the case, he cannot retire from it without the consent of the client or the permission of the court. However, a client has always right to withdraw his brief from the lawyer at any time. In *State of U.P.* v. *U.P. State Lawyers' Association,*[79] Mr. Justice P.B. Sawant observed that the client engages a lawyer for his personal reasons and is at liberty to leave him also, for the same reason. He is under no obligation to give reasons for withdrawing his brief from his lawyer.

Again, in *R.D. Saxena* v. *Balram Prasad Sharma*[80] the Apex court of India was of view that Article 22(1) of the Indian

77. (1999)1 S.C.C. 37.
78. See, *Mahboob Ali Khan, In the Matter of,* A.I.R. 1960 A.P. 116.
79. (1994)2 S.C.C. 204.
80. (2000)7 S.C.C. 264.

Constitution, entitles an accused to consult and be defended by a legal practitioner of his choice and therefore, a litigant must have the freedom to change his advocate when he feels that the advocate engaged by him is not capable of espousing his cause efficiently or that his conduct is prejudicial to the interest involved in the *lis*, or for any reason.

The above discussion depicts that advocate is an ultimate protector of his client's interest. It is true that relation between advocate and his client is a direct result of agreement, but it is also true that, a lawyer when entrusted with a brief is expected to follow the norms of professional ethics and try to protect the interest of his clients in relation to whom he occupies a position of trust.

(i) Advocate's Duty to Inspire Trust and Confidence

The relation between an advocate and his client is highly fiduciary in its nature and of a very delicate exacting, and confidential character requiring a high degree of fidelity and good faith. It is purely a personal relationship involving the highest personal trust and confidence which cannot be delegated without consent. This fiduciary relation creates a variety of duties of the advocate. Some of such duties are narrated below:

(1) Duty to Fairness

By the fact of agreement between on advocate and his client, not only the relationship of principal and agent is created, they are also governed by the relationship of trustee and beneficiary. The first and foremost demand of this fiduciary relation is that, an advocate must be fair with his client. It is not enough for him not to abuse that trust ultimately, but he is required by all the traditions of the profession not to exploit it even temporarily for his personal advantage.

By so doing he proves himself to be unfit, to be dependent on clients without reserve and to be incapable for acting in conformity with the standard which the profession as well as ethics expects to him.

The ethics demands that, if a counsel is holding any money on behalf of his clients, he is expected to return the same. It was pointed out by the Andhra Pradesh High Court, in the matter of *P.J. Butchleao, Advocate Gunffur,*[81] that, an advocate is not entitled to appropriate, use or pay himself monies which he holds on behalf of his client, towards his fees, unless the client has expressly instructed the advocate to so. To appropriate any money belonging to a client is not permissible as the relationship of an advocate and his client is fiduciary and it cannot be converted into a relationship of debtor and creditor by violating that fiduciary relation.

The rationales of the cases decided on this issue by the various High Courts and Supreme Court viz. *Amritlal C. Shah* v. *Ram Kumar, Advocate,*[82] *N.K. Sen Advocate, in re,*[83] and *V.C. Rangdorai* v. *D. Gopalan,*[84] reveal that the relationship of advocate and clients being fiduciary the advocate is strictly accountable for client's money and failure to return the same amounts to misconduct not only in connection with his fiduciary relationship but in the relation to his profession too.

The Disciplinary Committee of the Bar Council of India has the same opinion on this issue. In a case before the Disciplinary Committee of the Bar Council of India,[85] the advocate had deprived workers of their legitimate dues by retaining client's money for 14 years without proper authority. Respondent advocate recovered money from authority on behalf of his clients and had settled the matter. Only a portion of the amount was paid to clients and remaining amount was retained by him. It was later on after 14 years that he deposited the money with the Disciplinary Committee at the time of the hearing of the petition of the complainants.

His conduct was reprehensible and for that he was reprimanded.[86] It is also expected that an advocate should avoid business with his client not only in regard to matters in

81. A.I.R. 1962 A.P. 1.
82. A.I.R. 1962 Punj. 325.
83. A.I.R. 1952 Cal. 551.
84. A.I.R. 1979 S.C. 281.
85. *A.B.C.* v. *D.C.C.*, case no. 33/1965 M.P., Vol. 5 (1-3) J.B.C.I. 1976, p. 230.
86. For the same view, see, *Ram Sewak Patel* v. *Vir Singh*, D.C. Appeal No. 32/1992, dated : 11.12.1997.

suit, but also in relation to any other matters. It should always be remembered by the advocate that all transactions between them will be watched by the court with jealousy and suspicions.

Even though the transaction is not illegal, the court will scrutinize it most closely and require strict proof that no undue advantage has been taken by the advocate of the confidence reposed in him by the client.[87] An advocate is also prohibited from purchasing in court sale the property of his clients in respect of which he acted in a professional capacity.[88]

It is advisable, therefore, that the advocate as a rule should not enter into business transactions with his client. Law contemplates that the client is very much under the influence of his advocate and accordingly does not permit contractual freedom between them.[89] Normally that transaction will be set aside unless beneficial to the client. Where the transaction is to the advantage of the counsel, the court will presume bad faith and it will be for the counsel to establish that the transaction was just and fair.[90]

In a very famous case *P.D. Gupta* v. *Ram Murti*[91] the grievance of the complainant was, how could an advocate purchase property from his client which was subject matter of dispute between the parties in a court of Law. The Bar Council of India examined the facts thoroughly and suspected the bonafide of P.D. Gupta who seemed to be a family advocate. Disapproving the conduct of the advocate the Bar Council of India suspended him from practice for a period of one year. The Supreme Court approved of the stand taken by the Bar Council of India.

There may be other cases where the client proposes that the counsel should confer with the opposing counsel or others in order to secure a settlement or compromise. Regarding the

---

87. Section 136 of the Transfer of Property Act, 1882, provides that a legal practitioner cannot buy or agree to receive any share of an actionable claim.
88. 22, C.W.N. 491.
89. See, Section 16 of Indian Contract Act, 1872.
90. *B. Bhargava* v. *Ramchandra Kasriwal* (1998) 1 S.C.C. 169.
91. (1997) 1 S.C.C. 147.

powers of advocate to make or accept a compromise on behalf of a client, Lord Atkin, delivering the judgment of Privy Council in *Surendar Nath Mitra* v. *Tarubala Dasi*,[92] explained the foundation and scope of such authority Lord Atkin observed:

> "Their Lordships regard the power to compromise a suit as inherent in the position of an advocate in India. It is a power deemed to exist because its existence is necessary to effectuate the relations between advocate and client, to make possible the duties imposed upon the advocate by his acceptance of the cause of his client. The advocate is to conduct the cause of his client to the utmost of his skill and understanding and it must be in the interest of his client".

The aforesaid decision of the Privy Council has been followed by the Supreme Court of India in *Jamila Bai* v. *Shankarlal*.[93] The instant case dealt with scope and ambit of a lawyer acting and their competence to enter into compromise without the consent of client under order III, Rules 1 and 4 of the Civil Procedure Code, 1908, Supreme Court expressed the view that: "All legal practitioners have the actual though implied, authority of a pleader to act by way of compromising a case in which he is engaged even without specific consent from his client, but undoubtedly subject to two overriding considerations, *first*, he must act in good faith and for the benefit of his client, otherwise the power fails; and *second*, it is prudent and proper to consult his client and take his consent if there is time and opportunity".[94]

In any case, if there is any instruction to the contrary or withdrawal of authority, the implicit power to compromise in the pleader will fall to the ground, because he cannot take undue advantage of his position.

92. *S.C.I. L.R.* 57 Cal. 1311.
93. A.I.R. 1975 S.C. 2202.
94. *Id.*, p. 2206.

In *Ramasrey* v. *Deputy Director Consolidation, District Faizabad,*[95] an advocate entered into compromise without being authorized by the appellant to enter into compromise. It was found on enquiry by District judge that the appellants did not authorize the advocate, nor did they sign the compromise, nor they execute Vakalatnama in favour of the advocate so as to authorize him to verify the contents of the compromise.

The Supreme Court held that Advocate not authorized by party to enter into compromise was guilty of misconduct.

(2) Duty to Return Documents

The fiduciary relation between an advocate and his client also imposes a duty upon the advocate to return all the documents to the client, the moment the case was terminated. No paper should be retained without the consent of the client.

Any unauthorized use of that papers, will amount to not only the misconduct, but will also create the criminal liability. The paper in the brief being property of the clients, the counsel has no right to send them to any one else, without the proper authority.

In *R.D. Saxena* v. *Balram Prasad Sharma,*[96] Mr. Justice K.T. Thomas of the Supreme Court elaborately dealt with the duty of the advocate to return the document on demand by the client. The learned judge pointed out that for whatever reason, if a client does not want to continue the engagement of a particular advocate, it would be a professional requirement consistent with the dignity of the profession that he should return the brief to the client. Such obligation was declared not only a legal duty but also a moral imperative.

The Supreme Court also discussed the issue of returning the paper by the advocate on two rational bases, *first,* alternate remedy available to the advocate to recover his fee and *second,* right-duty correlativity. As to the former, Mr. Justice Thomas pointed out 'even if there is no lien on the litigation papers of his client an advocate is not without remedies to realize the fee, which he is legitimately entitled to and, as to the latter, he said but if he has duty to return the files to his client on being

95. (1998)6 S.C.C. 480.
96. (2000)1 S.C.C. 264.

discharged, the litigant too has a right to have the files returned to him. More so, when the remaining part of the *lis* has to be ought in the court this right of the litigant is to be read as the corresponding counter-part of the professional duty of the advocate.

(3) Duty to Maintain Secrecy

Both the fiduciary relation existing between lawyer and client and norms of proper functioning of the legal system require the preservation by the advocate of confidence and secrets of those who employed or sought to employ the advocate.

It is the necessity of the advocacy that, a lawyer should be fully informed of all the facts of the matter being handled in order for the client to obtain the full advantage of legal system: but it will be possible only when, if the client must feel free to discuss everything.

The observance of the ethical obligation of a lawyer to hold inviolate confidence and secrets of the client not only facilitates the full development of facts essential to proper representation of the client but also encourages non-lawyer to seek early legal assistance.[97]

An advocate cannot divulge his client's secrets even in the interests of justice. The privilege is on account of the client and can only be abandoned by him. For this reason, it is a general rule of advocacy that when a counsel has already been consulted by one party to the litigation and has given him his opinion, it is improper for him later on to appear for the opposite party; *firstly*, because such a position will force him to the unedifying spectacle of attacking his own opinion which would embarrass him in the discharge of his duty, and *secondly*, because it is possible that the client in taking his opinion may have disclosed confidential information which the advocate is duty bound not to use to his detriment. But if the client himself refuses to retain him, then the advocate is at liberty to appear for the opposite side but the confidential information obtained must not be used, and if that is found

97. See, Canon 4.1 of New York Bar Association.

impossible, then he should forgo the chance of appearing on the opposite side.[98]

Thus, in *Chandrasekhar Soni* v. *Bar Council of Rajasthan*[99] the Supreme Court held that "It is not proper for an advocate to change sides, as it is unprofessional to represent conflicting interests except by express consent given by all the concerned after full discloser of fact.

(ii) Advocate's Duty to Court

As a legal practitioner, an advocate is not only representative, adviser, trustee, agent or mere mouthpiece of his client, but he is recognized also as the custodian of law, leader of society, vehicle of the administration of justice and officer of the court. Therefore, his duty ends not with his client's interest but it runs with the profession itself and the court of law.

The duty of the advocates which, they owe in relation to the court is announced in the series of judicial pronouncements as well as in very authoritative forms in the Rules of Bar Council of India.

These duties run as under[100]—

1. An advocate shall, during the presentation of his case and while otherwise acting before a court, conduct himself with dignity and self-respect. He shall not be servile and whenever there is proper ground for serious complaint against a judicial officer, it shall be his right and duty to submit his grievance to proper authorities.
2. An advocate shall maintain towards the courts a respectful attitude, bearing in mind that the dignity of the judicial office is essential for the survival of a free community.
3. An advocate shall not influence the decision of a court by any illegal or improper means. Private

98. *Supra* note 28, p. 136.
99. A.I.R. 1983 S.C. 1012.
100. See, Section-I of the Bar Council of India Rules, 1975.

communications with a judge relating to a pending case are forbidden.

4. An advocate shall use his best efforts to restrain and prevent his client from resorting to sharp or unfair practices or from doing anything in relation to the court, opposing counsel or parties which the Advocate himself ought not to do. An advocate shall refuse to represent the client who persists in such improper conduct. He shall not consider himself a mere mouth-piece of the client, and shall exercise his own judgment in the use of restrained language in correspondence, avoiding scurrilous attacks in pleadings, and using intemperate language during arguments in court.
5. An advocate shall appear in court at all times only in the prescribed dress, and his appearance shall always be presentable.
6. An advocate shall not enter appearance, act, plead or practice in any way before a court, tribunal or authority mentioned in Section 30 of the Act, if the sole or any member thereof is related the advocate as father, grandfather, son, grandson, uncle, brother, nephew, first cousin, husband, wife, mother, daughter, sister, aunt, niece, father-in-law, mother-in-law, son-in-law, brother-in-law, daughter-in-law or sister-in-law.

   For the purposes of this rule, court shall ban a court, Bench or Tribunal in which above mentioned relation of the advocate is a judge member or the Presiding Officer.
7. An advocate shall not wear bands or gown in public places other than in courts except on such ceremonial occasions and at such places as the Bar Council of India or the court may prescribe.
8. An advocate shall not appear in or before any court or Tribunal or any other authority for or against an organization or an institution, society or corporation, if he is a member of the Executive Committee of such organization or institution or society or corporation. "Executive Committee", by whatever

name it may be called, shall include any Committee or body of persons which, for the time being, is vested with the general management of the affairs of the organization or institution, society or corporation: Provided that this rule shall not apply to such a member appearing as "*amicus curiae*" or without a fee on behalf of a Bar Council, Incorporated Law Society or a Bar Association.

9. An advocate should not act or plead in any matter in which he is himself pecuniarily interested.
   I. He should not act in a bankruptcy petition when he himself is also a creditor of the bankrupt.
   II. He should not accept a brief from a company of which he is a Director.
10. An advocate shall not stand as a surety, or certify the soundness of a surety for his client required for the purpose of any legal proceedings.

The above referred rules of the Bar Council of India emerge following duties of advocate which he owes in relation to the court.

(a) Duty to be Respectful

The first duty that an advocate owes to the court is to be respectful to it. He owes this duty not for the sake of the temporary incumbent of Judicial Office, but for the maintenance of its Supreme importance.[101] The verdict, therefore, that he is an officer of Justice does not mean that he is subordinate of the judge, it only means that he is an integral part of the machinery for the administration of justice. Thus, the conduct of an Advocate should, at all times, be characterised by candour and respect. A good advocate is in the ultimate analysis a good man. As the Supreme Court, *in Re Vinay Chandra Mishra*,[102] asserted that a lawyer has to be a gentleman first. To quote Ram Jethmalani in this regard "No lawyer can be a great one of his class unless he is at once a

101. *Supra* note 13, p. 96.
102. (1995) 2 S.C.C. 584.

gentleman.[103] The reason is obvious a gentleman does not go about insulting others or treading another people's corns".[104]

It is the duty of an advocate to maintain towards the judges and the court, a very courteous and respectful attitude and insist on similar conduct on the part of his client but at the same time maintaining a self-respecting independence in discharge of his professional duties.[105]

Although the advocate has right to convince the judge by his argument but he has no right to achieve his purpose by appeal to his sentiment. To say to the judge that unless he gives such and such order, it will cause hardship and injustice, amounts to disrespect of court. It is the prime duty of advocate, to balance his temper in a court. Even when the judge, forgetful of the fact that the advocate is an officer of the court and a counselor to it, treats the counsel with the same coin, a firm and temperate remonstrance is all that is needed to be made.

The Supreme Court in the matter *'D', An Advocate of Supreme Court*[106] pointed out that the conduct of an advocate in the criminal trial against him in the court of Magistrate was entirely indefensible and disclosed a contemptuous and persistent attempt on the part of the advocate to be rude and contemptuous of the Magistrate and attempt to do everything in his power to hold up the trial and bring the administration of justice into contempt.

The Counsel should bear in mind how wearisome is a judge's office and how much there is to try his temper and patience. In a case before the Bar Council of India, *A.K. Appellant* v. *R.S., Respondent,*[107] the advocate got provoked by certain remarks made by a district Munsif in his judgment. He issued notice under section 80, C.P.C. to the Munsif demanding

103. Jethmalani, Ram, "Courage And The Lawyers", Vol. (2) 1973, *J.B.C.I.* 133.

104. *Marsland V. Taggart* (1928) 2 K.B. 447 as per Shearman, J.

105. Quoted from an address delivered by an American Judge; cited in 'Legal World', Vol. I, page 124 reproduced in *Cr.L.R.*, Vol. XI, pp. 7-16.

106. A.I.R. 1956 S.C. 102.

107. D.C. Appeal No. 41/1986, Vol. XV, 1988, I.B.R. at 200.

the damages to the tune of Rs. 25,000. The matter was referred to Bar Council of Andhra Pradesh which found him guilty of professional misconduct. On appeal the Bar Council of India having regard to Rule No. 1 stated that Rule 1, clearly states the limit by which the advocate can conduct himself as a member of the noble profession. The advocate had exceeded his limits by giving notice under Section 80, C.P.C. for suing the Munsif for damages. Therefore, lawyer should not think that because he believes in a point, the judge must be of the same opinion. If, the point that the advocate seeks to make is really a good one, the repeated submission of it—with humility and modesty without taking up a challenging attitude will serve the purpose. For instance, in a case an advocate cited dozen of authorities in support of some elementary proposition. The judge interrupted 'you need not cite any more authorities; you may safely assume that the court knows something'. The lawyer without loosing the time retorted politely "If your honour will permit me to proceed, I should like to do so in my own way. I may say that the assumption, that the court knew something was the mistake, I made in the court below".[108]

The above approach is the real art of advocacy. It is likely to bring round the judge in his favour. On the other hand, an exhibition to surprise or of temper may strain them the judge in his conclusion to find against the lawyer. It has rightly been said that:

> "A good temper is an inestimable advantage to a lawyer, and whatever his position it will carry him, with ease, comfort and rapidity, over all obstructions to the end of his journey. A bad one will strew his way thought with thorns, will convert everyone with whom he has to deal into an enemy, and himself in short, into his greatest.[109]

It is an axiom that the lawyer should not interrupt the judge when he speaks. The lawyer may probably guess, possibly rightly, what the judge is going to say before he

108. *Ibid.*
109. Quoted from, 'Art of Advocacy'.

concludes and he may be ready with his answer. But, it is also possible that he may be wrong. Anyway it is proof of that calmness that he should posses, to wait for the judge to complete his statement. Interruption is permissible only to correct an erroneous statement of fact or to mention a preliminary objection. Thus, a reply, after the judge spoken, will be both dignified and weighty.

(b) Duty to Maintain Public Estimation

It is the duty of an advocate that, he must maintain public estimation and confidence in administration of justice. This duty demands that he will not indulge in insinuation against the judge. He will not question fairness and impartiality of the court. He will not impute racial and communal antipathy to the judge. He will not threat to the judge. He will not proclaim that, he has no faith in court of Law.

To be short he will not do anything which will lower the court or administration of justice in public estimation. It includes not to criticize the Judicial conduct, while the case is pending. However, after the case is decided, a fair comment may be justified. As Sarkar in his *Modern Advocacy* warns that "it is a serious thing to offer an imputation against the impartiality of the trying court or to make offensive remark when a ruling is given against the advocate's contention".[110]

Therefore, not only the advocate himself should avoid unjust criticism, but he should protest from the unjust criticism and complaint by 'Suitors' and others; as the lips of judges are sealed by their position and they are unable to defend them.[111]

It was pointed out by the Supreme Court in *Lalit Mohandas* v. *Advocate-General of Orissa*.[112] that when a lawyer makes imputations of partiality and unfairness against the judge in open court and suggest that he follows no principle in his orders he is adding insult to injury and is guilty of misconduct. The advocate grossly oversteps the limits of propriety. Therefore, scandalizing the court in such a manner is

110. *Sarkar's Mordern Advocacy*, Vol. 2, p. 121.
111. *Supra* note 28, p. 110.
112. A.I.R. 1957 S.C. 250.

really polluting the foundation of justice and bringing the whole administration of justice into disrepute.

Again, in *Padmahasini alia Padmapriya* v. *C.R. Sriniwas,*[113] the Supreme Court, was of the view that allegation against judge that he had thwarted justice, flouted law, denigrated the face of judiciary and ridiculed the sanctity of the mandatory provision and established dictates of law, it is beyond the permissible limits of fair criticism.

The study of above decisions makes it clear that an advocate should accept the verdict of the court right or wrong, gracefully. He should not criticize unfavourable ruling.

The reasons why the holder of a judicial office should be treated with respect, and a decision should not be criticized are condensed in the following para, taken from a passage occurring in Canadian Law Times.[114]

The respect enjoined by law for courts and judicial officers is exacted for the sake of the office, and not for the individual, who administers it. Bad opinion of the incumbent, however, well founded cannot excuse the withholding of the respect due to the office, while administering its functions. The proprieties of the judicial station in a great measure disables the judge from defending himself against structures upon his official conduct".

Thus, it is improper for an advocate to adopt an insulting attitude, towards the presiding officer of the court or impute motives to him. In a case[115] before the Calcutta High Court, an advocate made an imputation against the firmness and impartiality of the court and his conduct was sought to be justified by the specious plea of independence of the Bar. His conduct was held reprehensible and therefore he was suspended for a month. Chief Justice Sanderson of Calcutta High Court said that—

> 'I yield to none in my desire to see the independence of the Bar maintained. The independence of the Bar has been in the past, and I hope will be, in future, maintained,

113. A.I.R. 2000 S.C. 68.
114. For detail, see 28, *Canadian Law Review,* p. 369.
115. *Supra* note 52.

> without making gratuitous and unfounded imputation upon the fairness and impartiality of the tribunal'.

The aforesaid observation of the learned Chief Justice of the Calcutta High Court shows a good judicial gesture and is appreciable. We agree that the Bar have right to enjoy their independence, but privileges of the Bar should not be extended to right to attack on the dignity and status of the court.

Again in *Shambhu Ram Yadav* v. *Hanuman Das Khatri,*[116] an advocate wrote a letter to his client demanding money to bribe the judge, his conduct was also declared reprehensible and lowering the image of court. Similarly, the Division Bench of the Supreme Court in *Chandrasheker Soni* v. *Bar Council of Rajasthan,*[117] depreciated the conduct of a lawyer taking money from client for the purpose of bribe. The Bench consisting of A.P. Sen, Venkataramiah and R.B. Mishra, JJ., observed "nothing should be done by any member of the legal fraternity which might tend to lessen in any degree the confidence of the public in fidelity, honesty and integrity of the profession".

The above referred judicial pronouncements clarify that an advocate cannot play with the dignity of the court in the name of protecting his client's interest or his independence. To quote Gururajachari.[118]

> "In court you should not speak disparagingly of any judge. Judges for the best reason, esteem and respect are brethren on the Bench and it is a fatal mistake for advocate in an appellate court to impute to the court below a quo, prejudice, bias, unfairness or ignorance of elementary law".

(c) Duty Not to Mislead the Court

It is another duty as well as the ethics of the legal profession that, an advocate must not mislead the court. It

116. A.I.R. 2001 S.C. 2509.
117. A.I.R. 1983 S.C. 1012.
118. Gururajachari, K., *The Advocacy and Professional Ethics,* Ist ed., p. 119.

would not be professionally right to include in pleading facts which the practitioner knows personally to be false. Thus, in *Thangavela Mudaliar* v. *Chengalvaraya Gurukkal,*[119] Chief Justice, Beasley of the Madras High Court rightly pointed out that "with regard to the advocates, it is most improper for them to allege fraud on their behalf in written statement. Without satisfying him that there may some evidence which would reasonably justify such charge".

The learned judge also warned that "It will be professional misconduct to prepare and present to the court an affidavit or document sworn by a client containing statements which the practitioners knew, or must have suspected, to be false. The practitioners will not be excused merely because he has notified the falsity to the client, who insisted on swearing it. His duty is to withdraw from the case when the client takes up that attitude.[120]

Similar view was taken by the House of Lords, in *Myres* v. *Elman,*[121] which is an important decision on the legal profession as reinforcing the jurisdiction of the court over practitioners as an officer of the court and contains authoritative pronouncement in regard to the making of false affidavits or documents by practitioners. This case before the House of Lords itself related to a solicitor but the principles that were enunciated are applicable to advocates in India, who, both act and plead.

In the instant case, the jurisdiction of the court in the matter is not the same as the jurisdiction which entitled the court to strike off the name of a practitioner from the rolls or to suspend him; but it is founded on the right of the court to enforce the duty which an officer owes to it. Misconduct, default or negligence in the course of proceedings will justify an order by the court, even though no personal obloquy is involved. The jurisdiction is invoked not to punish the practitioner but more to give redress to the party injured by the conduct of the practitioner.

119. 69, M.L.J. 250.
120. *Ibid.*
121. 1940 A.C. 282.

It is not only punitive but also compensatory, though not as affording relief for breach of any duty that practitioner owed to the litigant. The jurisdiction will be exercised in proper case by ordering the practitioner to pay the cost of the opposite-party in the action.

As the obligation arises from the fact of the advocate being an officer of the court, he will be liable for acts done by his registered clerk under delegation, though the advocate himself was personally unaware of the proceedings, on the principle that "the principal is liable for all acts done by the agent within the scope of his authority". It was held by the House of Lord that "he cannot take shelter behind his clerk". Likewise in *D.P. Chadha* v. *Triyugi Narayan Mishra,*[122] the counsel conniving with opposite party brought about a compromise without authority of the client. Sri D.P. Chadha who was advocate, was in possession of a blank Vakalatnama and a blank paper both signed by the complainant. These documents were used for fabricating a compromise petition whereby the complainer had been made to suffer a decree of eviction.

Narrating the court and counsel as two wheels of the chariot of Justice, Mr. Justice R.C. Lahoti (as he then was) observed:

> 'Zeal and enthusiasm are the traits of success in profession but over zealousness and misguided enthusiasm have no place in the personality of profession. Yet a consel, in his zeal to earn success for a client, need not step over the well defined limits of propriety, repute and justness'.[123]

The learned judge further said that—

> "The court reposes great confidence in the counsel appearing from both sides. An obligation of telling the correct law flows from this confidence. A counsel shall always bear in mind that, independence and fearlessness

122. (2001) 2 S.C.C. 221.
123. *Id.*, p. 237.

are not licenses of liberty to do anything in the court and to earn success to a client whatever be the cast and whatever be the sacrifice of professional norms. Thus, being an officer of court he shall apprises the judge with the correct position of law whether for or against either party".[124]

It goes without saying that credibility and integrity is the highest virtue of the legal profession. Judges appreciate them and put the reliance on what the Advocate say. As Chief Justice Chagla wrote in his autobiography, 'Roses in December'; about the intellectual integrity of Sri H.M. Seervai that—

> "He is most hardworking and conscientious and never argues a point in which he does not believe, and which he thinks is untenable or inarguable. Judges can always depend on him not to mislead them or to lead them astray.[125]

It is advisable therefore; an advocate can gain his credibility to the profession only by his trust and confidence. While discharging duty to his client, he has right to do everything fearlessly and boldly that would advance the cause of client, but he should never forget that after all he is bound to present only the correct law and facts and always avoid those act or statement which may mislead the court.

But lawyer's duties towards five 'C's; viz. country, community, client, court and colleagues may aptly be called 'Lawyer Panch Sheela', reveals that his duties not ends here. A lawyer must not only know his client and the presiding officer of court, but also others.[126]

With the sweeping change in the concept of role of government and manifestation of the state, there has been an intense need for the demand on the diversification of the lawyer's attainments to be able to meet the demanding tasks

---

124. *Id.*, p. 238.
125. Chagala, M.C., *Roses in December*, 1974, p. 164.
126. Concept of 'Panch Seela'.

of protecting the citizen from abuse and improper use of power. In evolution of judicial techniques of legal control of government and disciplining public power and in responding to all pervasive constitutionalism, lawyer must update his intellectual skill and moral responses.

As N.R. Madhava Menon wrote in his article *Reforming the Legal Profession: Some Ideas*[127] with unprecedented changes introduced by technology and globalization, legal profession are forced to re-think their methods of management and delivery of service voicing concern over delay in dispensing justice, President Pratibha Patil also said that 'we cannot allow a situation where the common man is tempted to take the law into his own hands and subscribe to the deviant culture of the lynch mob'.[128]

How these expectations to the law, become true? Only an advocate can take the lead. For this purpose the ethics of the profession imposes some duties which an advocate should follow in relation to the others.

(iii) Advocate's Duty to the Others

The advocate owes duty in relation to his colleagues and others also, which need not be discussed in detail, as some duties have been discussed in Chapter III, therefore these duties of advocate are given in brief as under:

(a) Duty Towards Country

1. It is the first duty of advocate to suggest changes in the law to accord with the changes in social, political and economical need of the life.
2. It is his duty to take an interest in public affairs, to discuss important issue and to exert his influence for better, speedier administration of justice.
3. The meaning of Article 38 of Indian Constitution is that the goal of India is the welfare state, Lawyers, as a class, can and should, therefore take a leading part

127. *The Hindu*, dated 20.02.2008, p. 10.
128. *The Hindu*, dated 24.02.2008, p. 12.

in the work of national planning for they are endowed with intelligence and capacity for work.

4. He should set-up Civil Liberties Committee to deal with questions relating to the society.
5. He should also study the social and economic needs of the people, and should not only keep watch on the social legislations and take interest in them, but also take initiative in formulating schemes of national reconstruction.[129]

The Bar Council of India Rules narrate certain duties of advocates in relation to their opponent and colleague such duties are reproduced below:

(b) Duty to Opponent

1. An Advocate shall not in any way communicate or negotiate upon the subject matter of controversy with any party represented by an Advocate except through that Advocate.
2. An Advocate shall do his best to carry out all legitimate promises made to the opposite party even though not reduced to writing or enforceable under the rules of the court.

(c) Duty to Colleagues

1. An Advocate shall not solicit work or advertise, either directly or indirectly, whether by circulars, advertisement, touts, personal communications, interviews not warranted by personal relations, furnishing or inspiring newspaper comments or producing his photograph to be published in connection with cases in which he has been engaged or concerned. His sign-board or name plate should be of a reasonable size. The sign-board or name-plate or stationery should not indicate that he is or has

129. Quoted from, Ramchandran Raju, Legal Ethics, Lexis nexis, Butterworth Publication, 2006.

been President or Member of a Bar Council or of any Association or that he has been associated with any person or organization or with any particular cause or matter or that he specializes in any particular type of work or that he has been a judge or an Advocate General.

2. An Advocate shall not permit his professional services or his name to be used in and of, or to make possible, the unauthorized practice of law by any agency.
3. An Advocate shall not accept a fee less than the fee taxable under the rules when the client is able to pay the same.
4. An advocate shall not enter appearance in any case in which there is already a vakalatnama or memo of appearance filed by an advocate engaged for a party except with his consent; in case such consent is not produced he shall apply to the court stating reason why the said consent should not be produced and he shall appear only after obtaining the permission of the court.

(d) Duty Towards Community

(i) It should be the first duty of a member of the legal profession to compose family differences, and settle disputes, and controversies, by amicable settlement, and thereby prove how mistaken is the popular notion that lawyers foment dissensions for their own ends.

(ii) Lawyers can play an important role in organising Panchayats in villages on sound lines so that people may discharge their functions in an enlightened and responsible manner. They can instill into their minds respect for the rule of law, and inculcate the fact that its maintenance in administration is of paramount importance for maintaining the democratic structure of the State. Under the Second Five-Year Plan, which has been described as the horoscope of Mother India by our Prime Minister, great stress is laid on village

Panchayat or Nyaya Panchayat in pursuance of the policy laid down in the Directive in Article 40 of our Constitution.

(iii) In the still wider field of autonomous bodies, like District Boards, Municipalities, and Corporations, there are serious problems to be tackled, several reforms to be introduced and social amenities to be added to our civil life in order to raise the general standard of our living. Such local institutions are the true institutions of Self-Government where people most easily learn their first lessons in the art of governing themselves. It is on the foundation of local institutions that the superstructure of the Welfare State can be built. A Welfare State has to grow from below. In Universities also the question of education of our children, according to the changed conditions of our country, has to be tackled. Lawyers can very well focus the mind of the people to these problems and suggest suitable measures for their satisfactory solution.

(iv) There are many social ills from which people are still suffering. They have got to be eradicated. It is a colossal task. The entire mental make up of the people has to be changed. Social ideas must undergo revolutionary changes. In this task lawyers may take a decisive part. They can educate the masses on right lines, and help them to get out of the old rut of thinking and behaviour.

(v) It is the duty of lawyers to establish Legal Aid Societies for the purpose of rendering legal assistance to really poor and deserving persons, free of any charge. In England there is the Legal Aid and Advice Act, which enables people who cannot afford to pay a Barrister's full fee to draw on public funds. We know that the teeming millions of our country are poor. They cannot properly defend themselves against invasion of their rights and liberties due to heavy cost of litigations. Therefore, legal aid or assistance in conducting, or defending, proceedings in law courts should be given to all such persons as are poor, and cannot afford to plead their cases. People now consider Law courts as their own. People now know that judge is their own man, but administration of justice is costly, and people are poor. It is, therefore, an obligation resting upon lawyers to see "that the poor man will have as nearly as possible an equal opportunity in litigating as the rich man". It is really the problem of making justice easily accessible to all, and lawyers can make valuable contribution in solving this much vexed problem to a very great and appreciable extent.

(B) Propriety of Judges

The administration of justice is result of the proper cooperation between the Bar and the Bench. The bench is also required to maintain decorum, trust-worthiness and integrity so as to repose confidence in the system of administration of justice. The duties of judges towards the members of the Bar and others play an important role in the administration of justice. In a country, like India which is committed to democratic socialism and judicial independence, these duties of judges gain a great significance. As the sole machinery for safeguarding the constitutional guarantee and the rule of law, the learned judges have to play a pivotal role in imparting impartial justice and ensuring effective administration of justice.

The successfulness of the administration of justice depends upon the amicable relationship between the Bench and the Bar. It is the behaviour of the judges with the lawyers, which makes the atmosphere of the court quite cordial and congenial. It means the administration of justice is not something which concerns the Advocates only, but it is related with judges as well.

So, needless to say there is a symbiotic relation and this reciprocal relationship casts duties on judges also. In England, the traditions of the Bench, as to the Bar are well understood and no attempt has, therefore, been made to formulate these into writing. In India, where no such practices exist and the English traditions are not widely known, the necessity of formulating a code of judicial ethics is as essential as formulating a code of professional ethics for the Bar.[130]

(i) Propriety of Judges to Inspire Cordial Relation with Bar

As stated earlier that, the Bench and the Bar are the two wheels of chariot of justice and unless they work harmoniously justice cannot be properly administered. The effective and just administration can be possible only with the equal partnership and full cooperation between the Bench and the Bar.

For inspiring the cordial relation between these two pillars of justice, the following propriety is required from the honourable judges:

(a) Propriety to Give Patient Hearing to Advocates

The first propriety which is expected of a judge is to give a patient hearing to Advocates and to avoid improper interruption of the counsels in their argument and in the examination of witnesses. The judges should allow counsels to speak uninterruptedly bearing in mind that interruption may detract the counsels and may get them nervous.

This expectation from the judges towards Advocates is the foundation of administration of justice. This is so because truth will come out of the argument and advocates feel satisfied that they have been heard fully and that the judges followed them well.

It is important to note that in this regard, failure on the part of the judges to allow patient hearing may create unhealthy situation, as happened in *Jones* v. *National Coal Board,*[131] case before the Queens Bench of England. In the instant case the plaintiff and the defendant both were so much annoyed on too much questioning of Sir Hugh Imbert Parram Hallet, that they filed appeal and cross-appeal against his judgement on the ground of their grievance that interruption by the judge prevented the parties from having a fair trial. The controversy ultimately resulted into resignation of the judge.

130. *Supra* note 109.
131. (1975)2 Q.B. 55.

Lord Denning calls it a poignant case because he was able and intelligent but he asked too many questions.[132]

Regarding the propriety of judges to avoid interruption canon 4 of the judicial conduct of the American Bar Association says: "A judge may properly intervene in a trial of case to promote expedition and prevent unnecessary waste of time or to clear up some obscurity, but he should bear in mind that his undue interference, impatience or participation in the examination of witnesses or a serve attitude on his part towards witnesses, especially those who are excited or terrified by the unusual circumstances of a trial may tend to prevent the proper presentation of the cause or the ascertainment of the truth in respect thereto".[133]

While, the above canon of American Bar Association says that there should not be improper interruption on the part of judges but also indicated that, if the lawyers take too much time in their arguments, then there may be danger of overburdening upon the courts by arrears.

Thus, the question arises what is meant by such improper interruption? Mr. C.L. Anand has clarified the position as to propriety or otherwise of putting interrogation for the judges to put questions or express opinion to understand the exact position is not such interruption. For him to stop an improper argument or repletion, or appeal to feeling, or to attempt to misstate fact or the law or putting irrelevant questions to witness is not such interruption.[134] But no judge should interrupt as to make the argument a mere course of interrogation between the judge and the Advocate. Therefore, interruption may be good or bad according to the circumstances.

Lord Hailshman suggested a very good solution that—"The judges function is to listen intelligently and patiently to evidence and arguments using rival expert witnesses where specialized knowledge is required to identify the right points,

132. *The Due Process of Law*, p. 58.
133. See, Canon 4 of the Judicial Conduct, 1993 as adopted by American Bar Association.
134. Anand, C.L., *General Principles of Legal Ethics*, 1965 ed., Law Books Company, Allahabad, p. 39.

to evaluate the reliability and relevance of oral testimony and draw the right inference from primary fact and finally to reach a conclusion based on accurate knowledge of law and practice".[135]

Thus, the lawyer should be interrupted only after his narration of relevant facts and laying down proposition of law. There should be no interruption of the counsel except to prevent repetition or irrelevancy or to clear up some obscurity in Counsel's line of argument or representation of facts.

It should be always remembered by the judges that, undue interference merely tends to hinder the ascertainment of truth.

(b) Propriety to Remain Courteous

The other propriety expected from judges which is necessary for the cordial relation between Bench and the Bar. Is the consideration and courtesy to the member of the Bar? Mr. C.L. Anand suggested in his *General Principles of Legal Ethics*, that, when the Advocate is upset by discourteous treatment, it will prevent him from doing full justice to the client in arguing the case. No judge should desire that Bar should be servile.[136]

The attitude of judges towards the lawyers should be one of uniform respect. They should be moved by the brief not by the position of lawyers appearing before them. Whatever the status of the Advocate, whatever the judge's private opinion, they must not show it in their behaviour, because one of their foremost duties are to uphold the dignity of the Bar as an institution.

Judges should treat the lawyer as a gentleman and respectable person as they are. Innate sense of the fairness and justice makes the Bench very popular in the eye of the Bar. An incidence can be cited from the experience of Chief Justice of India, Mr. Justice B.P. Sinha. He had been arguing a case before Patna High Court as a counsel. He was arguing the case before Chief Justice Sir Dawson Miller. Mr. Justice Kulwant Sahay was so much impressed by his arguments in a difficult case

135. Lord Hailshan, Hamlyn, *The British Legal System Today,* 1983, p. 52.
136. Anand, C.L., *General Principles of Legal Ethics,* Vol. I, p. 219.

arising under the revisional jurisdiction of the High Court that he expressed his desire to see Mr. B.P. Sinha and went to his residence. The learned judge encouraged and said "Youngman, if you work like this with devotion to the perfection, you are bound to go very far.[137] It is submitted that, such attitude of judges will inspire not only the cordial relation with the member of the Bar, it will add great luster to the administration of Justice by encouraging promising and studious lawyers. The judges should also be polite towards the members of the Bar, and should do everything possible to advance its high traditions.

(c) Propriety to Ensure the Autonomy and Independence of the Bar

It is the cordial principle of the legal profession that Advocate should be allowed by the court to assert their points and perform their duties without fear and favour. Therefore, the next propriety which is expected from judges is to ensure the autonomy and independence of the Bar. However, independence should not be mistaken for insolence or impertinence or readiness to make reports to the judge.[138] It should be taken as the right of Advocates to do their duty to the client without fear and favour without being discourteous to the court.

Judges should be treating the lawyers as a friend of the court. Judges should remember that, they are the organ of the same machinery and both are equal and none of them is superior or inferior.

The above idea of equality will ensure the autonomy and independence of the Bar. The equal position and cooperation in administration of Justice of the both is re-enforced through certain practices of the court itself. In early times the England, sergeants-at-law were addressed by the judges as brothers.[139]

Likewise, the concept of *amicus curiae*[140] reinforces the cooperation of an Advocate to the court in administration of

137. Sinha, B.P., *Reminiscences And Reflections of a Chief Justice*, B.R. Publishing Corporation, 1985, p. 28.
138. *Supra* note 136, p. 223.
139. For detail see Chapter II.
140. Friend of the Court.

justice. This concept also indicates that when the honourable court feels that the advocacy on either side is not providing sufficient assistance in arriving at just conclusion it can seek the assistance of an Advocate as *amicus curiae.*

The above practice in India is followed mainly in those cases where one of the parties argues the case itself without taking the help of the legal practitioner. For example, in *Rajpal Verma* v. *Chancellor, Merrut University*[141] the appellant was appearing before the court himself in person. The court sought the help of Shri D.D. Thakur as a friend of court, which he complied gracefully in the case of *D.K. Basu* v. *State of West Bengal,*[142] the court realized the necessity of help from Bar and invited Dr. A.M. Singhvi to act as *amicus curiae*. The Supreme Court of India takes help of senior Advocates as *amicus curiae* when it feels essential.

As the sole machinery for safeguarding the Constitutional guarantee and rule of law the learned judges should never hate the lawyer's guts. The judge's eloquent silence and the lawyer's lucid arguments should result in a just judgement. It is necessary to maintain a high degree of mutually beneficial comfort level between the Bench and the Bar. A judge should never adopt a command made of functioning.[143] Judges should not take adversarial roles when hearing counsel. "The Bench should never attempt Bar annihilation. They should take care to set the mood of unity".[144] Judges should behave the way they are supposed to, without throwing barbs at the Bar and sans offensive manifestation of superiority.

There is need to arrest the harsh tone of judicial discourse from the Bench. There is absolute necessity to contain Bench-speak. It should be remembered that there are a bunch of obligations which are incumbent upon every judge and lawyer because of the profession's nobility. It should also remembered that no man, whether he be a lawyer or a judge, can be said to be ideally noble so as to keep equanimity and patience

141. (1997)6 see 365.
142. A.I.R. 1997 S.C. 610.
143. Nambiar Kelu T.P., "Bar Bench and Gap" (2002), *S.C.J.* 39.
144. *Ibid*, p. 40.

under every kind of provocation.[145] It may, however, be noted that the presence of professional etiquette coupled with recognition by judiciary of the importance of an independent Bar, will work together to minimize the possibility of confrontation between the Bench and the Bar.

(ii) Propriety of Judges to Inspire Confidence of the Society in Administration of Justice

The behaviour of a judge is the bastion for the people to reap the fruits of the democracy, liberty and justice and it's the antithesis rocks the rule of law. Judicial office is essentially an office of a public trust. Society is, therefore, entitled to expect that a judge must be a man of high integrity, honesty and high moral vigour, ethical firmness and impervious to corrupt or venial influences. He is required to keep most exacting standards of propriety in judicial conduct. Any conduct which tends to undermine public confidence in the integrity and impartiality of the court would be deleterious to the efficacy of judicial process. It is, therefore, a basic requirement that a judge's official and personal conduct be free from impropriety, the same must be in tune with the highest standards of propriety and probity. The standard of conduct is higher than that of expected from layman and so higher than that of expected of an Advocate.

In fact, even his private life must adhere to high standards of probity and propriety, higher than those deemed acceptable for others.

Therefore, the judge can ill-afford to seek shelter from the fallen standards in society. In India there cannot, however, be any fixed or set principles but an unwritten code of conduct of well established traditions is the guideline for judicial conduct.[146]

In India the canons of judicial ethics have been attempted, time and again, to be drafted as a code but nothing concrete has yet come out in writing. Mostly these canons have

145. See, *P. Das* v. *P.C. Aggrawal* (1975) 1 Cr.L.J. 659.

146. See, *R. Ravichandaran Iyer* v. *A.M. Bhattacharjee* (1995) 5 S.C. 467, Para, 23.

originated in and have been handed down by generation after generation of judges by tradition and conventions.

In this regard the following documents may be referred which is intended to impose several duties on the judges which they owe to society as well as the administration of justice itself.

(a) Restatement of Values of Judicial Life

On May 7, 1997 the Supreme Court of India in its Full court accepted a charter called the *"Restatement of Values of Judicial Life"* to serve as a guide to be observed by judges, essential for independent, strong and respected judiciary, indispensable in the impartial administration of justice. This Resolution was preceded by a draft statement circulated to all the High Courts of the country and suitably redrafted in the light of the suggestions received. It has been described as the 'restatement of the pre-existing and universally accepted norms, guidelines and conventions' observed by judges. It is a complete code of the canons of judicial ethics. It reads as under:

1. Justice must not merely be done but it must also be seen to be done. The behaviour and conduct of members of the higher judiciary must reaffirm the people's faith in the impartiality of the judiciary. Accordingly, and act of a judge of the Supreme Court or High Court, whether in official or personal capacity, which erodes the credibility of this perception, has to be avoided.
2. A judge should not contest the election to any office of a club, society or other association; further he shall not hold such elective office except in a society or association connected with the law.
3. Close association with individual members of the Bar, particularly those who practise in the same court, shall be eschewed.
4. A judge should not permit any member of his immediate family, such as spouse, son, daughter, son-in-law or daughter-in-law of any other close relative, if a member of the Bar, to appear before him

or even be associated in any manner with a cause to be dealt with by him.

5. No member of his family, who is a member of the Bar, shall be permitted to use the residence in which the judge actually resides or other facilities for professional work.
6. A judge should practice a degree of aloofness consistent with the dignity of his office.
7. A judge shall not hear and decide a matter in which a member of his family, a close relation or a friend is concerned.
8. A judge shall not enter into public debate or express his views in public on political matters or on matters that are pending or any likely to arise for judicial determination.
9. A judge is expected to let his judgments speak for themselves. He shall not give interviews to the media.
10. A judge shall not accept gifts or hospitality except from his family, close relations and friends.
11. A judge shall not hear and decide a matter in which a company in which he holds shares is concerned unless he has disclosed his interest and no objection to his hearing and deciding the matter is raised.
12. A judge shall not speculate in shares, stocks or the like.
13. A judge should not engage directly or indirectly in trade or business, either by himself or in association with any other person. (Publication of legal treatise or any activity in the nature of a hobby shall not be construed as trade or business).
14. A judge should not ask for, accept contributions of otherwise actively associate himself with the raising of any fund for any purpose.
15. A judge should not seek any financial benefit in the form of a perquisite or privilege attached to his office unless it is clearly available. Any doubt in this behalf must be got resolved and clarified through the Chief Justice.

16. Every judge must at all times be conscious that he is under the public gaze and there should be no act or omission by him which is unbecoming of the high office he occupies and the public esteem in which that office is held.

These are only the *"Restatement of Values of Judicial Life"* and are not meant to be exhaustive but illustrative of what is expected of a judge.

The above "restatement" was ratified and adopted by Indian Judiciary in the Chief Justices' Conference 1999. All the High Courts in the country has also adopted the same in their respective full court meetings.

(b) The Bangalore Draft Principles

The values of judicial ethics which the Bangalore Principles crystallizes are: (i) independence, (ii) impartiality, (iii) integrity, (iv) propriety, (v) equality, and (vi) competence and diligence.

The above values have been further developed in the Bangalore Principles as under:

1. Judicial *independence* is a pre-requisite to the rule of law and a fundamental guarantee of a fair trial. A judge shall therefore, uphold and exemplify judicial independence in both its individual and institutional aspects.
2. *Impartiality* is essential to the proper discharge of the judicial office. It applies not only to the decision itself but also to the process by which the decision is made.
3. *Integrity* is essential to the proper discharge of the judicial office.
4. *Propriety*, and the appearance of propriety, are essential to the performance of all of the activities of a judge.
5. Ensuring *equality* of treatment to all before the courts is essential to the due performance of the judicial office.

6. *Competence and diligence* are prerequisites to the due performance of judicial office.
7. *Implementation*—By reason of the nature of judicial office, effective measures shall be adopted by national judiciaries to provide mechanisms to implement these principles if such mechanisms are not already in existence in their jurisdictions.

The Preamble to the Bangalore Principles of Judicial Conduct states *inter alia* that the principles are intended to establish standards for ethical conduct of judges. They are designed to provide guidance to judges and to afford the judiciary a framework for regulating judicial conduct. They are also intended to assist members of the executive and the legislature, and lawyers and the public in general, to better understand and support the judiciary. These principles presuppose that judges are accountable for their conduct to appropriate institutions established to maintain judicial standards, which are themselves independent and impartial, and are intended to supplement and not to derogate from existing rules of law and conduct which bind the judge. There are a few interesting facts relating to the Bangalore Principles. The first meeting to prepare the Draft Principles was held in Vienna in April 2000 on the invitation of the United Nations Centre for International Crime Prevention, and in conjunction with several other institutions concerned with justice administration. In preparing the draft Code of Judicial Conduct, the core considerations which recur in such codes were kept in view. Several existing codes and international instruments more that three in number including the Restatement of Values of Judicial Life adopted by the Indian judiciary in 1999 were taken into consideration. At the second meeting held in Bangalore in February 2001, the draft was given a shape developed by judges drawn principally from Common Law countries. It was thought essential that it will be scrutinized by judges of all other legal traditions to enable it to assume the status of a duly authenticated international code of judicial conduct. The Bangalore Draft was widely disseminated amongst judges of both common law and civil law systems and discussed at several judicial conferences. The draft underwent a few revisions and was finally approved by a Round-Table meeting of Chief Justices (or their representatives) from several law systems, held in Peace Palace in The Hague, Netherlands, in November 2002. 'Accountability' as one of the principles which was included in the original draft was dropped in the final draft. It is apparently for two reasons. *First,* it was thought that the principles enshrined in the Bangalore Principles presuppose the 'accountability' on the part of the judges and are inherent in those principles. *Secondly,* the mechanism and methodology of 'accountability' may differ from country to country and therefore, left to be taken care of individually by the participating jurisdictions.

(c) The Oath or Affirmation by Judge

The Constitution of India obligates the Indian Judiciary to reach the goal of securing to all its citizens Justice, Liberty, Equality and Fraternity. How this goal is to be achieved is beautifully summed up in the form of oath or affirmation to be made by the judges of the Supreme Court and High Courts while entering upon the office.

Swearing in the name of God or making a solemn affirmation a judge ordains himself :

(i) that I will bear true faith and allegiance to the Constitution of India as by law established;
(ii) that I will uphold the sovereignty and integrity of India;
(iii) that I will truly and faithfully and to the best of my ability, knowledge and judgment perform the duties of office without fear or favour, affection or ill-will; and
(iv) that I will uphold the Constitution and the laws.

Mr. Justice R.C. Lahoti said that the oath of a judge is a complete code of conduct incorporates therein all the canons of judicial ethics.[147]

---

147. Quoted from, first M.C. Setalvad Memorial Lecture, held on 22nd Feb. 2005 at Gulmoha Hal India Habital Center, Lodhi Road, New Delhi.

It is clear from the above discussion that, the judges as the interpreter of law and also the innovator of case law have to perform the assigned duties with utmost care, decency, dignity and respectability in manner accountable to the society and public opinion. An ostensible duty also lies on the judges to provide speedy trial, just and equitable justice so as to satisfy the aspiration of the people well in time. The Bench should as far as possible give precise, specific and full-fledged decisions at all times and in all cases without leaving any room for its deviation by the respondent parties on any technical plea or administrative difficulty.

Adherence to the precedents of the courts, obsolescence with the laws and policies *vis-à-vis* the changing modes and needs of the society go a long way in reducing the increasing number of litigations well in time. The responsibility solely lies on the Bench and the success of the judiciary largely depends upon the speed with which the judicial proceedings are conducted.

The most important aspect of Bench-Bar relation relates to in cautious conduct either by a lawyer or a judge. However, it is worth-mentioning that foundation of our democratic system which is based on the independence and impartiality of those who are involved in justice delivery system. Therefore, an independent judiciary is of vital importance to any free society. Keeping in view that a free and fearless Bar is not to be preferred to an independent judiciary nor an independent judiciary to a free Bar. Neither should have primacy over the other. Both are indispensable to a free society. As Mr. B.R. Verma points out,[148] "the freedom of the Bar presupposes an independent. Judiciary through which that freedom may, if necessary, be vindicated, one of the potent means for assuming judges of their independence is responsible, well-behaved, cultured and learned Bar".

The proper conduct of Bar and Bench, ensures reciprocal adjustment, mutuality of faith and co-operation and thereby inspire the faith of the people at large in the healthy administration of justice.

148. Verma, B.R., *Law of Contempt of Court*, IInd ed., p. 271.

6

Professional and Other Misconducts of Advocates

Having regard to the unique place of advocates in justice distention system, society and law expects the highest standards of ethics, morality, propriety, integrity, hard work and good moral behaviour from them.[1] But if they fail to satisfy these expectations they become guilty of professional and other misconduct.

In the context of above background the natural question arises as to what is professional and others misconduct? When the court can declare the particular conduct of an advocate as misconduct? When such conduct comes within the preview of contempt of court? An attempt will be made in this chapter to discuss and examine the meaning of the word professional misconduct and illustrate the circumstances under which an advocate may be guilty of professional misconduct, other misconduct as well as contempt of court.

1. See, The Bar Council of India Rules, 1975.

I. PROFESSIONAL MISCONDUCT : MEANING AND SCOPE

In a general sense, the word "misconduct" usually implies an act done wilfully with a wrong intention. It is sufficiently a wide expression which includes any conduct that makes a man unfit for the exercise of his profession. If this general definition is applied to the legal profession, one can say that any conduct of advocates which brings disrepute to the administration of justice or likely to hamper or embarrass the justice delivery system or makes them unworthy of being in the profession, amounts to professional misconduct.

The *Corpus Juris Secundum,*[2] explains the professional misconduct pointing out that professional misconduct may consist in betraying the confidence of a client in attempting by means to practice a fraud or impose on or deceive the court or the adverse party or his counsel and, in fact, in any conduct which tends to bring reproach on the legal profession or to alienate the favourable opinion which the public should entertain concerning it". The *Law Lexicon* explains it in term of any wrongful action with wider connotations covering all actions unworthy of the profession. It reads "misconduct in a Solicitor justifying the disciplinary jurisdiction of the court is not confined to professional misconduct, but extends to conduct which shows him to be unworthy member of the legal profession.[3]

Professional misconduct is explained, evaluated and examined in view of the nobility of the profession. An advocate is a member of legal fraternity, as well as a member of society. He is expected to behave more responsibly than an ordinary man. The standard of conduct expected from an advocate is also different from an ordinary man. Thus, it is not necessary that professional misconduct should be of such gravity as to involve moral turpitude. The judicial appreciation of social and professional gravity attached with the conduct of advocates is well expressed in judicial decisions.

2. Corpus Juris Secundum (2000) 'Misconduct', p. 832.
3. Law Lexicon of British India (1940), p. 821.

The courts have refused to take restricted view of misconduct so as to limit it to the case of misconduct involving moral turpitude. Thus, in *Re Tulsidas Annamal Karim,*[4] the Bombay High Court took the view that a conduct may be taken as misconduct although it does not involve moral turpitude is that it aggravates the misconduct and leaves very little room for lenient view in awarding punishment and severe punishment is inflicted upon the delinquent legal professionals.

This attitude find place in the definition of the term given in *Black's Law Dictionary*. It defines it to mean "transgression of some established and definite rule of action, a forbidden act, a dereliction from duty, unlawful behaviour, wilful in character, improper or wrong behaviour, its synonyms are misdemeanors or misdeed, misbehaviour delinquency, impropriety, mismanagement and offence.[5]

Even the incompetence of a lawyer has come to be treated, in some countries, as misconduct. Thus, in a Canadian case *Baron* v. *F.,*[6] it was held to be 'good cause' to justify suspension of a member that the member was guilty of a series of acts of gross negligence which taken together would bring the legal profession to disrepute. The dictionary meaning of the term professional misconduct depicts that, it is wrongful and improper conduct of an advocate which adds disreputation to the justice dispention system. There may be two tests for the determination of misconduct. *Firstly,* the misconduct is such that it must be regarded as unworthy to remain a member of the honourable profession, and *secondly,* the misconduct is such that they must be regarded as unfit to be entrusted with the responsible duties that they are called upon to perform.

Rule 8.4 of Model Rules of American Bar Association[7] is worth quoting:

---

4. I. L.R. Bom. 548.
5. Henry Campbell Black (ed.) Black's Law Dictionary, St. Paul Mins West Publishing Co., U.S.A. (6th ed., 1999), p. 999.
6. (1954)4 D.L.R. 525.
7. See, Canon on 8.4 of American Bar Asscociation.

It is professional misconduct for a lawyer to:

(a) violate or attempt to violate the Rules of Professional Conduct, knowingly assist or induce another to do so, or do so through the acts of another;
(b) commit a criminal act that reflects adversely on the lawyer's honesty, trustworthiness or fitness as a lawyer in other respects;
(c) engage in conduct in involving dishonesty, fraud, deceit or misrepresentation;
(d) engage in conduct that is prejudicial to the administration of justice;
(e) state or imply an ability to influence improperly a government agency or official; or
(f) knowingly assist a judge or judicial officer in conduct that is a violation of applicable rules of judicial conduct or other law.[8]

However, in India there are no statutory example or Canons of Bar, which expressly illustrate the professional misconduct. At present the Bar Council of India Rules provided certain norms of ethics and the violation of which are usually considered as professional misconduct in India.[9] The Bar Council of India Rules has been prepared in response to the statutory requirement of section 35 of the Advocates Act, 1961. It says that a legal practitioner may be punished for professional misconduct as well as other misconduct. Therefore, an advocate invites disciplinary orders not only if he is guilty of professional misconduct but also if he is guilty of other misconduct, that is to say, misconduct which may not be directly concerned with his professional activity as such nevertheless is of such a dishonourable or infamous character as to invite the punishment due to professional misconduct itself. One example of such misconduct is conduct involving moral turpitude it makes clear that "conviction of an advocate

8. Legal Information Institute, Canell Law School, ed. 1995-96.
9. For details see, Chapter III.

for a criminal offence involving moral turpitude though it may not be connected with his professional work as such,[10] may invite punishment for misconduct under the category of other misconduct. It seems that misconduct may be unrelated to profession, but it should be such as to make the lawyer unworthy of remaining a member of the honourable profession.

In the *matter of P.*,[11] the Supreme Court of India again explained that 'misconduct may not be directly concerned with the professional activity'.

The expression professional misconduct got crystallized after a long span of time. The Legal Practitioners Act, 1879 provided for disciplinary actions against the advocates but did not define misconduct. It used the expression 'unprofessional conduct' and explained it. An advocate was held guilty of 'unprofessional conduct' if he—

(a) Took instruction in any case except from the party on whose behalf he was retained.
(b) Was guilty of fraudulent or grossly improper conduct in discharge of his professional duty.
(c) Tendered, gave or consented to the retention, out of any fee paid or payable to him for his services, or any gratification for procuring or having procured the employment in any legal business of himself or any other pleader or mukhtar, or
(d) Directly or indirectly, procured or attempted to procure the employment of himself as such pleader of mukhtar through, or by the intervention of any person to whom any remuneration for obtaining such employment had been given by him, or agreed or promised to be so given, or
(e) Accepted any employment in any legal business through a person who had been proclaimed as a tout under Section 36, or
(f) For any other reasonable cause.[12]

10. *In re* 'P', an Advocate, A.I.R. 1963 S.C. 1313.
11. A.I.R. S.C. 1313.
12. See, Section 13 of the Legal Practioners Act, 1879.

The expressions 'for any other reasonable cause' gave clue for expansive scope of misconduct. Though in an early case, *In Re Jogendra Narayan Bose,*[13] the Calcutta High Court took a restrictive view in view of the rule of interpretation popularly known as rule of *ejusdem generis*. But later on a bunch of cases decided by the High Courts[14] and the Privy Council[15] expanded the scope of misconduct by overruling the earlier view.

The expansive meaning of 'misconduct' got statutory recognition for the first time in the Indian Bar Council Act, 1926[16] and was duly recognized under Section 35 of the Advocates Act, 1961. But the said Act, itself does not define misconduct. It leaves to the Bar Council of India to provide for rules regulating the conduct of the advocates. The Bar Council of India gives illustration of different duties of an advocate[17] and violation of such duties may invite action against the advocate.

Anyway some attempts have been made to define professional misconduct by the English as well as Indian courts. According to judicial approach professional misconduct covers the case of infamous conduct, betrayal of confidence, disgraceful and dishonourable conducts.[18] The Supreme Court of India has agreed to the views of English Courts including the Privy Council and has treated misconduct sufficiently comprehensive to include misfeasance as well as malfeasance and applied to professional peoples it includes unprofessional acts even though they are not inherently wrong.[19]

Thus, inspite of the fact of statutory absence of the definition of 'Professional misconduct' judicial approach to adopt its meaning in ordinary and common parlance so as to mean improper conduct[20] or improper behaviour, intentional

13. 4, C.W.N. (Note CCXXX1).
14. *Le mesurier* v. *Wajid Husain*, 29 Cal. 890 (F.B.), see also *Matter of Tulsidas*, 1 L.R. 1941 Bom., 548.
15. *G.F. Grahame* v. *Attorney General*, A.I.R. 1936 P.C. 224.
16. Section 10 of the Indian Bar Councils Act, 1926.
17. For details see, Chapters IV and VIII.
18. *Allinson* v. *General Council of Medical Education and Registration* (1894), Q.B. 750.
19. *Ratanam* v. *Konikaram*, A.I.R. 1965 S.C. 713.
20. *U. Dashina Murty* v. *Commission of Inquiry*, A.I.R. 1980 Mad. 89.

wrong doing or deliberate violation of a rule or standard of behaviour,[21] is sufficient to decide the cases of misconduct committed by an advocate and punish him so as to ensure the smooth and unpolluted running of the stream of administration of justice.

It reveals from the above discussion that the misconduct by an advocate may be classified into three categories, namely:

(i) Professional misconduct,
(ii) Other misconducts, and
(iii) Contempt of court.

(A) Professional Misconduct Committed by Advocates

The duty of advocates towards the various components of administration of justice has been discuss earlier. The violations of such duties invite action against the advocates. Rendered their action as professional misconduct in relation to some components will be discussed here below:

(i) Misconduct in Relation to Clients

Rules 11 to 33 of the Bar Council of India Rules provide certain duties towards client. These duties and the personal contract between advocates and client give rise to various fiduciary obligations, which are enforceable at the suit by the client.[22] The sprit of Section 35 of the Advocates Act is that the advocate must avoid situation involving a conflict between his personal interest and his duties. He should always restrain from using the fiduciary relationship as conduit for personal gain, otherwise it will be a matter of professional misconduct. There are verities of conducts which have been pronounced by the courts as professional misconduct in relation to the client.

(a) Dereliction of Duty

Rule 15 of the Bar Council of India Rules provides that, it shall be the duty of an advocate fearlessly to uphold the interest of his client.[23] It is highly unprofessional for an

21. *Naratamal* v. *M.R. Murti,* A.I.R. (2004) 5 S.C.C. 689.
22. *Manjit Kaur* v. *Deol Bus Service Limited,* Civil Misc. No. 4905 C. II of 1988.
23. See, Rule 13 of the Bar Councils of India Rules, 1975.

advocate to handover his brief to another and allow to him to step into his shoes at hearing and to conduct the case as if the latter had himself been briefed as deviling is strictly prohibited. In *Prem Nath* v. *Kapil Dev Singh*,[24] the advocate failed to file a writ petition and handed over the brief to another advocate, even after accepting the fee. The Supreme Court of India found him guilty of professional misconduct and upholds the punishment by way of suspension from practice for three months.

Likewise, receiving the amount, failure to file the suit and giving fictitious number of the suit and making believe that a suit was filed are also constitute the same effect. In *V.C. Ranga Durai* v. *D. Gopalan*,[25] the appellant duped the complainants by not filing the suits on the promissory notes for Rs. 15,000. A suit filed by him was returned for presentation to proper Court. The appellant never represented the suit to the proper Court. But the appellant made false representations to the complainants that the suits had been filed and were pending, gave them the various dates fixed in the two suits, and later on, falsely told them that the suits were decreed. The complainants served a legal notice on the debtor called upon the debtor to pay the decretal debts. In fact, no such suits were filed nor were any decrees passed. The appellant pleaded that the complainants engaged one K.S. Laxmi Kumaran and thrown out mud on him to save his interest, and stated that he is nothing to do with the charges. Laxmi Kumaran pleaded that at the behest of the appellant, he signed vakalat as a matter of courtesy and that he was never instructed by the complainant. The Supreme Court found the advocate guilty of misconduct and directed the suspension along with undertaking to serve poor for a year.

Similar attitude has been adopted by the disciplinary committee of the Bar Council of India. Thus, in *C.L.* v. *N.T.S.*,[26] the complaint was that no proceeding was instituted by the advocate even after receiving fees. It was alleged that the advocate informed the complainant that a decree had been

24. (1995) Supp. (3) S.C.C. 717.
25. A.I.R. 1979 S.C. 281.
26. 16, I.B.R. (1989) 563.

passed in his favour. The Advocate in his reply stated that he offered to act as a mediator being a neighbour of both the parties, and not as an advocate and that he had received the amount towards his fees due to him for conducting petition under Rent Control Act. The Disciplinary Committee of the Bar Council of India, after going through the facts in detail, held that the advocate was guilty of gross professional misconduct.

Again in *Manjit Kaur* v. *Deol Bus Service Limited*,[27] an appeal was dismissed in default due non-appearance of counsel, it was ruled that the advocate was guilty of professional misconduct and that party suffering loss was at liberty to sue then for obtaining such loss. In *Smt. P. Parkajam* v. *B.H. Chandra Shekhar*,[28] the complainant engaged respondent advocate to defend him in court in a case of eviction from house. He intentionally did not attend the proceeding. As a result *exparte* decree for eviction was passed against complainant. Advocate was alleged to have entered into a compromise with landlord and complainants files were returned to her through the person who had introduced her to respondent. Advocate was held guilty of professional misconduct for deliberate absence and breaking confidentially by returning documents to some other party other than the clients himself.

(b) Changing the Sides

Relying again on the Rule 15 of the Bar Council of India Rules, the act of an advocate in accepting brief for plaintiff and appearing without valid formation of the authority in the suit for defendant is also said against the propriety of the legal profession. That is why, the courts have taken a very rigid approach on this point, so it is not only the matter of breach of contract but it is unethical towards the spirit of the legal profession. In *Emperor* v. *Rajani Kanta Ghose*,[29] a division bench of the Calcutta High Court held that a legal practitioner

27. Civil Misc. No. 4905 C-II of 1988.
28. B.C.I. T.R. No. 86/1992 dated 17.02.1997.
29. A.I.R. 1923 Cal. 106.

appearing on behalf of both sides was guilty of professional misconduct.

The full bench of the Lahore High Court in the *matter of Ramlal Anand,*[30] elaborated the issue in the following words:

> "change of sides as such by counsel is not forbidden by law; change of sides is forbidden if there are confidential communications by one side which may be made use of when the lawyer represent the opposite party. It is forbidden if the lawyer obtains his own discharge and acts for the opposite party. It is also forbidden if the lawyer accepts a retainer from the opposite party without first offering his service to his original client. If he fails to do so he will be guilty".

Again in the *matter of Gurubasappa,*[31] the respondent advocate appeared for the complainant at the early stage of the suit. At the instance of defendants No. 1 and 2 in the suit the Government was added as a party to the suit. At that stage the respondent without the knowledge and consent of the complaint filed a memo of appearance for the Government and contested the suit against the complainant. It was alleged that the respondent wilfully withheld the certified copy of a mortgage deed given for the purpose of filing in it the court along with other documents with a view to help the defendants in the suit. The Andhra Pradesh High Court though accepted the apology of a respondent and dropped the proceedings, held that the act of the counsel deplorable amounting to professional misconduct. The court observed:

> "An advocate or pleader, who has appeared on behalf of one party in a suit ought not allow himself to be placed in the position in which there might be some suspicion whether well or ill founded, that his knowledge of his client's case would be used by him on a subsequent

30. A.I.R. 1946 Lah. 301.
31. A.I.R. 1965, A.P. 261.
32. *Ibid.*, p. 266.

occasion in appearing for another party and against his original client".[32]

The decisions of the various High Courts, discussed earlier, found strong support in a famous case by the Supreme Court. In *Chandra Shekhara Soni* v. *Bar Council of Rajasthan*,[33] the advocate concerned was retained by one party and thereafter he accepted the brief of the other party and also took Rs. 300 for one doctor (Magal Sharma). He gave a letter to the client stating that "I am sending the man to you with X-ray plats. Your amount is lying with me. I will come to *Jalore* in evening and see you. Please do his work and it will be done positively. It was a case of injury of skull and he wanted to secure a favourable report from the doctor concerned by taking bribery amount on his behalf. On complaint the State Bar Council and Bar Council of India suspended his licence of practice for a period of three years on the ground of professional misconduct. In appeal under Section 38 of the Advocate Act, 1961 though the Supreme Court reduced the punishment to one year but observed:

> "It is not in accordance with the professional etiquette for an advocate while retained by one party to accept brief of the other. It is unprofessional to represent conflicting interests except by express consent given by all concerned after disclosure of full fact".[34]

Likewise, Mr. Justice Sabyasanchi Mukharji and Mr. Justice Saikia, took strong view on such point in the case of *B.L. Samdaria* v. *Harak Chand Jain and others*.[35] In this case the complaint was that the Advocate was habituated to ignore all the rules of professional conduct and in a particular case before the District Judge, Ajmer, a petition was filed under the Motor Vehicles Act through his junior advocate, who was not the real counsel and who never took interest in it. When the claimant, Smt. Chandu Bai, widow of the deceased, expired

33. A.I.R. 1983 S.C. 1012.
34. *Ibid.*
35. A.I.R. 1990 S.C. 2213.

after filing the claim petition, the Advocate filed the Vakalatnama on behalf of the legal representatives of Chandu Bai. In affect, he filed Vakalatnama and affidavit on behalf of the legal representatives and the insurance company. The order-sheet revealed that the claim of the widow Chandu Bai was dismissed for want of prosecution.

It was also complained that the Advocate had already been punished in a case by the Disciplinary Committee and another case was pending before it.

The complaint was investigated and the Disciplinary Committee of the Bar Council of India found him guilty. It was observed that it was not believable that the widow had engaged the junior, who was a novice to the profession. The junior had left the office of the Advocate and the Advocate had failed to produce him or the clerk or typist as witnesses. The advocate was suspended for two years. The Chairman of the Bar Council issued an order of stay for one month. Inspite of it, the Advocate was suspended. He preferred an appeal to the Supreme Court in Dec. 1985 which was dismissed. A review petition was also dismissed in Feb. 1986. In April, he filed a review petition before the Bar Council of India on the basis of fresh evidence. It was admitted but dismissed in Jan. 1987. He moved the Supreme Court by special leave petition in July 1987 against the order of the Bar Council of India.

Chief Justice Sabyasachi Mukharji and Mr. Justice Saikia, held that the Bar Council of India did not commit any error in passing the order against the advocate. As the petition was dismissed by the Disciplinary Committee on the merits and not on technical grounds, the Supreme Court dismissed the review petition.[36]

From the above decisions it is revealed that if an advocate believes reasonably that his accepting brief for a party may be prejudicial to his former client in litigation, it is not proper for an advocate to appear for opposite party in such a litigation. Failure of this duty may constitute professional misconduct. But it is not an absolute prohibition. Rule 20 of the Civil Rules of practice envisages the circumstances in which an advocate

36. *Id.*, p. 2221.

may appear for the opposite party.[37] Thus, where a client engages another counsel, the presumption is that the services of the former counsel were not needed and he is at liberty to accept brief from the opposite party.[38] When a legal practitioner does not hold a general retainer on behalf of a certain client but has merely been engaged in certain cases with separate vakalats, there is nothing to prevent to him from appearing against him. Where a legal practitioner in the absence of instruction from the first client appears for the opposite party in a subsequent connected proceeding, he cannot be held guilty of professional misconduct.[39] Similarly, he can certainly appear for the other side in a case not directly concerned with the earlier litigation.

The above instances make it clear that it is not that an advocate can in no case appear for the other sides. It is submitted that by allowing the advocate to represent other sides in suit, the court should be very careful. While we agree that in special circumstances an advocate may appear for the opposite party, but we never support to make it a general rule. The two reasons may be advanced for the same.

Firstly, an advocate from appearing for the opposite party against his former client, is that there is a likelihood or

---

37. The text of the Rule 20 runs as: "*except when specially authorized by the Court or by consent of the party, a pleader who was advised in connection with the institution of a suit, appeal or other proceedings acted for a party,. shall not, unless the first gives the party for whom he had advised, drawn pleadings or acted an opportunity of engaging or in any appeal or application of revision arising on in any matter connected there with for any person, whose interest is opposed to that of his formal client.* Provided that the consent of the party shall be presumed if he engages another pleader for him in such suit, appeal or other proceedings, without offering an engagement to the pleader whose services he originally engaged.

    Explanation: *Notwithstanding anything contained hereinbefore, a Practitioner who discloses to one client the information confided to him in his capacity as a legal practitioner of another without the latter's consent, shall not be protected merely by reason of his being permitted to appear for the other client under this Rule.*
38. Atchutaramiah *v.* Secretary of State for India, A.I.R. 1915 Mad. 552.
39. In the Matter of *A Mukhtar,* 13 A.L.J. 475 (F.B.).

possibility of misuse of the instruction given to him by his former client. It should be very clear that a question whether the misuse has been actually made; the mere possibility of such misuse in a matter, which is connected with previous litigation, is sufficient.

The *second* reason is that the advocate have had such confidential information from one of the party as would make it improper for him to appear for the other party.

Whether confidential information has been imparted or not would be a question of fact. It may, in certain cases, be the very antithesis of the privilege afforded under Section 126 of the Indian Evidence Act, 1872, to embark on an enquiry which necessarily must elicit the information which the court considers to be confidential and a protected privilege.

In order to prevent an advocate from appearing for the opposite party, what one has to see is whether in the circumstances of a particular case, having regard to the steps taken in the litigation or criminal proceedings, it can be reasonably inferred that confidential information could have been imparted to the advocate. In *Earl Cholmondeley* v. *Lord Clinton*[40] the Lord Chancellor said:

> "If there is any ground for this application, either as a motion in the cause or upon the general jurisdiction, it must be furnished by a general principle, not the particular circumstances of the case; otherwise the court must try every such case on its particular circumstances, and it cannot be so discussed without a disclosure from the solicitor of all he knows".

While, in civil cases consent of the party or the special permission of the court can permit a lawyer to act for the opposite party as well and the question of imparting any confidential information to the other party would only be a ground for professional misconduct. In criminal cases there is no provision for an advocate to appear for the opposite party with the consent of that party, though even in such cases the imparting of confidential information, protected under Section

40. (1815) 19 Ves. 261, p. 266.

126 of the Indian Evidence Act, 1872 to the other party would make him liable to a charge of professional misconduct.

It is requested in this regard that even where circumstances exist from which a reasonable inference can be raised that confidential information could have been imparted, that would preclude an advocate from appearing for opposite party, not on the ground of professional misconduct, but as an improper conduct for an advocate maintaining the highest traditions of the Bar. Hence it is not correct to say that only in such cases where he is liable for misconduct, can he be prevented from appearing for the opposite party. Even apart from any contractual obligation, the court will, in the exercise of their powers to maintain the highest standards of the profession, preclude advocates from appearing for the opposite party, if that is likely to embarrass the advocate or raise a suspicion in the mind of the client with respect to the conduct of his erstwhile advocate or that it is improper to do so, or the circumstances are such from which an inference of imparting of confidential nature of information can be raised.

Thus, in *Bawa Mohan Singh Sethi* v. *Baburam,*[41] *Saharanpur Grain Chamber Ltd., Saharanpur, through Manager, Sri Ram Gupta* v. *Maharaj Singh, Saharanpur,*[42] and Baijnath V. *'S', an Advocate of undo-opposite Party,*[43] it was held that if the former client conveys any confidential information from one of the parties, it is improper to appear for the other party.

It is also improper for an Advocate who held in office of the public prosecutor or was engaged as a special public prosecutor to accept an engagement for the defence in a case in which at an earlier stage he advised or gave opinion to the prosecution or appeared on behalf of the prosecution at the stage of interlocutory applications like application for bail. In *Emperor* v. *Brij Krishore Raj,*[44] in *Emperor* v. *Rajanikanta Ghose,*[45] and in *the matter of S.P., a pleader*[46] appearance for both the

41. A.I.R. 1959 Punj. 160.
42. A.I.R. 1940 All. 233.
43. A.I.R. 1934 Oudh. 58.
44. A.I.R. 1918 Pat. 265.
45. A.I.R. 1923 Cal. 106.
46. A.I.R. 1934 Pat. 352.

sides was held as amounting to gross misconduct and a pleader should as possible stick to one side who first employed him. It is his duty to inform his client where the other sides offer instructions, without information to the client he should not be allowed to change sides.

Thus, it is clear from the above discussion that in most of the cases the judiciary is of the opinion that advocate must not change side if he accepts the brief of his client. It is submitted again that in the interest of justice firstly, advocate should himself reject the proffered brief for the other sides. The question of propriety cannot depend upon the confidential communication. To quote Andhra Pradesh High Court,[47] "Advocate is the best person to Judge in what circumstances he should appear against the accused and in doing so, he must always interpret any particular situation against himself and his interest for the maintenance of the highest standards of professional ethics".[48] Thus, *Quod dubitas ne feceris* is a good rule for the regulation of one's own conduct and if the advocate fails to maintain self-dignity, then his act must be declared misconduct by the court of Law.

(c) Negligence

As discussed earlier the ethics of the legal profession not only expects from an advocate to be honest, but also demands that he should exercise reasonable skill and prudence to the case conducted by him. Hence the question arises: whether an advocate is expected to be infallible? To what extent the prudence is expected? If he fails to prove himself as a wise and able person, will it amount to misconduct?

In a series of judicial pronouncements the judiciary has negatively decided the above questions.[49] The courts have repeatedly taken the view that there must be the element of moral delinquency in the negligence, as negligence by itself does not amount to professional misconduct. Professional

47. *Public Prosecutor, Andhra Pradesh* v. *Kothakappu Venkata Reddi*, A.I.R. 1961 A.P. 105.
48. G. Geetish, "Professional Misconduct by Advocates", CULT, 2003, p. 183.
49. *In re Pran Narain, Advocate, Agra*, A.I.R. 1940 All. 280.

misconduct means conduct which would reasonably be regarded as disgraceful or dishonourable by legal practitioners of good repute and efficiency. It was held by the Supreme Court of India in the *Matter of P., an Advocate,*[50] that mere negligence or error of judgement on the part of the Advocate would not amount to professional misconduct. Error of judgement cannot completely eliminate in all human affairs and mere negligence does not necessarily render advocate guilty of misconduct".

The perusal of case law both in England and India reveals that though serious in nature negligence, itself cannot constitute professional misconduct. In this regard it will be useful to refer the case in *Myers* v. *Elman*[51] and in particular to the observation of Viscount Maghuam, L.C. In the above case a charge of negligence had been preferred against the solicitor. In the course of his judgement Lord Chancellor observed:

> "Apart from the statutory grounds, it is, of course, true that a solicitor may be struck off the rolls or suspended on the ground of professional misconduct—words which have been properly defined as conduct which would reasonably be regarded as disgraceful or dishonourable by solicitors of good repute and competency. Mere negligence, even of a serious character, will not suffice".

The same view was reiterated by Lord Esher, M.R. *in re,* G. Mayor Goope,[52] as;

> "The motion is made against a solicitor for such misconduct in his profession as would call upon the court either to strike him off the rolls or deal with him by way of punishment is some other manner. But when such a motion is made asking the court to exercise penal jurisdiction over a solicitor, it is not sufficient to show that his conduct is such as to support an action for negligence or want of skill. In order to support such a motion as the

50. A.I.R. 1963 S.C. 1313.
51. (1939) 4 All. E.R. 484, p. 488.
52. 33, S.J. 397.

present it must be shown that he had done something dishonourable to him as a man and also in his profession".

The view taken by the English Courts in the above cases has been also adopted by the courts in India. In the *matter of V.K. Narsinga Rao and Yusufddin*,[53] it was held by the Andhra Pradesh High Court that negligence in filing the appeal would not amount to professional misconduct. Similarly, in *matter of B. Munuswami Naidu*[54] it was ruled by a special bench of the Madras High Court that negligence of duties would not amount to professional misconduct, since the element of moral delinquency is an ingredient of professional misconduct.[55]

In similar vein the Andhra Pradesh High Court remarked *in Re, A Pleader, Tiruppur*:[56]

"It looks to us that an advocate who neglects to perform his duty does not come within the purview of clause (b) since the moral delinquency is absent in the neglect of duty. It is only in cases where moral turpitude is involved when such misappropriation or misuse of the funds entrusted to him or in analogous circumstance that the case falls within the ambit of clause (b)".

The aforesaid decisions of the various High Court were affirmed by the Supreme Court of India in the case of *V.P. Kumaravelu* v. *Bar Council of India*,[57] wherein the Apex Court summarized this matter by saying that negligence without moral turpitude or deliquency may not amount to professional misconduct. Therefore, the decisions referred above reveal that negligence will constitute misconduct only if the element of delinquency is also present there. The rationales of the cases in *Ali Mohd. Kashmiri* v. *An Advocate*,[58] *State* v. *Mahendranath Dutta*

53. A.I.R. 1959 A.P. 593.
54. A.I.R. 1926 Mad. 969.
55. *In the matter of a 'Vakil'*, I.L.R. 47 All. 729.
56. A.I.R. 1926 Mad. 568.
57. (1997) 4 S.C.C. 266.
58. A.I.R. 1953 Cal. 484.

& others,[59] *V.P. Kumaravelu* v. *Bar Council of India*[60] clearly indicate that mere negligence on the part of the advocate does not amount to misconduct. However, if it is accompanied by suppression of truth[61] or deliberate misrepresentation of fact[62] or involve moral turpitude[63] or gross negligence[64] then it may constitute the professional misconduct.

It is humbly submitted that the decisions referred to above do not express to be correct approach and are contrary to the high traditions of the legal profession. Therefore, a second look is needed on the view that "mere negligence cannot constitute professional misconduct". Such approach is supported by more than one reason.

Negligence is an act which itself invites action in the eye of law. Therefore, negligence by the member of legal profession should not go unpunished.

Different consideration may arise where the negligence of an advocate may be able to constitute the gross misconduct. Therefore, the court should make distinction between the negligence and gross negligence relying on the fact and circumstances of the cases.

(ii) Misconduct in Relation to Money

The relationship of an Advocate and client is unequal and the personal dependency of advocate over client is a factor which cannot be lost sight of. Therefore, an advocate is strictly accountable for client's money, one of such obligations is that he must promptly pay over to his client the money collected for him, and failure to return money, especially after demand has been made for it, amounts to professional misconduct. While the money remains with him, it has to be treated as a trust fund and he is its trustee. One of canons of ethics adopted by the American Bar Association as a general guide is:

59. A.I.R. 1975 Ori. 49.
60. A.I.R. 1997 S.C. 1014.
61. *Sardul Singh* v. *Pritam Singh,* A.I.R. 1999 S.C. 1704.
62. *V.C. Ranga Durai* v. *D. Gopalan,* A.I.R. 1979 S.C. 281.
63. *Hikmat Ali Khan* v. *Ishwar Prasad Arya* (1979)3 S.C.C. 131.
64. *Stephen & Company* v. *Allen,* A.I.R. 1921 P.L. 231.

> "Money of the client or other trust property coming into the possession of the lawyer should be reported promptly, and except with the client's knowledge and consent should not be commingled with his private property or to be used by him".[65]

Hence it is expected to the members of legal profession that they should keep themselves as for as possible at a respectable distance from using client's money and keep accounts for the same. The courts in England also insist that it is a barrister's duty to preserve a record of his dealings with his clients and any agreement between them should be in writing.[66]

In our country Rules 25 to 32 of the Bar Council of India Rules expressly relate with the duties of an advocate towards clients money and infringement of these duties will constitute professional misconduct.

Some instances of professional misconduct relating to client's money are given below:

(a) Financial Misappropriation

Rule 27 of the Bar Council of India Rules provide that where any amount is received or given to him on behalf of his client the fact of such receipt must be intimated to the client as early as possible. However, after the termination of the proceedings the advocate shall be at liberty to appropriate towards the settled fee due to him any remaining unspent out of the amount paid or sent to him as expenses, or any amount that has come into his hands in proceedings.[67] But he shall not adjust fee payable to him by his client against his own personal liability to the client.[68]

Any failure of this duty will invite action against the advocate. It is well established through a catena of cases that financial misappropriation of client's money is a grave

65. See, the Canon of American Bar Association.
66. *Anandu Devi* v. *Banchhanidu Sumanta Rao,* All. E.R. 27, p. 735.
67. Rule 28 of the Bar Council of India Rules, 1975.
68. *Id.,* Rule 23.

misconduct. No advocate therefore, is entitled to hold client's money in his hand and use it himself. This position of trusteeship in respect of money of the client in his hand is all the greater where the money represents the unspent balance of what was given for a specific purpose. In the *Matter of T.N.P., an Advocate,*[69] the Calcutta High Court held that where a client hands over to his counsel money for the purchase of Court fee, stamp, it is not permissible to the counsel to appropriate it towards his own fee.

Likewise, withdrawal of money from the court without the consent of client and appropriating the same towards the fee also constitute a grave professional misconduct. In *K.V. Umere* v. *Venubai O. Dase,*[70] in a claim the respondent was to get Rs. 11,760. Appellant advocate deprived the respondent who was a helpless widow of the said money legitimately due to her. He took false plea before the disciplinary committee of the Bar Council of the State that Rs. 6,000 were due to him towards fee and other miscellaneous expenses. But, ultimately accepted to pay Rs. 10,000 in two instalments. The Bar Council of India held the advocate guilty of professional misconduct for violating Rule 20 of the Rules of the Bar Council of India. It also expressed the view that there were a large number of claims for death or bodily injury resulting in motor accident in country and if lawyers were allowed to withhold payment of compensation awarded and pay the same in instalment, it would amount to misconduct.

Again, in *Devendra Bhai Shakar Mehta* v. *Ramesh Chandra Vithaldas Seth,*[71] the appellant advocate indulged himself in fraudulent activities by taking money from respondent on assurance to help him in getting loan of Rs. 12 lacks from a financer. But loan was never financed. The disciplinary committee found that there was a racket for defrauding and cheating the aspirant loanee and the alleged financier and the appellant advocate were parties to such racket. The Supreme Court of India observed:

69. 10 Cr.L.J. 412 (Cal.).
70. A.I.R. 1988 S.C. 1154.
71. A.I.R. 1992 S.C. 1398.

> "It is really unfortunate that a member of the legal profession has indulged in fraudulent activities in a calculated manner of financial gain at the cost of innocent person. To say the least, an advocate enrolled under the Advocates Act, 1961 having a licence to represent the case for litigants is expected to maintain high standard of morality and un-impeachable sense of legal and ethical propriety".

Yet in *J.S. Jadhav* v. *Mustafa Hazi,*[72] the Apex Court went to extent of passing a decree in favour of the client for the amount misappropriated by the advocate with interest at 9 percent per annum. In the instant case the advocate was found guilty for withdrawing money from Court on behalf of his client in pursuance of a compromise decree and returning only a small amount to the client and for misappropriating the balance. Such misappropriation of degree amount payable to the client was held to be grievous misconduct by the Apex Court.

The Bar Council of India in this regard also took a very serious view in most of the cases. Some instances are given here.

In *Mrs. M.S. Patwardhan* v. *V.V. Karmarkar,*[73] the complainant engaged respondent advocate in the process of purchase of 1000 acres land. She gave 2,45,000 to respondent for purchase to lands stamp duty, registration charges and other expenses. Respondent did not render accounts nor paid the balance amount lying with him. He was held guilty of professional misconduct on account of his failure to maintain proper account of his client's money. In *Upendra D. Bhatt* v. *Vijay Singh Kapadia*[74] the respondent advocate collected heavy amount by defrauding the complainant's mother. But the workers for which money was received were not done. He was found guilty of professional misconduct.

72. A.I.R. 1993 S.C. 1533.
73. D.C.I. T.R. case no. 93/1991 dated 7.5.1993.
74. D.C. Appeal No. 23/1993 dated 25.4.1995.

Again in *Allahabad Bank* v. *Girish Prasad Verma,*[75] the respondent advocate was engaged by the appellant Bank to file a number of cases. But he did not file suit in some of cases and remaining suits were filed with nominal court fees, though full court fees had been paid to him. He misappropriated huge amount and therefore, was found guilty by the Bar Council of India for misappropriating the amount of court fees of Rs. 1,36,441 and not filing suits in some cases.

In *Secretary, Karnataka Khadi Gram Udyog Samyukta Sangh* v. *J.S. Kulkarni,*[76] a registered society carrying on business of Khadi and Village Industries engaged the respondent advocate to file the execution proceedings in the competent Court for the execution of the decrees already obtained in the civil suit. He did so and received different amounts towards the decretal amounts in different execution proceedings. But he paid only a part of the amount to the society complainant. Respondent advocate was found to have failed to discharge his professional duty to the client by neither furnishing the accounts of amount nor refunding the said amount nor providing the claim of settled or payable by the client to him.

Thus, in the above referred cases the view taken by Bar Council of India reveals that client's money cannot be diverted at the will of the legal practitioner. Hence an advocate who receive client's money has the duty to pay the same.[77] In the plethora of decisions, the courts have repeatedly held that even if a counsel has not much work, he is bound to keep accounts for whatever work.[78] The purpose of these decisions are to prevent the advocate from diverting any portion of the client's money towards own pocket.

In *In Re an Advocate*[79] the High Court of Kerala observed that an advocate receives or realizes the amount in his capacity as his client's advocate and that *jural* relationship ought to determine the nature and character of his liability. If any amount is received or given to him on behalf of his client the

75. B.C.I. T.R. case no. 49/1993 dated 7.3.1996.
76. B.C.I.T.R. case no. 12/1990 12.8.2000.
77. D.C. No.31/1883 of Ker. Bar Council.
78. *Ibid.*
79. 1979 K.L.T. 236.

fact of such receipt must be intimated to the client as early as possible.[80] If any amount of fee remains unpaid, after the termination of proceedings the Bar Council Rules provides for deduction of such amount from any amount belonging to the client remaining in his hands. If the fee has been left unsettled, then he may deduct the fee payable under the rules of the court in force for the time being out of any money belonging to the client in his hands and the remaining shall be refunded to the client

It is important to note that any delay in rendering account or payment of balance to client on demand and the request of the advocates to entrust more cases so as to enable him to adjust the balance of client's money toward his fee or any other purposes may constitutes misappropriation and will amount to professional misconduct. As Mr. Justice Madhavan Nair of the Kerala High Court said that "in the matter of moneys of the litigant in the hands of his counsel the later must act in honest manner and all expenditure incurred by him for and on behalf of his client out of such money must be duly accounted for and the withholding of such moneys or their misapplication will clearly amount to professional misconduct".[81]

It is submitted that the act of professional misconduct committed by an advocate, specially misappropriation of considerable sum of his client's money is a very serious and grave one; and in these types of matters the advocate should not be allowed to continue in the honourable profession.

However, going through various decisions, it can be seen that Court makes a distinction between delayed payment (when the client makes demands) and the non-payment after request.

The court is taking a lenient view in the former case by giving a punishment of reprimand only.[82] But in latter cases courts do not take lenient view in the interest of justice.

(b) No Right to Lien as to Money or Papers

In *John D' Souza* v. *Edward Ani*,[83] where an advocate failed

80. See, Rule 27 of the Bar Councils of India Rules, 1975.
81. *In the Matter of 'R' an Advocate*, A.I.R. 1961 Ker. 209.
82. *Prahlad Saran Gupta* v. *Bar Council of India*, A.I.R. 1997 S.C. 864.
83. (1994)2 S.C.C. 64.

to return the Will (deed) even on demand, his conduct was held unworthy. He was held to be duty bound to return because the Will was entrusted to his custody by the testatrix, only on trust. In the circumstances of the case, the sentence of debarring him for one year was affirmed.

It is a settled principle that an advocate cannot hold lien over the case file on the plea that he was not paid his fee. The advocate can sue the client for recovery of fee, but in no way is authorized to hold his money or papers. The Supreme Court of India in *R.D. Saxena* v. *Balram Prasad Sharma*[84] and *New India Assurance Company* v. *A.K. Saxena*[85] repeatedly affirmed the view that advocates have no lien.

(c) Taking Signatures on Blank Paper and Misuse of Signed Document

It is highly unprofessional conduct on the part of an advocate to take his client's signature on a blank sheet of paper. For instance, when this is done in the case of a plaint there can be no proper verification as required by the Code of Civil Procedure, 1908. A practitioner who permits this to be done and induces his client to sign blank sheets of paper in order that they could be used for the preparation of a plaint, which would then be regard as having been duly signed and verified by the client is guilty of professional misconduct.[86]

In *Gianchand Goyal* v. *Bar Council of India*[87] the Supreme Court held a lawyer obtaining signature on blank papers and misusing the same to be guilty of professional misconduct.

Similarly in *Vikramaditya* v. *Smt. Jamila Khatoon*[88] complainant had engaged appellant advocate for mutation in her name a land purchased by her. Advocate obtained signature of the complainant on Vakalatnama and blank papers. He misused these documents for obtaining a compromise decree in favour of his own father. It was done by filing a false suit against the complainant that sale deed in her

84. A.I.R. 2000 S.C. 2912.
85. A.I.R. 2004 S.C. 311.
86. *In re a pleader*, Bellary, A.I.R. 1945 Mad. 130.
87. (1997)1 S.C.C. 108.
88. D.C. Appeal No. 21/1996 dated 21.09.1998.

favour was benami transaction and his father was the real owner. He was held guilty of professional misconduct.

In a famous case, *D.P. Chaddha* v. *Triyugi Narain Mishra*,[89] the appellant advocate got a blank Vakalatnama and a black paper signed by the complainant. He used these documents for fabricating a compromise petition, whereby the complainant was made to suffer a decree of eviction. The blank Vakalatnama was used for engaging Shri Anil Sharma, Advocate on behalf of the complainant, who got the compromise verified. Rajasthan State Bar Council found the appellant advocate guilty of professional misconduct, and punished with suspension from practice for a period of five years. Shri Anil Sharma, advocate was also proceeded against along with Shri D.P. Chaddha, appellant and he too having been found guilty was reprimanded.

An appeal was preferred by Shri D.P. Chaddha, advocate under Section 37 of the Act. The appeal was not only dismissed but the Bar Council of India had chosen to vary the punishment of the appellant by enhancing the period of suspension from practice to ten years.

It is submitted that the approach of the Bar Council of India in the above case is so good and consistent with the object of the Act.

(d) Charging Improper Fee

It is true that a client is duty bound to pay remuneration to his client for service rendered by him, but at the same time ethics demands that advocate should charge reasonable fees from his client. This is because "the prospect of extra ordinary high fees may cause the advocate to compromise his fiduciary obligation".[90] Mr. Harsh A. Desai wrote in this regard that, "what pinches litigants most are the fees that lawyers charge which are often exorbitant and unrelated to the amount to work that goes into the matter. It is tempting to say that as fees are known before hand the client can choose whether he goes to a particular lawyer or not. This is not the case. A litigant does not go to lawyers by choice and he may require

89. Civil Appeal No. 1124 of 1998 dated 5.2.2000.
90. Quoted from Gururajachari, K., Ist ed., p. 105.

the services of a particular lawyer which he cannot afford".[91] To quote Mahatma Gandhi "a true lawyer is one who place trust and service in the first place and emoluments of the profession in the next place only".[92] However, the ideal expectation peeping through Gandhian way of looking into the matter has undergone a change. The present day feeling is that an advocate's fee is related to the eminence and the standing of the lawyer at the Bar. Therefore, the size of fee in relation to the work done or the work undertaken may be unethical and open to criticism but it cannot amount itself to professional misconduct unless a scrutiny of the evidence in case discloses evidence to prove fraudulent conduct on the part of the lawyer.[93] Some extra element, therefore, should also be present to prove the professional misconduct of charging high fees. Thus, holding brief from another pleader on payment, but obtaining exorbitant fees from client separately was held as misconduct in *William Edward* v. *Judges of Supreme Court of Sierra Leone and others,*[94] by the Privy Council. In the instant case an advocate owing to his inability to attend a case requested another advocate to attend promising him to pay a portion of the fee, but the latter alleging that the case itself had been transferred, obtained fee from the client, who was an illiterate person. He charged again a large amount of fresh fee out of all proportions to the importance of the case and work done by him. The conduct of advocate was held to involve professional misconduct.

It is important to note that the Bar Councils of India Rules does not provide any standards of fee charged by the advocate. The Law Commission recommended for statutory ceiling on lawyer's fees in its 128th and 131st Reports, but such recommendations have not been accepted till now. At present in India there is only one provision under the Constitution which gives power to the High Court for regulation of fee. Article 227(3) reads: "The High Court may also settle table of fees to be allowed to the sheriff and clerk and officers of such

91. Desai, D.A. "Research For Justice", 3 *Lex Juris* (1988) 24.
92. See, 'Harijan' dated 26.11.1938, p. 2.
93. *Supra* note 90.
94. A.I.R. 1928 P.C. 264, p. 266.

courts and to attorneys, advocates and pleaders practising therein.

In earlier period in England, barrister's remuneration was called honorarium and not fees, counsel was entitled to refuse to accept a brief it the fee was not paid when brief was delivered, but if the Counsel had not so insisted the payment became a matter of honour and not of legal obligation. More or less the earlier rule is still prevailing in England and an advocate is at liberty to say that he will not practise in a particular court without a special sum amount.[95]

The issue arises as to the position enjoyed by an advocate in India. No. doubts the advocates in India can also charge high fees from his client, but according to the judicial approach failure of a lawyer to appear before the court only due to non payment of fee, is an act which amounts to professional misconduct. Thus, in *S.R.K.S. Chettiar* v. *V.K.N. Kodhandarmma,*[96] the Madras High Court held that if an advocate has accepted the brief of the case, he is duty bound to conduct the same, even if there is non-payment of fee. If he fails to obey this legal and moral duty, he will be punished due to his misconduct. Thus, on accepting Vakalatnama an advocate has to conduct the case irrespective of payment of fee by the client.

Similarly, it is not proper on the part of the advocate to charge contingent fee.[97] In India it is highly reprehensible for an advocate to stipulate or receive remuneration based on the result of litigation or claim. Thus, in *H.G. Kulkarni* v. *B.B. Subedar*[98] an advocate misused complainant's signed blank paper and also charged fees on percentage basis contingent upon the result of the case. He was found guilty of professional misconduct by the disciplinary committee of the Bar Council of India for violation of Rule 20 of the Bar Council of India Rules, 1975.

The question whether it is legal and proper for an advocate to make his remuneration in a case contingent on the

95. Article 227(3) of the Indian Constitution.
96. A.I.R. 1958 Mad. 122.
97. *Supra* note 90.
98. D.C. Appeal No. 40/1996 dated 22.8.1998.

success of the case was also discussed by the full bench of the Supreme Court in the case of *Ganga Ram* v. *Devi Das.*[99] Wherein the Apex Court observed:

> "agreements between practitioners and their clients making the remuneration of the advocate dependent to any extent whatever on the result of the case in which he is retained are illegal as being contrary to public policy and practitioners entering into such agreements are therefore, guilty of professional misconduct and render themselves liable to the disciplinary action of the court".

The court further held that a fee fixed by a lawyer contingent upon success of a suit is unenforceable being opposed to public policy.[100]

It is interesting to note that in England too, this practice of fixing contingent fee has not been allowed to grow by the English Bar. Of late in America contingent fee is permitted. There has grown a practice among lawyers working in the professional injury claims to accept brief in such cases on condition that their fees shall be measured by an agreed fraction of the benefits to the client resulting from the lawyer's prosecution of the claims. They justify the contingent fee on the ground that it enables a poor litigant with meritorious claim to obtain competent legal service, because the client pays no fees for the legal service if the claim does not succeed.[101]

It is submitted that even though this type of payment may be useful on some occasion, but it may result into two types of dangers:

(i) On the success of the claim advocate may claim heavy amount; and

(ii) It may become a tool of sharing in profits of the litigation, specially in India, where the tradition of Bar is not well established.

---

99. 61 P.R. 1907 (F.B.).
100. *Ibid.*
101. *Supra* note 90.

Thus it is further submitted that keeping in view that demanding exorbitant fee is unethical and sharing in profit of litigation is itself a professional misconduct. Therefore, the contingent fee should not be allowed in India. The advocate should fix his fee at the time of his engagement. The schedule of fee would ease the problem.

If any standard is needed we can take the help of the Rule 1.5 of the Model Rules of professional conduct, wherein certain factors are prescribed for determining the reasonableness of the fee charged by the Advocates. The factors enumerated are as under:

(1) The time and labor required, the novelty and difficulty of the question involved, and the skill requisite to perform the legal service properly;
(2) The likelihood, if apparent to the client, that the acceptance of the particular employment will preclude other employment by the lawyer;
(3) The fee customarily charged in the locality for similar services;
(4) The amount involved and the results obtained;
(5) The time limitations imposed by the client or by the circumstances;
(6) The nature and the length of the professional relationship with the client;
(7) The experience, reputation and ability of the lawyer, and
(8) Whether the fee is fixed or contingent.

It is to be noted that under Article 227(3) of the Indian Constitution various High Courts have formulated fee schedules. But it remains purposeless because of the failure to get them periodically revised. It is advisable, therefore, that the Bar Council of India should come forward and prescribe the highest amount of fee that is to be realized from the client in a particular case. This will certainly help in checking certain people carrying on the legal profession as a trade or shop of commercial nature.

(e) Taking Undue Advantage of His Position

The position of an advocate is so capable to abuse the profession, that law prefers in some respects the complete prohibition against taking undue advantage of his position. In a number of cases decided on this point the judiciary has taken view that if an advocate takes undue advantage of his position or ignorance, illiteracy or helplessness of the client, cheats them and thereby collects the money or serve any other purposes he would be guilty of fraudulent or grossly improper conduct.

In *M. Veerabhadra Rao* v. *Tek Chand,*[102] the appellant forged affidavit of the respondent and attested it on the basis of income tax clearance certificate. It facilitated registration of a sale deed in respect of which the licence consideration had not been paid to the respondent. Advocate was held guilty of professional misconduct by facilitating commission of fraud by becoming party to the forged document.

In *S.K. Nagar* v. *V.P. Jain,*[103] an advocate was engaged for the purpose of filing a suit which he never filed. He also gave false information and prepared false and fabricated document to convince client about pendency of case. He was found guilty of professional misconduct. In *R.N. Tewari* v. *Retan Shah,*[104] appellant advocate was defending the accused in the trial Court. Accused was sentenced to death against which he filed appeal before the High Court. He also filed a writ petition in the High Court along with his personal affidavit on behalf of the accused for better treatment. In his affidavit he had admitted that accused had shot dead the deceased. There was no instruction from the accused for doing so. He was found guilty of grave professional misconduct, as a lawyer should not play fraud upon his client. In *Brajendra Nath Bhargava* v. *Ramachandra Kasliwal*[105] the advocate played active part in suit property transferred in the names of their relatives by paying consideration from their own fund while representing. He was held guilty of professional conduct of

102. A.I.R. 1985 S.C. 28.
103. D.C. Appeal No. 14/1997 dated 31.7.1999.
104. D.C. Appeal No. 9/1999 dated 5.9.1999.
105. (1998)9 S.C.C.169.

infringement of Rules 9 and 22 of the Bar Council of India Rules.

Likewise in *Harischander Singh* v. *S.N. Tripathy,*[106] the appellant advocate was engaged by the complainant as a counsel to represent him in the consolidation proceedings. On the appellant's persuasion the complainant executed a mukhtarnama in favour of his junior. On the basis of such mukhtarnama the junior advocate executed a sale deed in respect of the complainant's land in favour of the appellant's father. The *kutumb register* showed that the appellant and his father were living in the same house.

It was held that the Disciplinary Committee was justified in taking the view that the complainant was duped by his advocate namely, the appellant who had misused the confidence reposed by the complainant in him and had tried to dispose of the property in favour of his own father. The sentence of suspension from practice for two years imposed on him cannot be treated to be harsh or grossly disproportionate in the light of the misconduct.

Again in *D.P. Chaddha* v. *Triyugi Narain Mishra,*[107] the respondent while himself busy in election campaign elsewhere had left with appellant advocate signed blank paper and blank Vakalatnama. Advocate misused them for a compromise detrimental to the interest of the complainant. He was held guilty of professional misconduct by the Supreme Court of India.

It is to be noted that in India an advocate combines the functions of that of a solicitor and a barrister in England. He does the solicitor's work and he pleads in court like barister. As he plays both the roles he must be subject to the disabilities of both. There would be nothing improper for a solicitor to advance moneys to his client for purposes of litigations but it would be improper for a barrister briefed by a solicitor to do so and the higher standard must be applied. By helping his client in this way the advocate acquires a personal interest in the litigation; in fact an actual interest in the subject-matter of the suit. This is surely not in keeping with the standard of

106. (1997)9 S.C.C. 694.
107. A.I.R. 2001 S.C. 457.

conduct which his profession demands of him. Hence it would be manifestly improper for a practitioner to advance money to a person for the purpose of the institution of a suit and it is difficult to see what difference there can be when money is advanced for the purpose of continuing litigation. Therefore, the only safe rule to lay down is that an advocate should not lend money to his client at any time for the purposes of an action in which he is engaged. He is also prohibited from purchasing the client's property.

The above position is affirmed by the courts in a catena of cases.[108] The courts have expressly prohibited an advocate from directly or indirectly bidding or purchasing either in his own name or in any other name, for his own or any other person benefit, any property sold in execution of a decree or order in any suit, appeal or other proceeding.[109]

The question that remains to be considered is whether the purchase by an advocate otherwise than in execution would be misconduct? The positive answer of this question was given by the Bar Council of India in the case of *Ajmer Singh* v. *Jagir Singh,*[110] wherein it was held that the act of purchase of client's property in his own name, when the title of property itself is the subject matter of pending litigation amounts to misconduct.

Even before the incorporation of this rule in the Bar Council of India Rules,[111] various High Courts had held that purchase of client's property amounted to misconduct. Thus, in *Quarban Ali Khan* v. *G., a pleader,*[112] the advocate was held guilty of professional misconduct, where he caused such property to be purchased by his own father. However, in that case, the advocate was not punished since the purchase was with the client's consent.[113] It is submitted that the above decision is erroneous because the standard of conduct was evolved for the preservation of the integrity of the profession

108. *Sheo Narain Lal* v. *Mir Amjad Ali,* 25 (Cr.L.J. 1151.
109. *New India Assurance Co. Ltd.* v. *A.K. Saksena,* A.I.R. 2004 S.C. 117.
110. D.C. Appeal No. 11/1998 of B.C.I, 22.09.2000.
111. It comes into existence in 1975.
112. A.I.R. 1938 Pat. 28.
113. The advocate was only reprimanded by the Patna High Court.

and therefore mere consent of client should not be sufficient to overcome such a *prima facie* suspicious conduct.

In *Sheo Narain Lal* v. *Ahmad Ali*,[114] the lawyer was found guilty of professional misconduct. In the instant case a legal practitioner who purchased Benami property in the name of another person and not only appeared as a legal practitioner in the legal proceedings regarding the property but also took his fee in his professional capacity in the courts, since he was really the *de facto* purchaser he committed an offence against property. He was found guilty of grossly improper conduct as a member of legal profession.

The Advocates Act expressly prohibit an advocate from doing anything whereby he abuses or takes advantage of the confidence reposed in him by his client. Summarising this issue in *P.D. Gupta* v. *Ram Murti*,[115] the Bar Council of India observed:

> "It is an acknowledged fact that a lawyer conducting the case of his client has a commanding status and can exert influence on his client. As a member of the Bar it is common knowledge that lawyers have started contracting with the clients and enter into bargain that in case of success he will share the result. A number of instances have been found in the cases of Motor Accident Claims. No doubt there is no bar for a lawyer to purchase property but on account of common prudence specially a law-knowing person will never prefer to purchase the property, the title of which is under doubt".

It is submitted that when a lawyer engages in a transaction with a client during the lawyer-client relationship and benefits thereby, in order to show that the benefit he received did not proceed from undue influence, he must prove that, *firstly*, he made a full and frank disclosure of all the relevant information that he had, *secondly*, the consideration was adequate, and *thirdly*, the client had independent advice before completing the transaction.

114. A.I.R. 1925 Oudh. 130.
115. (1997) 7 S.C.C. 147.

(f) Champertous Bargain

An agreement to share the benefit of client's litigation is called champerty. It is a bargain whereby a party is to assist another in recovering property and to share in the proceeds the action.[116]

Such conduct is offensive of the etiquette of legal profession and has been always condemned by the law and ethics. The Rules of Bar Council of India does not expressly uses the term 'champery' but provides that "an advocate shall not enter into arrangements whereby funds in his hands are converted into loan".[117] It further says that an advocate shall lend money to his client for the purpose of any action or legal proceedings in which he is engaged by such client.[118]

The purpose of the above rules is to maintain detachment and to ensure that the advocate must not get himself involved in the subject matter of the litigation. It is interesting to note that under the English law such agreements are struck down as illegal and void, on the ground of their being opposed to public policy, but the rigid English rules of champerty are not applicable in India.[119]

This point was considered as early as 1876 by the Privy Council in *Ram Coomar* v. *Chunder Cante,*[120] and since then it has never been doubted that the validity of champertous agreement under the Indian Law of Contract cannot be challenged on the technical grounds as they are understood under the English law. It may, however, be added that even though the English law of champerty and maintenance are not in force as specific laws in India, the judgement of the Privy Council in the aforesaid case itself emphasizes the fact that agreements of such kind ought to be carefully watched and when extortionate, unconscionable or made for improper object ought to be held invalid.

---

116. Advocates are some times tempted to enter into agreement with their clients regarding the subject matter of litigation. They finance the client in the litigation and agree that the expenses therefore would be reimbursed by the client later on
117. See Rule 31 of the Bar Council of India Rules.
118. *Id.*, Rule 32.
119. *Lala Ram Sarup* v. *Courts of Wards* I.L.R., 1940 Lah. 1 (P.C.)
120. 1876 (4) I.A. 23.

Relying on the above judgement, Privy Council once again, in *Raja Venkata Subhadrayamma Gaur* v. *Sree Pursapathi Venkatapati Raju,*[121] held that, in India courts will refuse to enforce Chamertous agreement only when they are found to be extortionate and unconscionable and not made with the *bonafide* object of assisting the claims of the person unable to carry on the litigation himself.

Thus, the both of the cases decided by the Privy Council depict that in India only those agreements which appear to be made for purposes of gambling and for injuring or oppressing others will not be enforced but not all agreements of champerty or maintenance.

However, with the passage of time and establishment of the Bar, the court changed their views and took more rigid approach on this point. *In the matter of G. Senior Advocate*[122], their Lordship of the Supreme Court condemned such type of agreement and held it as professional misconduct. In the instant case Mr. G., an advocate entered into an agreement with his client for his engagement stipulating that he would take 50% of the amount recovered through litigation.

Their Lordship of the Supreme Court observed:

> "It is highly reprehensible for an advocate to stipulate for, or receive a remuneration professional to the results of litigation or a claim whether in the form of a share in the subject matter, a percentage or otherwise. He will by so doing offend the rules of his profession and so render himself liable to the disciplinary jurisdiction of the court for professional misconduct".[123]

In *District Judge* v. *J.C. Gandhi,*[124] applying the above view on champertous agreement Bombay High Court ruled that an agreement between lawyer and client making payment of the lawyer's fee conditional upon the success of the suit and

121. 48, Mad. 230 (P.C.).
122. A.I.R. 1954 S.C. 557.
123. *Ibid.*, p. 559.
124. A.I.R. 1956 Bom. 739.

giving the lawyer the percentage of profit in the subject matter clearly constitutes professional misconduct.

The same view was expressed by a full bench of the Calcutta High Court *in the matter of an Advocate.*[125] Chief Justice Maclean, who delivered the principal judgment of the full bench, observed that it is professional misconduct for an advocate to agree with his client to accept as his fees a share of the property, fund or other matter in the litigation for his services as advocate in such litigation upon the successful issue thereof. Similarly, in the matter of in *R, an advocate*[126] a full bench of the Madras High Court has held that for an advocate to enter into a agreement by which he was to accept for his fees a certain proportion of the subject-matter of the suit amounted to professional misconduct of which the court would take serious notice. In this case there were two agreements which the advocate had made with his client. By the first agreement the advocate had undertaken the liability to maintain the client and carry on the litigation. But by the second he had merely agreed to receive for his fees a certain share in the proceeds of the litigation. His conduct was condemned not only in respect of the first agreement but also in respect of the second. The Punjab High Court expressed the same view in the matter of *Pleader of the Chief Court of Punjab*[127] and *Ganga Ram* v. *Debi Das.*[128]

(g) Advertisement and Solicitation

Profession of Law is firmly established on the strong winds of distorting commercialism, but, the winds of change that have been blowing by the forces of consumerism, and emerging globalised commercial culture are strong enough to overcome even the strongest of oppositions. Till the era of organized Bar in any part of the world, any form of advertisement[129] or solicitation[130] was considered abhorrent and unethical:

125. 4, Cal. L.J. 259.
126. A.I.R. 1939 Mad. 772.
127. 69, P.R. 1904.
128. 61, P.R. 1907.
129. Advertising is aimed at drawing attention of the Public and it is an advice for obtaining public favour of notoriety.
130. Solicitation.

The prime justification for the ban on the advertisement and solicitation is the potential adverse affect on professionalism. The rule against advertisement and solicitation has been given under Rule 36 of the Bar Council of India Rules, which prohibits all forms of such acts by saying that: An advocate shall not solicit work or advertise, either directly or indirectly, whether by circulars, advertisements, touts, communication, interview not warranted by personal furnishing or inspiring newspaper comments or produce photograph to be published in connection with cases in which he has been engaged or concerned. His sign board or name plate should be of reasonable size. The sign board or name plate or stationery should not indicate that he is or has been President or member of a Bar Council or any association or that he has been associated with any person, organization or with any particular cause or matter or specializes in any particular type of work or that he has been a Judge or an Advocate General.

Relying on the above Rule and nobility of the legal profession a five Judge Bench of the Supreme Court in the *matter of A, an Advocate,*[131] held that writing a postcard, to the Maharashtra Government, seeking briefs amounted to professional misconduct. The court observed:

"It was in utter disregard of truth. He has in this court, condemned himself as a liar and one who is either ignorant of the elementary rules of professional ethics or has no regard for them. In our opinion the advocate has mischosen his profession. Apparently he is a man of very weak moral caliber. If he is ignorant of the elementary rules of professional ethics he had demonstrated the inadequacy of training and education befitting a member of the profession of law. If he knew that it was highly improper to solicit brief and even then he wrote the post card in question, he is very unworthy member of the legal

131. A.I.R. 1962 S.C. 1337.

profession . . . by adopting the attitude of denial which has been demonstrated to be false in the course of the proceedings before the Tribunal, he has not deserved well of the court even in the matter of amount of punishment meted out to him. He fully deserves the punishment of suspension from practice for five years . . . *Let him learn that a lawyer must never be a liar"*.[132]

As advocacy is not a business it can be said that the Advocate is liable for misconduct if he advertises. It can be said that the Advocate is liable for misconduct if he advertises himself. It was held in *Kanepath Kaur* v. *Kasi Prasad Singh*,[133] that it is well recognized rule of etiquette in legal profession that no attempt should be made to advertise oneself directly or indirectly. Issuing of a circular, letters or election manifesto by a lawyer with his name, address and profession entered thereon and appealing for vote in Bar Council elections does not amount to misconduct but only a breach of professional etiquette.

Yet in a earlier case[134] the Allahabad High Court was also of the opinion that any attempt to advertise oneself directly or indirectly, tends to lower the dignity of the profession and amounts to touting, which is prohibited under the profession.

The above decisions found strong support in, *The Bar Council of Maharastra* v. *M.V. Dabholkar*,[135] wherein solicitation to seek work by snatching brief, standing at strategic places of Court and indulging in unedifying exhibition and advertisement had been held as violation of Rule 36 of the Bar Council of India. Rules and advocate indulged in such activities have been held guilty of professional misconduct.

Mr. Justice Krishna Iyer in his usual Judicial eloquence, came down heavily on idea of advertising and soliciting of legal service in following words:

132. *Id.*, p. 1341.
133. A.I.R. 1976 S.C. 106.
134. See, "The Matter of 13 Advocates of Allahabad High Court", A.I.R. 1934 All. 1067.
135. A.I.R. 1976 S.C. 242.

"The canons of ethics and propriety for legal profession totally taboo conduct by way of soliciting, advertising, scrambling and other obnoxious practices, subtle or clumsy for betterment of legal business. Law is not trade, briefs no merchandise and to the leaven of commercial competition or procurement should not vulgarise the legal profession.[136]

On this issue the Disciplinary Committee of the Bar Council of India is also of the view that advertisement and solicitation must not be allowed in the legal profession. In *J.N. Gupta* v. *D.C. Singhania and J.K. Gupta,*[137] respondent advocate made a publication in the International Bar Directory giving the names and addresses of their offices under the heading "Singhania & Company", "Firms Major Case" and "Representative Clients". The Bar Council of India found that the lone purpose of the publications was to give publicity to the fall that Singhania and Company have dealt with cases of importance and they have clients of eminence with a view to solicit more briefs and attract more clients.

Such publications were held to offend Rule 36 of the Bar Council of India Rules of Standards of Professional Conduct and Etiquette prohibiting advertisement and solicitation in any manner of a person of the legal profession.

It is evidently clear from perusal of the above case that in legal profession any attempt of advertising and soliciting amounts to professional misconduct in India. Though, in *Tata Press Limited* v. *Mahanagar Telephones Limited,*[138] the Supreme Court of India extended the protection provided under Article 19(1)(a) to commercial speech and advertising, but it is submitted that the above decision was not directly related to advertisement by advocate, and keeping in view that advocacy is not a business the advertisement should not be allowed in the legal profession.

However, it is interesting to note that although in United States Canon 27 of the American Bar Association severely

136. *Ibid.*
137. B.C.I.T.R. case no. 38/1994 dated 15.07.1997.
138. A.I.R. 1995 S.C. 2438.

restricted lawyer's right to advertise, but limited right to advertise is still permitted that is why the ratio of the decisions delivered by American Supreme Court in *Bates and another* v. *State Bar of Arizona*,[139] *Oharlik* v. *Ohio State Bar Association*[140] and in *Zaudere* v. *Office of Disciplinary Council of Supreme Court of Ohio*,[141] reveals that there are hardly any instances of imposing formal sanctions against act of self-publicity.

Likewise in England, the issue of advertising has been regulated under the Solicitor's Practice Rules, 1990 and the Solicitor's Publicity Code, 1990, which permit to advertise, provided that they do not compromise their independence and integrity.[142] Their plea in support of this campaign for advocate's advertisement is that this is an age of consumerism and hence we live in the usual mercantile methods for attracting their consumers, i.e. clients, the commercial means of advertisement by lawyer should be allowed.

It is submitted that there is basic difference between goods merchandise and the profession of law. To quote Mr. Justice M.C. Chagala:

> "In business your sole object is to make money. You owe no duty or obligation to any one except to yourself. You determine the means to achieve your aims and there are no standards to limit or restrict your actions. But in the profession you have traditions to which you have to be true".[143]

Moreover, lawyer's service for the cause of Legal Aid programme is also different from commercial attitude. In this programme he renders his services to the clients not out of commercial but social motive for indigent litigants. Similarly, a lawyer serves the court freely as *amicus curiae*.

---

139. 433 U.S. 350 (1977).
140. 436 U.S. 477 (1978).
141. 471 U.S. 626 (1985).
142. In England Baristers are prohibited from writing to Solicitors or even to brother practitioners, explaining his service, experience, ability or work.
143. Quoted from G. Geethisha, "Professional Misconduct by Advocates", 2003 C.U.L.R., p. 156.

Thus, in India advertisement and solicitation of legal profession has not allowed any advocate to advertise his profession to compete with fellow advocate within the knowledge of the public and denigrate the noble and learned profession of law into an ordinary commercial merchandise goods selling business.

(h) Carrying on Other Business

If a man enters the profession of law as an advocate, he must make up his mind to conduct the business of an advocate and nothing else. He is expected to fully devote his time for legal profession. To ensure it, restrictions are imposed on other employments or engagements by the Advocate. Rule 47 of the Bar Council of India Rules, expressly prohibits to carrying any other business along with the practice of legal profession. But certain exceptions have been recognized in this regard.

An advocate can participate in academic activities and also take up part-time teaching of legal and non-legal subjects,[144] but he cannot run any business simultaneously with legal profession. Similarly, charging fee for sitting as an ordinary director of a company is not misconduct under Section V Rule 41 of the Bar Council of India. But if the advocate becomes managing partner or secretary of a company he is liable for breach of his duty contemplated under Rule 44 of Section V of the Bar Council of India. Thus, *In re, a pleader,*[145] Chief Justice Leach of the Madras High Court held that a pleader can act as legal advisor of a company of which he is director, but he cannot act as a promoter or hold the seat of secretary. When a pleader acts as an insurance agent, it is injurious to the interest of the public and therefore, he was guilty of professional misconduct.[146] In the *matter of S, a Pleader, Raghunathpur,*[147] a pleader had been trying to run two businesses at the same time, the business of a pleader and the business of an insurance agent. It was held that such a practice

144. Gaur, K.D., "Professional Responsibilities of Lawyers", 9 C.U.L.R. 297, p. 314 (1985).
145. A.I.R. 1943 Mad. 665.
146. A.I.R. 1984 S.C. 110, p. 114.
147. I.L.R. 15, Pat. 175.

was, in the highest degree, injurious to the interest of the profession and to the interest of the public and that the pleader was guilty of professional misconduct.

Likewise, in *Babulal* v. *Subhash Jain,*[148] a practising lawyer was also working as an editor, printer and publisher of a weekly called "Aaj Ki Janta", and was owner of the press, which executed printing. He was held guilty of professional misconduct for violation of Rule 47 of the Bar Council of India.[149]

The views taken in the above cases by the different judicial agencies reveal that carrying on of a trade or business is ordinarily inconsistent with practice of the legal profession. Therefore, the conduct of a practising lawyer to become a *partner in firm,*[150] carrying a *Grocery and Provisions Store,*[151] *carrying Photocopy Center,*[152] *P.C.O.,*[153] *Taxi business*[154] also have been held as professional misconduct by the various High Courts as well as the Supreme Court.

However, in *N.A.H.* v. *M.R.S.*[155] the complaint was that the advocate had obtained licence for running an arrack shop in his name in 1985-86 and he carried on the sale of arrack while practicing as an advocate. The advocate contended that he had obtained licence in his name as he belonged to the ruling AIDMK party and that the licence was obtained for the benefit of his father. He expressed his regrets about what had already been done. In this case the complainant stated that though he had no grievance personally, he made a complaint as the dignity of the profession has become so low in the eyes of the public. The Disciplinary Committee of State Bar Council observed that lending the name in getting licence for running

148. B.C.I. T.R. case no. 115/1986, dated 2.2.1997.
149. *Babulal* v. *Subhash Jain, B.C.I.TR.* case no. 115/1986, dated : 2.02.1997.
150. In the matter of B, an Advocate, A.I.R. 1935 All. 1023.
151. In the matter of Ramachandra Jayannadh Mundade, A.I.R. 1956 Bom. 174.
152. A.I.R. 2000 S.C. 47.
153. *Yadhav J.S.* v. *Mustafa Fiazi,* A.I.R. 1993 S.C. 1535.
154. *Pawan Kumar Sharma* v. *Gurudial Singh,* A.I.R. 1999 S.C.
155. B.C.I.T.R. case no. 45/2004 dated 5.4.2006.

arrack shop, while practising as an advocate is inconsistent with the dignity of the legal profession and it amounted to professional misconduct. The advocate was suspended from practice for 5 years.

On appeal, the Bar Council of India preferred to take a lenient view, saying that ends of justice would be served if the advocate is reprimanded.

Again in *D. Saibaba* v. *Bar Council of India*[156] a handicapped advocate charged with professional misconduct of running a S.T.D. booth was debarred by the Bar Council. The Apex Court taking a sympathetic view that the advocate was handicapped and could not clear the arrears in time restored his licence as he produced proof of surrendering the same.

Recently, in *Madhav M. Bhakarikar* v. *Ganesh M. Bhakarikar,*[157] the issue was whether an advocate who secured a dealership of retail Petrol Pump and also entered into a partnership with his brother agreeing to be a sleeping partner, can be allowed to plead the same to get over the bar under rule 47? The Supreme Court allowed the matter to be remanded to the State Bar Council observing that the advocate had already suffered 5 years suspension, but held that advocate carrying on any business is guilty of professional misconduct.

(i) Touting

The term 'tout' is used in a common parlance in order to confer on it a meaningful context.[158] Accordingly, it refers to such a category of personnel as are utilized by advocates to get business on payment of a share of fees received by them from their clients.

However, in commercial life, or other competitive intercourse it may not be morally wrong to pay a portion of the benefits to a person who fetches the business. But in the legal profession, the practice of toutism is strictly prohibited. Touting or employment of touts is not consistent with the rule

156. A.I.R. 2003 S.C. 2502..
157. A.I.R. 2004 S.C. 1877.
158. Touts are persons who procure business in consideration of Commission Moving from Legal Practitioners.

36 of the Bar Council of India Rules and contrary to the professional heritage of the Bar. So to do or cause to do or allow to be done anything for the purpose of touting directly or indirectly constitutes professional misconduct.

In the matter of Peary Moha Ghoo,[159] it was held that a pleader who pay commission to a mukhtar, instructing him was guilty of professional misconduct. Likewise giving present or sending notices to solicitors and other notifying his intention to practice in particular branch of law and offering percentage of fee has also held professional misconduct.[160]

Thus, it is the tradition of Bar that the lawyer should not seek business but that business must seek the lawyer. So the lawyer must not apply others to weight his capacity, he must wait until his merits are discovered and appreciated, because employment of touts will brings discredit to advocate and immediate gain will result into continuous loss. The judiciary always condemn this practice.

In re Jaikishan, an Advocate,[161] a villager, Jailal, who went to Patiala with a letter of introduction from his pleader at lower court to Amarnath, an advocate. He straightway went to the High Court from Railway station. He met one, Baldev Kishan, a declared tout, and enquired about the address of Amarnath. The tout offered to take him to Amarnath, but took him to the house of another Advocate, Jaikishan. The brief, along with the required fees, was handed over to Jaikishan. Subsequently, Jailal came to know about the mischief played by the tout in getting him engaged to a different lawyer. Jailal identified the tout and complained against him to the President of the Bar Association. Jailal and Amarnath filed a joint complaint under Section 420 of the Indian Penal Code. The tout was convicted and sentenced to six months R.I. He had already been arrested and convicted for cheating earlier.

On the question of accepting employment through a tout declared by the High Court it was held that the Advocate committed professional misconduct and deserved to be suspended.

159. 11 B.L.R. 312
160. *Ibid.*
161. A.I.R. 1954 (pep). 47.

Evil of deviling is a meanance and has been growing now like a cancer and our unified bar till today did not take step to eradicate evil of touting or to ameliorate the conditions of the members of the Bar.

Mr. Justice Sen of the Supreme Court in *Poona Collectorate Bar Case,*[162] observed:

> "we are constrained to say that evil of touting has been in existence since ancient times and still is a growing menance and the bar is open to accusation of having done nothing tangible to eradicate. This is unmitigated evil. Some lawyers may well expound unblushingly the doctrine of getting on, getting honour and at last getting honest. If it is generally known that a person however honest has get on and get honour through the patronage of touts, the bar should decline to show such a man any honour of consideration whatsoever".

Thus, it is submitted that keeping in view the fact that 'law is a profession not trade or business', the Bar Council of India should take strong action to eradicate the practice of touting. This would lead to a high standard of propriety and professional rectitude which would make it impossible for a tout to turn a penny within the precincts of the law Court.

(j) Seeking Money from Client to Bribe the Judge

Bribe to any one itself is an act punishable under the law. Hence, being a member of honourable profession it is expected to an advocate that he took himself far away from using this tactics. If a lawyer collects money from his client for the purpose of paying it as bribe to obtain judgement in his client's favour his conduct is highly unprofessional and he is guilty of professional misconduct.

It is worth to note that to bribe the Judge is not only an act which is inconsistent with rule 3 of the Bar Council of India Rules,[163] it also amounts to betrayal of justice if the advocate

162. A.I.R. 1984 S.C. 110, p. 114.
163. An Advocate shall not influence the decision of a court by any illegal or improper means, private communications with a Judge relating to a pending case are forbidden.

manages the result by such means. In a case[164] legal practitioner advised his clients to offer the conclusion of the case in which they had been acquitted to present some gratification to the Magistrate, who decided the case. It was held by the Patna High Court that conduct on the part of advocate was disgraceful and the practitioner was liable to be suspended from practice for three years.

However, the cases are to be decided in facts and circumstances of each case. Where an advocate receives money for bringing the police officer an acts as a go between in the matter, his conduct was held grossly improper in discharge of his profession duty.[165] But where a practitioner was suspected of having bribed the record keeper and to have attempted to remove certain words from a document, it was held that the conduct had no bearing to the professional duties of the practitioner and, therefore, instead of taking disciplinary action against him there should have been trial and conviction for the criminal offence.

It is important to note that in the such type of cases the Bar Council of India and State Bar Councils can also take disciplinary action under Section 35 of the Advocates Act, 1961 after the decision of a regular Court's finding that he was guilty of any offence punishable under any law of the land.[166]

In *Chandrashekher Soni* v. *Bar Council of Rajasthan,*[167] the Supreme Court of India observed that offering of bribe or giving bribe or taking money from the client for the purpose of giving bribe to Judge amounts to grave professional misconduct. In the instant case, the complainant and his wife were assaulted and received injuries on head and were examined by a doctor who referred them to a Radiologist. The Radiologist sent a report to the station house officer stating that he found nothing abnormal in the X-ray plate of the complainant, but from the X-ray plate of complainant's wife he suspected fracture of skull and suggested that he should refer

164. *In the matter of Babu Awadh Bihari Lal,* A.I.R. 1932 Pat. 356.
165. In the matter of 'V', an advocate, A.I.R. 1935 Rang. 178.
166. See, Section 35 of the Advocates Act, 1961, Disciplinary Committee can take action, also in other misconducts.
167. A.I.R. 1983 S.C. 1012.

the matter to a specialist. The appellant approached the complainant with X-ray plates and promised to get a favourable report and said that Rs. 300 had to be paid to the Radiologist. Later on receiving his letter the Radiologist sent another report to the station house officer stating that there was evidence of fracture of the skull.

The State Bar Council and also the Bar Council of India held that appellant was guilty of professional misconduct and suspended him from practice for three years. The appellant preferred second appeal to the Supreme Court. Supreme Court also upheld the findings of the Disciplinary Committee, but reduced the sentence of suspension from three years to one year.

It is interesting to note that for a member of the Bar to suggest only that an official or any one is prone to be affected by such act also constitutes the said misconduct. In *Shambhu Ram Yadav* v. *Hanuman Das Khatry*,[168] an advocate wrote to his client that his another client had told him that the concerned Judge accepted bribe and either he should influence the Judge through someone himself or send him Rs. 10,000 so that the suit got decided in his favour. The conduct of advocate was irresponsible and amounted to professional misconduct.

(iii) Professional Misconduct in Relation to the Court

The advocates are considered as an important wheel the chariot of Justice. They are also recognized as an officer of the court. That is the reason why the Rule 1 of the Bar Council of India Rules provides certain duties of the advocates in relation to the court. The underlying purpose of these duties to the court is to enforce appropriate behaviour by the advocates so as to achieve the goal of just operation of the legal system.[169] *G. Geethisha* has classified these duties into five categories namely, duty of disclosure, duty not to abuse the court process, duty not to corrupt the administration of Justice, duty to conduct cases efficiently and duty to respect the court.[170]

168. A.I.R. 2001 S.C. 2509.
169. David (J), "Lawyers' Duties to the Court", 114 L.Q.R. 63, p. 6 (1998).
170. G. Geethisha, "Professional Misconduct by Advocates", C.U.L.R. 2003, p. 204.

Any violation of these duties amounts to professional misconduct. A study of the same is presented here:

(a) Misleading the Court

An advocate is obliged to act honestly in all positive statements he makes in the court room. The duty of confidentiality owed to the client is subjected to the duty of disclosure owed to the court. Both non-disclosure and disclosure of wrong fact or law is not expected from an advocate. Therefore, it is hardly necessary to say that it is the part of the etiquette of the advocate to tell only true in the court and should never give perjured evidence on behalf of their client. Thus, the conduct of an advocate who makes palpably false statement recklessly or knowingly is reprehensible and tantamounts to moral depravity, amounts to professional misconduct.

In *D.P. Chadha* v. *Triyugi Narain Mishra,*[171] the Supreme Court of India found the deliquent lawyer guilty of professional misconduct for deliberately attempting to mislead court into accepting position that personal presence of parties was not a mandatory requirement for verification of compromise. It was observed by the Apex Court that a lawyer must not hesitate in telling the court the correct position of law when it is undisputed and admits of no exception. He is not entitled to drag a settled and non-controversial point of law into doubt solely to mislead or confuse court so as to gain an unfair advantage for his client.

It is interesting to note that "suppression of truth" which is called "Offence of Perjury" in England always involves moral turpitude in varying degrees depending upon the particular facts of each case. Thus, *in the matter of M, a first grade pleader,*[172] in answer to a notice from the Bar Association the practitioner had falsely stated that he had dispensed with the service of a 'Tout' he had engaged and struck to that statement, in subsequent inquiry. It was held that advocate was guilty of professional misconduct.

171. (2001) 2 S.C.C. 221.
172. 214 P.L.R. 1915 (F.B.).

Again *In the matter of District Judge,*[173] the legal practitioner had committed a technical offence but instead of admitting it frankly he told unnecessary lies and shuffled in a very discreditable manner and thereby aggravated his offence. The High Court taking a serious view of the matter suspended him for a period of two years. Where a bail application having been refused by the Session Judge the practitioner made another application for the same purpose to the District Magistrate without informing him about the previous application, he was held guilty of professional misconduct.[174] In *Smt. Suresh Rani* v. *Munish Chandra Goel,*[175] respondent advocate signed as a witness in agreements of sale of plots a land sold by his father-in-law and received consideration money by way of compromise decree in 11 suits filed by 11 complainants. Complainants constructed houses on their plots. Thereafter respondent advocate filed eviction suits showing all complainants as tenants. He was held guilty of professional misconduct for having failed in his duty towards the court by suppressing fact of decrees which were known to him before as he was an advocate in the earlier cases and had received decretal amount.

Again in *Chandrika Prasad* v. *State of Madhya Pradesh,*[176] an advocate filed a writ petition knowing well that earlier identical writ had been dismissed before another Bench. He was held guilty of professional misconduct by the Madhya Pradesh High Court.

The aforesaid decisions depict that disclosure of wrong fact is professional misconduct on the part of advocates but it is interesting to note that even non disclosure of fact may constitute professional misconduct too. In *Ratnamma* v. *Abdul Khader,*[177] while ordering to suspend delinquent advocate, the Andhra Pradesh High Court held that it is professional misconduct for an advocate to apply for a succession certificate in the name of the daughter of the deceased without

173. A.I.R. 1930 Pat. 493.
174. B.C.I.T.R. case no. 43/1995 dated 9.12.1998.
175. B.C.I.T.R. case no. 48/1996 dated 9.1.2.1998.
176. A.I.R. 1983 S.C. 1012.
177. A.I.R. 2005 A.P. 736.

reference to the widow when he well knew the fact that both were interested in the matter.

Thus, there can be no justification at all for not speaking the truth. The fact that a man is going to be injured professionally if he does speak the truth is no valid excuse for telling a lie.

(b) Corrupting the Administration of Justice

More than 100 years ago it was said that "Counsel's signature on a pleading is a voucher that the case is not a mere fiction.[178] Therefore, making false statement in pleading,[179] giving false certificate to a person,[180] giving false identification,[181] etc. amounts to professional misconduct. Further swearing of untrue affidavit or documents is perhaps the obvious example of conduct, which a lawyer cannot knowingly permit.

It is also extremely objectionable and serious offence on the part of a legal practitioner to temper with the court's record. Hence it has been held *in the matter of pleader*[182], that where the clerk of a legal practitioner alters the record to conceal error, due to carelessness and the alteration is initiated by the legal practitioner without inquiry or care, though bonafide, the legal practitioner was guilty of professional misconduct. Where a member of the legal profession added to the names, that were already entered in the Vakalatnama, his own name and also altered certain words in the content of vakalatnama, it was held by the Calcutta High Court that his conduct was within the four corners of the term professional misconduct.[183] Tempering with Court's record and documents or alteration of the same is a serious matter and when it is done by an advocate who got facilities to deal with them, in

---

178. Great Abrelian Gold Mining Co. v. Martin (1877)$_5$ Ch.D.1.
179. *Gurucharan Kaur* v. *Devakinandan Kaur,* A.I.R. 1920 All. 212.
180. *Jadubansi Sahay* v. *Barhamdeo Narayan Singh,* A.I.R. 1960 Mad. 268.
181. *Mrs. Ratnamam Breganya* v. *Abdul Khader Kureshi,* A.I.R. 1959(1) Anwr 137.
182. I.L.R. 15 Pat. 175.
183. In the Matter of Purna Chandra Chetterji, 17 C.W.N. 328.

view of its position for handling such records his conduct cannot be easily excused.

It is interesting to note that in such circumstances the rigid rule of guilty mind or 'intention' which is the basis of criminal law shall not be applicable and advocate may be punished even without intention. Thus, in *Secretary of State* v. *Jogendra Chandra Das*[184] wherein a mukhtar after filing the petition under Sec. 144 Cr. P.C. into the court discovered that he made a mistake in description of the court and instead of filing a new petition for amendment, he made a correction in the petition already filed. The act of mukhtar was held reprehensible though there was lack of malafide intention. *In the matter of B, a Pleader of Gaya,*[185] a pleader of decree holder made correction in an execution petition filed by him after the attachment was made and after the papers became part and parcel of the court record. It was held as professional misconduct. His lordship Fazal Ali, J., in course of the judgement held:

> "It is perhaps true that the pleader had no malafide intention in the sense that he did not try to get any under advantage over his adversary and made the corrections probably with a view to avoid any objection being raised by the judgement debtor in future; but at the same time it cannot be overlooked that to tamper with public records is a serious matter and when it is done by a pleader who has particular facilities afforded to him by reason of his position for handling such records, the conduct cannot be excused".

In the aforesaid circumstances the lawyer must assist and advise his client as to the latter's bounden duty in that matter. But what if the lawyer believes initially that original affidavit is true, but before the trial discovers that it was untrue? In such situations lawyer has to advise the client that the opponent's lawyer must be informed of the omitted documents and if this course is not assented to, he must cease

184. A.I.R. 1926 Cal. 223.
185. A.I.R. 1936 Pat. 418.

to act for the client. Otherwise the conduct of lawyer would be considered as professional misconduct. The judiciary has to take into consideration the facts of each case. In view of the matter it has concluded committal of professional misconduct in a number of cases. Thus, *an act of Cheating the client,*[186] *giving false information to the court,*[187] *misleading the court,*[188] *giving false certificate,*[189] *forged signature,*[190] *baseless charge against public officer,*[191] *instituting false cases*[192] are also considered as corrupting the administration of justice which has been held professional misconduct by the various High Courts and also the Supreme Court of India.

(c) Disrespect to the Court

Rule 2 of the Bar Council of India Rules, provides that "an advocate shall maintain towards the court a respectful attitude bearing in mind that the dignity of a judicial office is essential for survival of a free community. So it is most irregular and unfair for members of the legal profession to make personal attack or make reckless and unfounded charges of corruptions and improper imputations against court.

While the act of disrespect to the court is also considered as contempt of court thus, this point will be discussed later in this chapter.

(B) Other Misconducts Committed by Advocates

It is well established that the court has a right to expect a higher standard of loyalty to the advocates than ordinary man of the society. That is why section 35 of the Advocates Act covers not only the professional misconduct but the other misconducts too. It means any conduct of advocate which in

186. *N.B. Mirzan* v. *D.C. Bar Council,* A.I.R. 1972 S.C. 46
187. *Emperor* v. *Jodh Singh,* A.I.R. 1923 Lah. 211.
188. V.C. Rangadurai v. D. Gopalan (1979), S.C.C. 1054.
189. *Vijay Singh* v. *Murari Lal,* A.I.R. 1979 S.C. 1712.
190. *D.P. Chandha* v. *Triyugi Narain Mishra* A.I.R. 2001 S.C. 457.
191. In the matter of 'K', A.I.R. 1934, Pat. 518.
192. *M. Veerabhadra Rao* v. *Tek Chand,* A.I.R. 1985 S.C. 28.

any way renders him unfit for the exercise of his noble profession may be subject matter of Advocates Act, 1961. What court has to consider in all these cases, is the conduct of the advocates, and its affect on their profession and position.

The conduct involved in professional misconduct comes as primary conduct before the Bar Council. However, in other misconduct cases it comes as secondary. The prime distinction between professional misconduct and other misconduct is that in former case the conduct of advocate must be directly related to his profession, which attracts the motion of disciplinary committee either on basis of complaint or *suo-motu.*[193] In such cases Bar Council may refer the matter to the disciplinary committee and award punishment accordingly. But in latter case, i.e. other misconduct, the conduct of advocate may not be directly related to his profession. However, keeping in view the nobility of profession and section 35 of the Act, disciplinary committee can take action in these cases also. In such cases misconduct firstly has to proved before a regular court of law and depending upon conviction or otherwise the committee of Bar Council deals with matter.

In a catena of cases several conducts of the advocates have been held as a misconduct which is not directly related with profession. Some of them are as under:

(i) **Obscene Behaviour**

It is said that a lawyer should be a gentleman first. Any obscene speech or behaviour of the advocate may invite action. In, *P.B. Jog* v. *The Bar Council of Maharastra,*[194] an advocate who was also a Deputy Mayor of a Municipal Corporation, at a public meeting addressed by him used extremely obscene and vulgar language. He was convicted under Sections 294 and 153 of the Indian Penal Code. The Bar Council of Maharastra initiated *suo-motu* action for speech under section 35 of the Advocates Act, 1961. Advocate made objections that his speech was not made in capacity of an advocate but as the Deputy Mayor and his conduct did not amount to misconduct within the perview of Advocates Act, 1961.

193. For more discussion on deterrence between these two terms see, *P.J. Ratnem* v. *Kanikam,* A.I.R. 1964 S.C. 22.

194. D.C. Appeal No. 10/1970 (1972 J.B.C.I., 105).

Rejecting his objections Disciplinary Committee of the Bar Council of India held him guilty and ruled:

> "the misconduct in respect of which the Bar Council has jurisdiction need not necessarily relate to professional matters. The same test as to conduct as is applicable to moral man generally, applies to the conduct of an advocate. Lawyer's position in society is unique in this, that the things that man in a free society holds dearest on earth—their fortunes, reputations, domestic peace, the future of their dearest and nearest, why their liberty and life itself they confide to the integrity of their legal advisors. The public image of propriety must not only be without stain but without room for suspicion".[195]

Likewise in *U.N. ... Appellant* v. *B.C.M. ... Respondent,*[196] appellant advocate gave a speech exhorting the people of the country to collect arms and go for a direct-armed conflict against the government established by law. She was convicted and sentenced under different sections of Indian Penal Code. The Bar Council of Maharastra issued a show cause notice to her and thereafter held her guilty of misconduct. In *Smt. Farida Choudhry* v. *Dr. Achyut Kumar Thakuria,*[197] an advocate not having good relations with complainant—neighbour, filed a false case against her. With a view to harm her reputation he wrote to the employees in the department obscene letter and he also wrote letters to her containing vulgar and obscene language with remark and sketches and pictures in his own writings. The Bar Council of India held him guilty of other misconduct as his conduct was unbecoming of an advocate.

(ii) Criminal Conduct

When a person enters into the noble legal profession, he undertakes faithfully to maintain the existing law and to assist in its enforcement. No reputable advocate would claim to be entitled to assist in breach of the law for the sake of his client's

195. *Ibid.,* p. 109.
196. D.C. Appeal No. 45, 1974, Vol. 15, 1988, I.B.R. 182.
197. B.C.I.T.R. case no. 1/1993, dated 11.09.1999.

interest. His personal behaviour should also be as obedient of law. If he did anything against the law of land he will be guilty of other misconduct under section 35 of the Advocates Act, 1961.

Where an advocate is found guilty of criminal conduct finally under Criminal Procedure Code, then Bar Council of India can also take disciplinary action against him. To initiate disciplinary proceedings against him in the circumstances and the evidence on record in the criminal proceedings, it must be proved that offence alleged to have been committed is one which implies a defect of character which unfits him to be an advocate. There are variety of instances wherein the courts reached on the conclusion that advocate was guilty of others' misconduct.

Thus, in *Saiyed Anwar Abbas* v. *Shri Krisna Singh and two other*,[198] the complainant had filed a suit. An advocate sought adjournment on behalf of other. Complainant raised objection against it stating that advocate had no authority to move such application. Outside the court room respondent Advocate and his colleagues manhandled the complainant. In District Bar Office, they also surrounded him and exhorted him saying *"Agar Aaj Ke Bad Yhan Dikhayee Diye To Tange Torwa Dunga"* FIR was lodged for the same.

In disciplinary proceedings before the Disciplinary Committee of the State Bar Council respondents took the plea that their conduct did not fall within the ambit of section 35 of the Advocates Act as it related to private affairs and not with professional duty. States Bar Council did not take decision within a year therefore, matter reached to the Bar Council of India. Holding respondent advocates guilty of other misconduct, the Bar Council of India said:

> "Lawyers being the members of the noble profession are supposed to behave like gentlemen with the litigants or any other persons inside the court room while conducting the proceeding and also outside the court. They are not supposed to take law into their own hands even if they

198. B.C.I.R.R. case no. 62/1991 dated 14.05.2000.

are provoked by anybody while dealing with the cases inside the court or outside".[199]

In this regard a question arises whether conviction for an offence under criminal law itself be evidence of other misconduct under section 35 of the Advocates Act? There are difference of opinion on this point. In *Advocate-General of Bombay* v. *Phiroz Rustomji Bharucha*.[200] In *the matter of N, an Advocate,*[201] and *in Re a pleader*[202] criminal offence were held as evidence of misconduct. But it was held by the Madras High Court *in Bar Council, Madras* v. *K. Raghavaiah,*[203] that the rule that conviction for an offence under criminal law itself be evidence of other misconduct could not be applied merely to a departmental enquiry. All criminal offences do not necessarily call for disciplinary measures.

It appears from the view taken by the Madras High Court that propriety of the conviction cannot be considered in disciplinary proceedings, before the State Bar Councils or the Bar Council of India. It is submitted that while deciding the other misconduct nature of offence and special fact of the case should always be taken into consideration for the disciplining the lawyers.

Thus, where an advocate was convicted and sentenced with rigorus imprisonment under section 165-A of the Indian Penal Code, he must be declared guilty of other misconduct.[204]

Likewise, a legal advisor to Maharastra State Road Transport Corporation was convicted by a special Judge, Bombay for illegal gratification under section 161 of the Indian Penal Code. He was sentenced to nine months rigorous imprisonment with fine. His appeal was rejected. Leave to special appeal to the Supreme Court was also rejected. About eight months after serving out imprisonment, the advocate

199. *Ibid.*
200. A.I.R. 1935 P.C. 168.
201. A.I.R. 1936 Cal. 158.
202. A.I.R. 1946 Mad. 247.
203. A.I.R. 1964 Mad. 488.
204. *Ishwar Bapuji* v. *Disciplinary Committee of Bar Council of Maharastra,* D.C. Appeal No. 11/1971 Vol. (1) 1972 J.B.C.I. 111.

started practice. The Disciplinary Committee of the Bar Council of India, held that the conduct of advocate was highly depreciable and deplorable, deserving deterrent punishment.

Similarly, and act of *Moral turpitude,*[205] *misappropriation of money,*[206] *inciting others to break the law,*[207] *organized breach of peace,*[208] *incitement to acts,*[209] *tending to subvert the law and order*[210] are also held misconduct though they are not directly related to the professional duty under the Rules of Bar Council of India.

(iii) ***Sexual Misbehaviour***

In, *Bar Council of the State of Andhra Pradesh* v. *Sri G. Lingareddy*[211] an advocate who was widower took shelter as tenant in house of his colleague advocate's brother who gave him front room in his house for his office and residence and their after was giving him Rs. 3 for his daily expenses. One day when landlord went out along with his two children in evening and his wife remained alone, respondent advocate knowing well that she was alone entered the room, bolted the door of the main hall and attempted to committed rape on her. He was convicted under sections 450, 376 read with sections 511, 354 and 323 of the Indian Panel Code.

The disciplinary committee of Andhra Pradesh State Bar Council held it as a clear case of other misconduct within the meaning of Section 35 of the Advocates Act, 1961.

Likewise in *Kamal Prasad Mishra* v. *Methilal,*[212] complainant engaged the appellant advocate in a case. He filed vakalatnama in the court of Munsif, Gonda. Advocate required Rs. 20,000, complainant agreed to pay by going out of station for earning the money and keep on sending money. Complainant went to Ludhiana for earning money and keep

205. *In the matter of Barrister at law,* I.L.R. 15 Lah. 354.
206. *Shambhu Ram Yadav* v. *Hanuman Das Khatry,* A.I.R. 2001 SC 2509.
207. *Local Government* v. *N.B. Despande,* (32) Cr.L.J. 604 (Nag.)
208. *Ibid.*
209. *In the matter of Mahadev Singh, Vakil,* A.I.R. 1923 Pat. 185.
210. *In Re, Harbux Raj,* A.I.R. 1931, Sind, 33.
211. C.C. No. 3/1968 Vol. (2) J.B.C.I., 461.
212. D.C. Appeal No. 45/2000 dated 15.12.2004.

on sending money from there for two year. During this period the advocate developed illicit relation with the wife of complainant and kept her as his concubine along with sons of the complainant in his house. The appellant advocate in connivance with the wife and sons of the complainant declared him dead in the record. It was held that the advocate was guilty of misconduct.

But in another case[213] before the Bar Council of India, an advocate however had been found guilty of attempt to rape of his client's wife; but no action had been taken against him, and he was simply reprimanded. Though the Bar Council of India thought that it was the case called for drastic action of removal of name of the advocate from rolls. But it could not resist itself from clarifying its soft approach "It is always open to reinstate the advocate on prayer of that he is a changed man and fit to be admitted into profession.

(iv) Physical Assault

Being itself an offence, physical assault is another instance of other misconduct. In N... Petitioner V. S... Respondent,[214] an advocate abused the complainant and assaulted her by tearing her blouse and snatching the saree to force ejectment from the house of his client-relative. Again at night the opposite party advocate went to the residence of the complainant along with 2-3 companions. He was fully drunk and started abusing the complainant and her family members. The Bar Council of India held him guilty of other misconduct, as he had gone to the extend of identifying himself with the interest of his client and giving threats and assaulting the client at residence of the complainant.

In *Hikmat Ali Khan* v. *Ishwar Prasad Arya,*[215] the advocate assaulted his opponent with a knife. A Pistol shot was also said to have been fired by him at the time of incident. He was prosecuted for offence under section 307 of the Indian Penal Code and section 25 of the Arms Act and was sentenced to undergo rigorous imprisonment for three years for the offence

213. III. J.B.C.I. 461 (1973).
214. B.C.I.T.R Case no. 9/1983, Vol. 12(4) 1985 I.B.R. 528.
215. A.I.R. 1986 Pat. 65.

under section 307 I.P.C. and for nine months for offence under section 25 Arms Act.

Mr. Justice S.C. Agrawal of the Supreme Court of India held that the conduct of advocate was unbecoming and of serious nature. The punishment of removal of the name from the roll was held to be appropriate.

(v) Abuse of Privileges

The Advocate Act, 1961 confers certain rights and privileges to the practising advocates, but misuse of the same are not permitted. Where an advocate abuses, his rights and privileges provided by the said Act, he becomes guilty of misconduct.

However, an advocate has right to put any question to his client and their opponent, but where an advocate is in habit of putting scandalous and obscene questions to women witness say victims of rape despite warnings from the court, amounts to professional and other misconduct under section 35 of the Act.

In *Shiv Narayana Jafe* v. *Hon'ble Judges of Allahabad High Court*[216] one Ganesh was prosecuted under Sec. 376 of I.P.C. for an attempt to commit rape upon a chamar woman, Himman. Shiv Narain Jafe was the Advocate at the trial. The Assistant Sessions Judge complained to the High Court against the Advocate on several charges. The main charge being that he was habituated to putting scandalous and obscene questions to woman witnesses like Himman, in the course of cross-examination, which were indecent and unnecessary. In this case the questions related to the physical condition and character of the accused Ganesh.

Mr. Justice Gulam Hussan held that the substance and the manner in which the questions were put suggested that the advocate exceeded the legitimate bounds of his privilege and therefore he was warned.

A gross abuse of the right of cross-examination by a legal practitioner is abhorrently not proper conduct in discharge of his duties.[217] Anything done or said which may amount at

216. A.I.R. 1953 S.C. 368.
217. In the matter of a 'Vakil', I.L.R. 47 All. 729.

criticism any proceedings pending in a court of justice is calculated to hinder the even and impartial administration of justice. It was held in *Government Pleader, High Court, Bombay* v. *Vinayak Balwant Chaukar,*[218] that to congratulate and sympathies with an under trial prisoner amount to misconduct inasmuch as such conduct is, to all intents and purpose a criticism of pending proceeding. Similarly, to publicity glorify as a Marty, a man who is on his trial, tends to hinder and embarrass the proper administration of justice.

In such circumstances advocate cannot claim the right to free speech. A plea that he was acting in personal capacity also did not lies in such case.

Thus, the office of an advocate is was created in furtherance of the administration of justice. Therefore, advocate privileges, but they have responsibility too. An advocate who acts so as to hinder and embarrass the administration of justice is guilty of improper conduct and such conduct furnishes reasonable cause for the exercise of disciplinary jurisdiction. Appearance and prosecution of proceedings in a court when the presiding officer is one among his kith and kin, entering into service without the sanction of Bar Council, wearing the dress prescribed for appearance in court in public places, seeking adjournments only to delay the course of justice and attending the court in drunken state or some unprofessional conduct on the part of the advocate which comes under the preview of section 35 of the Advocates Act.

(vi) Political Activities and Civil Disobedience

Before India became free the lawyers were in the vanguard of the freedom movement and advocates at various levels throughout the country participated in civil disobedience movement and also defied unjust laws. Those were the days of sacrifice. They claimed themselves as civil resister. After India became free and the Constitution guaranteed several rights under Article 19, which do not affect the working of the court certainly would be protected. It is debatable as to how for the decisions rendered by the courts in British India dealt with lawyers can be considered still valid in post-independence era.

218. A.I.R. 1922 Bom. 361.

The Bar Council is not concerned with the political opinions of the members of the legal profession unless the expression of it involves the commission of an offence or amounts to the conduct improper on the part of a legal practitioner who is a part of the machinery of the administration of justice. A legal practitioner, as any other person, has a right to entertain political activities, but having obtained licence to practice, if he acts inconsistently with the position, he abuses it and is liable to disciplinary action.

In *Ram Govind Verma and others,*[219] some pleaders, were arrested but released as consequence of a settlement between the Viceroy and the Congress party, which had become popular as "Irwin-Gandhi Pact". A question arose whether their certificates entitling them to practise should be renewed or not. The District Judge ordered that their certificates should not be renewed until a guarantee was given by them that they would not engage themselves in any political or other activity of a kind subversive of Government. They refused to do so. It was held that there was nothing in the Act to prevent an action being taken by the practitioner being convicted of an offence committed in the course of civil disobedience movement.[220]

The rationales of the decisions in *Emperor* v. *Rajni Kanta Bose,*[221] *Shankar Ganes* v. *Secretary of State,*[222] *Advocate-General of Bombay* v. *Phiroj Rustomji,*[223] are also based on this view that if an advocate deliberately joins or continues to be a member of unlawful association, he renders himself liable to disciplinary action. A speech calling upon the audience to break laws will

219. A.I.R. 1931 Pat. 360.
220. A.I.R. 1931 Patna 360. See also *Government Pleader* v. *Jagannath Maheswar* where a pleader presided over a public meeting held for expressing sorrow for and sympathy with Lokamanya Tilak was suspended for six months, (1909) 33 Bomb. 252. In *Second Grade Pleader, Ramachandrapuram,* a pleader was imprisoned for inciting public not to pay taxes and to boycott courts. In his show cause he expressed no regrets for his tone of speeches nor promised for future behaviour. The court refused to renew his certificate, A.I.R. 1924 Mad. 129.
221. A.I.R. 1922 Cal. 515.
222. A.I.R. 1922 P.C. 351.
223. A.I.R. 1935 P.C. 168.

also render the practitioner amendable to the disciplinary jurisdiction.[224]

One cardinal principle emerges from the above decisions that an advocate who wishes to remain on the rolls has to remember that those *who live by the law must respect the law.* They should never show hearty sympathy towards seditious and disloyal movements.

The recent judicial trends in this regard also upholding the same view. Thus, the opinion of a bench of five judges in the case of *Harish Uppal* v. *Union of India,*[225] that advocates have no right to abstain from working in court and if they have any grievances they should pursue other avenues of settlement. However, the Constitution Bench did concede that where the dignity, integrity and independence of judiciary is threatened the Bar as a mark of protest, can abstain from work for not more than a day.

(C) Contempt of Court Committed by Advocates

Smooth functioning and development of society is largely based on the respect of law. It is emphasized in the verdict of Hon'ble Mrs. Justice Ruma Pal, that "a civil society is founded on respect of law. If every citizen chooses to break the law, there would be no society at all, at least not a civil one".[226] The duty to respect the law is relied firstly upon the advocates who are the honourable members of justice dispension system. If they lose their equipoise and err in doing disrespectful act or using indiscreet language, the courts resort to the exercise of their powers to declare such acts as contempt of court.

In India, the law relating to contempt of court is embodied in contempt of Courts' Act, 1971. The Bar Council of India Rules do not contain any express provision as to the contempt of court, but judicial decisions in this regard say that contempt committed by advocates will be treated as

224. (2003) 2 S.C.C. 45.
225. A.I.R. 2003 S.C. 739.
226. *J.R. Parasar* v. *Prasant Bhusan* (2001) 6 S.C.C. 735.

professional misconduct.[227] However, as discussed earlier professional misconduct is a wide term which includes all unprofessional attitudes whether or not directly related with the profession of law; but the term contempt of court is narrower than that It contains only such conducts which are against the honour and integrity of the court.

Here the pertinent question arises that what constitutes contempt of court? The simple answer of this question may be that any thing which tends to bring the administration of justice into disrespect or interferes with the due administration of justice constitutes the contempt of the court.

The significant principles governing the contempt of court are given below:

(i) Contempt of court which is characterized as scandalizing a court or a Judge consists of an act done or writing published which is calculated to bring the court or the judge into contempt or lowers his authority.

(ii) Contempt may be committed as *Ex Facie* contempt and also constructive contempt. A reflection on the court or the judge imputing dishonesty, partiality, unfairness or incompetence are the general example of committing contempt.

(iii) The elements of *mens rea* is not necessary for the contempt.[228]

(iv) The purpose of punishment for contempt is not to protect the court or the Judge from a repetition of attacks and interference but to protect any one from the mischief they will incur if the authority of the court is undermined or impaired.

(v) There is a clear distinction between libel and contempt. The former is a wrong done to the Judge personally while the latter is a wrong done to the public. So it is the subject matter of Contempt of Court Act, 1971.

227. *Event* v. *Willions* (1893) L.Q.R. 197.

228. *Perspective (Pvt.) Ltd.* v. *State of Maharastra*, 1971 Cr.L.J. 288, S.C.

(vi) In that connection the nature and circumstances under which the allegations are made, the extent and character of the word spoken written and similar other considerations have to be taken into account.[229]

As has been shown earlier the act of contempt may be divided into two categories, namely, *exfacie* contempt[230] and constructive contempt,[231] hence, there are irremovable ways in which attempt can be made to hinder or obstruct the judicial system in court.

Recently the Delhi High Court held guilty of contempt of court a senior advocate R.K. Anand and I.V. Khan and two other lawyers arising out of a sting operation that claimed to have exposed an alleged nexus between defence and prosecution lawyers in winning over an eye witness in the B.M.W. hit-and-run case of 1999.

A Division Bench of the Delhi High Court comprising Mr. Justice Manmohan Surin and Justice Manmohan observed that "We are *prima facie* satisfied that you have widely and deliberately tried to interfere with the due course of Judicial proceedings and administration of justice by the courts and your acts and conduct were intended to subvert the administration of Justice in the pending trial and, in particular influence the out come of the on going proceedings".[232]

It depicts that any interference with due course of Justice may constitute contempt of court, but one such method which is universally defined is known as scandalizing the court. Scandalizing the court is specie of contempt and it is worst kind of contempt. Making imputation, touching the impartiality and integrity of a Judge or making sarcastic remarks about judicial competence constituted contempt of court. In a series of judicial pronouncements the aforesaid conducts of advocates have been declared by the judiciary as contempt of court. Some of the cases of contempt are discussed here below:

---

229. This position is changed now by the Amendment in 2005.
230. Contempt which committed on the face of the court.
231. Contempt which committed, out of the court, by publication, etc.
232. *The Hindu*, dated 26.06.2008.

(i) Imputation of Partiality

To impute partiality to a Judge in discharge of his official duty is actionable as contempt. In *Vidya Sagar* v. *R.*,[233] it was held by the Privy Council that the allegation of the counsel in the court that the judge was partial and that he and his client were thereby compelled to withdraw from the case was an allegation of partiality. It was a case of scandalizing to court, hence a contempt of court. Further, an allegation of undue favour shown by a judge to a particular counsel was treated to be an allegation of partiality on the court. Hence it was a clear case of contempt.[234]

In *Lalit Mohan Das* v. *Advocate General*,[235] the legal practitioner imputed partiality and unfairness against the magistrate in an open court. He suggested that the Magistrate followed no principle in his order. It was held by their Lordships of the Supreme Court that:

> "It is a human weakness to throw the blame on others, but scandalizing the court is really putting the very font of justice and brings disrepute to the whole administration of justice. Therefore, the conduct of advocate was absolutely reprehensible, and that conduct was no doubt contempt of court".

In *G.V. Ramamurthy Patnaik* v. *P. Pani, Migistrate Ist Class*,[236] merely because many of the cases in which the pleader had appeared for a party were decided against that party, he jumped at the conclusion that the judgements were partial, though he seems to have recognized that on appeal some of those judgements were upheld. He did not hesitate to say that the Munsif had spoken falsehood. The language used was extremely unbalanced and even in his show-cause petition before the Judicial Officer he characterized him, along with his clerks, as 'miscreants'. It was held by the Orissa High Court that he overstepped the limits of propriety expected from a members of the Bar. He sent a representation to the District

233. (1968) A.C. 589 (P.C.).
234. *State of Gujrat* v. *Narayan Bhai Parmar* (1982) Cr.L.J.1872.
235. A.I.R. 1957 S.C. 250.
236. A.I.R. 1959 Ori. 26.

Judge, painting the stationary Sub-Magistrate in the blackest colour possible, and imputing to him partiality and prejudice in passing judicial orders against the pleader.

In *L.D. Jaikwal* v. *State of U.P.*,[237] an advocate who appeared in shirt and trouser in court, the learned Judge asked him to appear in proper dress. The advocate took umbrage and left the court. The appellant made a written application to the special judge couched in scurrilous language. He made imputation that the Judge was a "corrupt Judge" and was also contaminating the seat of justice. Application also contained a threat to lodge a complaint to higher authorities that he was corrupt and did not deserve to be retained in service.

The High Court initiated contempt proceeding under Section 2(c)(1) of the Contempt of Court Act, 1971. After giving him full opportunity of hearing the High Court imposed a sentence of simple imprisonment of one week and a fine of Rs. 500 and in default of payment to undergo a further term of simple imprisonment for one week. The advocate felt no remorse, no sorrow and tendered no apology even before the High Court and sought to justify his conduct on the ground of the treatment alleged to have been meted out to him by the learned judge. In appeal he expressed sorrow before the Supreme Court saying that he had lost his mental balance.

The Supreme Court found that apology was not sincere as it was a mere paper apology and expression of sorrow had come from his pen, not from his heart. The court noted—*"It is one thing to say sorry and it is other to feel sorry"*. Rejecting the apology the court observed:

> "If such an apology were to be accepted, as a rule, and not as an exception, we would in fact be virtually issuing a licence to scandalize courts and commit contempt of court with impunity. It will be rather difficult to persuade members of the bar, who care for their self-respect, to join the judiciary if they are expected to pay such a price for it. No sitting Judge will feel free to decide any matter as per the dictates of conscience on account of the fear of being scandalized and persecuted by an advocate who

237. A.I.R. 1984 S.C. 1374.

does not mind making reckless allegations if the Judge goes against his wishes".

The Hon'ble Court also pointed out the other danger of ill impact of such tendency:

> "If this situation were to be countenanced, advocates who can comedown the judges, and make them fall in line with their wishes, by threats of character assassination and persecution, will be preferred by the litigants to the advocates who are mindful of professional ethics and believe in maintaining the decorum of courts".[238]

It seems that the liberty of free expression is not to be confounded or confused with license to make unfounded allegations against the judges or judiciary.

In *Pritam Pal Singh* v. *High Court of Madhya Pradesh, through Registrar,*[239] the appellant was disturbed by dismissal of his writ petition and moved a contempt petition making some serious allegations against two judges of the High Court. A show cause notice was issued against him *suo motu*. Finally, High Court held the contemner guilty of criminal contempt of not only scandalizing the court and lowering its authority but also substantially interfering with the due course of Justice. The contemner added fuel to fire by defiant attitude. The High Court sentenced the contemner to suffer simple imprisonment of two months. His attitude did not change even before the Supreme Court in appeal. He had ventured into another bont of allegation against the High Court Judges and persisted in his campaign of vilification, the Apex Court confirmed the sentence awarded by the High Court.

Thus, decisions referred above indicated clearly that imputation of partiality is a serious offence against the propriety of the law courts, as it amounts to contempt of court.

(ii) Allegation of Corruption

Making an statement to allege corruption against judges

238. *Id.*, p. 1354.
239. A.I.R. 1992 S.C. 904.

also stands the risk of an action in contempt. In *U.P. Sales-Tax Service Association* v. *Taxation Bar Association*.[240] certain advocates made wild allegations of corruption against appellate authority functioning under Section 9 of the U.P. Sales Tax Act and demanded enquiry and transfer of its functions to another jurisdiction. It was held to be a case of attributing improper motive to the court. Hence, it was contempt of the court.

In *Dr. J. Jayalalitha* v. *Dr. M. Chenna Reddy*,[241] news paper collecting opinions on questions which were *subjudice* from different persons including lawyers and publishing before argument and indulging in yellow journalism and gossip about the members of the Bench, amounted to scandalising or tending to scandalize or lowering the authority of the court.

It is also a grave misconduct on the part of the legal practitioner to make unfounded allegations of bribery against judicial officer which not only he knew to be false but also to make charges which he must know that he has no reasonable prospect of substantiating.[242]

In *Advocate General, Kerala State* v. *John*,[243] the contemner advocate made certain allegations of bribery and corruption against a Judicial Officer. On receipt of a show-cause notice; he at first tendered an apology which was unconditional. But, he subsequently withdrew apology and wanted to lead evidence to substantiate the imputation of bribery. It was held that the scurrilous attack of corruption constituted *ex facis contempt* and as advocate's behaviour and conduct did not show contrition a different punishment of penal servitude was called for. In *State* v. *R.N. Patra*,[244] allegation against the District Judge was made in a letter written to the Chief Justice of India and it was suggested that the High Court would not act because District Judge was related to the Chief Justice of the High Court. It was treated to be a scurrilous abuse of the District Court hence contempt of court.

240. (1995) 5 S.C.C. 716.
241. (1995) A.I.H.C. 5875 (Mad.).
242. *C.N. Presannean* v. *K.A Mohammed Ali*, 1991 Cr.L.J. 2205.
243. A.I.R. 1965 Ker. 49.
244. (1976) Cr.L.J. 440 (Ori.).

So when scurrilous allegations are made that a Judge has taken bribe and illegal gratification from the other party, such scandalizing the court cannot be purged by apology of contemner. Such acts were also held contempt of court in *B.R. Nikung* v. *Vipin Bansraj Tewari,*[245] by the Madhya Pradesh High Court, in *State of Gujarat* v. *Pravin Kumar Patel,*[246] by the Gujarat High Court, in *Re Sriman Bose,*[247] by the Calcutta High Court and in U.P. *Sales Tax Servie Association* v. *Taxation Bar Association*[248] by the Supreme Court of India.

In the above referred decisions the common question arose: whether it was permissible for a contemner to attempt to establish the truth of his allegation, as that would in itself be a fresh contempt? According to the judicial view when an allegation of corruption is made in open court when the Judge was discharging his judicial duties there can be no doubt it is contempt. To further allege in open court to prove it is indeed a fresh contempt. It can be no defence in contempt action in such cases, to plead truth.[249]

In *ex facie* contempt truth or otherwise of the allegation is quite immaterial.[250] It is contempt even if the judicial officer is later on found in an administrative enquiry to be corrupt. The proper thing for the person is not to allege it in open court, but submit a carefully worded petition to the superior officer of the judge requesting an enquiry. If such a petition is *bonafide* and is intended merely to call for an enquiry, the petitioner stands protected. But, if under the guise of such a petition, scurrilous attacks are made against the judge, the risk of contempt action is largely present.

However, when allegations made against a judicial officer in an application for transfer of a proceeding from his court are found to have been based on mistaken and misconceived view of the facts the offence of contempt of court cannot be said to have been committed substantially. It amounts to no

245. (2000) 1 M.P.L.J. 105 (D.B.).
246. (1996) 1 G.L.H. 358.
247. Cal. L.T. (1994) 2 231.
248. (1995) 5 S.C.C. 716.
249. *V.N. Kanade* v. *Mahadev Gadkari* (1990) Cr.L.J. 190 (Bom.).
250. (2000) M.P.L.J. 105 (D.B.).

more than a technical fault therefore does not amount to contempt of court.[251] Likewise in *Brahma Prakash Sharma* v. *State of Uttar Pradesh*,[252] the Apex Court said that a defamatory attack on the judges unless it is also calculated to interfere with the due course of Justice or proper administration of law by such court will not be treated as contempt of court. Criticism of judges in relation to something done by them which has absolutely no relevance to their position as judges does not amount to contempt.[253]

But in *State* v. *Radha Kishan Khanna*,[254] it was held that casting aspersion on the integrity or impartiality of the courts in rendering decision is clear example of the contempt of court.

Thus, what is protected is the seat of justice. Now the question arises: if the above rule also applies in the matter of retired judges?

Contempt proceeding can only be started against a sitting Judge, as the protection is aimed to be given to the functioning of the court. So defamatory statement made against a retired Judge relating to his judicial character cannot interfere with or obstruct due course of justice. Any libelous and defamatory statement made against a retired judge relating to his judicial conduct and character cannot be scandalizing of court as such. It is immaterial whether a Judge retired recently or has been on the retirement list for a long time. In *S. Gyan Singh* v. *Ram Bhya Lal Malik*[255] the Punjab High Court and in *Registrar, Assam High Court* v. *Bharat Chandra Das*,[256] the Assam High Court held that there can be no contempt of court as regard a retired Judge. In other words, the privilege of committing for contempt belongs to sitting judge. The contempt is the contempt of the court as a collective body and the immunity is not personal to the judges as individuals. "In substance contempt of court consists of disrespect to the fountain-head of

251. *Sher Singh* v. *Raghupati Kapur*, A.I.R. 1968 Pun. 217.
252. A.I.R. 1954 S.C. 10.
253. *Ibid*.
254. A.I.R. 2004 S.C. 575.
255. A.I.R. 1959 Pun. 319.
256. A.I.R. 1962 Ass. 96.

justice, or to the authority of sovereign State exercised through court of law; and court means the judges who constitute it for the time being".

(iii) Unsavory Language

An advocate is a person educated and trained in law. The choice of language in the matter of drafting the legal documents and arguments has to be careful. It should be balanced, respectful and in fitness of things within the framework of the law of the land. There are barriers, which are known to an advocate and those have not to be crossed, advocates have not to ever-step the limits of decency and ethics in the matter of their behaviour towards the judges and their decisions.

In *K.A. Mohd. Ali* v. *C.N. Prasamau,*[257] in the course of argument, the counsel raised his voice unusually high to the annoyance of the Magistrate and used derogatory language against the Magistrate before whom he was conducting the trial of an accused. He was held guilty of contempt of court.

In an earlier case[258] Mr. Sham Lal, an advocate made a statement before the judges of a full bench that his client did not wish the matter to be argued before the bench as constituted. It was held deliberate and intentional insult to the court.

However, in *Arun Kumar* v. *Ashutosh Guha,*[259] a pleader while arguing the case in the court of a Munsif put forward a copy of Magistrate's order under Section 144 of Criminal Procedure Code against his client and called it an act of executive *goondism* and *zabberdastism* of the S.D.M.

Speaking for the Supreme Court Mr. Justice K.C. Das Gupta observed:

> "In deciding whether characterization of action of this kind as executive goondaism or 'executive zubberdastism' impaired the dignity of the court, we have to remember that the remark was made in course of arguments. High

257. (1994) Supp. (3) S.C.C. 509.
258. *Sukhdev Raj* v. *Emperor,* A.I.R. 1932 Lah. 485.
259. A.I.R. 1955 Cal. 368.

> flown language has often to be used in trying to persuade a court to a particular view. Some amount of latitude must be allowed to lawyers when addressing arguments in court of law. We think that the use of the words 'executive goondaism' would be very improper: the use of the words executive zabberdastism' would be less objectionable. But whether one or other word was used, it was a trivial matter. If we take action for contempt of court for use of such words it will amount of such interference with the activities of counsel in court that the effect on the administration of justice may well nigh be disastrous".[260]

The observation of the Supreme Court in *D.C. Saxena* v. *Chief Justice of India*[261] in this regard is worth mention:

> The Supreme Court held that when an advocate or a party appearing before the court conducts himself in a manner not befitting to the dignity and decorum of the court, he cannot have a free license to indulge in writing the pleading, the scurrilous abuse or scandalisation of the Judge or the court. In the referred case, the Supreme Court further held that the right to freedom of speech is subject to Article 19(2) and Articles 129 and 215 of the Constitution. Article 19(2) imposes restriction on the right to freedom of speech and expression, if such speech amounts to contempt of court. The provisions of Articles 129 and 215 are independent and are not subject to Article 19(1)(a). When contempt of court is committed through contemptuous expression, it becomes punishable under Article 129 of the Constitution under the powers conferred to the court in Section 12 of the Contempt of Courts Act, 1971.

In a famous case *Charan Lal Shahu* v. *Union of India*[262] a petition was filed by an experienced advocate of the Supreme

260. *Ibid.*
261. A.I.R. 1996 S.C. 2481.
262. A.I.R. 1988 S.C. 107.

Court by way of public interest litigation. It was couched in unsavory language and the petitioner seemed to have made an intentional attempt to indulge in mudslinging against the Judge, the Supreme Court in particular as also other Constitutional institutions. Many of the allegations in his writ petition were likely to lower the prestige of Supreme Court as the Apex Judicial institution. At one place in the writ petition he had alleged:

> "Thus the working of the judges are cocktail based on western common laws and American techniques, as such unproductive, and outdated according to socio-economic conditions of the country".

At another place the petitioner had stated that Court is sleeping over the issues like *kumbhakarna*. The reading of the writ petition gives the impression that it clearly intended to denigrate the court in the esteem of the people of India. The Supreme Court observed that the petition has been drawn up with a designed purpose of bringing the court into contempt and the petitioner, is therefore, *prima facie* guilty of contempt.

The aforesaid decisions make it clear that there is limit to the liberty of advocates. They cannot use language which is personally insulting or scandalous against any judge or the court. The use of insulting language by the advocate against judge upon failure to obtain the desired order,[263] raising the pitch of his voice to unusual level and using derogatory language in court,[264] abusing and slapping the presiding officer of a court,[265] counsel shouting and abusing a High Court Judge who had put a question to him during the course of hearing and threatening to get him transferred,[266] failure to maintain dignity, decorum and order in the court proceedings,[267]

263. *M.B. Sanghi, Advocate* v. *High Court of Punjab & Haryana* (1991) 3 S.C.C. 600.
264. *K.A. Mohammad Ali* v. *C.N. Prasanan,* 1994 (Supp.) (3) S.C.C. 509.
265. *Shamsher Singh Bedi* v. *High Court of Punjab & Haryana* (1996) 7 S.C.C. 99.
266. *Vinay Chandra Misra,* Re (1995) 2 S.C.C. 554.
267. *D.C. Saxena* v. *Hon'ble Chief Justice of India* (1996) 5 S.C.C. 216.

attempting to overawe the court,[268] leaving the courtroom without listening to the order being passed and thus showing discourtesy[269] have all been held to be contempt of court.

(iv) Threatening

Advocates should generally be respectful in their attitude towards courts and judges. It is unbecoming to their status to give threat to any judge. Any threat to a judge or act of influencing the decision of the judge including private communication is contempt as it diverts the course of justice.

In a series of judicial pronouncements the courts have declared such acts as a contempt of court. *In Re Vinay Chandra Mishra*[270] is the famous case on this point. In the instant case M/S Bansal Forgings Limited took loan from U.P. Financial Corporation and it made default in payment of instalment of the same. Corporation proceeded against the company under Section 29 of the U.P. Financial Corporation Act. The company filed a civil suit against the corporation and it has also filed an application for grant of temporary injunction. The counsel for the corporation *suo motu* put appearance in the matter before Trial Court and prayed time for filing of reply. The learned trial court passed an order on the said date that corporation will not seize the factory of the company. The company shall pay the amount of instalments and it will furnish also security for the dispute amount. The court directed to furnish security on 31.01.1994 and the case was fixed for hearing on 5.3.1994. Against the said order of the Trial Court an appeal was filed and arguments were advanced that the court had no jurisdiction to pass the order for payment of instalment of loan and further no security could have been ordered. One of the honourable judges of the Allahabad High Court constituting the bench sought some clarification.

On a query from the counsel, Shri Misra under which provisions that order had been passed, he started to shout and said that no question could have been put to him. He would get him transferred or see that impeachment motion was

268. *Ajay Kumar Pandey Re* (1996) 6 S.C.C. 510.
269. *M.M.P. Sinha* v. *Steel Authority of India* (1997) 10 S.C.C. 191.
270. A.I.R. 1995 S.C. 2348.

brought against him in Parliament. He further said that he had turned up many judges. He created a good scene in the court. He asked the learned judge to follow the practice of the court. In sum and substance it was a matter where except abusing him of mother and sister he insulted him like anything. What he wanted to convey to him was that admission was a matter of course and no argument could be heard at that stage.

In a contempt proceeding, the Supreme Court of India held that while hearing a case if some question is asked by a judge to be disrespectful to him, to question his authority to ask the question, to shout at him, to threaten him with transfer and impeachment, to use insulting language and abuse him, to dictate the order that he should pass, to create scenes in the court, to address him by losing temper, are all acts calculated to interfere with and obstruct the course of justice. Such acts tend to overawe the courts and to prevent it from performing its duty to administer justice. Such conduct brings the authority of the court and the administration of justice into disrespect and disrepute and undermines and erodes the very foundation of the judiciary by shaking the confidence of the people in the ability of the court to deliver free and fair justice.

If the judiciary is to perform its duties and functions effectively and true to the spirit with which they are sacredly entrusted to it, the dignity and authority of the court have to be respected and protected at all costs. Otherwise, the very cornerstone of our constitutional scheme will give way and with it will disappear the rule of law and the civilized life in the society. It is for this purpose that the courts are entrusted with the extraordinary power of punishing those indulge in acts whether inside or outside the courts which tend to undermine their authority and bring them in disrepute and disrespect by scandalizing them and obstructing them from discharging their duties without fear or favour. When the court exercises this power, it does not do so to vindicate the dignity and honour of the individual judge who is personally attacked or scandalized, but to uphold the majesty of the law and of the administration of justice. The foundation of the judiciary is the trust and the confidence of the people in its ability to deliver fearless and impartial justice when the foundation itself is shaken by acts which tend to create disaffection and disrespect for the authority of the court by creating distrust in its working, the edifice of the judicial system gets eroded.

The contemner, therefore would be guilty of the offence of the criminal contempt of the court for having interfered with and obstructed the course of justice by trying to threaten, overawe and overbear the court by using insulting, disrespectful and threatening language. Since the contemner is a senior member of the Bar and also adorns the high offices such as those of Chairman of the Bar Council of India, the President of the U.P. High Court Bar Association, Allahabad and others, this conduct is bound to infect the members of the Bar all over the country, therefore, an exemplary punishment has to be meted out to him. The Supreme Court, therefore, sentenced the contemner for his conviction for the offence of criminal contempt.[271]

However, the Supreme Court has been cautious to ensure procedural safeguards provided to contemner. Thus, in *Dr. L.P. Mishra* v. *State of U.P.,* [272] the Supreme Court did not allow holding of the appellant guilty of Contempt of court without following the procedure prescribed by law. It is most unfortunate case in which the appellant L.P. Mishra advocate along with some other advocates entered into the court room when the Division Bench consisting of Mr. Justice B.M. Lal and Mr. Justice A.P. Singh was hearing a writ petition. They raised slogans and asked the court to rise and stop functioning. The court did not do so. Thereafter, they reached on dais and tried to manhandle and in that process Dr. L.P. Mishra caught hold of Justice A.P. Singh forcing the court to rise and used abusive language against Justice B.M. Lal in following words:

> "TUM SHALE UTH JAAO NAHIEN TO JAAN SE MARR DALENGE. THUMNE CHIEF JUSTICE SE KAHA HAI KI LUCKNOW JUDGES 5000/- RUPYA LE KAR STAY GRANT KARTE HAIN AUR EXTEND KARATE HAIN. AAJ DO BAJE TAK AGAR TUM APNA BORIYA BISTAR LEKAR YAHAN SE NAHIEN BHAG JAATE TO TUMHE JAAN SE MAAR DALENGE".

---

271. *Ibid*.
272. A.I.R. 1998 S.C. 3337.

In view of the alarming and threatening situation, the court was forced to retire and consequently both the judges retired in the chamber. Dr. L.P. Mishra then entered the chamber and repeated the same uncivilized language and extended the same threat. The ugly scene was averted by the intervention of Shri H.N. Bhalla, additional chief standing counsel, State of U.P. and some members of the staff who persuaded Dr. L.P. Mishra to leave the room.

After some time the court reassembled and taking serious note of contemptuous conduct on the part of appellants, it passed following order in exercise of its power under Article 215 of Constitution:

> "this clearly amounts to grossest contempt of the court, interference in the administration of justice and insult to the court as it scandalizes the court and lowers the authority of the court. Therefore, in our considered opinion Dr. L.P. Mishra and other advocates are *ex facie* guilty of contempt of court.

In appeal filed by the appellants they assailed the order principally on the ground that the court while passing the order did not follow the procedure prescribed by law.

The Supreme Court did not go into the merit of the case, and the bench consisting of Mr. Justice M.K. Mukherjee, Mr. Justice S.P. Kurdukar and Mr. Justice K.T. Thomas passed the judgement:

> "We are of the opinion that the court while passing the impugned order had not followed the procedure prescribed by law. It is true that the High Court can invoke powers and jurisdiction vested in it under Article 215 of the Constitution of India, but such a jurisdiction has to be exercised in accordance with the procedure prescribed by law".

The Supreme Court remitted the case to be heard by some other bench of the High Court at Allahabad following the procedure prescribed in High Court's Rules.

It is submitted that the above decision of the Supreme Court was based on technicality and may have ill impact on the administration of justice. While we agree that High Court should follow the High Court's Rules, but it was an *ex facie* contempt case and clear evidence of threatening to the judge. Therefore, the Supreme Court should not have been very technical on this point.

(v) Unbecoming Behaviour

It is highly unprofessional and objectionable on the part of the member of noble profession to show an unbecoming behaviour before the court of law. The term unbecoming behaviour is a wide expression and includes in its ambit the different types of conducts. Therefore, entering the chamber of the presiding officer after delivery of judgment shouting at him assaulting him and snatching and taking away the original judgment from the Reader,[273] refusing to argue the case while continuing to represent a party,[274] entering the courtroom of the CJM in drunken state, remaining there for sometime vomiting and spitting and thus interfering with judicial proceedings,[275] abusing judicial officer in his chamber, assaulting him and tearing judicial record,[276] imputing partiality and prejudice to the Metropolitan Magistrate,[277] making wild allegations of corruption against presiding officer, shouting in court and thumping the rostrum during the argument[278] are the several instances of unbecoming behaviour amounting to contempt of court.

Recently, in *Prem Surana* v. *Additional Munsif and Judicial magistrate,*[279] an unfortunate incident took place in the court of additional Munsif and Judicial Magistrate, Jaipur. In the instant case an advocate whose application for exemption from

273. *Swami Nath Yadav, In re,* 2000 All. L.J. 2985 (D.B.).
274. *Parsvanath Developers Ltd.* v. *New Okhla Industrial Development Authority,* 2000 All. L.J. 3160 (D.B.).
275. *State of U.P.* v. *Rajendra Singh Chaudhary* 2000 All. L.J. 815.
276. *State of U.P.* v. *Satendra Singh Tomar,* 2001 All. L.J. 1041.
277. *B.A. Shelar* v. *M.S. Menon* (2001) 3 M.L.J. 105.
278. *B.R. Nikunj* v. *Vipin Bansraj Tiwary* (2000) M.P.L.J.557 (D.B.)
279. (2002) 6 S.C.C. 722.

appearance in court in a criminal trial was dismissed by the court started abusing the Magistrate and said, "How you dared, to disallow my application for exemption of my presence. He also reached to dais and gave a slap on left check of the Magistrate and told that "just come out, I show to you". Taking note of seriousness of the issue, the Supreme Court observed:

> "Slap on the face of the judicial officer is in fact slap on the face of the judiciary and entire justice delivery system. Therefore, no leniency can be shown as regard the sentence of six months simple imprisonment imposed by the High Court".

An unprecedented incident about the unbecoming behaviour of a lawyer took place in the case of *R.K. Garg, Advocate* v. *State of Himanchal Pradesh.*[280] In the instant case the appellant was an advocate practising at Solan, Himachal Pradesh. He was representing the petitioner in relation to a petition under the Rent Control Act. Hearing was taking place before Shri Kulpid Chand Sud, the presiding officer of the court. When the case was called out for hearing the learned judge noticed that the petitioner had not paid the process fee as a result of which the summons could not be issued to the respondent. As a consequence the judge proceeded to dismiss the petition under order IX Rule 2 of the Civil Procedure Code.

Taking umbrage at the dismissal of the petition the appellant—advocate hurled his shoe at the judge which hit him on shoulder. Taking the strong view of the conduct of the advocate and punishing one month of imprisonment and fine of Rs. 200, Supreme Court of India observed:

> "In the opinion of the court, the appellant is guilty of conduct which is highly unbecoming of a practising lawyer. He hurled his shoe at the judge in order evidently to overawe him and to bully him into accepting his submission that the case should not be dismissed. The

280. (1981) 3 S.C.C. 166.

appellant did his best or worst to see that the petition was not dismissed for non-payment of process fee and finding that the judge was not willing to accept his argument, he took out his shoe in show of his physical process. Such incident can easily multiply considering the devaluation of respect for all authority.[281]

Again, in the *Municipal Corporation of Greater Bombay* v. *Smt. Annatte Remound Uttanwall*,[282] hurling of shoe at the presiding officer of the court was held as contempt of court.

In Re Nandlal Balwani,[283] Mr. Nand Lal Balwani, who claimed to be an advocate since 19 year and had apparently no case on the Board of Bench, shouted slogan in the open court and thereafter hurled his shoe towards the court thereby interrupting the court proceedings it was informed that his action was aimed at intimidating the court and causing interference in conduct of judicial proceedings. The Supreme Court noted that it was no way to ventilate his grievances against the police agencies and it was most unbefitting for an advocate to act in the manner in which the contemner acted. He was found guilty of committing gross criminal contempt.

The court said, "Law does not give a lawyer, unsatisfied with the result of any litigation, licence to permit himself the liberty of causing disrespect of the court permitting in any manner, to lower the dignity of the court. A lawyer does not enjoy any special immunity under the contempt of courts Act where he is found to have committed a gross contempt of court, courts cannot be intimidated to seek favourable orders.

The court noted that it is unfortunate that a person belonging to the Bar should have behaved in that manner. The action of the contemner advocate was most reprehensible and had the tendency to interfere with the administration of justice and undermine the dignity of the court and the majesty of law. From the manner in which the contemner had behaved a deliberate, motivated and calculated attempt to impair the

281. *Ibid.*, p. 169.
282. 1987 Cr.L.J. 1038.
283. (1992) 2 S.C.C. 315.

administration of justice is discernible. Fact that he appeared to be aggrieved of alleged suffering at "the hands of all police agencies", is however, no way to ventilate his grievances against the police agencies. As a lawyer, he should have known better.

The court refused to accept his apology as the apology tendered by the contemner could not be accepted as it did not appear to be at all *bona fide* and genuine in view of his attitude exhibited in court during his questioning and seemed to have been made only to escape punishment. He did not appear to be repentant at all. Keeping in view the seriousness of the offence committed by the contemner a deterrent punishment was necessary to be imposed on him so that to serve as an example to other and no one indulges in repetition of such acts.

State of U.P. v. *Rajendra Singh Chaudhary*[284] is another instance of misbehaviour. In the instant case contemner advocate under intoxication entered and remained in court of Additional Chief Judicial Magistrate vomited out and spitted the court. His behaviour had interfered with course of judicial proceeding on that day as well obstructed administration of justice in preventing from functioning. The court found the contemner guilty of contempt of court.

In *Sukhdevraj* v. *Emperor,*[285] the counsel at the hearing of a criminal revision, in the High Court stated that he was instructed to say that his client did not wish to him to argue the case before the Bench as at present constituted. This statement was held to be a deliberate and intentional insult to the court and the counsel in making the statement was guilty of contempt of the court. Thus, counsel's privilege does not extend to stating his instructions when these instructions involve an attack on the dignity of the court and no litigant is entitled to have any say in the selection of judges who are to constitute any bench.

(vi) Criticism of Judges and Judicial Conduct

An advocate may also commit contempt of court by

284. (2000) All.L.J. 815.
285. A.I.R. 1932 Lah. 485.

criticizing the judges and judicial conduct. It may be either by *ex facie* contempt or by outside the court utterances and publications. A perusal of cases relating to contempt of court in the face of court and allegation of such contempt through publications reveal that in the case of former the courts are very particular about declaring the contempt, but in the case of latter they take rather lenient view by giving due credence to freedom of speech and expression and public interest.[286]

In the case of publication advocate is on part with the common people and contempt of court is viewed in light of the dimensions of the fundamental right under Article 19 of the Indian Constitution. Need not to say that in India Article 19(1)(a) gives the right of freedom of speech and expression to all citizens. But Articles 129 and 215 give the power of contempt of court to the higher judiciary, and this power, limits the freedom granted by Article 19(1)(a). Therefore, the question arises: how are these two provisions to be reconciled?

The test to determine whether an act amounts to contempt of court or not, as pronounced by the various High Courts and Supreme Court, is this: Does it make the functioning of the judiciary impossible or extremely difficult? If it does so, it may amount to contempt of court; but if it does not then it does not amount to contempt, even if it is harsh criticism.[287]

Thus, what amounts to contempt of court and when it crosses the limits of reasonable courtesy is very critical issue to be decided in the contempt cases. It involves two very important questions; *firstly,* whether there is any difference between libel and contempt of court? And, *secondly,* what is the border line of situation under which an act falls within the preview of the contempt of court?

The judiciary has taken a clear approach that contempt exist to protect public confidence in the administration of justice and not the individual judges. Chief Justice Griffith pointed out in an Australian case of *Nicholl*[288] that:

---

286. *Ajay Kumar Pandey* v. *Virendra Saran,* A.I.R. 1998 S.C. 32.
287. *M.B. Sanghi, Advocate* v. *High Court of Punjab & Haryana,* A.I.R. 1991 S.C. 1834.
288. (1911) 12 C.L.R. 280.

"In one sense, no doubt, every defamatory publication concerning a judge may be said to bring him into contempt as that term is used in the law of libel, but it does not follow that everything said of a judge calculated to bring him into contempt in that sense amount to contempt of court.

There are two primary considerations which should carry weight with the court in such case viz., whether a reflection on the conduct or character of the judges is within the limits of fair and reasonable criticism and whether it is a more libel or defamation of the judge or amounts to a contempt of court? Where the question arises whether a defamatory statement directed against a judge is calculated to undermine the confidence of the public in the competency or integrity of the judge, or is likely to deflect the court itself from a strict and unhesitant performance of the duties, all the surrounding circumstances under which the statement was made and the degree of conduct would be relevant circumstances. The question is not to be determined solely with reference to the language or contents of the statement. Mere publication to a third party, which would be sufficient to establish an ordinary libel may not be conclusive for establishing contempt. That would depend upon the nature and extent of the effect of such conduct.

In this regard it is worth to quote the report of the Sanyal Committee:

"A matter to be taken into account in considering the law relating to contempt by scandalizing is the need for drawing a clear cut distinction between comment or criticism affecting judges in their representative capacity on the one hand and those affecting them in their personal capacity. Personal attacks against the judges should be susceptible to punishment in the same way as attacks upon any other individual. But there would hardly be any justification for treating such attacks as standing on a higher footing than attacks against ordinary individuals. Redress in respect of such attacks has necessarily to be left to the general law of defamation.

> This position viz. that mere personal attacks on judges will not amount to contempt is so well established by a long line of decisions that it is hardly necessary to re-state it in so many words. If, it is feared that there may still be cases where a judicial personage is galled by public criticism against himself to such a degree that he is led to mistake the criticism as directed against the administration of justice, and instead of pursuing the remedies available to him as an individual, he may resort to his powers to punish for contempt, the answer in that such cases would be exceptional and the remedy, therefore, should be found elsewhere rather than in a definition".[289]

Mr. Justice Krishna Iyer of the Supreme Court has very well summarized this issue *in Re S. Mulgaoker,*[290] by considering under which circumstance a conduct may be called contempt of court. His Lordship clarified different considerations in considering the matter of contempt:

Firstly, there should be a wise economy of use by the court of this branch of its jurisdiction. It will act with severity where justice is jeopardized by a gross and unfounded attack on judges, and also where the attack is calculated to obstruct or destroy the judicial process. However, the court may ignore by a majestic liberalism trifling and venial offences *"the dogs may bark, the carvan will pass"*.

Secondly, the courts are to harmonise the Constitutional values of free criticism. *Thirdly,* the court should avoid confusion between personal protection of a libelled judge and prevention of obstruction of public justice and the community's confidence in that great process. The former is not contempt,[291] the latter is. *Fourthly,* the court should not be hypersensitive even where distortions and criticism overstep the limits, but to deflate vulgar denunciation by dignified bearing condensing indifference and repudiation by judicial rectitude. And, *lastly,* after evaluating the totality of factors, if

289. *Ibid.*
290. (1978) 3 S.C.C. 339.
291. *Ibid.*, p. 347.

the court considers on the judges scurrilous, offensive, intimidatory or malicious beyond condonable limits, the strong arm of the law must, in the name of public interest, strike a blow on him who challenges the supremacy of the rule of law by fouling its source and stream on the second question that when the criticism crosses the border line the courts have taken a view that a mere abuse of process of court is not contempt.[292] In *Moazzen Hossain* v. *State*,[293] it was held that writing of a letter by a lawyer to other lawyer highlighting the growing tendency to hurl abuses on Judges and undue criticism of the judges did not constitute contempt.

But critism constitutes contempt if there is an unfair imputation of corruption or conscious or unconscious bias to a court or to a judge acting in his official capacity or if the criticism is not made in good faith or exceeds the limits of reasonable courtesy and amounts, therefore, to scurrilous abuse. Thus, *In re S. Mulgaokar*,[294] the conduct of a senior advocate in publishing a pamphlet imputing improper motives to the Magistrate, who decided his case, was held to constitute substantial interference with the due administration of justice, therefore, the Contempt of court. To quote from Oswald,[295] "To charge a Judge with injustice is a grievous contempt. To accuse him of corruption might be a worse insult, but a charge of injustice is as gross as insult as can be imagined short of that. The arraignment of the justice of the judges is arraigning the King's justice; it is an impeachment of his wisdom and goodness in the choice of his judges and excites in the minds of the people a general dissatisfaction with all judicial determinations and indisposes their minds to obey them".

To quote again from Oswald:

> "To keep a blaze of glory around them (Judges) and to deter people from attempting to render them contemptible in eyes of the public. A libel upon a court is a refection upon the King and telling the people that the

292. *Ibid.*, p. 349.
293. (1983) 35 Dhaka L.R. 290, (S.C.).
294. (1978) 3 S.C.C. 339.
295. 'Oswald' "Contempt of Court" III ed., p. 50.

administration of justice is in weak or corrupt hands, that the fountain of justice is itself tainted and consequently that the judgments which stream out of that fountain must be impure and contaminated".

Prejudicing the public when a matter is pending before court is also held contempt, however, the impugned publication need not necessarily be in connection with any pending case. It can be on the judiciary as a whole and in some cases that too without any reference to any particular judge. In *EMS Namboodripad* v. *T.N. Nambiar,*[296] the contemner was held guilty of contempt of court for his general remarks against of judicial system viz. 'judiciary is an instrument of oppression' "judges are dominated by class hatred and class interest". "Judiciary works against workers, peasants and other section of working class and the law and system of judiciary essentially serve the exploiting class". In this case Marxian philosophy was narrated by the Supreme Court and treated the general remarks amounting to contempt. It is submitted that the judicial outlook was not in tune with the general ingredients of contempt. The case though not overruled has been *subsilentio* modified to great extent in subsequent rulings of the Supreme Court. There are not much cases of publications of scandalous allegation about Judges in personal article or in news paper by advocates. But the principles evolved for general public or press persons will be applicable in cases of such publications by the advocates.

It is important to note that, what is not permissible to a member of the Bar is equally not permissible, when it is a Bar Association acting as such and passing resolution affecting a judge.

In *Brahma Prakash Sharma* v. *State of Uttar Pradesh,*[297] the Supreme Court of India laid down two considerations. For determining what amounts to permissible publication and what amounts to contempt of court. In the first place the reflection on the conduct or character of a Judge in reference to the discharge of his judicial duties would not be contempt, if

296. A.I.R. 1970 S.C. 2015.
297. A.I.R. 1954 S.C. 10.

such repletion is made in the exercise of the right of fair and reasonable criticism which every citizen possesses in respect of public acts done in the seat of justice. Secondly, when attack or comments are made on a judge or judges disparaging in character and derogatory to their dignity care should be taken to distinguish between what is libel on a judge and what really amounts to contempt of court.

If, however, the publication of the disparagingly statement is calculated to interfere with the due course of justice or proper administration of law by such court, it can be treated as contempt. The aforesaid principles were applied and reaffirmed *In Re, Hira Lal Dixit and Two Others,*[298] where statement did not amount to scandalize the court but tend to hinder or interfere with the due course of administration of justice by the court. In this case a poster published had the necessary implication that judges who decided in the favour of the Government were rewarded by the government with appointments to the Supreme Court.

In *Perspective Publication (P) Ltd.* v. *State of Maharastra,*[299] the Supreme Court referred the principle evolved in *Brahma Prakash Sharma's*[300] case and held the publication of article *Story of a loan and Blitz-Jhackersey libel case,*[301] containing scandalous statement calculated to obstruct the administration of justice. The article contained insinuations that there was a connection between a loan of Rs. 10 lakh, granted to a firm in which the judge's brother was a partner and the judgement in the defamation case and that the judges knew about the loan having been granted to the firm.

The limits of criticism of the judges also were pin pointed by the Supreme Court in *Rustom Cowasjee Cooper* v. *Union of India,*[302] where the court recognized that it does not enjoy immunity from fair criticism. It further observed, that the Supreme Court does not claim to be always right although it does not spare any effort to be right according to the best of

298. (1955) 1 S.C.R. 677.
299. (1969) 2 S.C.R. 779.
300. A.I.R. 1954 S.C. 10.
301. 281, U.S., 559.
302. (1970) 2 S.C.C. 298.

its ability, knowledge and judgement of the judges, while fair and temperate criticism of the Supreme Court or any other court, even if strong may not be actionable, attributing improper motives or tending to bring judges or courts into hatred and contempt or obstructing directly or indirectly with the functioning of courts is serious contempt of which notice must and will be taken.

Again in *Uma Dutt* v. *R.K. Sardana,*[303] the Delhi High Court emphasized that contempt action can be resorted to only in cases of gross affront to the dignity of the court or in cases where the judicial process has been sought intentionally to be seriously interfered with.

In *Abdul Jabbar* v. *R.K. Karania,*[304] the Supreme Court explained the situation when unjustified and excessive criticism of the judiciary is treated as contempt of court. The ground on which it is so treated is that such unwarranted, unjustified and unoccasioned malicious criticism tends to undermine the prestige and dignity of the judiciary. This is only one effect. Such criticism if passes unnoticed has also the tendency to shake the confidence of the common man in the impartiality of the judiciary.

The above discussion of case law reveals that if a lawyer chooses to exercise his freedom of speech and expression by exposing judicial corruption and general deplorable condition of judiciary he will be out of the clutches of the contempt of court. But the exposure of the corruption or misconduct of individual judges has been put on different footing.

In *State of Hyderabad* v. *C. Natarajan,*[305] an advocate of 32 years standing in his communication addressed made scandalous allegation against Chief Justice of Hyderabad, that Chief Justice was an outsider, a job-hunter, a dictator, an autocrat and Jaffry of Irish Fame and his behaviour was contradicted with the previous Chief Justices. Copies of the letter were dispatched to the Prime Minister of India, the Home Minister of India, the Rajpramukh of Hyderabad and

303. A.I.R. 1969 Del. 6.
304. A.I.R. 1970 Bom. 48.
305. A.I.R. 1984 Hyd. 180.

the Chairman of the Anti-Corruption Committee. Mr. Justice Mukherjee of the Hyderabad High Court held that the communication was scurrilous and extremely offensive and that amounted to gross contempt of court.

Again, In *C. Ravichandran Iyer* v. *Justice A.M. Bhattacharjee,*[306] the Supreme Court derided lawyers—on pain of contempt the right to publicly expose judicial corruption. It limited the freedom of bar to bring the matter to the notice of Chief Justice of India through a High Court Chief Justice. The court ruled:

> "This procedure would not only facilitate nipping in the bud the conduct of a Judge leading to loss of public confidence in the courts and system, public faith in the efficacy of the rule of law and respect for the judiciary, but would also avoid needless embarrassment of contempt proceedings against the office-bearers of the Bar Association and group libel against all concerned".

A close reading of the above cases raise one very pertinent question, whether justified and truthful imputation of bias or production of the proof is protected from contempt of court?

There is conflict of opinions on this point in different countries. In United States truth is a defence in contempt case wherein contempt power is used only if there is a clear, imminent and present danger to the disposal of a pending case. Criticism, however, virulent or scandalous after final disposal of the proceedings will not be considered as contempt.[307]

In European democracies such as Germany, France, Belgium, Austria and Italy, there is no power to commit for contempt for scandalising the court. The Judge has to file a criminal complaint or institute an action for libel. Summary sanctions can be imposed only for misbehaviour during court proceeding. So is the case with the Commonwealth of

306. (1995) 5 S.C.C. 457.
307. 'Contempt of Court': Need for a second look, "*The Hindu*, dated 22.01.2007.

Australia. In the *King* v. *Nicholls,*[308] Chief Justice Griffith did not accede to the propositions that an imputation of want of impartiality to a Judge is necessarily a contempt of court. He allowed such comments if it was for the public benefit. The report of the Inter-Departmental Committee on The Law of Contempt,[309] approving the opinion of Griffith, C.J. said, "In most unlikely event, however, of there being just cause for challenging the integrity of a Judge or of a member of a tribunal of inquiry it could not be contempt of court to do so. Indeed it would be public duty to bring the relevant facts to light".

In England there is some ambiguity on this point. Three reports expressed three different approaches there.

1. In 1969, Salmon Committee said that "In the most unlikely event, however, of there being just cause for challenging the integrity of a judge it could not be contempt of court to do so. Indeed it would be a public duty to bring the relevant facts to light.[310]
2. The Justice Report on Contempt of Court also conceded the opportunity of making *bonafide* charges of partiality or corruption against a judge. But, it said that the appropriate purpose for this means was not the press but a letter to the Lord Chancellor.[311]
3. The Phillimore Committee on Contempt of Court did not consider that truth alone should be defence, but if in addition to proving the truth of his allegation; a defendant can also show that its publication was for the public benefit he should be entitled to an acquittal. The committee added an important proviso that public interest requires that normally allegations of judicial corruption or lack of impartiality should be submitted to the Lord Chancellor.[312]

308. (1911) 12 C.L.R. 280.
309. See, Report of 1969.
310. The Salmon Committee Report, 1969, p. 15.
311. Contempt of Court, page 15, a report by Justice Chairman, Lord Shaw, 1959.
312. Commd. 5794 at Par. 164 p. 70 (1975).

In India before the commencement of the Indian Constitution, the almost uniform view of the High Courts was that the truth of the matter said to constitute contempt was no defence.[313] *In re K.L. Gauba,*[314] the Hon'ble Judge of the Lahore High Court Young C.J. and Justice Monore themselves acted against an advocate K.L. Gauba who had published a book under caption *"The new Magna Charta"* containing allegations against the said judges. They said to have done so to vindicate the prestige of the court. It did not show any inclination to allow truth as defence. In case of truth as plea, the answer of the court was:

> "Even assuming that the writer of a manifesto believes all he states therein to be true, if anything in the manifesto amounts to contempt of court, the writer is not permitted to lead evidence to establish the truth of his allegation".

The post-Constitution judicial outlook believes in putting old wine of non-allowing the truth as defence in contempt case in the new bottle. However, some rays of hope were aroused by the decision of the Supreme Court in *Bathina Ramakrishna Reddy* v. *State of Madras,*[315] but it died away after some time. The spirit flied off when in *Perspective Publication* v. *State of Maharashtra,*[316] on the question of truth as defence in contempt case the Supreme Court said, "It may be that truthfulness or factual correctness is a good defence in an action for libel, but in the law of contempt there are hardly any English or Indian cases in which defence is recognized".

The above view was again fallowed in *C.K. Daphatry* v. *O.P. Gupta*[317] by the Supreme Court.

The chief reasons for not allowing allegations to be substantiated by leading evidence appears to be that every

313. See, *Tushar Kanti Ghose* case, A.I.R. 1935 Cal. 419.
314. A.I.R. 1942 Lah. 105.
315. A.I.R. 1952 S.C. 149.
316. (1969) 2 S.C.R. 779.
317. A.I.R. 1971 S.C. 1132.

attempt to justify would constitute a new offence of contempt.[318]

It is submitted that in a democracy there is no need for Judges to vindicate their authority or display majesty or pomp. Their authority will come from the public confidence and this in turn will be an outcome of their own conduct, their integrity, impartiality, learning and simplicity. If truth is no defence in a contempt case then the freedom of speech and expression and right to know will go far.

"A fresh, modern, democratic approach like that in England, the United States and Commonwealth countries is now required in India to do away with the old anachronistic view".[319]

It is matter of satisfaction that our parliament has now intervened and radically changed the law by Act 6 of 2006 by amending section 13 of the Contempt of Courts Act, 1971. It reads:

> "Notwithstanding anything contained in any law for the time being in force, the court may permit, in any proceedings for contempt of court, justification by truth as a valid defence if it is satisfied that it is in public interest and the request for invoking the said defence is *bonafide*".

It is submitted that our parliament, by the recent amendment has attempted clearly to bring our law in line with European and American standard. The statement of Objects and Reasons to the said amendment states that the amendment would introduce fairness in procedure and meet the requirements of Article 21 of the constitution.

When the provisions of the Bill were discussed in the Lok Sabha, Law Minister H.R. Bharadwaj said—

> "Suppose, there is a corrupt judge and he is doing corruption within your sight, are you not entitled to say

318. Soli, J. Sorabjee, "The Law of Contempt: Some Anomalies", *The Indian Advocate* (17), p. 19.
319. *The Hindu*, dated 22.01.2007, p. 10.

that what you are saying is true and should prevail. That is also in public interest".[320]

Thus in India truth is now a defence in contempt of court proceedings if it is in the public interest and is *bonafide*. This amendment is in the right direction and was long overdue.

(vii) Contempt During Conducting Cases

The Advocates Act, 1971 provides full liberty to advocates to conduct their cases to the best of their ability in the interest of their clients, without fear and favour. But they have to observe the rules of procedure applicable to that forum and should in no way act so as to bring their profession or the court into contempt.

Now it is well settled principle that an advocate is not exempt from the ordinary disability which law imposes and his position is not inviolable and his privileges cannot be extended to interfering with the administration of justice. He is also expected to help in subsewing the course of justice and not to impede it in any manner.[321]

Thus, in *Rajendra Singh* v. *Uma Prasad*,[322] an advocate during the pendency of a suit sent a notice on behalf of his client to the defendant threatening him that unless he withdrew the plea and paid him a certain sum of money as damages he would be prosecuted criminally for defamation of the plaintiffs, the Allahabad High Court held that the advocate who drafted the notice was clearly liable in contempt since the act amounted to an interference with the administration of justice.

The aforesaid case also make it clear that if a litigant makes contemptuous statement against any person, the advocate who drafts or settles the document also commits the contempt. In *Shamsher Singh Bedi* v. *High Court of Punjab and Haryana*,[323] a notice was drafted by advocate but was sent to Magistrate by the party who was refused bail in criminal

320. 'Contempt And Truth', *The Hindu* dated 29.10.2007.
321. *Court on its own motion* v. *Radhakrishna*, A.I.R. 1957 Punj. 105.
322. A.I.R. 1935 All. 117.
323. A.I.R. 1991 S.C. 2176.

case—Allegations in notice was that in refusing bail, Magistrate acted with *malafide* intention and with a view not to displease local police.

The Supreme Court held that such remarks are scandalous and with references to judicial function of Magistrate which reference interfered with administration of justice and therefore, could not be said to be aimed at the individual. Advocate who had drafted the notice in his professional capacity could not escape the responsibility. So the court upheld the conviction of the advocate.

The aforesaid decision was affirmed by the Supreme Court *In Re Sanjiv Datta,*[324] wherein, the advocate filing the affidavit of the contemner was issued show cause notice for contempt as the affidavit contained contemptuous statements. He was found guilty of contempt. However, having regard to explanation submitted by the advocate that he had no opportunity to pursue the affidavit before filing the same and the fact that his conduct as practising lawyer in the court had been fair, his unconditional apology was accepted.

But in *Radhakishan case,*[325] it was a prosecution for blackmail in a Magistrate's court when after the complainants first witness was examined in Chief, advocate for the accused furnished an envelope, containing sixteen photos, to the witness and said that unless he withdrew the case it will be bad for the family of the witness. The court at once drew up proceedings against advocate for contempt as the words uttered by advocate amounted to nothing short of intimidating the witness. Advocate denied such intention but later tendered an apology. Mr. Justice Kapur of the Punjab High Court held it was contempt.

An advocate has necessarily to be protected when he is *bonafide* discharging his duty to the court. When a court questions counsel, the answer given by the latter cannot be attacked by opposing party as interfering with administration of Justice and is therefore, contempt.

---

324. (1995) 5 S.C.C. 457.
325. *Supra* note 321.

The principle however was recognized that when a matter is *subjudice* nothing should be done which might disturb the free course of justice. The Patna High Court in *King* v. *Parmanand,*[326] said:

> "This court will discountenance any attempt on the part of any executive official, however high he may be, to prejudge the merits of a case and to usurp the functions of the court which has got seisin of the case".

The observation of the Patna High Court reveals that advocate must be careful as to when and what he says to the court.

In *Nirmal Singh* v. *Gainda Mal,*[327] the Public Prosecutor applied for withdrawal of a case from a First Class Magistrate's court, on the ground that there was no evidence in support of it. He also added that the District Magistrate had come to the opinion that the case was false and should be withdrawn. Sanction of the First Class Magistrate was necessary under law for such withdrawal and so to influence that court by stating that some other court or public official thought the case to be false, was clearly influencing the court. The learned Chief Justice of the Pepsu High Court deprecated this in strong terms:

> "It must be remembered that once a case is before a court of law, it is for that court and that court alone to decide whether the case is true or false, and if any other person ventures to form an opinion on this point and communicates that opinion to the court during the pendency of the case his conduct amounts to interference in the administration of justice and consequently to contempt of court. The same remarks apply to a person who communicates to the court someone else's opinion about a pending case in the court".

326. A.I.R. 1949 Pat. 222.
327. A.I.R. 1954 (pep.) 91.

It should be noted that in such cases the honesty of the motive of the contemner can be no defence to action in contempt. Therefore, it is the duty of counsel to be careful and accurate in the statement of facts in order to assist the court and not to do anything to deceive or overreach it, but that does not mean that he is under an obligation to state the facts or the legal position favourable to his opponent and that an omission to discharge that supposed obligation would amount to contempt. Simply because a ground taken is eventually repelled as based on incomplete statement of facts or on an erroneous view of the law, it cannot be stated that counsel is liable for comment. But not placing material parts of a document (matter written on the overleaf of remand report filed with a bail application) before the court rendered the counsel liable for punishment for contempt.[328]

Tutoring a witness outside or in the court,[329] writing of letters by the plaintiffs advocate to probable witnesses of the defendant saying that the defendant has robbed the estate[330] and thereby trying to influence them have also been held to contempt of court.

(viii) Strike and Boycott of Court

Strike reported by advocates has many long ranging repercussions and as such it needs serious considerations. It is true that in every democratic set-up, protest is an essential weapon in the armory of every citizen. It is also true that we have found our freedom by way of 'satyagrah'. Like other forms of protest the right to strike places pressure on those in power to recognize dissent and respond to just demand. But the court process stands on different footing and has not to be obstructed by strikes or boycotts.

It should always be remembered that when lawyers go on strike it is only the litigant who suffer. During the strike, in the guise of taking urgent matters of injuction, bail, etc. lawyer can remain monetarily very comfortable. They earn a well-paid

---

328. *A.T.M. Rangaramankjan* v. *State of Andhra Pradesh,* 1998 (1) ALD 797 (J.B.).
329. *In the matter of a Pleader,* A.I.R. 1942 Mad. 701.
330. *Welby* v. *Still* (1892) 66 L.T. 523.

rest. Similarly, the judges are also not at a loss. So every body is happy at the cost of the poor litigant, who has no alternative except to wait and wait till the strike is called off.

As a result of strike and boycotts the regular work in the courts comes to stand-still resulting in delaying the justice, causing hardship to the clients. The worst sufferers are the poor litigants. Can we afford these strikes and boycotts? Due to the backlog of cases in each and every court lawyer's strike is making thing much worse day by day. It is rightly pointed out by Mr. Naresh Sujana, an advocate that, there is an impending danger of the whole of judiciary gets 'collapsed'. It's a highly deplorable behaviour to be condemned by all classes of people.[331] Today many feel that lawyers' strike is both unethical and illegal".[332]

The Law Commission in its 131th Report recommended that lawyer should never go on strike as such a thing had pernicious tendency of eating into the vitals of independence of judiciary.[333]

Our judiciary is also not an exception. So it has never been in favour of strike by advocates. In *Emperor* v. *Rajani Kanta Bose,*[334] the Calcutta High Court held that a pleader being an officer of the court is bound to submit to its authority. He cannot join any action to boycott the court or political or other character.

Over the last few years the Higher Judiciary has taken a very serious view of advocates boycotting the court. In *S.J. Chaudhary* v. *Delhi Administration.*[335] the Supreme Court observed that absenting from court on a particular day in pursuance of a concerted movement on the part of the lawyers to boycott a court amounts to professional misconduct. The court also opined that having accepted the brief, if the advocate abstains from attending the court then he will be committing a breach of his professional duty.

331. S.C. Mukherjee "On Cease Work", A.I.R.(J) 1990, 88.
332. Mahesh Jethmalani, 'The Lawyers, Strike', Ed. 3 Lexet Juris, March 1988.
333. See the report.
334. A.I.R. 1922 Cal. 515.
335. (1984) 1 S.C.C. 722.

Raising the pitch of its view to condemn the strike in *Mahabir Prasad Singh* v. *Jack Aviation Private Limited*[336], the Supreme Court held that the strike by lawyers amounts to contempt of court. The court ruled:

> "No court is obliged to adjourn a case because of strike call given by any association of advocates or a decision to boycott the courts in general or any particular court. It is the solemn duty of every court to proceed with the judicial business during court hours. No court should yield to pressure tactic or boycott calls or any kind of brow beating".

In *Roman Services Private Limited* v. *Subhash Jack Aviation Private Limited*[337] the Supreme Court again emphasized that "Inaction will surely attribute to the erosion of ethics and values in legal profession. The defaulting court may also be contributory to the contempt of court". Thus the last sentence gives enough indication that strike in response to the call of strike by bar association may amount to contempt of court.

The decisions pronounced by the Apex Court in *K. John Roshy* v. *Dr. Tarakeshwar Prasad Shaw*[338], *Koluttu Mottil Razak* v. *State of Kerla*[339], *Uttar Pradesh Sales Tax Service Association* v. *Taxation Bar Association*[340] and *Supreme Court Bar Association* v. *Union of India*[341] are also indicator to the same effect that strike by the lawyers will be dealt as contempt of the court.

The Constitution Bench of the Supreme Court in *Harish Uppal* v. *Bar Council of India,*[342] held that the strike by lawyers *perse* is illegal. In the instant case a bench of five learned judges[343] held that advocates have no right to go on strike and

336. (1999) 1 S.C.C. 37.
337. (2001 1 S.C.C. 118.
338. (1998) S.C.C. 624.
339. (2000) 4 S.C.C. 465.
340. (1995) 5 S.C.C. 716.
341. (1998) 4 S.C.C. 409.
342. A.I.R. 2003 S.C. 739.
343. The Bench constituting of Mr. Justice G.B. Patnaik (C.J.I.), Justice S.N. Variava, Justice Dorai Swamy Raju, Justice Sham and Justice D.M. Dharmadhikari.

if they have any grievance they should pursue other avenues of settlement. However, the bench conceded that where the dignity, integrity and independence of judiciary is threatened, the Bar as a mark of protest can abstain from work for not more than a day. Thus, the court has recognized the right to protest but at the same time said that in case any Bar association calls for a strike or boycott the concerned State Bar Council and on their failure the Bar Council of India immediately take action against the advocates who give a call for strike.

Therefore, the protest, if any is required can only be by giving press statements, T.V. interviews carrying out on court premises banners and placards, wearing black or white or any colour arm bands, peaceful protest marches outside and away from court premise, going on *Dharnas* or relay fasts, etc.

Hence protest must be resorted to on a non-coercive basis as a last resort for a limited duration bearing in mind the workload of the courts and the effect of protest on the administration of justice.

The above decisions make clear that our judiciary always condemns the call of strike by lawyer and even it declares such act as contempt of court. Some practical problems still remain unresolved. It is submitted with due regards to the judiciary, that mere declaration is not enough; the major problem is the implementation of such declaration. In case of countrywide call of strike judiciary becomes helpless.

The country wide strike by lawyers in the year of 2002 was the clear evidence of the aforesaid problem. A countrywide strike was held by the lawyers on the call of the Bar Council of India on 18 December, 2002. The Supreme Court of India banned the proposed strike one day before, but lawyers across the country struck to protest against the amendments introduced to the Legal Service Authority Act and the Civil Procedure Code.

The pertinent and most significant question arises: have the lawyers privilege to disobey the order of the highest court of the land? Does not strike *enmasse* by the lawyers' amount to interference with the administration of justice? Will not such type of judicial helplessness to enforce its order create many recurring problems?

Mr. K. Pradeep views that lawyers not heeding the Supreme Court's ban of their strike is the height of contempt.[344]

However, reacting on country wide strike on 18.12.2002 on call of the Bar Council of India despite the Supreme Court ban on such strike a five Judge bench speaking through Mr. Justice Variava warned that if lawyers did not observe self-restraint and resorted to strike courts may think for ban on their practice.[345]

Again question arises that how it will be possible for Hon'ble Supreme Court, when it involves a large number of advocate. Certainly it will be very difficult task. Further in view of the Supreme Court decision in *Supreme Court Bar Association* v. *Union of India*[346] it will not be legally permissible for courts to do so.[347] If courts treat strike by advocates as contempt of court they can punish only with imprisonment or fine. Thus, only disciplinary committee of State Bar Council or the Bar Council of India will be competent to put ban on practice. It is submitted that where the Bar Council of India itself becomes interested in the strike, how the above dream will become true. In such a situation we agree with the decision given by the Supreme Court in Harish Uppal's case[348] that "in respect of disciplinary jurisdiction, the Supreme Court is the final appellate authority by virtue of section 38 of the Advocates Act, 1961".

Thus, even if the Bar Council do not rise to the occasion and perform their duties by taking disciplinary action on a complaint against a boycott Supreme Court can and should take action against advocates. However, the problem will not be overcomes. Section 38 of Advocates Act can be used by the Supreme Court only in appellate capacity in cases coming from Bar Council itself by way of appeal. The remedy has to

344. Pradeep, K. 'Lawyers Strike', (in) Letters to the Editor Column, *The Hindu*, 25.12.2002, p. 10.
345. See *Harrish Uppal* v. *Union of India* (2003) 2 S.C.C. 45.
346. A.I.R. 1998 S.C. 1895.
347. In the instant case, Supreme Court held that the power of the courts are subject to Advocate's Act, 1961.
348. *Supra* note 345.

be searched out somewhere else. In grave situation like countrywide strike, that too on call of Bar Council itself, the court may seriously think to resort to its power under Article 142 of the Constitution,[349] so as to meet out the need of absolute justice. Still the problem will not be satisfactorily solved and Bar Council should be persuaded to cooperate in national interest.

An unfortunate trend we see now a day is that advocates are indiscriminately indulging in boycotting courts on various grounds causing disruption in court work and difficulties to the clients. In most cases the reasons for such boycott are flimsy like an advocate being beaten by police, want of proper posting of Judges in courts, demand for new courts, etc.

(ix) Disturbing the Court Proceedings

The prestige of the courts rests on three pillars; independence, integrity and impartiality. It also depends upon the traditional atmosphere of dignified calm surrounding of the law courts. Therefore, conduct of advocates which disturbs its proceedings or otherwise interferes with the due administration of justice can also invite action in contempt of court.

Such disturbance or interference with the course of justice may even be through loud talk. As pointed out by the Hon'ble Allahabad High Court in *State* v. *Sundar Lal Srivastav,*[350] that a person who creates around the court an atmosphere resembling that a market place by talking loudly in the corridor of the court commits contempt. Again *In re Swaminath,*[351] the same High Court emphasized that where a person or organization obstructing working of the court and preventing lawyers from attending courts to plead for their clients is grave misconduct against the gravity of the court, amounts to contempt.

349. Under Article 142 the Supreme Court in the exercise of its jurisdiction may pass such decree or make such order as is necessary for doing complete justice in any cause or matter pending before it.
350. (1963) 2 Cr.L.J. 62 All.
351. (2000) All. L.J. 2985.

In a famous case, *Courts of its own motion* v. *B.D. Kaushik,*[352] it was held by a special Bench of 23 Judges of the Delhi High Court, that if a group of advocates stormed into various court rooms of the High Court shouting abusive slogans against Judges and disturb the functioning of the court they absolutely commit contempt. So also the action of an advocate slapping and abusing a presiding officer in court,[353] disturbing the proceedings of court by a counsel raising the pitch of his voice to an unusual level,[354] and using derogatory language and abusing a High Court Judge in the court and threatening to get transferred and impeached have been also held to be contempt.[355]

The act of disturbance may also be created by the helping another person. An interesting instance came before an American case, namely *Ex party Terry,*[356] wherein an attorney's wife jumped up when the judge was reading the judgement in a case and shouted that justice was bought. The Marshall went to remove her under order of court but the attorney assaulted the Marshall saying that no living man could touch his wife. The attorney was convicted for contempt.

In *U.S.* v. *Sacher,*[357] during a disorder in the courtroom, one lawyer made no attempt to have his clients resume their seats, while two another lawyers failed to take seats to help restore order. They were also found guilty of contempt.

It is interesting to note that, since an advocate participating in a trial has a duty not only to refrain from disorderly conduct but also to aid the court in preserving order in the court room. The decisions in *State of Andhra Pradesh* v. *J. Venkataraman,*[358] In *re Swaminath Yadav,*[359] and *State of U.P.* v. *Satendra Singh Tomar,*[360] are also based on this view

352. 1993 Cri.L.J. 336 (Delhi).
353. *A.M.J.M., 9 Jaipur City* v. *Prem Surana,* (1994) 1 R.L.R. 8.
354. *K.A. Mohammad Ali* v. *C.N. Prassannan,* 1994 supp. (3) S.C.C. 509.
355. *In re Vinay Chandra Mishra* (1995) 2 S.C.C. 584.
356. (1888) 1 28 U.S. 289, 32 L.E.D. 405.
357. 1950 C.A. 2 N.Y. 182.
358. (1997) 2 A.L.T. 456 (D.B.).
359. (2000) All. L.J. 2985 (D.B.).
360. (2001) All. L.J. 1041.

that preventing judicial officer from entering chambers and court room to discharge their duties are clear evidence of the contempt of court.

Where group of advocates enter the courtroom, hurled abuses and disrupt the court proceedings it has been held to be gross contempt.[361] So is the case of abusing and slapping of a Presiding Officer of a court. *In Re Nandlal Bulwani,*[362] an advocate who had no case on the Board shouted slogans in open court and hurled a shoe towards the court interrupting the court proceedings. Treating it to be gross contempt and rejecting the unqualified apology tendered by him as it did not appear to be *bonafide*, the Supreme Court punished him with imprisonment and fine.

(x) Influence by Private Communication

An advocate may meet the Judge in chamber on matter relating to such work of the court which has necessarily to be in chambers. He may meet socially in any place short of abusing that privilege to this professional advantage. He may also write to a Judge and receive letters from him in matters personal and not touching any aspect of court work, pending or dispose of or on the general aspect of judicial administration. But, if the purpose of doing so is to influence the Judge then he cannot do anything referred above. Private communication to a Judge seeking to influence him on any matter *subjudice* is grave misconduct amounted to contempt of court, and it is reprehensible as it tends to divert the course of justice.

Private letters to a judge to influence him on any matter *subjudice* is grave contempt of court. It is reprehensible as it tends to divert the course of justice.

In *Emperor* v. *Tushar Kanti Ghosh,*[363] Allahabad High Court held that any act or conduct with reference to a pending proceeding which has a tendency to deprive the court of the power to administer justice duly and impartially and to reduce it to impotence as regards effectual elimination of prejudice

361. *Supra* note.
362. (1999) 2 S.C.C. 315.
363. A.I.R. 1946 All. 298.

and prepossession amounts to contempt. A superior executive authority who sends a letter to the Magistrate dictating the terms of the order which is to be passed in pending proceeding commits contempt.

In *Rizwan-ul-Hasan* v. *State of U.P.*,[364] the Supreme Court has held that writing a recommendatory letter to a judicial officer about the facts of a case is a communication for the purpose of influencing his decision and hence amounts to a high contempt of court.

In *Advocate General of Madras* v. *S.V. Thonthi*,[365] the respondent to an appeal pending before the District Judge, wrote a letter to the Chief Justice of Madras High Court containing the allegations (without any attempt at its justification) that the District Judge was corrupt and that he was apprehending that a just decision would not be rendered by him in the pending appeal. It was held that the respondent was guilty of gross contempt.

In re Wallace,[366] a Barrister who was a party to suit wrote a letter to the Chief Justice casting aspersions on the administration of Justice. This was clear contempt, but the Privy Council held that the proper punishment was usual fine or imprisonment for contempt and not suspension of practice since the act indulged in was as a suitor and not as a Barrister.

But *in re Tulsidas Amanal Karam*[367] counsel had under cover of giving notice under Section 80 CPC to a Judge made sandbags allegations attributing prejudice, malice and dishonesty to a judge. The court felt that here counsel had exceeded his privilege and had made unbecoming and deliberate aspersions on judge that called for suspension of practice for six months.

Regarding the private communication with judges, the *Halsbury* say:

> "Every private communication to a Judge for the purpose of influencing his decision upon a pending matter

364. A.I.R. 1953 S.C. 185.
365. A.I.R. 1965 Mad. 415.
366. (1866) L.R. I.P.C. 283.
367. I.L.R. 1941 Bom. 548.

> whether or not accompanied by the officer of a bribe or personal abuse is contempt of court tending to interfere with the course of justice.[368]

Thus, in *Tuljaram Rao* v. *Sir James Taylor*,[369] a special Bench of the Madras High Court was clearly of the view that to comment on a case which is *subjudice* or to suggest that the court should take a certain course in respect of a matter before it undoubtedly constitute contempt and honesty of motive cannot remove it from this category. Further it is not necessary to consider in such matters whether the judge will be likely to be influenced or not by such letter. The criterion is whether the act complained of is likely to *prejudice* the course of justice.

It seems from the decisions referred above that private communication to court is most reprehensible. In such circumstances an apology tendered have also not been accepted by the court. Thus, the test of contempt is its tendency to interfere with justice. The intention of the contemner advocate and ignorance of law is of no account whatsoever.

In *Advocate General, Madras* v. *S. Sundaran*[370] it was pointed out again by the Madras High Court that every private communication to a judge with a view to influence him in a pending matter will constitute contempt of court. This is so even if the substantial allegations in the letter are contained in the pending processing it. The issue is not whether the judge is in fact influenced. The criterion is whether the act complained of is likely to prejudice the course of justice.

Thus, it is clear from the varieties of instances of professional or other misconducts discussed above that advocates who are at the center of administration of justice have been indulging into such acts, which are against the propriety and dignity of the legal profession.

368. See, Halsbury's Laws of England, Vol. 10, IIIrd ed., p. 319.
369. A.I.R. 1985 Mad. 567.
370. A.I.R. 1965 Mad. 336.

7

Ill Health of the Judiciary and Unbecoming Behaviour of Judges

The act of administering justice is considered to be a divine function. Therefore, the persons who discharge this function are expected to conduct themselves in a manner which befits to their position. The unbecoming conduct of the advocate as discussed in the last chapter was the one side of the coin of the emerging ill-health of judiciary. The other side of the coin is that our judges also are involved in such activities which are adding fuel to the fire by further accelerating the disease.

Hence, if an independent judiciary and honest Judges are regarded as the heart of a Republic then the Indian Republic is at present suffering from serious heart ailment. In fact, "the Indian Judiciary has of late, been under constant attack both external as well as internal, which is bound to cripple the health and progress of our body politic, as an ailing heart cannot ensure vigorous blood-supply for the sound health of the society".[1]

1. Gupta, Apar, 'Need to Judge the Juges', available on www.indlaw.com. Visited on 25.7.2008.

There are numerous reasons for the ill health of the judiciary but the main reason is the deviant and unbecoming behaviour of those persons who are administering justice in the court of law. Sometimes the conducts of judges are not upto mark. A number of instances occur wherein the administration of justice becomes subject of disbelief due to the conduct of the judges themselves. Some of such occurrences and instances are discussed in the present study.

I. CORRUPTING THE ADMINISTRATION OF JUSTICE

Judiciary was once considered to be a holy cow.[2] Of late, going by the reports in the news media, there have been several serious allegations of corruption against Judges in and out side the courts. While it is true that at present the cases of unbecoming behaviour of judges are increasing day by day, the instances of unbecoming behaviour of judges are not product of abrupt misdeeds. The story of the conduct of judges corrupting the administration of justice in India can be seen to have began with the report of Federal Court in respect of charges made against justice Shiva Prasad Sinha, a Judge of the High Court Judicature at Allahabad.

On 20th July, 1948 a reference was made to the Governor-General of India under Clause (b) of Section 22(2) of the Government of India Act, 1935 as adopted by the India (Provisional Constitution) Order, 1947 and the India (Provisional Constitution) Amendment Order 1948, that while hearing a case related with the Gorakhpur District[3] and two other criminal appeals,[4] Mr. Justice Sinha gave vent to a violent outburst of temper in court and great annoyance to his fellow judge Mr. Justice 'Waliullah'. His behaviour was improper and the cumulative effect of which was to lower the dignity of his office and undermine the confidence of the public in the administration of justice.

---

2. See, Report of Center for Media Studies, 'India's Corruption Study, 2005, p. 10.
3. See Padrauna case, available on www.judgesplot.com. Visited on 2.7.2006.
4. Criminal Revision no. 1150 of 1945.

There were several other charges against the learned Judge, viz.:

1. The aforementioned appeal was to be dismissed by him without arguments and irrespective of its merits.
2. He had earned for himself the reputation of having his favourites, and taken favour of his brother Mr. Shambhu Prasad who had appeared as a counsel in appeal,
3. He had been guilty of conduct outside the court because when Mr. M.C. Gupta was candidate for the post of the Executive Officer of the Allahabad Municipal Board, Mr. Justice Sinha went to the house of Mr. Khan Mazahar Husain, Superintendent of the High Court to canvass his support and to secure the votes of other members of the Municipal Board for Mr. M.C. Gupta, and lastly,
4. Mr. Justice Sinha gave an incorrect declaration that he was born on 26th February, 1894, but the correct date of birth was found to fall in the month of February 1891.

After giving the most anxious consideration to the above charges in view of this being the first case of its kind in the history of the Indian Courts Chakravarti Rajagopalachari, Governor-General of India accepted the report of the Federal Court and removed Mr. Justice Shiva Prasad Sinha from his office. However, self-respecting judge himself resigned.

The incident of Justice Sinha took place, in Independent India but at that time the Constitution of India had not come into force. The independent and democratic India adopted its Constitution on January 26, 1950, deemed to be an epoch and liberally embodying the doctrine of separation of powers, ascribed to *Montesquieu* and establishing an independent judiciary, to discharge its functions without fear or favour. Its considerable autonomy has been utilized by the judiciary for flowering *pro bono Publico*[5] causes and engineering devices for special safeguard.

5. For the public good, for the welfare of the whole.

Therefore, constitutionally the Indian Judiciary has been assigned with the role of sentinel the *qui-vive* to protect the fundamental rights and to hold even the scales of justice between the citizens and the State. But, it is also true that, the law of human conduct has laid down considerable precedent that for the use of a device there also exists its abuse. To cite a primitive and simplistic illustration, *a fire cooks as well as destroys*. Thus, has this autonomy to the judiciary, become a vassal of prerogative, a fiefdom of personal fashion. The same has been succinctly stated by Justice Frankfurter, "that man being what he is, cannot be safely trusted with the complete immunity from outward responsibility in depriving others of their rights".[6] Recent cases of misconduct have raised serious doubts as to the absence of accountability.[7] The masses have started questioning and proposing that whether the malady of corruption has crept in the judicial system and whether there, exist sufficient and adequate checks and balances to absolute exercise of judicial power. It is unfortunate that in Independent India there are enough indication that corruption in higher judiciary has reached the alarming stage.

Today, the decline in the moral ethics of judges of constitutional courts in India is visible, visceral and venomous, and what we are witnessing is the transformation of the country into a predatory society, where the corrupt and their enforcers prey on the hopeless and the helpless. There has been a central loss of character among the judges of higher courts too. Some of such shocking instances are as under:

> To begin with the Madras scandal, in the year of 1974 at Madras (Chennai) a case arose from the discovery of huge quantities of money in the residence of Justice K. Veeraswamy, then Chief Justice of the Madras High Court. However, when Central Bureau of Investigation prosecuted him for corruption, the Supreme Court of India ruled that no First Information Report can be registered against a Judge, nor a criminal investigation be initiated without prior consent of Chief Justice of India.[8]

---

6. *Supra* note 1.
7. *Ibid*.
8. For detail see, chapter IV also.

Likewise, the mysterious involvement of Mysore High Court Judges in a sex-scandal, where even the Supreme Court refused to release the committee's report on ground of confidentiality and exonerated them.[9] The case of additional District Judge of Mumbai is no less astounding.[10] The judge was accepting bribes from the enemies of the nation and was acting hand-in-glove with them to facilitate their illegal designs.[11]

The result of these misdemeanors has been to camouflage rather than to expose corruption in the judiciary. Only those cases, where there has been considerable debate and patent misconduct, have been exposed and in very few cases Judges have been prosecuted. There exist some documented cases, where judges of the higher judiciary have been charged for accepting illegal gratification or involvement in financial misappropriation or moral turpitude. Some instances are as under:

> Firstly, reference can be made to the case of Mr. Justice V. Ramaswamy. In this case for the first time since the Constitution came into force, the procedure laid down in 124(5) to remove a Supreme Court judge was put in motion.

Justice Ramaswamy, whose Madras residence is incidentally named 'Coin House' hit the national headlines in 1992-93 when as Supreme Court judge his parliamentary removal process came before Parliament. The issue related to his days as the Chief Justice of Punjab and Haryana High Court in Chandigarh.[12] 108 members of the Ninth Lok Sabha gave notice to the speaker of a motion for presenting an address to the President for removal of Justice Ramaswamy on the report of Comptroller and Auditor General, wherein he found serious discrepancies in the account relating to the furnishing and carpeting of Chief Justice's residence and also

9. "The Judiciary", *Frontline*, Vol. 19, issue 21, Oct. 12-25, 2002, p. 13.
10. *Id.*, p. 15.
11. *Ibid.*
12. During November 11, 1981 to October 6, 1989.

claiming reimbursement for telephone calls made to his family members in Madras.

The allegations against Mr. Justice V. Ramaswamy were:

1. That he personally got purchased carpets and furniture for his residence and for the High Court costing about Rs. 50 lakhs from public funds from hand-picked dealers at highly inflated prices. This was done without inviting public tenders and by privately obtaining a few quotations, most of which were forged or bogus.
2. That he also got payments made to hand-picked dealers for furniture and carpets ostensibly purchased for his residence which were never delivered.
3. That he misappropriated some of the furniture, carpets and other items purchased from court funds for his official residence costing more than Rs. 1,50,000 and did not account for the same at all.
4. That he replaced several items of furniture, carpets and suitcases, etc. of a value of more than Rs. 30,000 which had been purchased by him for his official residence from public funds, by old and inferior quality items, with the object of deriving under benefit for himself.
5. That he purchased from public funds more than Rs. 13 lakhs worth of furniture and other associated items for his official residence at Chandigarh even though he was entitled to furniture worth Rs. 38,500 only. That in the process, he wilfully evaded several rules, and sanctioned money for such purchases by splitting up bills.
6. That he got purchased 25 silver maces for the High Court at a cost of Rs. 3,60,000 from a firm at his home town in Madras at highly inflated prices without inviting competitive quotations. This was done even after the other Judges of the High Court had opposed the purchase of these maces on the ground that were wholly unnecessary and appeared to be a relic of the colonial past.

7. That he misused public funds to the extent of Rs. 9.10 lakhs by making the court pay for non-official calls made on his residential telephones at Chandigarh during his $22^1/_2$ months in office as Chief Justice of Punjab and Haryana High Court.
8. That he abused his authority of Chief Justice to make the Punjab and Haryana High Court pay Rs. 76,150 for even his residential telephones at Madras.
9. That he misused his staff cars provided to him by taking them from Chandigarh to hill stations for vocations and to Madras for his son's wedding and spent more than one lakh of public money for paying for the petrol of these staff cars. He even got himself paid for false petrol bills and other false bills relating to car repairs, etc.
10. That he gave four unjustified promotions each within 18 months to several members of the subordinate staff of the High Court whom he misused for aiding and abetting his above acts done for his personal pleasure.

In response to public opinion Chief Justice Sabyasachi Mukharji passed an order in open court, requesting Justice V. Ramaswami to proceed on leave during pendency of the enquiry into the serious allegations made against him. During the pendency of the enquiry he was requested not to discharge judicial function.[13]

Thereafter, a committee of three Judges of the Supreme Court consisting of Mr. Justice B.C. Ray, Mr. Justice M.N. Venkatachaliah and Mr. Justice Jagannatha Shetty was appointed to advise the Chief Justice on the future conduct of the case. On the report of the three judges committee the then Chief Justice Ranganath Mishra stated that the only option left in the circumstances is that to campaign for the institution of impeachment proceedings.

The impeachment motion was admitted on 12 March, 1991 by the Lok Sabha Speaker Rabi Ray. He proceeded to constitute an Enquiry Committee consisting of Justice P.B.

13. *'Impeachment of Justice* v. *Ramaswami'*, The *Lawyers*, 1993, May, p. 19.

Swant, a sitting Judge of the Supreme Court, Chief Justice Desai of the Bombay High Court and Mr. Chinnapa Reddy, a retired Supreme Court Judge as a distinguished Jurist. Before the committee could present its report, the 9th Lok Sabha was dissolved.

In this regard a question arose in *Sub-Committee of Judicial Accountability* v. *Union of India*,[14] whether dissolution of Lok Sabha put an end to motion for removal of the concerned Supreme Court Judge? The court's response to this question was that the motion for removal of judges under Article 124 of the Constitution does not lapse with the dissolution of the House. The Apex Court reached this conclusion as a result of interpretation of Sections 3(1) and (6) of the Judges (Inquiry) Act. Referring to these statutory provisions, the court observed: "The effect of these provisions is that the motion shall be kept pending till the committee submits its report and if the committee finds the judge guilty, the motion shall be taken up for consideration". In the long and arduous process of removal of the Supreme Court Judge, the third stage was reached when the Inquiry Committee reported that acts committed by Justice Ramaswamy were of such a nature that his continuance in office will be prejudicial to the administration of justice and public interest.

With the tenth Lok Sabha the report of the committee was tabled in Parliament on December 17, 1992. Thereafter, the motion was debated in the Lok Sabha. The case of Justice Ramaswamy in the House was ably argued by lawyer-politician and member of the Rajya Sabha, Mr. Kapil Sibbal. Ultimately, the motion was put to vote in the House, but Justice Ramaswamy escaped impeachment by inches, because the motion was lost as it could not receive the requisite votes in the House because of the absence of the Congress Party members "under pressure from it's A.I.A.D.M.K. and its own Tamilnadu unit".[15] Recent incidence of impropriety committed

---

14. A.I.R. 1992 S.C. 320, see also *Krishnaswami* v. *Union of India* (1999) 4 S.C.C. 605. In the instant case the functioning of the committee was challenged, but Supreme Court held that petitioner had no *locus standi*.
15. *The Hindu*, dated 26.12.1992, p. 12.

by Mr. Justice S. Sen of Calcutta High Court and consequent communication of Chief Justice of India to Prime Minister of India to initiate impeachment process after his refusal to resign has added fuel to the fire of Judicial Credibility.[15a]

In 2009 very acute controversy arose as to the elevation of the Chief Justice *Dinakaran* of the Karnataka High Court to the Supreme Court bench in view of allegation of graving governments' land in Karnataka. Though Chief Justice *Dinakaran* could not be alevated to could not find it controversial to take effective measure against Chief Justice *Dinakaran*. The controversy took a new twist and removal process has been intiated against him on the basis of a motion admitted by the chairman council of the State who has appointed a three member panel headed by Justice *V.S. Sirpurkar* of the Supreme Court of India. The members being *J.A.R. Dave,* Chief Justice of Andhra Pradesh High Court and *P.P. Rao,* senior advocate of the Supreme Court. The investigation is in progress.

The above case of Justice V. Ramaswamy gave the clear indication that in India the cumbersome procedure laid down by the Article 124 is not able to discipline the erring judges. Again, the public interest litigation filed by Mr. C. Ravichandran Iyer,[16] against Mr. Justice A.M. Bhattacharjee, Chief Justice of the Bombay High Court raises the question of the credibility of the judges.

In the aforesaid case, the petition concerned the resolution passed by the Bombay Bar Association against Mr. Justice A.M. Bhattacharjee. It was stated that Mr. S.S. Musafir, Chief Executive of Reebuck Publishing, London, paid eighty thousand U.S. dollars by way of royalty for two years for a book named 'Muslim Law and The Constitution" authored by the learned Chief Justice. There was also an inconclusive negotiation for seventy-five thousand U.S. Dollars for overseas publishing rights of his book "Hindu Law and the Constitution". He did not divulge the information but had kept it confidential.

15a. *Id.,* dated 09.09.2008, p. 12.

16. *C. Ravichandran Iyer* v. *Justice A.M. Bhattacharjee & Others* (1995) 1 S.C.C. 447.

Since late 1994 there was considerable agitation amongst the members of the bar that certain persons whose names were known and who were seen in the court and were being openly talked about, were bringing influence and could influence the course of judgements of the former Chief Justice of Bombay. As a consequence of the Bar resolution, the Chief Justice had to resign. Even his resignation did not satisfy as the amount involved was disproportionate. It was alleged to be for a purpose other than the extensible purpose and thereby raising a serious doubt as to the integrity of the Chief Justice.[17]

There are visible signs of decline in judicial prestige. In March 2003, Mr. Justice Shamit Mukherjee of the Delhi High Court was arrested by the Central Bureau of Investigation under the Anti-Corruption Act, 1988 and Criminal Procedure Code, 1973 for Criminal conspiracy and allegedly involving in serious graft charges including womanising and involvement in the multi-crore Delhi Development Authority Corruption ultimately he resigned.[18] In Chandigarh there was also considerable Furor over three judges of the Punjab and Haryana High Court accepting membership from the golf course club, namely, the *Forest Hill Club*.[19]

The question arises, should the judges have accepted *ex-officio* or honorary membership of a club mirrored in litigation and controversy? When the Chief Justice issued notice to two judges to explain their membership of such club, was it right for the judges other than the two to write back? If the Chief Justice can't question fellow judges, who else can? After all, to re-paraphrase William Shakespeare, "wrong doers for their wrong doing have authority when Judges wrong themselves". Later when the Chief Justice sought the explanation from some others on matters of legal propriety, as many as 25 Judges submitted leave application. Even though these applications were sent in individually, similar wording on most

17. Prasad, Anirudh, *Principle of the Ethics of Legal Profession In India*, IInd ed. 2006, p. 109.
18. Goyal, K.N., "Judicial accountability *v.* Independence", available at www.hindustantimes.com., visited on 2.7.07
19. Judicial conduct in India, available at www.mortgage-vortex.com., visited on 15.5.2008.

applications indicated common intent. What does this mean? If government or private employees had done so, it would amount to trade union activity. In the military it could amount to collective insubordination. Perhaps the judges themselves need to ponder over the rectitude of their action, whatever the provocation. "Nobody has a more sacred obligation to obey the law than those who make the law", said the Greek philosopher, Sophocles, long ago.[20]

However, in Madhya Pradesh signaling a strong warning to the corrupt persons in all sectors, including judiciary Madhya Pradesh Chief Minister Babulal Gaur on September 16, 2004 said that 22 judges have been dismissed on the recommendation of the High Court for alleged corruption and irregularities.[21]

The Punjab and Haryana High Courts was again highlighted when the Bar association of the said High Court demanded action against the three judges after reports about their alleged involvement in the scam began to appear in the media. It was alleged that Mr. Sidhu had organized the manipulation of marksheet and pre-delivery of examination paper in order to help Mr. Justice Amarbir Gill's daughter Amol Gill and Mr. Justice M.L. Singhal's daughter Sapna Singhal to get a government job. The third judge, Mr. Justice Mehtab Gill allegedly tunneled several candidates through Mr. Sidhu's enterprise of fraud and promised legal protection for Sidhu and his aides. In their testimony, Mr. Sidhu and co-accused confirmed the involvement of these three Judges.

The then Chief Justice of the Punjab and Haryana High Court Mr. Justice Aran B. Saharya, had submitted a report to Chief Justice of India, Mr. Justice B.N. Kirpal on the allegations against three Judges in connection with the Punjab Public Service Commission case for jobs scam. Chief Justice Kirpal retired without taking any follow-up action on Mr. Justice Saharya's report. He reportedly[22] recommended transfer of one of the tainted Judges, Justice Amarbir Singh Gill, to the Guwahati High Court and asked Mr. Justice S. Rajendra Babu

20. *Supra* note 1.
21. *Supra* note 19.
22. *Frontline,* December 6, 2002, p. 12.

of the Supreme Court to study the report to arrive at the guilt of the other two judges.

However, Justice Amarbir Singh Gill was not transferred because of opposition to the proposal from the Guwahati Bar, which felt that the Guwahati High Court was being considered a 'dumping place' for tainted judges.

Besides, transfer was never intended as a punitive measure either under the transfer policy enunciated by the Supreme Court, the second and third judges cases or under the in-house procedure, evolved by the Supreme Court in 1995.[23] However, in the aforesaid case a committee was constituted comprising the Chief Justice of the Andhra Pradesh High Court, A.R. Laxman, the Chief Justice of Madras High Court, B. Subhashan Reddy, and Justice Sachidanand Jha of the Allahabad High Court, to study Justice Saharya's report and examine the veracity or otherwise of the allegations against the three Judges. The committee submitted its report to the Chief Justice of India.

As revealed by Chief Justice Patanaik a day before his retirement, the in-house committee appointed by him in the Punjab Judges case had concluded that the judges misconduct did not warrant their removal. The committee exonerated Justice M.L. Singhal, while holding Justices Mehtab Gill and Amarbir Singh Gill guilty of misconduct.[24] Justice Patanaik, in an interview to a newspaper, declined to go into the basis of the committee's findings. While he claimed that: "He was bound by the committee's report and his only option was to call the two Judges found guilty by the committee and advice them accordingly".[25]

Following this, Justice Amarbir Singh Gill wrote to Justice Patanaik that he would be taking leave from December 16, 2002 until his retirement in May, 2003. As Mehtab Singh Gill did not get back to justice Patanaik on what he intended to do, Justice Patanaik passed an order on December 15, 2002 depreciating his misconduct. In his order he also warned

23. *Supra* note 16.
24. *Supra* note
25. *Frontline*, February 16, 2003, p. 9.

Mr. Justice Mehtab Singh Gill to be careful in future but no further action was taken against three judges.

Now-a-day, "Gaziabad judges scam" is pending before the Supreme Court of India.[26] The case allegedly involves 26 Judges—one Supreme Court Judge, seven High Court Judges, six retired High Court Judges, ten serving district Judges and two retired district Judges. This case is related to alleged misappropriation of 23 crore Rupees from the Provident Fund contributions of class IVth employees with the connivance of officials and Judges.

The Supreme Court on 17th July, 2008 posted this interesting case for hearing. The decision to hear the matter in an open Court was taken after a brief hearing in the chambers of Chief Justice K.G. Balakrishnan. The Bench included Mr. Justice P. Sathasivam and Mr. Justice J.M. Panchal. Later on Chief Justice withdrew from the bench hearing the case and court ordered that judges should not be interrogated like common men by the police.

Though the above case is *subjudice* before the Supreme Court, but one thing is clear that the instances discussed above are potentially taint the image of the Judiciary. The cases discussed above are related to the financial misappropriation and bias, etc. however, there exist multifarious causes of malaise in judiciary. It is submitted that illegal gratification are not only the sole corruptor. There may also be a judge who is not of good moral character, such as not being above board in the matter of integrity and honesty, showing favour to a section of the members of the Bar, or he being a casteist or parochial in his approach in the administration of justice. It has been rightly pointed out by Mr. Justice P.N. Bhagwati, that "*I think it was Mr. Justice Jackson who said that Judges are more often bribed by their ambition and loyalty than by money*".[27]

It is indeed a historical truth shrewdly observed by Ehrilch that "in the long-run there is no guarantee of Justice, except the personality of the judge". In this regard the Rajasthan and Karnataka scandals are worth mention.

---

26. *The Hindu*, dated 16.12.2008, p. 1.
27. *Union of India* v. *Sankal Chand Himmatlal Sheth*, A.I.R. 1977 S.C. 2328.

In Rajasthan case an allegation was made against the Mr. Justice Arun Madan that he was involved in a proposition to a lady doctor to have sex with him in exchange for a judicial favour.[28] The lady doctor was prosecuted for running clinic where the unlawful abortion was taking place and the case was in the Bench of Mr. Justice Madan. It was alleged that he offered judicial favour by saying that:

> "AGAR SAJA SEY BACHENA HAI TO MERE SATH SEX KARO".

A three Judge committee set-up by Justice Patanaik, confirmed the above allegations against Justice Madan. The committee headed by the Chief Justice of the Punjab and Haryana High Court, Justice B.K. Roy submitted its report to Justice Patanaik indicting Justice Madan on a complaint made by lady doctor. But again no effective action could be taken against the judge.

Similarly, in Karnataka Scandal, the complaint was made that a group of judges of the Karnataka High Court were involved in sexual misconduct. This case again did not result into any deterrent example. The Bench had dismissed the petition filed by senior advocate *Indira Jai Singh* to make public the in-house-inquiry committee's report on the Karnataka scandal on the grounds that the Chief Justice of India had set-up the committee only under moral authority and report was confidential.[29] The Bench also overlooked the fact that the in-house-inquiry committee had its legal basis in the Apex Court judgement in Bhattacharjee case in 1995. Looking after the growing tendency of corruption in Judiciary a former Chief Justice *Som Piroj Bharucha* suggested that while upto 20 percent of the judges become corrupt, there was virtually no way to discipline the black sheep in the court.[30] Justice V.N. Khare (former C.J.I.) said:[31] Karnataka scandal, Rajasthan scandal,

28. Venkatesan V., "Judging the Judges" available at www.ind.law.com. Visited on 2.7.2006, pp. 1-6.
29. *Supra* note 1.
30. 2002(2) SCALE J-1.
31. *Supra* note 28, p. 6.

Punjab scandal and the Delhi scandal—all hit at the image of the Judiciary. He puts the question crisply *"who will Judge the judges"*?

The question of credibility of the higher judiciary has once again come into focus with a report suggesting that substantial number of High Court Judges and the machinery appointing them have disregarded the requirement of Bar Council of India Rules as well as the ethics provided by the restatement of value of Judicial life[32] adopted by the Supreme Court in 1997. What is shaking is that in a number of cases relatives of the working Judges are indulged in practising before them. This may be found across the country. On July 28, 2003 the Bar Council of India forwarded to the Union Law Ministry a list of 131 judges (out of a total 499) in 21 High Courts and 180 advocates with their names and nature of relationship. Bar Council of India, Vice-Chairman Adish C. Aggarwala released the list, compiled on the basis of inputs supplied by the State Bar Councils, to the media. The Bar Council of India appealed to the centre and the Supreme Court to transfer such judges to other States. It had threatened to take disciplinary action against the Advocates concerned, and suspend their licenses if the centre and the Supreme Court did not respond forthwith.[33]

During last two decades the degradation in Judges' morality has not affected only the national scenario but International scenario also. An article published in a magazine, opens thus:

> "There were dark hints of a high level deal for Justice Pathak's nomination for the International Court of Justice at Hague".[34]

---

32. Under code 3 of those values, judges should eschew close association with individual member of the Bar, particularly those who practise in the same court. Code 4 says a Judge should not permit any member of his immediate family, if a member of the Bar to appear before him.
33. Venkatesan, V., "The question of credibility" available at, http://india.eu.org, visited on 2.7.2007.
34. see, "Lid off the Pandera's Box of Judicial Corruption", *The Lawyers'*, January 1990, p. 25.

These are but a few instances of the lack of public morality that has crept into our judicial system and are also a pointer to the fact that even the presiding duties of Higher courts are not immune from the glamour, glitter and galloping corruption in the society. Thus, the corruption in the Judiciary is reaching height day-by-day.

A study conducted by the Centre for Media Studies[35] in 2005 reveals that, value of corruption in the judiciary on the country level is estimated at Rs. 2630 crores per annum. Around 13.37% of households claimed to have interacted with judiciary in the last year. This figure is higher in urban areas (15.73%) than rural areas (12.43%). 6.3% of the households interviewed have claimed to pay bribes.

The said study also claims that on question: is judiciary corrupt? More than three-forth (79%) of the respondents, who had been interacting with the judiciary agree with the statement that corruption was prevalent in the department. Surprisingly, only 8% of those respondents felt that there was no corruption in judiciary. However, not much difference is seen in perception of corruption the judiciary for status having low/high strength of judiciary per lakh of population.

Perception of Corruption	*States : Judicial Strength*			*Total*
	High	*Medium*	*Low*	
Disagree	9	5	7	6
Not say	16	11	14	13
Agree	74	83	76	79

Nearly three fourths of the respondents, who have been interacting with judiciary, were of the opinion that judiciary was not committed to tight corruption. However, 21% felt that they were committed. Around 26% respondents in the states having judicial strength per lakh of population believed that judiciary was committed, against 18% in states having low strength of judiciary.

35. Available at www.indlaw.com.

Level of Commitment	States : Judicial Strength-wise			Total
	High	Medium	Low	
Not committed	56	61	54	58
Indifferent	15	13	21	16
Committed	26	19	18	21

On the question has corruption increased or declined in last one year? More than half of the respondents (64%) who have been interacting with department believe that corruption has increased during last few years.

However, more than one fourth believed that corruption has actually declined. The reason for decline in corruption, according to respondents, is due to strict control over officials (52%), honest working of officials (42%) and increase in awareness among public (6%).

II. UNBECOMING BEHAVIOUR OF JUDGES AND CONTEMPT OF COURT

The instances of unbecoming behaviour of the judges discussed earlier related to their conduct outside the court. Sometimes their misconduct may arise in course of the administration of justice and therefore, may involve their conduct in the court itself.

The natural question arises if parties, witness, press and even lawyers can be proceeded against for contempt of court for interfering the course of law or for bringing into disrespect the fountain of justice, may judges also be proceeded for committing the contempt of court? A very clear answer of this question was given by the Joint Committee of Parliament[36] by including the statutory provision, Section 16(1) in the contempt of Court Act, 1971. It runs as under:

> "Subject to the provisions of any law for the time being inforce, a judge, magistrate or the persons acting

36. Committee Presided over by Dr. Bhargava, Member of Parliament in 1969.

judicially shall also be liable for contempt to his own court or any other court in the same manner as any other individual is liable and the provisions of this Act so for as may apply accordingly".

However, it immunizes certain remarks or observations made in discharge of official duty by saying that, "Nothing in this section shall apply to any observation or remarks made by a judge, magistrate or other person acting judicially, regarding a subordinate court in an appeal or revision pending before such judge, magistrate or other person against the order of judgement of the subordinate court".[37]

It is most pertinent to note that this statutory provision is very necessary in view of growing tendency on the part of some Judges, indulging in unbecoming language against lawyer or party or even another judges or court, or his involvement into insubordination or any act which brings disrepute to the administration of justice or shakenes the public confidence in judiciary. By virtue of the aforementioned section the judges seem to only a part of the court and like any other person it is their duty to maintain the dignity and decorum of the court. They too should do nothing which may obstruct or interfere with the due course of justice. If they do so they should be liable for contempt of court.

It goes without saying that, the concept of contempt of court is not meant to protect the judges personally but is conceived that it must never be allowed to be ridiculed or interfere with so as to make the common man feel that the halo of divinity and justice adorning the seat is always kept pure and unsullied and that they can always look to the person enthroned in that seat of justice as a divine, impartial, unruffled emblem of justice.

Therefore, the judges can be punished for contempt of their own court or any other court for acting unjustly, oppressively or irregularly in the execution of their duties by colour of judicial proceedings wholly unwarranted by law. However, for the purposes of the contempt of court by judges, a clear distinction is drawn between judges who is presiding

37. Section 16(2), Contempt of Courts Act, 1971.

officers of the lower judiciary or inferior courts and judges of the superior courts like High Courts and Supreme Court. The former are held to commit contempt of their own courts and as well as superior court, but, latter are not held to commit contempt. The judicial approach drawing a distinction between the judicial behaviour of the subordinate court's judges and the superior courts judges needs a thorough critical exposure. Therefore, the study will be conducted into different categories-first judicial conduct of subordinate courts' judges involving contempt of court and judicial conduct of superior courts judges, not being treated as committing contempt of court, so far.

(A) Conduct of Subordinate Court Judges Amounting to the Contempt of Court

The judicial outlook, so far, has been to keep the stream of justice pure by discipline the subordinate judges. For doing so, it has interpreted the expression 'Judge used in Section 12', the Contempt of Courts Act, 1971 strictly so as to include only Judges of the inferior courts.[38] The contempt committed by subordinate Judges may arise in a number of situations. The same are dealt herewith. In respect of contempt committed by a Judge, it is very difficult to define the exact area wherein the contempt arises.[39] The definition in section 2 of this Act can hardly suffice. Thus, it is not possible to give a tight jacket circumstances wherein a judge may be guilty of contempt of its own court or others. Therefore, it appears that the Supreme Court will be right, if it holds that section 2 of this Act cannot be considered as an exhaustive definition.[40] Some instances of unbecoming behaviour of judges which invite action in Contempt of Courts Act are given below:

(i) Unseemly Behaviour Against Advocates

It is accepted that the best way to sustain the dignity and status of judges' office, is to deserve respect from the public at large by the quality of judgement, fearlessness and objectivity

38. *G. Raja Kumari* v. *B. Krishna Rao* (1996), 3A.L.D. 848.
39. *Noorali Babul* v. *K.M.M. Shetty,* 1990 Cr.L.J. 316 (S.C.).
40. *Rama Dayal Markarha* v. *State of M.P.,* 1978 Cr.L.J. 917 (S.C.C.).

of their approach and by the restraint, dignity and decorum which they observe in their judicial conduct. Like the judges, advocates are also officers of the court, so there are reciprocal duty on Judges to maintain dignity and honour of the Bar. To quote, Supreme Court of India: "nothing is more destructive of public confidence in the administration of justice than incivility, suddenness or disrespectful conduct on the part of a counsel towards a court or disregard by the court of the privileges of the Bar".[41]

If the judges become too inhuman, lose their temper and use arduous words and indulge in unseemly and indecent language against advocates, then the impersonal concept of the seat of justice comes to be offended. If the judges bring the administration of justice into disrepute or interrupt in clean flow of the stream of justice, how can justice are administered? Can Judges in such circumstances escape from the liabilities of the contempt of court? A very clear answer was given by the Lahore High Court, even, when the Contempt of Courts Act, 1971 had not come into existence.

In *Mohammad Shafi, Advocate v. Chaudhari Qudir Baksh,*[42] a piquant situation was created by the unseemly conduct of a Judge. In the instant case rival lessees of a cinema were arraigned in a proceeding under Section 145, Criminal Procedure Code before the respondent Magistrate. On the date of hearing the counsel for appellant, represented that his client had obtained an *ad-interim* injunction in the sub-Judge's Court against the petitioner from prosecuting the proceedings till the disposal of the suit. Thereupon, the Magistrate lost his temper, got up from the chair and told the counsel:

> "This is a foolish order passed by a foolish sub-judge in a suit filed by a foolish lawyer. From where have you come? What is your standing? You seem to know nothing of law. You are instrumental in procuring this foolish order and as such you have committed a crime for which you could be sent behind prison-bars.[43]

41. *Supreme Court Bar Association* v. *Union of India,* A.I.R. 1998 S.C. 1895, p. 1918.
42. A.I.R. 1949 Lah. 270 (F.B.).
43. *Id.,* p. 274.

The Magistrate further told the counsel in a very contemptuous and furious manner that he wanted to teach him a lesson so that he could be careful in the future and that he was playing with the fire and the consequence of playing with fire was obvious.[44]

The advocate was admirable in his conduct. He cooly took down word by word what the learned Magistrate pronounced in such intemperate language and moved the High Court for a rule of contempt.

The full Bench of the Lahore High Court took a very serious view on the matter and held that remarks of Magistrate amounted to contempt of court on two counts, *firstly,* it was contempt against the sub-judge and *secondly,* it was contempt against the lawyer, an officer of the court. With regard to the former, the Bench opined that any remark made against the sub-judge who was doing his duty would excite in the minds of the people a general dissatisfaction against all judicial proceedings and that after all the injunction was against the party and the learned Magistrate could have proceeded as if no injunction was passed against his court as such and that his conduct in telling foul of another judge acting in his judicial capacity was wholly unbecoming. On the second count of contempt, i.e. against the lawyer, their Lordships observed:

> "The magistrate also committed contempt of court against the lawyer, who was after all doing duty by representing facts. If abuse of witness regarded as contempt of court on the grounds that it would intimidate other witness and thus, impede the course of justice, the intimidation of a lawyer who is representing one of the parties is also contempt as it would interfere with the administration of justice".

The magistrate had insulted the advocate without rhyme or reason and did not tender him an apology or redress till the application was heard. The court ruled that:

44. *Ibid.*

> "In all cases the prestige and dignity of the court as well as the course of justice must be preserved from all interference. No judge or magistrate has any business to lose his temper in a court of law, get up from his chair and make contemptuous remarks about other judges or counsel appearing on either side. If parties to a litigation feel that they are likely to be subjected to insulting behaviour at the hands of presiding officer of the court it would shake all confidence in the administration of justice and would thus, pollute the stream of justice".[45]

It is evident from the decision of Lahore High Court that if a judge shows unseemly behaviour against the advocate he becomes guilty of contempt of its own court. Regarding the above ruling of the Lahore High Court Justice William Douglas in the *Tagore Lecture* delivered in 1955, adverted to American conditions and said: The decision would come as a surprise to the American Bar that is accustomed only to judges holding lawyers in contempt. But it is sound theory and consistent with the concept of contempt developed in Anglo-American Law".[46]

This concept of contempt by judge against lawyer is same even after the constitution of India came into vogue. That a Judge can be guilty of contempt of its own court for his unseemly behaviour, was further supported by the decision of Allahabad High Court in *Bar Association, Moradabad* v. *Kothari Sub-Divisional Magistrate*,[47] as first time by the Indian courts. In the instant case, when the Public Prosecutor was conducting a criminal prosecution, the counsel for accused was registering his protest, addressing the Public Prosecutor and not the court. The Magistrate got agitated and ordered the defence counsel peremptorily to leave the court hall. Counsel obeyed and after some time the Bar Association took action by initiating contempt proceedings.

The Allahabad High Court observed that, a counsel has as much right to remain in the court room as the presiding officer

45. *Id.*, p. 276.
46. Vide, Studies in 'American and Indian Constitution Law', p. 278.
47. 1996 All. W.R. (H.C.) 197

himself, and so an order by presiding officer ejecting the counsel from the court room during the progress of a cause would not only pollute and *prejudice* the fair administration of Justice, but would violently shake the faith and confidence of the litigant public in the sublimity of the process of law. The court ruled: "If the presiding officer acts in such outrageous and undignified manner he can verily be held guilty of contempt of its own court for him is only one of the component parts which constitute the comprehensive and manifold concept of a court".[48] It appears from both of the decisions referred above, that when a judge uses intemperate language against lawyer without any provocation on the part of lawyer or ordered him to go out of the court-room, he is doing something which can be said as outrageous act. No rule can support his action and he have no power to do so, unless it is a case of 'laws order situation'. It is submitted that such acts are *malafide* on the part of judges and when it is *malafide* there can be no good faith, hence it constitutes contempt of court and there are no question of protection under the provisions of Judicial Officers Protection Act, or Judges Protection Act, 1985 or under section 77 of the Indian Penal Code, 1860.[49]

However, it is important to note that, when the advocates are attacked in an unbecoming way in open court by the presiding officer they should not despair, what is required of the advocate is that he need not lose his own decorum or poise on that court. If he does otherwise he will be contributing to the offence of contempt and in such an event very often it may be difficult for the higher forum of justice to held guilty of judges. As said by the Allahabad High Court in *Prag Das, Advocate* v. *P.C. Agrawal*,[50] that if a lawyer exceeds his bound to intimidate a court forgetting favourable orders and goes to the extent of calling external agencies to *overawe* the court, and court merely called in the police guard but did not order any ejection of the lawyer; then it was no contempt on the part of the judge.

48. *Ibid.*
49. Section 77 of the Indian Penal Code reads.
50. 1975 Cr.L.J. 659.

However, taking drastic action against advocate by the judge may constitute contempt. In *Hakumat Rai v. Crown*[51] an advocate, Mr. Hakumat Rai filed a bail application before a Magistrate for his client. During the cross examination the Magistrate objected to that cross examination remarking that unnecessary questions were put by the advocate, Mr. Rai. So saying the Magistrate ordered for adjourning the case and dismissed his bail application. Advocate resented such observations. The court asked advocate to reduce his protest to writing to which the latter said it was quite unnecessary and that the Magistrate's remark was improper. Advocate was thereupon ordered by the Magistrate to be kept in custody. The case was adjourned and another case was called. At this time another advocate possibly astounded by the order of the court rushed into the court room, but the chaprasi pushed him out roughly under the magistrate's order. Hakumat Rai protested against this treatment meted out to a respectable advocate. The learned magistrate took this also to be an interruption to his court work and asked Hakumat Rai to resume his seat, at which the latter said, "This was strange": All this further infuriated the Magistrate who forthwith framed six charges against Hakumat Rai under Section 228(1) of the Indian Penal Code. He pleaded not guilty but he was fined Rs. 100.

In appeal Justice Din Mahammad, held:

> "I am of opinion that in this case the magistrate was not in any way justified in taking the drastic action. It is true that lawyer should always conduct himself properly in a court of law, but the court should not be discourteous to a lawyer and should also try to maintain his respect in the eye of his clients and general public. Hypersensitiveness on the one side and rudeness on the other must be avoided at all costs".

On the merits, the learned judge found all six charges to be groundless and held that the behaviour of the magistrate was unbecoming, amounting to contempt of court. Can a Judge who punished an advocate for contempt of court, itself

51. A.I.R. 1943 Lah. 14.

be held guilty of contempt because of death of that very advocate in custody?

This interesting question arose before the Apex Court in a petition recently filed therein by advocate of Allahabad High Court, Mr. Altemish Rein. The petition related to Mr. Awasthi, an advocate of Allahabad High Court who was found guilty of contempt of court by the Allahabad High Court for attributing motives to Judges, accusing them being biased and scandalising the court. Mr. Awasthi was sentenced one month imprisonment on April 22, 2008 by the same High Court and ultimately died under custody.[52]

The petition alleged that due to cruel treatment in jail, victim died as the victim was illegally chained, handcuffed and tortured by the jail authorities. It also alleged that two High Court Judges, namely Mr. Justice B.S. Chauhan and Mr. Justice Arun Tondon as themselves had committed contempt by awarding drastic sentence to contemnor advocate.

The petition is however, *subjudice* but in view of the question raised in the petition it may be submitted that for the death of the victim, jail authorities may be held guilty as they have illegally chained and handcuffed the victim. However, we agree that contempt jurisdiction could be and should be invoked in rarest of the rare cases and that too on sound basis, but whether a judge of courts of record, would be held guilty of contempt, this question is not authoritatively decided till now.

(ii) Abusing the Decorum of the Court

Like the advocates the judges are themselves required by their self-imposed code of conduct[53] to protect and maintain their own dignity by proper conduct and behaviour in and outside the court, every where and all the time. They must regulate their behaviour and dealings the cases or with the persons those who have come in contact with them. The judges should behave in such a way that there can arise no occasion when their free and fair mind and sense of impartiality may become subject of criticism or speculation.

52. *The Hindu*, dated 15.5.2008, p. 1.
53. See, Statement of the Value of Judicial Life, 1997.

There are verities of instances wherein the judges are held guilty of contempt of court for abusing the decorum and dignity of the court. Thus, in *Subhash Chand* v. *S.M. Aggarwal*,[54] the Additional Session Judge, after awarding death sentence to the accused person submitted the record to the High Court for confirmation of the death sentence. During the pendency of reference the Additional Session Judge gave interview to the Press and Doordarshan in which he commented on merits of the case and described the accused as worst criminal. It was held by the Delhi High Court that the conduct of the Additional Judge verges on contempt and was also violative of judicial propriety.

Arriving at the court in intoxicating stage by the judge is also an act of abusing the decorum and dignity of the court. In a Canadian case, namely, *Rodgers* v. *Ra Reynolds*,[55] a Juror committed to prison for some thirty days after he had arrived at court having drunk two quarts of beer.

A judge may be liable to criminal contempt if his act or conduct amounts to the interference with the course of justice or obstruction in the administration of justice or scandalizing or lowering the authority of the court in any way. In *State* v. *P.C. Mall*,[56] a Magistrate was held guilty of contempt of its own court for delivering a reserved judgement after eight months having a lot of adjournments without any reasonable cause. Similarly, in *State* v. *Viswanath Prasad Sharma*,[57] wherein an accused, who was on bail, he was tempered and intimidated by the prosecution witness and their counsel that the complainant's request for cancelling bail was accepted by the Munsiff Magistrate. A Sub-Inspector not only evaded fulfilling the arrest but maneuvered a petition being given to the Sub-Divisional Officer and persuaded him to order the accused to be in the lockup. Though the Sub-Divisional officer was fully aware by the fact that no order was passed by magistrate, he ordered to sent the accuse to the regular Jail.

54. (1984) Cr.L.J. 1181.
55. (1952) 103 C.C.C. 168.
56. (1973) 39 Cut. L.R. 358.
57. 1951 Pat. 451.

In such circumstances the Patna High Court was satisfied that the Sub-Inspector who had persuaded to the Sub-Divisional Officer, had flouted the order of the Munsiff Magistrate and he was guilty of contempt of court. However, on the matter of Sub-Divisional Officer, the unconditional apology tendered by him was accepted by the Patna High Court.[58]

Likewise if the court does not function as per office hours, the dignity and prestige of the court in the minds of the common man will greatly suffer. The question arises; is it not contempt? However, the law on this point is not well settled but it is submitted that when there is no valid reason for the late coming, any judge cannot be reasonably be excused.

An interesting instance in this regard may be cited. There is a matter of judges Ralph Kohn of Adrian (Michigan, U.S.A.). He came ten minutes late, for a case, he was hearing. He expressed regret in open court and fined himself $50. The charge to which he pleaded guilty was contempt of his own court.[59]

It may be debatable question, can a Judge fine himself, but it is humbly submitted that such Judges should adorn the Indian courts. Often there are lapses in court attendance by judges even by hours. Sticking to court time, with lunch on interval is very healthy. If judges fine themselves for their lapses in attendance like the Michigan Judge, law's delay may be reduced to some extent.

However, a judge may be guilty of contempt of his own court by his very act of delay in disposal of cases. In an earlier referred case,[60] the magistrate heard parties in proceedings under Section 145 Criminal Procedure Code. The judgement was given after eight months after nearly thirteen adjournments. When asked to explain by the superior court, the explanation was that he was having lot of administrative work and had to visit high officers often.

The Calcutta High Court found him guilty of contempt of his own court and held "it is shocking to the sense of justice

58. *Id.*, p. 459.
59. Vide, Reuter news flash 'Judge fines himself' from Adrian on March 8, 1974, vide *The Hindu*, 9.3.1974, p. 7.
60. *State* v. *P.C. Mall* (1973) 39 Cut. L.R. 358.

that a magistrate in seisin of judicial proceedings would prefer administrative work and visit of higher officers to rendering judgement in cases which he has heard. By the process which has been adopted in this case not only the confidence in the judiciary is likely to be lost, but the image of the Magistracy is also lowered. This ultimately is bound to lower the authority of the court and effect the administration of Justice".

Again, in *G. Raja Kumari v. B. Krishna Rao,*[61] it was held by the Allahabad High Court that, delay in disposal of an injunction matter and adoption of dilatory tactic by a judicial officer amounted to contempt of court. He was directed to dispose off at the earliest without delay.

(iii) Insubordination

The very idea of judicial supremacy rests on the foundations of discipline and respect for its decision. Therefore, it is province and solemn duty of the subordinate judges to obey and pay regard to the decisions and directions of superior courts, otherwise the system cannot be run smoothly and even course of justice will be thwarted. Hence a subordinate judge commits contempt of court, if he disobeys the order of his superior courts.

In *Satinath Sikdar* v. *Ratanmani Nasker,*[62] a rule was issued by the High Court of Calcutta staying certain proceedings before a District Munsiff. The party who obtained the rule also moved to the Munsiff for adjournment of the proceedings and supported his application by an affidavit and a letter written by his Vakil of the High Court. The Munsiff rejected the application and proceeded with the case and passed final orders. Their Lordships of the Calcutta High Court found that the act of the Munsiff was unsatisfactory and that his behaviour amounted to contempt of court. The court deprecated his conduct as open to the gravest censure and added:

"We trust he will profit by the warnings given now, that

61. (1996) 3 A.L.D. 848 (D.B.).
62. 15 C.L.J. 335.

> the arm of this court is long enough to reach any person who may behave in this manner".[63]

It is also an act of insubordination and contempt for the judges of inferior court to demand of the superior court, the law under which stay order has been passed before complying with it.[64] The judges of lower judiciary should always keep in mind that subordinate courts have a prime duty to carry out and obey the superior court's order and they should not demand that the superior court's should say under what law, the directive was issued.[65] In *Session Judge, Meerut v. Fanthone City Magistrate, Meerut,*[66] the Allahabad High Court held that the magistrate cannot challenge the order of High Court even when he commit error of refusing to comply with the order, which he think is without jurisdiction. The learned judge held that, the judges of the inferior court cannot ask any question about the correctness of the decision taken by the higher court. If they did so they will do so at their peril. His Lordship further suggested that:

> "If they think the order of the superior court is without authority, should presume for the time being that the order is lawful, unless the contrary appears. Any discourtesy exhibited can only land then in contempt proceeding and will be it visited by the higher court with several penalties.[67]

So, when a presiding officer of the tribunal refused to apply the law as laid down by the High Court, for the reason that an application for leave to appeal to the Supreme Court was pending, it was held that act of the presiding officer was likely to insubordination amounting to contempt of court.[68]

---

63. *Ibid.,* p. 339.
64. *Session Judge, Meerut v. Fanthone, City Magistrate, Meerut,* A.I.R. 1958 (All.) 161.
65. *State* v. *N.C. Chaki* (1988), Cr.L.J. Cal. 47.
66. *Supra* note 64.
67. *Ibid.,* p. 169.
68. *Bhimsen Dixit* v. *B.K. Mishra,* I.L.R. Cut. 986.

In *Mahatri Prasad* v. *State,*[69] a District Magistrate made a reference under Section 439 of the Criminal Procedure Code, to the High Court in respect of an order of Additional District Magistrate, who had granted bail on the authority of a High Court decision. The reference sought was on the ground that the wording of section 497 of the Criminal Procedure Code, do not admit of grant of anticipatory bail and that therefore, grant of bail was wrong in law. The primary purpose of the reference was, to suggest that the prior decision of the High Court was obviously not correct and that the points mentioned by the District Magistrate may be taken into consideration for reconsidering that decision.

Rejecting the contentions Mr. Justice Dixit expressed condemnation of the conduct of the District Magistrate and held that, it was a very extraordinary and unwarranted reference and that the District Magistrate appeared to have transgressed all limits of balance and all proprieties expected from Judicial Officers and Magistrates, subordinate to the High Court. Rejecting his apology also the learned Judge observed:

> "In view of the apology tendered by him, I do not wish to pursue the matter further and dismiss it as a lapse on the part of an officer whose zeal as an officer responsible for maintaining of law and order has out weighted his duties as a Magistrate subordinate to his court. I must add for the benefit of Judicial Officers and Magistrate to this court that a decision of this court may not appear to them as laying down the correct law.. It may be subsequently overruled by this court or set aside by the Supreme Court. But so long as it has not been overruled or set abide it is binding on all Judicial Officers and Magistrates. They have no liberty of criticising the decisions of the higher court, much less can they deliver to higher court a homily on the matters it should take into consideration while examining the correctness of any decision. If they do so, their act is no doubt, in common parlance an act of insubordination and in law, it amounts to contempt of court and they are liable to be dealt with

69. A.I.R. 1953 M.B. 60.

as such for that act. The fact that criticism or the suggestion have been made by the Judicial Officer or a Magistrate in the course of judicial proceedings cannot alter the nature of act".[70]

The above decisions of the various High Courts found strong support in *Prithwi Nath Ram v. State of Jharkhand*,[71] wherein it was ruled by the Supreme Court that dealing with an application against alleged non-compliance with its earlier order cannot examine the rightness or wrongness of that order nor can it add or delete any direction.

Again in *B.P.L. Limited* v. *R. Sudhakar*,[72] the order of reference to Industrial Tribunal of a dispute was stayed by the High Court by an interim order. The Tribunal passed an order on an application of the management under proviso to Section 33(2) of the Industrial Disputes Act, 1947. The court pointed out that there was possibility of tribunal committing contempt of the order passed by the High Court. It cited with approval, the observation of the Supreme Court in a *earlier case*,[73] to the effect that 'It is a common place that where the superior court's order staying proceeding is disobeyed by the inferior court to whom it is addressed, the latter court commits contempt of court for it acts in disobedience to the authority of the former court. The act of disobedience is calculated to undermine public respect for the superior court and Jeopardizes the preservation of law and order".[74]

It is also an act of insubordination, if a subordinate court recorded contrary finding as recorded by the High Court. In *Kanti Devi* v. *Sarju Prasad*,[75] a subordinate Judge recorded findings contrary to the High Court in litigation about the same premises, on the same issue, without there being any new material. The Allahabad High Court felt that the presiding

70. *Ibid.*
71. A.I.R. 2004 S.C. 718.
72. (2004) 7 S.C.C. 219.
73. *Badrakanta Mishra* v. *Registrar of Orissa High Court* (1974), S.C.C. 374.
74. *Ibid.*
75. A.I.R. 1997 A.I.H.C. 4042 (All.).

officer of the subordinate court was *prima facie* liable for contempt as well as insubordination. His Lordships ruled:

> "Unless subordinate court to obey and pay regard to the directions and decisions of the higher court there would be confusion in the administration of law and respect for law would irretrievably suffer. The High Court has always the right to punish the presiding officer of a subordinate court for disobedience of its orders by action in contempt. It is not the province of the subordinate judiciary to be critical of superior judge to whom they are subordinate. If that were allowed, the common man will lose all regard for the sanctity of the High Court if its directions are disobeyed or criticized by inferior courts".[76]

The learned High Court further observed:

> The idea of judicial corrective rest on the foundations of discipline and respect for decision and directions of the superior courts. If the subordinate judge contravene this principle, they cannot be efficient and relied upon for the maintenance of the rule of law. An ordinary citizen may plead ignorance of the law but how can a Judicial Officer? He cannot in all conscience, plead that he did not understand the implications of an order of the High Court".[77]

It appears from the above decisions that the presiding officers of the subordinate courts are bound to respect and give effect to all orders passed by the higher courts. While it is also true that presiding officer are not bound to obey any order until it is officially communicated to them and they are not bound to accept the assurance of any interested party in that regard.

But in regard to the 'Stay Order' the court of India and England have taken a very strict view by saying that when an order of stay or other such prohibitory order has been made

76. *Id.*, p. 4059.
77. *Ibid.*

by the High Court and when the subordinate judge or magistrate is informed of the order by an advocate he ought ordinarily to accept what is stated by the advocate.[78] If, the subordinate judge or magistrate disregards such information and continues the proceeding he may be guilty of contempt of court.[79]

The reason for this reliance on counsel's statement is that he is considered as an officer of the court and is not likely to supply information as to the correctness of which he is not himself completely satisfied. As Mr. Justice Shearer said in *Harkushum Singh* v. *Chhotan Mathon*[80] that if an advocate act improperly or carelessly and it eventually turns out that no prohibitory order has been made by the court, suitable action can be taken against him.

So, also where the officer in spite of the fact they were already aware of the stay order in force upto a certain date and were informed by a responsible person early on the next morning that the stay order had been extended for a further period by the High Court. Thereupon carried out the action with the police help, were held contempt of court.[81]

Likewise in *Ponnuswamy Iyer* v. *K. Ganapathy Iyer*,[82] Mr. Justice Venkata Subbarao of the Madras High Court held that, in regard to the prohibitory orders it is not necessary ingredient that the order should have been officially communicated to the Magistrate. Notice of an order can be given otherwise than by an official communication of it. Under certain circumstances a telegram may constitute such a notice of an order of a court to make a person who disregards the notice and acts in contravention of the order liable for contempt of court".

It is submitted that the view taken by the English and Indian courts in the above cases, is not free from doubts.

---

78. *Rameshwar Singh* v. *A.N. Chaubey*, AI.R. 1954 Pat. 554.
79. *Bryant, In re* (1876) 4 Ch.D. 98.
80. A.I.R. 1951 Pat. 494.
81. *K. Kutumba Rao* v. *M.B. Subba Rao*, A.I.R. 1969 A.P. 47.
82. A.I.R. 1924 Mad. 393.

However, if the judge had no actual knowledge of such notice then contempt did not come out. In *H.P. Singh* v. *Thakur Prasad Tiwari*,[83] the District Magistrate was absent at the time when the High Court's order ordering release of the prisoner was received. So when he was asked to show cause for having not released, his defence was that he had no actual knowledge of the order of the High Court and he had no intention to flout the order. He also tendered an apology to the Patna High Court which held that he was guilty of contempt. In appeal Supreme Court held that apology should not be taken as an admission of guilt as he had no knowledge of the order of release, he cannot be charged with the order of release, he cannot be charged with contempt of court.

Likewise in *B.K. Kar* v. *Chief Justice of Orissa*[84] a stay order by the High Court was communicated by counsel to local counsel who filed it before the Sub-Divisional Magistrate who ordered "No action can be taken on telegram File", and pronounced his orders on the opposite party's application for restitution. The High Court held this was contempt of court and refused to accept the conditional apology and fined the Magistrate Rs. 100. The conviction was set aside in special leave appeal by the Supreme Court. Mudholkar J. observed:

> "Before a subordinate court can be found guilty of disobeying the order of the superior court and thus to have committed contempt of court, it is necessary to show that the disobedience was intentional. There is no room for inferring an intention to disobey an order unless the person charged had knowledge of the order. If what a subordinate court has done is in utter ignorance of an order of a superior court, it would already not amount to intentional disobedience of the court's order and would therefore, not amount to a contempt of court at all. There may perhaps be a case where an order disobeyed could be reasonably construed in two ways and the subordinate court constructed it in one of those ways, but in a way different from that intended by the superior court. Surely

83. A.I.R. 1953 S.C. 436.
84. (1962) 1 S.C.R. 319.

it cannot be said that the disobedience of the order by the subordinate court was contempt of the superior court. There may possibly be a case where disobedience is accidental. If that is so there would be no contempt".

It is clear from the above discussion that contempt by subordinate judge is heinous since in the nature of things, he is an educated public servant who should have known his duties. However, some leniency has been be shown by the court to the judges for his unintentional disobedience of the order of the higher courts, but it is submitted that any deliberate or wilful disobedience cannot and should not be go unpunished.

(iv) Influencing Another Judge

The act of influencing another Judge is also considered as Contempt of Court. Hence it is highly objectionable on the part of a judge to influence another Judge extraneously or privately. In *King* v. *Moulah Bux*,[85] a Sub-Divisional Magistrate issued instructions to the trying Magistrate to adjourn all rioting cases connected with the disturbances in the Tata Factory as the accused had moved the Government for withdrawal of cases. Successive adjournments were given ultimately resulting in the withdrawal of the cases by the public prosecutor. The Patna High Court issued a rule for contempt against the Sub-Divisional Magistrate for influencing the trial Magistrate and interfering with the course of Justice in the trial court. Though the High Court accepted the apology of Sub-Divisional Magistrate, their Lordships gave a definite finding that it was clear contempt to fetter the jurisdiction of trial court.

It is to be noted that no other judge, however high placed, can attempt to influence another judge who may be equal, superior or inferior in status to him. In *Jawand Singh Hukum Singh* v. *Om Prakash Agrawal, Sub-Judge, Jagadhri*,[86] the Punjab High Court was of the opinion that, it is gross contempt of court for such a judge to communicate with another Judge for the purpose of influencing on the subject-matter of a case

85. A.I.R. 1949 Pat. 253.
86. A.I.R. 1959 Punj. 632.

pending before the latter. Describing it a dangerous act court ruled:

> "Among a large variety of acts and conduct which amount to contempt of court, whereby due administration of Justice is obstructed, interrupted, embarrassed or impeded, an attempt to corrupt a judge is perhaps most serious offence. It is a dangerous assault upon the integrity of the court. Every public office is a public trust, but judicial office is more than that—it is a sacred trust".[87]

His Lordships further observed:

> "It is abhorrent to the conception of the public justice that a judge should be influenced in making his decision by extraneous influence to corrupt him or out of feeling for personal relation. Courts have shown scant mercy to those who have attempted to deter a presiding officer of a court to performance of his duty by attempting to influence his decision by means of private communication".[88]

It is also improper and contemptuous on the part of a Judge to advice the lower courts' judge and thereby interfere in their judicial duties.[89] Giving bribe or illegal gratification is also an act which may influence the judgement of the court. Therefore, courts have taken a view that no officer of court or subordinate should ask or seek illegal gratification. *In re Abdul*[90] such an act was considered as contempt of court. In the instant case Sir Barnes Peacock was of the opinion that giving or taking bribe is contempt whether it was asked for or received before or after judgement or order in any suit, appeal, proceeding or matter. Thus, in such cases the giver as well as taker of bribe or any illegal gratification are both guilty of contempt of court.

87. *Ibid*, p. 639.
88. *Ibid*.
89. *Brij Kishore Mehrotra* v. *G.P. Srivastav*, A.I.R. 1956 (All.) 117.
90. 8, W.R.C.R. 32.

In *Abhijit Tea Company Private Limited* v. *Terai Tea Company Private Limited*,[91] the Supreme Court without recording a finding of contempt, directed that an adverse entry be made in the confidential roll of the Registrar of a High Court, when it found that his conduct were against the propriety of an officer.

(v) Attributing Bias on Superior Judges

The subordinate court judges may also commit contempt by attributing bias or by labeling scurrilous allegations against the superior judges. In *State* v. *Nagamani*,[92] under the directions of the High Court one of the judges of the bench of that court inspected the Criminal Courts of a certain district and made a report to the High Court. A copy of the report was sent to the District Magistrate of that district, who on perusal of the report thought fit to write a letter to the Registrar of the High Court. The letter was couched in strange, labeling bias and unbecoming language, including phrases as "I am surprised to find. . . etc. . . ." a distorted version based probably on statements, made by some interested parties" and has jumped to certain conclusion as also the word 'absurd'.

It was held by the Patna High Court that, such word applied to a judge of a High Court by an inferior judge was quite disrespectful and as such cast a reflection on the dignity of the High Court and also caused obstruction to the course of justice, amounting to the contempt of court.

It is unethical for any educated person like lawyers or judges if they commit contempt. It appears to be worse if a District Judge commits such offences. Such was the celebrated case of *Badrakanta Mishra* v. *Registrar of Orissa High Court*.[93] In the instant case a District Judge who had quite unsatisfactory record as a District Judge, had been more than once reverted, suspended and subjected to disciplinary proceedings during his career. Once he was suspended by the High Court under Article 225 of the constitution and disciplinary proceeding was started. Against this the appellant Judge appealed to the Governor which appeal later was withheld by the Registrar,

91. (1996) 1 S.C.C. 589.
92. A.I.R. 1959 Pat., 372.
93. (1974) 1 S.C.C. 374.

High Court. After charges were framed the appellant challenged the jurisdiction of the High Court and the competency to initiate action for contempt on the specious plea that the acts done by the High Court were on the administration side and were not judicial actions.

A three judge bench rejected the plea and convicted the District Judge under section 12 of Contempt of Courts Act, 1971. The matter was referred to constitution bench of the Supreme Court, which considered the grave men to the imputations and held that the allegations made against the court in the memo submitted to the Governor constituted scurrilous allegations against the High Court. Not only this, some of the allegations to the Supreme Court were held to constitute contempt of court.

The Supreme Court confirmed the conviction, and held that imputation of improper motives, bias and prejudice constitutes contempt under Section 2(c) of the Contempt of Courts Act, 1971.

Speaking for majority of the Constitution Bench Mr. Justice D.G. Paleker placed emphasis on scandalization of the High Court and observed "the judges of the High Court and especially the Chief Justice are charged with maladies, improper motives, bias and prejudice by a District Judge". It is insinuated that they are oppressing the appellant have become vindictive and are in capable of doing him justice. It is also suggested that they do not administer justice fearlessly because in one matter affecting the appellant they dropped charges against him for fear of the Supreme Court. All this *prima-facie*, amounts to gross scandalization of the High Court. On a query that "can the suspension of the District Judge be regarded as not purely an administrative act but a para Judicial function? Mr. Justice Krishna Iyer, answered the query in the affirmative. The action was clearly for acts of judicial misconduct. The conduct was hence judicial and so the unbriddled attack on the High Court for the step was punishable as contempt.

Relying on the judgement of *Jugal Kishore* v. *Sitamarhi Control Cooperative Bank*,[94] Mr. Justice Krishna Iyer also said that, the right of appeal to the Supreme Court does not give

94. A.I.R. 1967 S.C. 1994.

the right to commit contempt of court nor can it be used as a cover to bring the authority of the High Court into disrespect and disregard. In this case, the very appeal grounds contained contumacious averments.

In awarding the punishment, the Supreme Court noted that appellant had been an incorrigible contemnor with a very unsatisfactory record and had been reverted, suspended and subjected to disciplinary proceedings during his career. In the present matter he had been reckless, persistent and guilty of undermining the High Court authority in his intemperate averment. However, having regard to the fact that he was a senior Judicial Officer, the two months simple imprisonment inflicted by the High Court was substituted with a fine of Rs. 1,000.

In *State* v. *N.C. Chaki,*[95] an Assistant Sessions Judge was held liable for criminal contempt by the Calcutta High Court. In the instant case he had written a letter to Session Judge in inductive language, to decide whether he was competent to deal with the Revision application before entering into its merit. He also wrote a letter to the High Court requesting it to exercise its power under Article 227 of the Constitution for quashing the provisional proceeding initiated by the Session Judge.

Use by a Judicial Officer of scandalous language against High Court Judges attributing bias and motive to them was also held contempt of the court by the Supreme Court in *Rolekar Adalat* v. *B.B. Singh, Munsif, Judicial Magistrate, Ist Class*.[96] In the instant case the Supreme Court made clear that in hierarchical structure of courts a disciplined and willing acceptance of the higher courts is the fundamental feature of the system and Judges who fail to maintain such discipline will be liable for contempt of court. This is so because superior courts have duty to exercise disciplinary control. To quote again Mr. Justice D.G. Pateker, "If superior courts neglect to discipline subordinate courts, they will fail in an essential function of judicial administration and bring the whole

95. (1988) Cr.L.J. (Noc) 47 (Cal.).
96. (1992) Cr.L.J. 16 (S.C.).

administration of justice into disrepute and contempt.[97]

In *Wazir Ahmed Khan* v. *Mohammad Anwar Ali,*[98] an order of remand was passed by the High Court and it was placed before the District Judge. The District Judge criticized such remand in a language which was not respectful. He also suggests that the order of remand was not called for and it should not have been made. The Rajasthan High Court was satisfied that the conduct of the District Judge was contumacious, however no action could be taken as the District Judge had retired from service on the date of judgement.

Thus, it is clear from the above discussion that if the judges of the subordinate judiciary involve himself in any activities, which lowers the image of the judiciary they will be held guilty of contempt of court. Can the judges of higher judiciary also come within the preview of the Contempt of Courts Act, 1971? The coming discussion will be focus on this issue.

(B) Conduct of the Superior Court Judges and Contempt of Court—An Unresolved Issue

By virtue of Section 16 of the Contempt of Courts Act, 1971 and the length of cases discussed earlier, it is well established that if the judges of the lower courts cross the boundary of their propriety and calmness then they are held liable for contempt of own courts or their superior courts. However, a question arises: whether contempt proceeding can also instituted against the superior courts' judges for their undignified acts, conduct or behaviour?

Though, this question has not been authoritatively settled till now, but preponderance of judicial opinions appear to favour the complete exclusion of superior court's judges from liabilities under the Contempt of Courts Act, 1971.

It is interesting to note that, the Parliament by enacting the said Act, does not make any clear distinction between Judges of the inferior courts and the judges of superior courts. Section 16 of the Act uses simply the term 'judges and magistrate', and it may be taken into its literal or simple

97. *Supra* note 73.
98. (2001) Cr.L.J. 1607 (Raj.).

meaning as Judges means all the judges'. But, in a series of judicial pronouncements courts have repeatedly taken the view that, the language of Section 16 gives statutory recognition in respect of contempt committed only by those judges who presided over subordinate courts.[99] The court have taken also the view that judges of courts of record[100] cannot be held liable for contempt of their own court and Section 16 does not purport to enlarge the scope of the Act by including even the judges of the court of record.[101]

In *Harish Chandra Mishra* v. *The Hon'ble Mr. Justice S. Ali Ahmed*[102] is a very important and leading case on this point. In the instant case an incident took place as advocate Sadanand Jha insisted upon hearing of revision on admission matter on merits. Thereupon, Mr. Justice S. Ali Ahmad remarked to advocate Jha, "You are present in court physically but mentally you are elsewhere and therefore, you missed my observation". Advocate Jha then replied. "My Lord, it is really uncharitable that your Lordship says that I was present in the court physically but was mentally somewhere else. I was both physically and mentally present in the court".

Learned Judge, became very angry upon this and he stated that it has become your habits to insult the court. He said 'Peshkar' "call the constable", I will have him arrested. He spoke for about ten minutes in which he used the following terms and expressions towards Advocate Jha:

> "You are a small fry and I would not even like to harm you because you are such a small fry. You have no knowledge and no understanding. With your habit you

---

99. *Harish Chandra Mishra* v. *Hon'ble Mr. Justice S. Ali Ahmed,* A.I.R. 1968 Pat. 65.
100. A court of record is a court, where of the acts and judicial proceedings are enrolled for a perpetual memory and testimony, the records of which are admitted to be of evidentiary value and are not to be questioned when produced before any court. A court of record has power to determine its own jurisdiction and it has power to punish for its contempt. See, M.P. Jain, Indian Constitutional Law, Fifth ed. 2003, p. 239.
101. *M. Ranka* v. *Hon'ble Chief Justice P.S. Mishra* (1992) 2 L.W. 110.
102. A.I.R. 1986 Pat. 65.

are doomed. I will not harm you but you will suffer from within and be doomed. I can tolerate a lot but there is limit to it and once the limit is reached. I am a very hard nut and remember that I tell you that you will suffer internally and be doomed. Now-a-day it has become the fashion of the Bar to insult the judges. I tell you, you will weep"—

Advocate Jha said I am sorry.

The judge again said, "You should be sorry and you would be sorry. You will suffer and you are doomed. Do not think with the attitude you will flourish or prosper".[103]

The contention of the petitioners was that by the aforesaid remarks made by the learned judge he committed contempt of his own court by interfering and obstructing the administration of Justice. The contention was based on the use of expression 'Judge' in Section 16(1) of the Act. It was argued that the expression Judge used in Section 16(1) shall include a judge of higher judiciary too. Such conclusion was drawn from the use of expression Judge or Judges in Section 14 of the said Act. It was submitted that if the expression judge or judges used in Section 14 does not refer to the judge or judges of the High Court and Supreme Court, even that the expression 'Judge' used in Section 16 should be interpreted to include not only a judge of the subordinate court but even a judge of a High Court or Supreme Court.

The Bench of five judges of the Patna High Court examined the following questions:

Whether such contentions of petitioner can be accepted? Whether a contempt petition against a sitting judge of a High Court is maintainable without the consent in writing of the Advocate General? Can a judge of a High Court be tried under the Contempt of Courts Act, 1971? By a 4:1 the Patna High Court rejected the contention of the

103. *Ibid.*

petitioner and answered all the questions in negative. Speaking for the majority Mr. Justice N.P. Singh said:

> "In view of Section 9 and the language of Section 16 itself it has to be held that Section 16 does not purport to enlarge the scope of the Act by including even the judges of the court of record. In my opinion, it only gives statutory recognition in respect of contempt of court committed by judges and magistrates presiding over subordinate courts and not the court of record".[104]

The reasons given by the majority rest on the following grounds:

1. The Supreme Court and High Courts are the court of records in view of Articles 129 and 215 of the Constitution and have all powers of such a Court including the power of punish for contempt itself. In England Court of records have always been treated in respect of contempt proceeding on a different footing from ordinary courts because it was not expected that judges presiding over the different courts of record shall not maintain the dignity of their own court.
2. Superior courts judges are not subject to contempt proceeding because absolute freedom and independence of such judges is necessary for the administration of justice.
3. At the time of enforcement of the said Act the judges of the Supreme Court or High Court could not be charged for having committed the contempt of the High Court or the Supreme Court.
4. Neither the preamble of the Contempt of Courts Act, 1971 nor any other provision gives any indication that the scope of the Act was enlarged. Rather contrary is true. Section 16 is subject to the provisions of any law for time being enforced.

104. *Ibid.*

Section 9 of the Act reads: "Nothing contained in this Act shall be construed as implying that any disobedience, breach, publication or other act is punishable as contempt of court which would not be so punishable apart from this Act". And Section 22 clearly states that the provisions of the Act shall be in addition to, and not in derogation of the provisions of any other law relating to contempt of court. Since the act or conduct of the judges of the Supreme Court and High Courts did not amount to contempt of court, they cannot be included under the Contempt of Courts Act, 1971.

5. The conduct of judges of the superior courts have been declared immune from parliamentary and legislative discussion (Articles 121 and 211). Not-only-this Judges of such courts are removable on the ground of proved misbehaviour or incapacity by a special procedure to be followed by Parliament.
6. Such thing happened in court room in the past as well but they were happily buried in the spirit of forget and forgive. This is so because the system through which justice is being administered cannot be effectively administered unless the two limbs of the court act in harmony.
7. On the basis of above elaborated reasons the majority (N.P. Singh, S.K. Chaudhari, Udai Sinha and P.S. Sahay, JJ. held that the judges of the Supreme Court and High Courts are not subject to contempt of court.

However, Mr. Justice *Birendra Prasad Sinha* did not agree with the majority's proposition. He observed:

> "With greatest of respect to my learned Brethren it is not possible for me to agree with the proposition that the judges of the High Courts and Supreme Court are immune from contempt of courts proceedings, nor do I agree that an application filed without the consent in writing of the Advocate General is not maintainable".

Though, for the above mentioned minority decision of Mr. Justice Birendra Prasad Sinha, no reason has been given by him, but it is humbly submitted that the minority view of Justice Sinha is more convincing and carries more weight than many majority decisions of the Supreme Court. Thus, it is submitted that Judges of the High Courts and Supreme Court should not be immune for the contempt proceedings.

However, in *Sikandar Khan* v. *Ashok Kumar Mathur,*[105] the Rajasthan High Court again accepts the majority view and held that contempt proceedings are not maintainable against a judge of court of record.

Likewise, in *M. Ranka* v. *Hon'ble Mr. Justice P.S. Misra,*[106] a Full Bench of Madras High Court took a similar view as stand taken by the Patna and Rajasthan High Courts.

Following the aforesaid decisions Mr. Justice Srinivasan of Madras High Court held that petition to punish a judge of a High Court for committing contempt of his own court was not maintainable.

Learned judges also said that intention of the Parliament is made clear by the Sections 9 and 212 of the Act that a judge of the High Court and Supreme Court cannot be proceeded against for contempt of his own court.

In *Vishwanath* v. *E.S. Venkataramiah,*[107] the Apex Court did not accept a contempt petition against former Chief Justice of India. While the court did not express its view on the question that contempt proceeding against a superior Judge lies or not? In the instant case, the fact was that, former Chief Justice of India, E.S. Venkataramiah gave an interview to a noted journalist Kuldeep Nayar which was published in several Newspapers, following portion gave rise to contempt petition by a private person:

> "The Judiciary in India has deteriorated in its standards because such judges are appointed, as are willing to be "influenced" by lavish parties and whisky bottles". In every High Courts there are at least four or five Judges

105. (1991) 3 S.L.R. 236 (Raj.)
106. *Supra* note 101.
107. (1990) Cr.L.J. 2179 (S.C.)

who are practically out every evening, wining and dining either at a lawyer's house or a foreign embassy. "He also stated that the way of appointments of majority of judges goes through glittering parties and expensive liquor bottles".[108] The contention of petitioner was that the former Chief Justice had crossed the boundary between fair criticism and contempt of court.

But without saying that a contempt proceedings cannot lie against Judges of Superior courts, the Apex Court held that:

"We do not think, there is any substance in this contention. We are reminded of Chinese proverb "As long as you are up-right, do not care if your shadow is crooked". It is not possible to appreciate as to how every judge would become vulnerable mainly because the names are disclosed. Having regard to these facts, we do not think it is a fit case where *suo-motu* action for contempt is called for".[109]

The same thing happened in next case before the Supreme Court.

In *Sub-committee of Judicial Accountability* v. *Justice V. Ramaswamy*,[110] when the Supreme Court was approached to take action against Mr. Justice V. Ramaswamy for contempt as he had written a letter to members of the Enquiry Committee set-up under the judges (Enquiry) Act, 1968. During proceedings for his removal initiated by Parliament he made reckless allegations against Judges and the Judiciary as a whole. But Supreme Court decided not to take contempt proceedings against him in large public interest without saying that such proceedings did not lie against a superior court judge.

In *State of Rajasthan* v. *Prakash Chand*,[111] the Supreme Court

108. As quoted (in) Justice J.D. Kapoor, Contempt of Court, 2004 edition, p. 141.
109. *Ibid*., p. 243.
110. (1995) 1 S.C.C. 5.
111. A.I.R. 1998 S.C. 1344.

of India approved the above decisions by saying that no contempt petition lie against the superior court judges.

In the instant case Mr. Justice Mukul Gopal Mukerji, the Chief Justice of Rajasthan High Court had transferred a writ petition from the Board of Mr. Justice Sethna to the Division Bench.

Justice Sethna issued contempt notice against the Chief Justice as to why the contempt proceedings should not be initiated against him for committing criminal contempt under the Contempt of Courts Act, 1971. He also casted aspersion on the learned Judges constituting the Division Bench and he made comment and allegations against some of the former Chief Justices of Rajasthan High Court including the then Chief Justice of India, Mr. Justice J.S. Verma, charging them of criminal misappropriation of public funds by enjoying the Guest House facility and drawing daily allowance of Rs. 250 per day.

A three judge bench of Supreme Court found that the last allegation was factually and legally incorrect. As to the second charge the court took the view that it was example of lacked judicial self-restraint and amounted to abuse and misuse of judicial authority and betrayed the lack of respect for judicial institution.

As to the first issue, speaking for the three judge bench of Supreme Court Mr. Justice Dr. A.S. Anand observed:

> "The issuance of a notice to show cause by Justice Sethna in the facts and circumstances of this case is thus wholly illegal, unwarranted and without jurisdiction. Thus, the court arrived at conclusion that "It is a fundamental principle of our jurisprudence and it is in public interest also that no action can lie against a Judge of a Court of Record for a Judicial act done by the judge.[112] This immunity is essential to enable the judges of the court of Record to discharge their duties without fear and favour, though remaining within the bounds of their jurisdiction. Immunity from any civil or criminal action or a charge of contempt of Court is essential for maintaining independence of judiciary and for the strength of the administration of justice.

Likewise in *Tarak Singh* v. *Joyti Basu,*[112] the division bench of the Supreme Court did not choose to start contempt proceedings against Mr. Justice B.P. Banerjee of Calcutta High Court, who had kept the allotment of plots of land in *Salt Lake City* stayed for more than a decade and had got plot number 1 allotted in his name from the Chief Minister quota. He had also filed false affidavit during the hearing of the case before the Supreme Court.

Speaking through H.K. Sema the Supreme Court noted the damage done to the administration of justice by such conduct on the part of a judge with tendency to compromise his divine duty with his personal interest and declared the conduct of the learned judge beyond condonable limits. The court ordered building constructed on the said plot to be auctioned with condition that no relative of the judge or the judge himself should be allowed to bid in auction sole. It thought that contempt proceeding was not necessary as the order would serve the end of justice.

The successive decision of the Supreme Court speaking on the issue of contempt of court by the superior courts' judges present important message for what they have not decided is more important than what they have decided. A time may come when the Supreme Court would like to consider the issue a fresh keeping in a view the contemptuous conduct of the superior courts' judges.

112. (2005) 1 S.C.C. 201.

8

Mechanism for Maintaining Accountability of Bench and Bar in India

When we think of the term 'Accountability' in relation to the administration of justice, the first image comes to mind that of holding advocates and judges responsible for their actions and consequences their of. The accountability here is the degree to which such persons have to explain or justify what they have done or failed to do. If the independence of the Bench and the Bar is important virtue of the democratic society, then accountability of these two wings is also essential requirement of a sound democratic polity.

Therefore, the core principle of the Rule of Law, which says "*Be you ever so high, the law is above you*",[1] is applicable to the members of the Bench and the Bar. Once it is established that advocates and judges should be and must be accountable, next question arises: how and to whom? An attempt will be made in this chapter to discuss and examine the status of

1. Quoted from Raju Ramchandran, *Legal Ethics*, Lexis nexis, Butterworth Publication, 2006, p. 233.

mechanism, as existing in India with a view to elaborate the above question, under the following heads:

I. MECHANISM PROVIDED FOR MAINTAINING ACCOUNTABILITY OF ADVOCATES

We have discussed earlier how in India the rules made by the Bar Council of India under Section 49(1)(c) of the Advocates Act, 1961, prescribe the standards of conduct and etiquette for advocates.[2] The violation of the standard of conduct affects the prestigious image of the profession and hence is treated as professional misconduct in India.[3] In *R.D. Saxena* v. *Balram Prasad Sharma*,[4] Mr. Justice R.P. Sethi observed that "an advocate is liable to disciplinary action if he departs from the high standards which the profession has set for itself and conduct himself in manner which is not fair, reasonable and according to law". Therefore, it is necessary that every advocate on the roll should strictly follow the standards prescribed by the Bar Council of India and maintain the dignity of the legal profession. With a view to make these expectations reality, certain control mechanism become imperative. The prime question arises, what form of mechanism will best advance the availability, competence, integrity and independence of the profession which the public needs?

In India, prior to the enactment of Advocates Act, 1961 the disciplinary control was vested in the High Courts.[5] There existed a tribunal of the Bar Council for the purpose of conducting inquiry into misbehaviour of advocates.[6] The High Court had discretion to refer the matter either to the tribunal or to a District Judge for the purpose of inquiry. The tribunal was only a fact finding body and did not have any power to impose punishment.[7]

2. See, Bar Council of India Rules, 1975.
3. For details, see Chapter VIth.
4. (2000) 7 S.C.C. 264.
5. Prior to the Advocates Act, The Bar Councils of India Act, 1926 was enforced.
6. Section 11 of the Bar Councils of India Act, 1926.
7. For detail see, Chapter IInd.

With the enactment of the Advocates Act, 1961 a self-regulatory mechanism is provided for the maintenance of ethics of the profession and for ensuring the accountability of the members of the Bar.

By virtue of the said Act, though, the sole authority to take disciplinary action against advocates is vested in the Disciplinary Committee of the Bar Councils, but there are also a traditional control on advocates in India, which are governed by the regular courts. It is important to note that District Courts and High Courts do not have primary jurisdiction in disciplining lawyers, except the jurisdiction of the courts by way of contempt proceedings.[8]

The Supreme Court exercises an appellate jurisdiction over the lawyer's conduct by the virtue of section 38 of the Advocates Act. In addition to it, it may exercise jurisdiction by virtue of Article 142 of the Indian Constitution also. Apart from matters connected with complaints and discipline, the regulatory function referred to are now performed by the Bar Councils either as a matter of self-regulation or in the exercise of powers conferred by the Act. In addition to self-regulation there is institutional regulation of lawyers by courts.[9]

Therefore, broadly speaking in India, there are three types of the mechanism for the maintenance of accountability of the members of the Bar, namely:

(i) Disciplinary proceedings.
(ii) Appellate Jurisdiction of the Supreme Court.
(iii) Contempt Proceedings.

(A) Disciplinary Proceedings by the Bar Councils and Its Committees

Professional status, public trust and confidence are the essential elements of any profession. In legal profession another essential elements may be added in the form of the element of independence and autonomy. Keeping in view these elements and gravity of the matter legislature kept out any outside control on the advocates and by enacting the

8. Section 35 of the Advocates Act, 1961.
9. *Id.*, sections 37-38.

Advocates Act, 1961 provided for self regulatory system. For this purpose the Act provided two layers of Bar Councils, namely, State Bar Council at the State level and Bar Council of India at the national level to deal with disciplinary matters through their respective committees.

The Act casts multifarious obligations and duties on the both Bar Councils.[10] The State Bar Councils maintain the roll of the advocates. The complete control and jurisdiction regarding enrolment of advocates and the matter of their discipline is vested in State Bar Councils and its Disciplinary Committee. It has been given powers to entertain and determine a case of misconduct against advocates on its rolls and to safeguard the rights and privileges of the advocates on rolls. The Act casts duty on the Bar Council of India, such as to lay down standards of professional conduct and etiquette for advocate, procedure to be followed by Disciplinary Committees, to promote and support law reforms, to deal with any matter arising under the Act, which may be referred to it by a State Bar Council, to exercise general supervision and control over State Bar Councils, to recognize the degree of law for admission of advocates, to prescribe standards of legal education, to perform all other functions conferred on it by or under the Act and to do all other things necessary for discharging the aforesaid function.[11] The power to take cognizance of professional or other misconducts lies with both the Bar Councils. Every Bar Council is a body corporate having perpetual succession and common seal. It has power to acquire and hold property both movable and immovable, to contract and may by the name which it is known sue and be sued.[12]

(i) State Bar Council and its Disciplinary Committees

Section 3 of the Advocates Act, 1961, provides for the establishment of the Bar Council for each State. The State Bar Councils are named after their State though, a few Bar Councils are common to two or more States and in some cases

10. *Id.*, section 6 and 7.
11. *Ibid.*
12. *Id.*, section, 5.

union territories have also been covered by a State Bar Council.[13] Union territory of Delhi, now called the National Capital Territory of Delhi, has a separate Bar Council. In 1999 there was a re-organisation of three major States of the country, out of the existing Bihar, Madhya Pradesh and Uttar Pradesh certain areas were carved out and three new States were created namely, Jharkhand, Chhattisgarh and Uttranchal respectively and separate Bar Councils were constituted for these States with separate High Courts.

(a) Constitution of State Bar Councils and its Disciplinary Committees

Every State Bar Council consists of the following:[14]

(a) Ex-officio members:

- (i) In the case of the Bar Council of Delhi—the Additional Solicitor-General of India.
- (ii) In the case of the State Bar Council of Assam, Nagaland, Meghalaya, Manipur and Tripura—Advocate General of each State.
- (iii) In the case of the State Bar Council of Punjab and Haryana—the Advocate General of each of the State.
- (iv) In the case of any other State Bar Council, the Advocate General of the State.

(b) Elected members :

- (i) For a State Bar Council having electorate not more than five thousand—15 members.
- (ii) For a State Bar Council with an electorate exceeding five thousand but not exceeding ten thousand—20 members.
- (iii) For a Bar Council exceeding ten thousand electorates—25 members.

The election of members shall be in accordance with the system of proportional representation by means of the single transferable vote from amongst advocates on the electoral roll

13. *Id.*, section 4.
14. *Ibid.*

of the State Bar Council. As for as possible one half of elected members shall be advocates of at least ten years standing on State roll. There shall be Chairman and the Vice-Chairman of each of State Bar Council elected by the Council. Every Bar Council shall appoint a secretary and may appoint an accountant and such number of other persons on its staff as it may deem necessary. Every State Bar Council has an executive committee consisting five members, an enrolment committee consisting three members, one or more legal aid committees and such other committees as it may deem necessary for the purposes of carrying out the provisions of the Act.

State Bar Council shall also constitute one or more Disciplinary Committees. Each committee shall consist of three members. It contains two types of members.

Elected members—Two members are elected by the Bar Council from amongst its members.

Co-opted members—One member of the Disciplinary Committee is co-opted by the Council from among advocates who have standing of 10 years as advocate on state roll and who are not members of the Council.

(b) Disciplinary Powers of the State Bar Councils and Their Committee

Once a person enters into the legal profession he is assumed to be competent and capable of giving legal service. The regulations then focus its attention on the standards of character. He is punished for his professional or other misconduct. In this regard the legislature has entrusted responsibility for maintaining standards of professional conduct and discipline for lawyers to the Disciplinary Committees of the respective State Bar Councils.[15] But the power to inquire whether there is a *prima facie* case against an advocate regarding his misconduct is with the State Bar Council. Section 35 of the Advocates Act, 1961 reads:

> "Where on receipt of a complaint or otherwise a State Bar Council has reason to believe that any advocate on its roll has been guilty of professional or other misconduct it

15. *Id.*, section 66.

shall refer the case for disposal to its Disciplinary Committee".[16] The State Bar Council may, either of its own motion or on application made to it by any person interested, withdraw a proceeding pending before its Disciplinary Committee and direct the inquiry to be made by any other Disciplinary Committee of the State Bar Council.[17]

The Disciplinary Committee of a State Bar Council may make any of the following orders, namely:

(i) dismiss the complaint or, where the proceedings were initiated at the instance of the State Bar Council, direct that the proceedings be filed.
(ii) Reprimand the advocate.
(iii) Suspend the advocate from practice for such period as it may deem fit.
(iv) Remove the name of the advocate from the State roll of advocates.

Thus, the above section provides that all cases of professional or other misconduct shall be disposed of by the Disciplinary Committee of the State Bar Council concerned, but before Bar Council refers a complaint against an advocate, to its Disciplinary Committee, it is essential that it should be satisfied that there is a *prima facie* case against the advocate. There are two steps for proceeding of the disciplinary action.

(c) Procedure Before the State Bar Council

The disciplinary proceedings may start either on receipt of a complaint or otherwise by the State Bar Council.[18] A complaint against an advocate shall be in the form of a petition duly signed and verified as required under the code of civil procedure. The complaint could be filed in English or in Hindi or in regional language. Where the complaint is in Hindi

16. *Id.*, 35 (1).
17. *Id.*, 35(1) (1-A).
18. Rule (1)(1) of the Bar Council of India Rules, 1975.

or in any other regional language, the State Bar Council shall translate the complaint in English, whenever a disciplinary matter is sent to the Bar Council of India under the Advocates Act. On receipt of the complaint, the Secretary of the Bar Council may require the complainant to pay prescribed fees, if not paid. He may also require to remove any defect and may call such particulars or copies of the complaint or other documents as may considered necessary.[19]

On a complaint being found to be in order, it shall be registered and placed before the Bar Council of state for such order as it may deem fit to pass. The Council may at any stage of a proceeding appoint an advocate to appear as *amicus curie*. Regarding the initiation of disciplinary proceedings it is important to note that, the initiation of disciplinary action lies under the power of the Bar Council as a unit and not in the hands of any office bearer, how so ever high he may be.

In a case *A . . . complainant* v. *B . . . Respondent*,[20] the complaint received against the advocate was not placed before the Bar Council. It was placed before the Chairman of the State Bar Council with a note that it may be referred to the Disciplinary Committee. Chairman made the order that due to serious allegations having been made against the advocate the matter may be placed before the another Disciplinary Committee for early disposal. The said Disciplinary Committee found the advocate guilty of professional misconduct and suspended him from practice for a period of one year. In the appeal filed against the order of the Disciplinary Committee, the appellant raised objection to the procedure adopted by the State Bar Council.

The Bar Council of India after making a reference to Section 6(1)(a), Section 9 and 35, noted that disciplinary power under the Act is by statute, shared between the Bar Council and the Disciplinary Committee, the Bar Council acting as the referring body if it has reason to believe that advocate is guilty of a professional misconduct. Parliament has constituted the State Bar Council as the authority to refer cases of misconduct

19. *Id.*, Rule 2.
20. D.C. Appeal No. 5/1970 (Raj.) Vol. (2) 1973 J.B.C.I. 266.

to the Disciplinary Committee. The Bar Council of India observed:

> "In our view when Parliament intends that a reference to the Disciplinary Committee has to be made by the State Bar Council, a reference by the Chairman of the State Bar Council would be clearly without jurisdiction because the Chairman is not the State Bar Council. The entire proceedings of the Disciplinary Committee was void and nullity".[21]

It must be noted that the Bar Council on receipt of complaint or otherwise, in not to transmit it to its Disciplinary Committee, but it is obligatory on the part of the Council to see if there is reason to believe, that an advocate on its roll is guilty of professional misconduct. On a complaint, the Bar Council has to proceed on the matter. It has to work under two constraints, *first,* no matter taken up by a State Bar Council *suo moto* or arising on a complain made under Section 35 of the Act shall be dropped solely by reason of its having been withdrawn, settled or otherwise compromised or the complainant does not want to proceed with inquiry. *Secondly,* the State Bar Council should itself satisfy as to reason to believe as to the guilt of professional misconduct.

The words 'reason to believe' imposed upon the Council a duty to apply its mind to the matter before the professional life of an advocate is put in Jeopardy. They are strong words casting on the body, having responsibility. Thus, in *Bar Council of Maharashtra* v. *M.V. Dabholkar,*[22] the Apex Court examined the meaning of the words 'reason to believe' and observed that, "the State Bar Council on receiving a complaint has to apply its mind to find out whether there is any reason to believe that advocate has been guilty of professional or other misconduct. The State Bar Council must act on that reasoned belief".

The court also added that "requirement of reason to believe cannot be converted into a formalized procedural road

21. *Ibid.*
22. A.I.R. 1975 S.C. 2092, p. 2097.

block, it being essentially a barrier against frivolous enquiries". The court attached importance to the decision of the Bar Council to refer the matter to the Disciplinary Committee by pointing out that "It is implicit in the resolution of the Bar Council, when it says that it has considered the complaint and decided to refer the matter to the Disciplinary Committee, that it had reason to believe as prescribed by the Statute".

The above decision was upheld in *Nandlal* v. *Bar Council of Gujarat*.[23] In the instant case, there was nothing evident from the record of the case to suggest that before referring the complaint to the Committee, the Bar Council applied its mind to the allegation made in the complaint to find that, there was a *prima facie* case to go before the Disciplinary Committee. So the Supreme Court held that the reference made by the State Bar Council to the Disciplinary Committee was incompetent. The court concluded that the proceedings before the Disciplinary Committee of Bar Council of Gujarat and also before the Disciplinary Committee of the Bar Council of India on transfer were invalid.

It seems that, the Bar Council, before it could act under Section 35, should have examined, material which will with some certainty, lead to the conclusion that misconduct was actually committed. It should be noted in this regard that, the Bar Council performs an administrative function when exercising power under Section 35, but when the matter goes to the Disciplinary Committee then *quasi-judicial* proceedings begins.

Again in a very famous case, *N.G. Dastane* v. *Shrikant Shivade*,[24] the Supreme Court considered the significance of the expression 'reason to believe' and made clear. The expression reason to believe is employed in Section 35(1) of the Act, only for the limited purpose of using it as a filter for excluding frivolous complaints against advocates. It asserted that if the complainant is genuine and if the complaint is not lodged with the sole purpose of harassing an advocate and it is not actuated by malafides, the Bar Council has a statutory duty to forward the complaint to the Disciplinary Committee.

23. A.I.R. 1981 S.C. 477.
24. A.I.R. 2001 S.C. 2026.

Likewise in *A.K.Subbaiah* v. *Karnataka Bar Council, Bangalore,*[25] Mr. Justice H.L. Datta of the Karnataka High Court summarized the issue by saying that "one of the functions of the Bar Council is to entertain and determine the cases of misconduct against advocates on its roll. The Mandate of Section 35(1) to refer the matter to Disciplinary Committee on having reason to believe the guilt of professional misconduct committed by an advocate and such believe may not be easily open for scrutiny". The Learned Judge observed:

> "The expression 'reason to believe' occurring in Section 35(1) is a combination of two words, 'reason' and 'to believe'. The word reason means cause or justification and the word 'believe' means to accept as true or faith in it. It means coming to a conclusion on the basis of the information that a thing, condition, statement or fact exist. In other words, it only means facts, which *prima facie* will convince any reasonable person under the circumstance of the case to form a belief that will impel him to take action under law".

The court also drew a distinction between the situation requiring no interference by the court and the situation warranting interference. It observed that before the Bar Council has faith or accepts a fact to exist there must be a reasonable justification for it. The belief may not be open for scrutiny of the court as it is the final conclusion arrived by it as a result of mental exercise made by it on the information received by it. But the reason due to which decision is reached can always be examined by the court.[26]

The learned judge further clarified that when I say, the reason to believe is open to scrutiny of this court, I mean that the satisfaction arrived at by the Bar Council is immune from challenge, but where the satisfaction is not based on any material or it cannot withstand the test of reason which is

25. A.I.R. 2002 Kant. 410.
26. *Id.*, p. 412.

integral part of it then if falls through and court is empowered to strike down such opinion.[27]

It is submitted that the above decision of the Karnataka High Court seems to be good approach. We agree with the view that the proceedings before the State Bar Council are administrative in nature and therefore, the court should not interfere with the decision of State Bar Council, except in very extraordinary situation. But, we never support to granting unlimited power to the Council in regard to the reference of the matter to the Disciplinary Committee.

Thus, it is clear from the above discussion that, though, section 35 of the said Act confers a very wide power to the State Bar Council, but such power in no sense is unlimited or unaccountable. The Bar Council may reject the complaint only when if it finds that no *prima-facie* case is made out by the complainant and the Bar Council has not sufficient reason to believe that professional misconduct has been committed by the advocate. Hence, only when a *prima facie* case is made out against advocate and where there is reason to believe that any advocate has been guilty of professional or other misconduct it shall refer the case for disposal of its Disciplinary Committee. After the reference the Bar Council has no control over the Disciplinary Committee.

(d) Procedure Before the Disciplinary Committee

When a matter is referred by the State Bar Council under Section 35 of the Advocates Act, then Disciplinary Committee comes into picture. On a receipt of complaint the Disciplinary Committee shall fix a date for the hearing of the case and the Registrar shall expeditiously send a notice to the advocate concerned. The notice may require him to show cause within a specified date on the complaint made against him and to submit the statement of defence, document and affidavits in support of such defence and further informing him that in case of his non-appearance on the date of hearing fixed, the matter shall be heard and determined in his absence. The Disciplinary Committee of a State Bar Council shall dispose of the complaint received by it under Section 35 expeditiously and in

27. *Id.*, p. 415.

each case the proceedings shall be concluded within a period of one year from the date of the receipt of the complaint or the date or initiation of the proceedings at the instance of the State Bar Council, as the case may be.[28]

The Chairman of the Disciplinary Committee shall fix date, hour and place of enquiry. The date fixed shall not ordinarily be later than thirty days from the receipt of the reference. Registrar shall give notice to the complainant, other person aggrieved, the advocate concerned and to the Advocate General (in relation to Delhi to Additional Solicitor General of India).[29]

The parties can appear in person or by an advocate. If in an enquiry on a complaint received, either the complainant or the respondent does not appear before the Disciplinary Committee in spite of service of notice the committee may proceed *exparte* or direct fresh notice to be served.[30] However, any such order for proceeding *exparte* may be set aside on sufficient cause being shown, when an application is made supported by an affidavit within 60 days of the passing of the *exparte* order.[31]

The committee shall hear the Advocate-General and determine the matter on documents and affidavits unless it is of opinion that it should be in interest of justice to permit cross examination of the defendent or to take oral evidence, in which case the procedure for the trial of civil suit shall as far as possible be followed.[32]

It should be noted that no disciplinary enquiry shall be dropped solely by reason of its having been withdrawn, settled or otherwise compromised or that the complainant does not want to proceed with the enquiry. It shows that the misconduct case involves public concern and not only individual's grievance, like civil matters.

After giving a full opportunity of hearing of the both parties, the finding of the majority of the members of the

28. Section 36-B of the Advocates Act, 1961.
29. Rule 5(1) Chapter I Part VII, the Bar Council of India Rules, 1975.
30. *Id.* Rule 7(1).
31. *Id.*, Rule 7(2).
32. *Id.*, Rule 8(1).

Disciplinary Committee shall be finding of the Committee. The reason given in support of the finding may be given in the form of a judgement.[33]

For a final order involving dismissal of the complaint, reprimand of the advocate, suspension of advocate or removal of the name of an advocate from roll, the presence of the Chairman and other members of Disciplinary Committee is essential.[34] If no final order involving any action referred above is arrived at, the case with their opinion thereon shall be laid before the Chairman or Vice-Chairman of the Bar Council, who after such hearing as he think fit, shall deliver his opinion and the final order of such Disciplinary Committee shall follow such opinion.[35]

The Registrar of the Disciplinary Committee shall send free of charge of each of the parties in the proceedings, a certified copy of the final order or judgement.[36] The Disciplinary Committee of a Bar Council may, of its own motion or otherwise review any order passed by it within sixty days of the date of the order. However, such order of review shall have effect only by the approval of the Bar Council of India.

(B) Disciplinary Proceedings by the Bar Council of India and its Committee

The Bar Council of India is the second authority under the Advocates Act, 1961, having been constituted for the maintenance of accountability of the members of the Bar. Section 4 of the Advocates Act runs as: "there shall be a Bar Council for the territories to which this Act extends to be known as the Bar Council of India". The Bar Council of India consists of Attorney General and Solicitor General as ex-officio members and one member elected by each State Bar Council from amongst its members.[37] Chairman and Vice-Chairman of the Bar Council of India are elected by the Council in

33. *Id.*, Rule 14(1).
34. Proviso to Section 42(4) of the Advocates Act, 1961.
35. *Ibid.*, Section 42(5).
36. Rule 14(2) of the Bar Councils
37. Section 4(1) of the Advocates Act, 1961.

prescribed manner for the period of two years.[38] In addition to various committees as under the State Bar Councils,[39] the Bar Council of India has a Legal Education Committee also. Under Section 4 of the Act, the Bar Council of India may constitute one or more Disciplinary Committees. A Disciplinary Committee shall consist of three members of whom two persons shall be elected by the Council from amongst its members.[40] The other members shall be co-opted by the Council from amongst advocate of ten years standing and who are not members of the Council.[41] The senior most advocates amongst the members of the Disciplinary Committee shall be the Chairman.[42]

(C) Disciplinary Powers of the Bar Council of India and its Committees

Under the Advocates Act, 1961 the Bar Council of India enjoys two types of disciplinary powers, firstly under its original jurisdiction[43] and secondly, under appellate jurisdiction.[44]

(i) Disciplinary Powers Under Original Jurisdiction

Under its original jurisdiction, the Bar Council of India can take action against deliquent advocate in three ways, viz:

- (i) Where the matter is not disposed of by the State Bar Council within one year,
- (ii) Where the matter is referred by the State Bar Council to the Bar Council of India, and
- (iii) Where the Disciplinary Committee of the Bar Council of India withdraw the matter, pending

---

38. *Ibid.*
39. These respective committees are, Legal Aid Committee, Executive Committee, Special Committee, Disciplinary Committee and Enrolment Committee.
40. *Supra.*
41. Section 4(2) of the Advocates Act, 1961.
42. *Id.*, Section 4 (2-A).
43. *Id.*, Section 36.
44. *Id.*, Section 37.

before the Disciplinary Committee of the State Bar Council.

In this regard Section 36 reads as:

"where on receipt of a complaint or otherwise if matter is not disposed of by the State Bar Council within a year, the matter is transferred to the Bar Council of India. The Bar Council of India has reason to believe that advocate whose name is not entered on any State roll has been guilty of professional misconduct it shall refer the case for disposal to its Disciplinary Committee.[45]

It seems from the above provision that section 36 confers similar power to the Bar Council of India as have the State Bar Council under Section 35 of the Act. But in respect of any advocate whose name is not entered on any state roll, there appear to be some contradiction. How the Bar Council of India will have power to take action against any advocate (person) whose name is not entered on any state roll?

It is to be noted that even though, Section 36(1) gives power to the Bar Council of India to refer the case against a deliquent advocate for disposal to the Disciplinary Committee, the wording 'whose name is not entered on any state roll' is inconsistent within the definition provided in Section 2(a) of the Advocates Act, 1961.[46]

The plain reading of the Act in context of the definition of Advocate may clarify that a person whose name is not entered on any state roll, is not an advocate and hence immune from any action under the Act. If it is interpreted in this way it is humbly submitted that the words "whose name is not entered on any state roll": in Section 36(1) is to be deleted by making an amendment in this regard. On the other hand, if literal interpretation rule is applied to Section 36(1) the words used therein shall not be rendered otiose. It speculates a situation where a person is practising before any court in India

45. *Id.*, Section 36(1).
46. Advocates means, an advocate, entered in any roll under the provisions of this Act.

pretending as an advocate without enrolment anywhere. In such cases he should not go undisciplined and unpunished. Section 36(1) may stipulate such a situation.

Under its original jurisdiction the Bar Council of India can also take action against an advocate if the matter is referred to it by the State Bar Council. The Bar Council of India can refer the case to its Disciplinary Committee if has reason to believe that professional or other misconduct has been committed by such advocate or advocates. However, no reference to the Disciplinary Committee will be made if the Bar Council of India comes to the conclusion that the complaint is unfounded. On receipt of a reference regarding the misconduct of any advocate, the Disciplinary Committee of the Bar Council of India, in disposing of any case under Section 36 shall observe the procedure similar to the procedure to be observed by the State Bar Council. The only difference will be that reference to Advocate General in relation to the State Bar Council should be construed as reference to the Attorney General of India.

On the receipt of a reference the Disciplinary Committee then fixes a date for the hearing of the case and shall cause a notice thereof to be given to the advocates concerned and to the Attorney General of India.[47] The Disciplinary Committee after giving the advocates concerned an opportunity to be heard makes an order. Such order may dismiss the complaint, where the proceedings are founded to be not fit for consideration.

Further, Section 36 empowers the Disciplinary Committee of the Bar Council of India to withdraw, *suo motu* or on a report by any State Bar Council or on any application by any interested person, any proceedings for misconduct, pending before the Disciplinary Committee of any State Bar Council to its own file and dispose of the same.[48] Where any proceeding has been withdrawn for inquiry before the Disciplinary Committee of the Bar Council of India, it shall remit the order to that Council who shall give effect to any such order made by the Disciplinary Committee of the Bar Council of India.

47. Section 36 (3).
48. Section 36 (2).

The Disciplinary Committee while disposing the proceedings may make any order like the State Bar Council, where the Committee finds the advocate guilty, it may reprimand him or suspend him from practice for such period as it deems fit or may remove him altogether from the roll of advocates. While disposing of the matter the Bar Council of India is required to act as *quasi-judicial* body. In *Meghraj Calla* v. *Kajodi Mat,*[49] the Rajasthan High Court held that in disposing of the complaint of litigant against any advocate, the Disciplinary Committee acts as a *quasi-judicial* body.

(ii) Disciplinary Powers Under Appellate Jurisdiction

By the virtue of Section 37 of the Advocates Act, the Bar Council of India and its Disciplinary Committee enjoy superior power in as much as it hears appeals from the orders of the Disciplinary Committee of the State Bar Councils. The appeal may be preferred by any person aggrieved by the order of the Disciplinary Committee of the State Bar Council made under Section 35 of the Act.

It is to be noted carefully that the expression 'aggrieved person' may include both parties separately or jointly even with same order. It may relate to order dismissing the complaint in which case complainant may be aggrieved. If the Disciplinary Committee awarded inadequate punishment the complainant may also feel aggrieved with the same order. It may relate to action against deliquent advocate, in which the advocate may be aggrieved.

In this regard an interesting question came for consideration before the Supreme Court of India in *Adi Pheroz Shah Gandhi* v. *H.M. Seervai,*[50] whether an Advocate-General of the State can also come within the ambit of the expression 'aggrieved person'? The fact of the case was that, an advocate was on the roll of Maharashtra State Bar Council, charged with professional misconduct, was exonerated by the State Disciplinary Committee. The Advocate-General of Maharashtra filed an appeal before the Bar Council of India where the advocate's objection, that the Advocate-General was not an

49. A.I.R. 1994 (Raj.) 11.
50. A.I.R. 1971 S.C. 385.

aggrieved person, was negatived and the advocate was suspended for a year. He then appealed to the Supreme Court.

The Supreme Court held that Advocate-General is not included in the expression 'aggrieved person'. By a Majority of 3:2 consisting Chief Justice Hidayatullah, Mr. Justice Mitter and Mr. Justice Shelat, of the hon'ble Supreme Court observed:

> "Advocate-General appearing in a disciplinary proceeding in pursuance of a notice under Section 35(2) is not a person aggrieved and as such he has no right to file an appeal. Speaking for the Majority Mr. Justice Mitter explained "an Advocate-General is not the guardian of the Bar nor is he the champions of the public interest in any matter save as specified in the statute".

However, in its minority view Mr. Justice Ray and Mr. Justice Vaidyalingam disagreed and said that the Advocate-General and the Attorney General represented the standard to be maintained in the profession. "If a public servant is competent to file a complaint, there is no reason why for the purpose of appealing to the Bar Council of India, he is not a person aggrieved".[51]

The majority decision of the Supreme Court was nullified by an amendment to the Advocates Act in 1973, i.e. only after two years of the judgment. It is interesting to note that after the two years the minority view of the above judgement became statutory provision by the way of amendment made in Sections 37 and 38 of the Advocates Act.[52] Thus, after 1973 Advocate-General is competent to appeal against the order of the Disciplinary Committee of the State Bar Council. After the aforesaid amendment the term 'aggrieved person' came to examined before the Bench of Seven judges in the case of *Bar Council of Maharashtra* v. *M.V. Dadholkar*.[53] In the instant case, the question arose whether Bar Councils may also be included in the term 'person aggrieved'. The then Chief Justice A.N. Ray, who wrote the judgement for himself and five other

51. *Id.*, p. 395.
52. See, The Advocate (Amendment) Act 60 of 1973.
53. A.I.R. 1976 S.C. 242.

justices held that the task of the State Bar Council to watch and maintain does not cease on placing a matter before the Disciplinary Committee. It has an abiding interest in the proceedings and a more liberal approach is required in the back-ground of statutes which do not deal with property right but deal with professional conduct and morality.

The Supreme Court held that the Bar Council is an aggrieved person because of:

(a) These are words of wide import,
(b) The Bar Council represents the collective conscience of the standard in the proceedings for vindicating discipline, dignity and decorum of the profession,
(c) A decision of the committee can only be corrected by appeal, and
(d) The Bar Council is vitally concerned with the decision.

(iii) Procedure to be Followed by Bar Council of India

The Bar Council of India rules deal with the procedure to be followed in appeal to the Bar Council of India under Section 37 of the Act.[54]

Every such appeal has to made within sixty days of the date of communication of the order, to the party concerned. The date of communication is not the date of the dispatch of the order but the date of its receipt.[55]

(D) Award of Punishments

Every appeal under Section 37 shall be heard by the Disciplinary Committee of the Bar Council of India which as an appellate body may pass under noted orders as it may deem fit:

(i) It may dismiss the appeal and uphold the orders of the Disciplinary Committee of the State Bar Council, or
(ii) It may allow the appeal and set aside the order of

54. Rule, 19-23 of the Bar Council of India Rules, 1976.
55. Section 37 of the Advocates Act, 1961.

the Disciplinary Committee of the State Bar Council, or

(iii) It may vary the punishment by way lessening the punishment or enhancing it, awarded by the Disciplinary Committee of the State Bar Council.

It is revealed from the above provision that the words "as it deem fit" confer power of wider jurisdiction. In *Narendra Singh* v. *Chottey Singh*,[56] Mr. Justice Desai, has rightly observed:

"The word as it deems fit" conferred jurisdiction of the widest amplitude. The appellate body enjoys wide jurisdiction as it is competent to pass any order which it may deem fit, and is relevant to the function of the Bar Council. However, he cautioned the order must be germane to the Act and its purpose and latitude cannot transcend those limits.

Thus, the Disciplinary Committee of the Bar Council of India can modify the punishment awarded by the Disciplinary Committee of the State Bar Council both by reducing and enhancing the punishment. In *Professor Krishnaraj Goswami* v. *Viswanath D. Mukasikar*[57] the complainant had paid sum to advocate who had not filed suit in time and deposited less court fee, refused to return papers and refused to give no objection certificate, had been punished by the Disciplinary Committee with suspension of licence for three years. The Bar Council of India set aside the order of the State Bar Committee and noting the fact that he had returned money. Consequently, the advocate was reprimanded and was given warning not to repeat such type of misconduct.

On the other hand in *S.K. Nagar* v. *V.P. Jain*,[58] where the deliquent advocate had given false information and prepared false and fabricated document to convince client about pendency of case when no case was filed in court. The Disciplinary Committee of the State Bar Council found him

56. A.I.R. 1983 S.C. 990.
57. D.C. Appeal No. 40/1995, dated 13.11.1999.
58. D.C. Appeal No. 14/1997, dated 31.7.1999.

guilty of professional misconduct and punished him with suspension from practice for two years. The Bar Council of India upheld the decision of State Bar Council and enhanced the punishment from two years to five years suspension from practice as well as a cost of Rs. 5000.

The Bar Council of India observed:

> "However, regarding the punishment of only two years we are of the opinion that it is too lenient considering the gross misconduct. Exercising our powers under Section 37 we feel that punishment be enhanced".

It is important to note that, before enhancing the punishment the Bar Council of India shall issue a show cause notice that, why the punishment should not be enhanced and must give a reasonable opportunity to be heard to the deliquent advocate.

Further, under the Act the Bar Council of India has power of review its own orders and decisions. Section 44 empowers the Disciplinary Committees of both the Bar Councils to review their own order and decisions within sixty days of the date of order. However, an order passed on revision by a Disciplinary Committee of a State Bar Council is subject to approval by the Bar Council of India. Both the Disciplinary Committees can review on being applied to by someone. They can also review *suo motu*. By the virtue of the decision of the Supreme Court in *O.M. Mahindroo* v. *District Judge, Delhi,*[59] matter has been decided by the Disciplinary Committee and has gone to higher authority provided under the Act still the power of review can be entertained by the Disciplinary Committee.

In the instant case while pointing out the wide ramification and significance of review exercised by the Disciplinary Committee, the Supreme Court observed:

> "The powers of review are not circumscribed by the Act. The analogy of Civil Procedure Code must not be carried

59. A.I.R. 1971 S.C. 107.

too far. Such powers may be exercised in a suitable case for or against an advocate even after the matter has gone through the hands of the Disciplinary Committee at some stage or even through this court. These matters are also not governed by the analogy of *autrefois convict or autrefois acquit* in the Code of Criminal Procedure".

However, on receipt of the application the Disciplinary Committee of a Bar Council may summarily reject the same under Section 44 of the Act, or it may wish to exercise its powers *suo motu*.

The foregoing discussion reveals that under the Advocates Act, 1961, a wide power is conferred on the State Bar Council and Bar Council of India alongwith their Disciplinary Committee to deal with the professional or others misconduct committed by the Advocates. While before discussing the sortcoming of the disciplinary proceedings and other mechanism for regulation of the conduct of the advocate it will be necessary to focus on the nature of the disciplinary proceedings under the Act.

(E) Nature of Disciplinary Proceedings and Standard of Proof

The disciplinary proceedings before the State Bar Council and Bar Council of India are *sui generis*, neither it is purely civil, nor criminal in nature. It is to be noted that under the Advocates Act, 1961, once the complaint is lodged and proceedings has started compromise between parties or withdrawal of charge will have no effect on the continuance of proceedings and taking action accordingly.[60] As in *M/s. Mottomal Ramchand & Sons* v. *U.N. Ajawani*,[61] the Bar Council of India emphasized that mutual compromise or settlement which is in some degree permitted in civil matter, is immaterial in the cases involving professional or others misconduct under the Advocates Act, 1961.

Similarly, disciplinary proceedings under the Act are not subject to the ordinary criminal procedure safeguards. The

60. See, Rules 11(3) and 26(1) of the Bar Councils of India Rules, 1975.
61. B.C.I.T.R. 61/974 Vol. 3(1) 1974 J.B.C.I. 508.

main disciplinary sanction under the Act is the removal of the name of advocate from the state roll. In addition, lesser punishments like reprimands and suspension from the practice may also be awarded. The Supreme Court in its decisions has consistently held that neither punishment nor deterrence is the aim of professional disciplinary mechanism. In *V.G. Rangadurai* v. *D. Gopalan,*[62] Mr. Justice A.P. Sen of the Supreme Court observed that "The purpose of disciplinary proceedings is not punitive but to inquire, for the protection to the public, the courts and the legal profession, into fitness of the subject to continue in the capacity of an advocate".

It appears that, there is difficulty to determine an exact nature of proceedings relating to professional and other misconducts under the Act. The answer may vary and it is not easy to define, like water tight comportment. Therefore, it may be said that the disciplinary proceedings under the Act, is quasi-criminal in nature, where the procedure contains in code of criminal procedure need not to be strictly followed. The principle of natural justice has to be applied and the Disciplinary Committee must frame a charge specifying the misconduct against the advocate before recording evidence.

However, it is also true that the proceedings dealing with professional misconduct does not have only litigation dimension. It also has to affect the society in general and legal profession in particular view of its effect an administration of justice. Here the question arises: what should be the degree of proof in the proceedings involving the professional or other misconducts?

In this regard the earlier view was that, the findings in disciplinary proceedings be sustained by a higher degree of proof than that required in civil suits, but shorter than that required to sustain a conviction in a criminal prosecution.[63]

It is submitted that the earlier view on this point was not a good approach that is why it is no longer considered to be a good law. The charge of professional misconduct is a stigma on the face of not only the particular advocate but entire legal profession. So charges must be clearly proved and should not

62. (1979) 1 S.C.C. 308.
63. *V.C. Rangaduri* v. *D. Gopalan,* A.I.R. 1979 S.C. 281.

be inferred from mere ground of suspicion. That is the reason why the courts have changed their views and said that charges of misconduct requires the same degree of proof as in the case of a criminal charge.

In *Pawan Kumar Sharma* v. *Gurdial Singh,*[64] Mr. Justice Anand (as he then was) of the Supreme Court held that a charge of professional or other misconduct is quasi-criminal in nature and has to be established beyond reasonable doubt and not by preponderance of possibilities as in civil cases.

Thus, the courts now by and large require the same degree of proof as in the case of criminal offence. But some flexibility is always attached differing from case to case. Thus, In *L.C. Goyal* v. *Suresh Joshi,*[65] an advocate was charged of misappropriating the client's money and the cheque through which money was refunded, bounced due to insufficient fund. He had denied his signature on cheque and receipts alleged to have been issued by him to client. It was held that opinion of handwriting expert was not necessary because other facts showed that the signature was of the appellant. The Supreme Court itself compared signature on the cheque with appellant's admitted signature and found striking similarities. The court held that the established circumstances spoke for themselves and candidly pointed towards appellant misconduct—*Res Ipsa Loquitor*.

But in a subsequent case it took a different approach. Thus, in *Bhupinder Kumar Sharma* v. *Bar Association, Pathankot*[66] an advocate had engaged himself in three different businesses like, P.C.O., Photo copier and Taxi driving, along with legal profession. *Mr. Justice Shivraj* v. *Patil* declared it a clear case of professional misconduct. The learned Judge observed:

> "Having perused both the orders and the evidence placed on record, we are of the view that the finding recorded, holding the appellant guilty of professional misconduct is supported by and is based on cogent and convincing evidence even judged by the standard required to

64. (1999) 3 S.C.C. 376.
65. A.I.R. 1999 S.C. 98.
66. (2002) 1 S.C.C. 470.

establish misconduct as required to prove a charge in a *quasi-criminal* case beyond reasonable doubt".[67]

Thus, the decisions referred above depict that, though, the exact nature of the disciplinary proceedings is not clear but the courts considered it as *quasi-criminal* in nature and ruled that charges of misconduct should be proved beyond reasonable doubt. Having regards to the *quasi-criminal* nature of the proceedings the courts also emphasise that, if any doubt comes in evidence, the benefit of doubt should be given to the deliquent advocate. Thus, in *L.D. Jai Shinghani* v. *Narain Das*,[68] finding the advocate guilty of not filing a suit on behalf of his client after taking moneys for the same and perpetuating gross misconception that suit was filed but in reality no suit being filed, the Disciplinary Committee had ordered removal of his name from the roll of advocate. In appeal the Supreme Court found some doubt as to the truthfulness of the complainant's version which had come with considerable delay. It set aside the order and said "we think that in a case of this nature, involving possible debar of the advocate concerned the evidence should be of a character which should leave no reasonable doubt about the guilt".

The above decision of the Apex Court found strong support in *Mrs. R.D. Bhatia* v. *Smt. Rajinder Kaur*,[69] wherein, respondent had engaged appellant as her advocate. She alleged that while conducting her case the appellant had committed professional misconduct by going hand in glove with defendant. Disciplinary Committee of the Bar Council of India found the appellant guilty and suspended from practising for two years. On scrutiny of evidence the Supreme Court found that evidence of the complainant herself was very shaky and unacceptable and failure of the Disciplinary Committee of the Bar Council of India to properly appreciate it resulted in miscarriage of Justice. Speaking for the court Mr. Justice Faizan Uddin of the Supreme Court observed:

67. *Id.*, p. 473.
68. A.I.R. 1976 S.C. 373.
69. (1996) 6 S.C.C. 627.

> "It is a cardinal principle of law that in case of misconduct or allegations of any guilt against any person involving his indictment or infliction of punishment the evidence adduced should be of such character and intrinsic value which may not admit any element of reasonable doubt about alleged misconduct or guilt. In other words, the evidence should be beyond all reasonable doubt"[70].

The Chief Justice of India, Mr. Justice R.C. Lahoti, in *D.P. Chandra* v. *Triyugi Narain Mishra*,[71] summarized the above principle in these words:

> "We are aware that a charge of misconduct is a serious matter for a practising advocate. A verdict of guilt of professional or other misconduct may result in reprimanding the advocate, suspending the advocate from practice for such period as may be deems fit, or even removing the name of the advocate from the roll of advocate which would cost the counsel his career. Therefore, an allegation of misconduct has to be proved to the hilt".

The ratio of the decisions in *Prahalad Saran Gupta* v. *Bar Council of India*,[72] *H.V. Panchaksharappa* v. *K.G. Iswar*[73] and *Bijay Kumar Mahanty* v. *Jadu Alias Ramchandra Sahoo*,[74] are also based on this view that, the disciplinary proceedings under the Act are *quasi-criminal* in nature and standard of proof should be beyond reasonable doubt.

(F) Quantum of Punishment Under Advocates Act

The ethics of punishment as a measure for maintaining discipline in legal profession is more akin to that "*Patria*

70. *Id.*, p. 631.
71. (2001) 2 S.C.C. 221.
72. A.I.R. 1997 S.C. 1338.
73. (2006) S.C.C. 721.
74. (2003) 1 S.C.C. 644.

Potestas" [75] for keeping discipline in the family than that of a theologian or a criminologist, though, the underlying idea in all the three is the same, that is to say, to maintain and stabilize a good social order. Just as the head of the family expects from its members good behaviour not only towards his own self but towards one and another also, similarly in the field of legal profession Bar Councils have power to direct its normal behaviour and etiquette. Under the Act Bar Councils functions are related to internal discipline and control over the profession. By virtue of Section 35 of the Act it has power to take disciplinary action against deliquent advocates if they are found guilty of professional or other misconduct. Under this section Bar Councils have power to take following action against deliquent advocate, viz.

(a) reprimand of the advocate,
(b) suspension of the advocate from practice for such period as it may deem fit, and
(c) removal of the name of the advocate from the state roll of advocates.

However, it is not clear as to guiding principles for inflicting punishments on erring and deliquent advocate? It is true that in every profession it is essential that there must be a certain amount of discipline without which the profession cannot run smoothly. The society has recognized the power of the Bar Councils to take action against advocates who commit a misconduct, which are likely to threaten and hamper the gravity of the profession. But, at the same time the society also demands that in doing so the Bar Council's actions should be fair, *bonafide*, just and commensurate with the guilt of misconduct. In *L.C. Goyal* v. *Suresh Joshi*,[76] Mr. Justice V.N. Khare (as he then was) very well summarized the principle of quantum of punishment. In his own words:

> "By doing any act which is contrary to the accepted norms and standards of the profession, a member of the

75. Head of the Family.
76. (1996) 3 S.C.C. 376.

> profession not only discredits himself, but also brings disrepute to the profession which he belongs. By such acts, the credibility and reputation of the profession as a whole comes under a cloud. If any member of the profession falls from such standards, he deserves punishment commensurate with the gravity of the misconduct".[77]

However, when a punishment may be said commensurate or what should be the ontological approach towards the award of punishment for professional or others misconduct is not very much clear. It is important to note that degree of misconduct is a question of fact, and there is no single yardstick to determine that a misconduct is minor in nature or serious. As *Lord Jems Hereford* said that "There is no fixed rule of law defining the degree of misconduct therefore each case must be decided on its own special facts.[78] In dealing with the misconduct of the advocates the courts have taken a view that the gravity of misconduct should be taken into account with the other situations of the case and ontological approach should be deterrent. However keeping a view the past record of advocate or age or any other similar situation the courts may take the reformatory approach also.

Thus, there is no statutory rule, or any perfect and final decision of Supreme Court or High Courts, by which the justness or wrongness of punishment can be tested. The appropriateness of the punishment will depend on the fact and circumstance of each case, specially the nature and gravity of the misconduct.

A few instances of guiding factor for awarding punishment collected from various cases, so far decided by the courts and the Disciplinary Committees of the Bar Councils are given below:

(i) ***Deterrent Approach to Punishment***

The Disciplinary Committee of the State Bar Councils and the Bar Council of India do not favour any leniency to the

77. *Ibid.*
78. *Cluston & Company* v. *Corry* (1906) A.C. 122 (P.C.)

advocates if they are found guilty of gross professional misconduct and grant deterrent punishment to the deliquent advocates. Thus, in *P.J. Ratnam* v. *D. Karikaran,*[79] an advocate got into his hands considerable sum of money belonging to his client. He did not return him on demand. He put forward false defence of payment and sought to sustain his defence by stuborning witness. Advocate was found guilty of gross professional misconduct and was punished with suspension from practice for five years. In appeal the Supreme Court of India confirmed the punishment and said that the punishment granted by the Council was proper, having regard to the gravity of the offence.

Again, in *John D'Souza* v. *Edward Ani,*[80] advocate did not return *Will* of testatrix despite repeated demands. He was punished with suspension for one year from practice. So also where an advocate purchased property from his client which was subject matter of dispute between the parties, he was suspended from practice for a period of one year.[81] In *Smt. Farida Chaudhari* v. *Dr. Achyut Kumar Thakuria,*[82] an advocate wrote obscene letters against his neighbour with whom he was not having good relations. He was suspended from practice for a period of four months with a cost of Rs. 10,000 payable within two months. Likewise in *Shambhoo Ram Yadav* v. *Hanuman Das Khatri,*[83] an advocate wrote a letter to client seeking money to bribe the judge, was punished with suspension from practice for two years.

It is to be noted that while awarding the punishment of suspension for professional misconduct the punishing authority, of the State Bar Councils and Bar Council of India as well as the Supreme Court have some discretion. If the authority found that the misconduct was serious in nature it can award more serious punishment depending upon the nature and gravity of the misconduct. Thus, in *Sardul Singh* v. *Pritam Singh,*[84] advocate was accused of practising despite an

79. A.I.R. 1964 S.C. 244.
80. A.I.R. 1994 S.C.975.
81. *P.D. Gupta* v. *Ram Murti,* A.I.R. 1998 S.C. 283.
82. B.C.I.T.R. Case No. 1/1993, dated 11.9.1999.
83. A.I.R. 2001 S.C. 2509.
84. (1993) 3 S.C.C. 522.

order of suspension from practice in a proceeding relating to suppression of facts at the time of enrolment. He was awarded suspension from practice for three years.

In *M.S. Patwardhan* v. *V.V. Karmarkar,*[85] where the advocate received heavy amount for purchase of stamp duty and other charges he did not render account nor paid the amount lying as balance with him. He was suspended from practice for a period of five years.

In *Mrs. Suresh Joshi* v. *L.C. Goyal*[86] an advocate realized an amount of Rs. 25,102 as Court fee and in the suit for declaration and damages, he paid only Rs. 100 as Court fee. On demand of complainant he issued cheques twice which were dishonoured on account of insufficient funds. His name was ordered to be struck out from the roll of the Bar Council of Delhi and cost of Rs. 5000 was also ordered to be paid.

Likewise in *Bar Council of Andhra Pradesh* v. *Kurapati Satyanarayana,*[87] an advocate had received a total sum of Rs. 14,600 belonging to payable to the *defacto* complainant on different dates. He had received the said amount on behalf of the complainant in the execution proceeding. He retained the said amount with him. The Supreme Court of India approved the decision of the State Bar Council of Andhra Pradesh punishing the deliquent advocate by removal of his name from the roll of the Bar Council. The Supreme Court expressed its opinion that for such a grave professional misconduct removal of name from the roll of Bar Council would be the only appropriate punishment.

Recently, in *Vikas Deshpande* v. *Bar Council of India*[88] an advocate solicited for himself for filing appeal to the High Court against the death sentences passed by trial court against three complainants. He had also obtained power of attorney or misrepresentation in his favour. On that basis he sold their property and fraudulently appropriated sole proceeds for his gain. The Bar Council of India permanently debarred the advocate and directed State Bar Council of Maharashtra and

85. B.C.I.T.R. Case No. 93/1991, dated 16.8.1999.
86. B.C.I.T.R. Case No. 44/1995, dated 2.3.1998.
87. A.I.R. 2001 S.C. 798.
88. A.I.R. 2003 S.C. 308.

Goa to remove the name of the advocate from the roll. The Supreme Court confirmed the punishment.

It appears to be clear from the decisions referred above that no hard and fast rule or strait jacket formula can be laid down regarding the punishment for professional and other misconduct. However, the State Bar Councils and the Bar Council of India are of the view that if the misconduct is of serious nature then no leniency should be shown to the deliquent advocate. Much will depend upon the misconduct committed. The expression commensurate may require aggravated as well lesson punishment. Thus, in some cases keeping in view that punishment should be commensurate with the gravity of offence the State Bar Councils and the Bar Council of India can and may award the lesser punishment, including the reprimand to the Advocates.

(ii) ***Reformatory Approach of Punishment***

In imposing punishment on an earning advocate an enlightened approach informed with the demands of the situation and the philosophy and spirit of times requires to be made. It cannot be a matter of the *ipsofato* of the disciplinary authority depending on his whim or caprice.

It has been said that be it administration of criminal Law or the exercise of disciplinary jurisdiction in departmental disciplinary proceedings punishment is not and cannot be the 'end' in itself. That is why in cases of minor misconduct the Bar Councils only reprimand the advocates. Thus, in *J.N. Gupta* v. *D.C. Sighania,*[89] where the respondent advocate made an advertisement in the International Bar Directory, he was reprimanded for the same and was warned that he should be more careful in future.

Likewise, in *Prahlad Saran Gupta* v. *Bar Council of India,*[90] an advocate wrongfully detained the amount of Rs. 1500 which was deposited with him in connection with the proceedings. He did not pay it for a period of eight months inspite of repeated request and in order to harass him, instead of handing over to him, he deposited the said amount in Court.

89. B.C.I.T.R. Case No. 38/1994, dated 15.7.1997.
90. A.I.R. 1997 S.C. 1388.

The Supreme Court found him guilty of misconduct and imposed the penalty of reprimand on the appellant advocate for the said misconduct.

What should be the guiding principle in these types of cases, Mr. Justice Krishna Iyer well summarized the issue by saying that "every punishment has a functional duality deterrence and correction. Deterrent approach is visible in awarding punishment for professional misconduct commensurate to the gravity of the misconduct grave the misconduct severe the punishment and negligible the misconduct lighter the punishment".[91]

The learned judge further observed:

> "Conventional penalties have their punitive limitations and flaws viewed from the reformatory angle. A therapeutic touch, a correctional twist and a locus penitential may have rehabilitative impact if only we may experiment unorthodoxly, but within the parameter of law" .[92]

Therefore, in extraordinary and special situations the courts take some lenient view to the advocates. Some instances are given below:

(1) where the advocate detained the client's money but deposited after demand;[93]
(2) where the advocate is too young;[94]
(3) where the advocate is old in age;
(4) where the advocate is handicap;
(5) if the advocate tenders unconditional apology. But it is not matter of right;
(6) if the deliquent advocate have good past record;
(7) and last but not least, some good gesture shown by deliquent advocate may provide good opportunity for showing leniency.

91. *Supra* note 63.
92. *Ibid.*
93. *Supra* note 65.
94. *Chandra Shekhar Soni* v. *Bar Council of Maharastra,* A.I.R. 1983 S.C. 1012.

II. APPELLATE JURISDICTION OF THE SUPREME COURT

The provisions in the Advocates Act, 1961 irresistibly establish the supremacy of the courts,[95] in giving final decision on question of misconduct of an advocate. Though, under the Advocates Act State Bar Councils and Bar Council of India are empowered to take action against the deliquent advocate, but by the virtue of Section 38 the final word on the punishment of an advocate for professional or others misconduct is still with the Supreme Court of India. Therefore, by the way of appellate jurisdiction of the Supreme Court, the Act provides second mechanism to deal with the misconduct of the members of the Bar.

From the decision of the Disciplinary Committee of the State Bar Councils, an appeal lies to the Bar Council of India.[96] Such appeal may be made to the Bar Council of India or to the Supreme Court as the case may be within the sixty days of the date of communication of the order to the aggrieved person.[97]

It is important to note that Section 38 provides that orders made by the Disciplinary Committee of the Bar Council of India under Sections 36 and 37 are appealable to the Supreme Court of India. Therefore, the Supreme Court has to hear to appeal by the way of the first and second appeal both. It is so because the first appeal against the order of the Disciplinary Committee of the State Bar Council lies to the Bar Council of India[98] and the appeal against the order of the Disciplinary Committee of the Bar Council of India lie to the Supreme Court of India.[99]

95. Section 32 of the advocates act empowers the court to permit appearance in cases and section 34(1) declares that High Court is competent to make rules for implementing the provisions of the act. Further, rules made by the Bar Council of India as to standards of professional conduct and etiquette to be observed by advocate by virtue of section 49(1)(c) in subject to the approval of the Chief Justice of India.
96. Section 38 of the Advocates Act, 1961.
97. *Ibid.*
98. *Id.*, section 36.
99. *Id.*, section 37.

Further, there is also an additional channel of appeal to the Supreme Court i.e., appeal against the order of the Disciplinary Committee of the Bar Council of India passed in exercise of the disciplinary powers of the Bar Council of India.

The above provisions of Sections 36 and 37 of the Advocates Act reveal that under the Advocates Act the Apex Court is the court of first appeal as well as the court of second appeal. To elaborate it if an advocate, whose name is not entered on state roll and his case was heard by the Disciplinary Committee of the Bar Council of India within its original jurisdiction and disposed of the appeal lies to the Supreme Court under Section 36(1) of the said Act, and in that case Supreme Court will be the court of First appeal.

Further, the second appeal is entertained by the Supreme Court when it hears appeal against the order of the Disciplinary Committee of the Bar Council of India passed under Section 37 of the Advocates Act, 1961. This is so because the Bar Council of India through its Disciplinary Committee hears the appeal against the order of the Disciplinary Committee of the State Bar Council and passes order which is appealed in the Supreme Court of India.

(A) Persons Who May Preferred Appeal

Under the Advocates Act, 1961 any person aggrieved by an order made by the Disciplinary Committee of the Bar Council of India under Sections 36 or 37 can prefer appeal to the Supreme Court.[100] Further, the amendment made in 1973 has inserted Advocate-General[101] and Attorney-General,[102] as persons competent to prefer appeal against the order of the Disciplinary Committee of a State Bar Council or the Bar Council of India, as the case may be. They are made party to the proceedings. However, the Advocates Act as well as the Bar Council of India rules does not reveal under what capacity and for whom they appear before Disciplinary Committee or for whom they prefer an appeal to the Supreme Court. Not

100. *Id.*, section 38.
101. For the other States.
102. For the Delhi only.

only this an issue has also arisen as to the *locus standi* of the State Bar Council itself.

In this regard another interesting issue came before the Supreme Court in the case of *Andhra Pradesh* v. *Kurapati Satya Narayanan*,[103] wherein the question was: can a State Bar Council file an appeal in the Supreme Court against the order of the Bar Council of India? In other word, whether a State Bar Council can be treated as a person aggrieved within the meaning of Section 38 of the Act?

Mr. Justice Ashok Bhan, speaking for the Division Bench of the Supreme Court, observed:

> "The role of the Bar Council is of dual capacity, one as the prosecutor through its executive committee and the other quasi-judicial performed through its Disciplinary Committee. Being the prosecutor the State Bar Council, would be an 'aggrieved person' and therefore, it can prefer an appeal to the Supreme Court".[104]

The above decision was based on an earlier view of the Supreme Court in *Bar Council of Maharashtra* v. *M. Dabholkar*.[105] In that case Mr. Justice Krishna Iyer was also of the view that the Bar Council may be treated as aggrieved person, and elaborated a number of reasons for his conclusion, which has been discussed earlier in this chapter.[106]

(B) Procedural Aspect of Appeal Before the Supreme Court

The Bar Council of India Rules, deal with the procedural aspects for filing and disposal of appeals. According to the Rules, application for appeal shall be in the form of a memorandum in writing.[107] If it is in a language other than English it shall be accompanied by translation thereof in

103. A.I.R. 2003 S.C. 175.
104. *Ibid.*
105. (1975) 2 S.C.C. 702.
106. *Supra* note.
107. Rule 19(1) of Part III, Chapter II, the Bar Council of India Rules, 1975.

English.[108] In every appeal, all persons who were parties to the original proceedings shall alone be impleaded.[109] Provision exist for the continuance of the proceedings after the death of the complainant,[110] for mode of presentation,[111] condonation of delay,[112] payment of fee,[113] rectification of defects, allocation of the matters to the Disciplinary Committee[114] and sending of notices to the parties.

Some procedural formalities regarding the appeals under Section 38 of the Advocates Act are also given in the Supreme Court Rules, 1966. These rules say the memorandum of appeal shall be in the form of a petition. It should state all the relevant facts leading up to the order complained of and shall set forth in brief the objections to the decision appealed from and the grounds relied or in support of the appeal.[115] The petition should be accompanied by an authenticated copy of the decision appealed from and atleast seven spare sets of the petition and the paper filed with it.[116]

After giving notice to the appellant or his advocate on record, if any, the Registrar shall post the appeal before the court for preliminary hearing and for orders as to issue of notice. Upon such hearing, the Supreme Court, if satisfied that no *prima facie* case has been made out for its interference, may dismiss the appeal, or direct that notice of the appeal be issued to Advocate-General of the State concerned or to the Attorney-General of India or to both and to the respondent.[117] Though,

---

108. *Ibid.*
109. *Id*, R. 19(2).
110. *Id*, R. 19(3).
111. *Id*, R. 20(1).
112. *Id*, R. 20(2).
113. *Id*, R. 21(3).
114. *Id*, R. 21(4).
115. Rule 19(1) and (2) of part VII, Chapter II, the Bar Council of India Rules, 1975. The petition should also state the date on which the order complained was received by the appellant. The allegation of facts contained in the petition which cannot be verified by the reference to duly authenticated copies of documents accompanying it shall be supported by affidavit of the appellant.
116. *Id.*, R. 5.
117. *Id.*, R. 7.

there is not time prescribed by the Act or Bar Councils of India rules, but Section 39 of the Advocates Act specifically provides that the provisions of Section 5 and 12 of the Indian Limitation Act, 1963 shall apply, so far as may be, to appeal under the Act.[118]

(C) Exercise of Appellate Jurisdiction

An appeal under Section 38 is not on law alone and by exercising its appellate jurisdiction the Supreme Court is empowered to pass any order as it deems fit, including an order varying the punishment awarded by the Disciplinary Committee of the Bar Council of India.

These words confer ample and flexible power on the Supreme Court. Thus, the court may pass the following orders:

(i) It can dismiss the appeal and uphold the orders of the Disciplinary Committee of the Bar Council of India.

(ii) It can allow the appeal and set aside the order of the Disciplinary Committee of the Bar Council of India.

(iii) It can vary the punishment awarded by the Disciplinary Committee of the Bar Council of India. Order may be varied either by reducing the quantum of punishment or by enhancing it. However, the Supreme Court will not vary the order of the Disciplinary Committee of the Bar Council of India so as to prejudicially affect the person aggrieved without giving him a reasonable opportunity of being heard.

It seems that in its appellate jurisdiction Supreme Court can interfere with the findings of the Bar Council of India. Though the grounds of interference are not prescribed by the Act or Rules, therefore, not clear. A few grounds collected from

---

118. Section 5 of the Limitation Act enables the extension of the prescribed period in certain cases, provided there is sufficient cause for not preferring the appeal or making the application within such period. Section 12 deals with the exclusion of certain periods in computing the period of limitation prescribed.

various cases so far decided by The courts are given below in brief:

(i) Where the error is expressed on face of record.[119]
(ii) Where the judgements have been given in violation of any statutory requirement.[120]
(iii) Where the findings of the Bar Council is perverse.[121]
(iv) Where the findings of the Bar Council is improper.[122]
(v) Where the punishment imposed by the Bar Council is found disproportionate.[123]
(vi) Where the Bar Councils take the grave professional misconduct in lighter vein.[124]
(vii) And last, but not least, where the approach of the Bar Council is found to be unsatisfactory.[125]

III. CONTEMPT PROCEEDINGS

Even Though, Advocates Act, 1961 gives power to discipline the members of the Bar to the professional body i.e., Bar Councils and also to the Supreme Court of India, but in legal world there are another mechanism by which the courts can deal the conduct of the members of the Bar. It is known as contempt proceedings. The Advocates Act, 1961 is silent as to the contempt by the advocates hence the said mechanism is regulated through the Contempt of Courts Act, 1971 as well as the Constitution of India.

In India High Court[126] and Supreme Court[127] both have power to punish for contempt. They are regarded as a court of record by the Indian Constitution and are vested with the

119. *Hikmat Ali Khan* v. *Ishwar Prasad Arya*, J.T. 1997 (2) S.C. 182.
120. *D.P. Chadha* v. *Triyugi Narain Mishra*, A.I.R. 2001 S.C. 457.
121. *Bar Council of Andhra Pradesh* v. *Kurapati Saqtya Narayanan*, A.I.R. 2003, S.C. 175.
122. *Prahlad Saran Gupta* v. *Bar Council of India* (2000) 1 S.C.C. 450.
123. *Rajendra V. Pai* v. *Alex Fernandez* (2002) 4 S.C.C. 212.
124. *Haris Chandra Tiwari* v. *Baiju* (2002) 2 S.C.C. 67.
125. *Sardul Singh* v. *Pritam Singh* (1999) 3 S.C.C. 522.
126. Article 215, Constitution of India.
127. *Id.*, Article 129.

power to punish for contempt of its own and its subordinate courts.

Under Section 10 of the Contempt of Courts Act, 1971, every High Court has the same power to punish for contempt of courts subordinate to it as it has in respect of contempt itself.[128] Section 15(1) of the Act, authorizes the courts of record to take action either on its own motion or on motion made by the Advocate-General or any other person with the latter's consent. Clause 2 of Section vests similar power in the High Courts on the report of the latter court's report or on the motion of the Advocate-General or authorized law officer of the Union Government. The *suo motu* exercise of all powers by courts of record is thus, constitutionally[129] and statutorily[130] permitted.

It is important to note that, the Contempt of Courts Act, 1971, reaffirms and reiterates the jurisdiction and power of a High Court in respect of its own contempt and of subordinate courts. "The Act of 1971 does not confer any new jurisdiction instead it affirms the High Court's power and jurisdiction for taking action for the contempt of itself as well as the subordinate courts".[131]

While, the High Court can exercise jurisdiction to punish contempt of subordinate courts over which it has supervisory jurisdiction, yet where in a statute, there is provision dealing with contempt of tribunals, the High Court cannot intervene in its inherent jurisdiction.[132] Besides, this every High Court in India has jurisdiction to punish for contempt. This special jurisdiction is inherent on account of court record from the very nature of the court itself.[133]

In any case, so far as contempt of a High Court itself is concerned it has been distinct from that of a subordinate court.

---

128. *State of Rajasthan* v. *Prakash Chand* (1988) 1 S.C.C. 1.
129. *Supra* note 126 & 127.
130. Section 10, Contempt of Courts Act, 1971; see also *Arundhati Roy, In Re* (2002) 3 S.C.C. 343.
131. *Delhi Judicial Service Association* v. *State of Gujarat*, A.I.R. 1991 S.C. 2191.
132. *'Hayles', In the matter of,* A.I.R. 1955 (Mad.) 1.
133. *Supreme Court Bar Association* v. *Union of India* (1998) 4 S.C.C. 409.

Article 215 vests these rights in every High Court, hence no Act of Legislature could take away that jurisdiction and confer it a fresh by virtue of its own authority. "Neither the Supreme Court nor the Legislature can deprive a High Court of the right which is so vested in it".[134]

However, the special jurisdiction of the High Court in respect of contempt can be used only when it is necessary in the interest of administration of justice. "It can be exercised only the cases of clear and beyond reasonable doubt".[135] Need not to say that, the power under Article 215 is vested in the High Court, hence a judge of the High Court can exercise the power only as judge of that court. So if a judge of the High Court is appointed to an Industrial Tribunal,[136] any contempt committed before the tribunal can only be contempt of that tribunal. It cannot become contempt of the High Court simply because a judge of the High Court is a presiding officer of the tribunal. So the latter cannot use the power of the High Court in dealing with contempt of the Tribunal.

The High Court as a court of record can also punish for contempt committed outside its territorial jurisdiction, if the contempt happens to be within its jurisdiction, however, there is not power to arrest a person who is outside its jurisdiction.

Under Indian Constitution the Supreme Court is also recognized as court of record so as a court of record has power to determine its own jurisdiction and has power to punish for its contempt. In *Naresh Shridhar Mirajkar* v. *State of Maharashtra,*[137] the Supreme Court has asserted that "In the absence of any express provision in the Constitution the Apex Court being a court of record has jurisdiction in every matter and if there be any doubt, the court has power to determine its jurisdiction. The Supreme Court has a summary jurisdiction to punish contempt of its authority.

The Supreme Court can also take cognizance *suo motu* of the contempt of a High Court under Article 129.[138] The

134. *Ajay Kumar Pandey, In Re,* (1996) 6 S.C.C. 510.
135. *Aaloji Rao Shitole* v. *Matkan, L.G.,* A.I.R. 1953 (M.B.) 245.
136. *'Harniman', In Re,* 1943 Bom. L.R. 94.
137. A.I.R. 1967 S.C. 1.
138. *V.C. Mishra, In Re,* (1995) 2 S.C.C. 584.

Supreme Court is the highest court of record. It is charged with the duties and responsibilities of correcting the lower courts and tribunal and of protecting them from those whose misconduct tends to prevent the due performance of their duties. Article 129 vests powers in the Supreme Court to punish for contempt of itself in its capacity as the highest court of record and also as a court charged with the appellate and superintending powers over the lower courts and tribunals as detailed in the Constitution.

Contempt of courts are either civil in nature or in criminal. Summary procedure is adopted in such cases. Contempt may be committed either on the face of the court or outside the court. It is also clear that the High Court can punish for its own contempt as well as contempt committed against its subordinate courts. The Supreme Court can punish for its own contempt as well as contempt of High Courts inspite of Article 215 and all the courts within the territory of India. Cognizance of contempt can be taken either after complaint is made about the contempt or *suo motu*. Procedural as well as substantive safeguards are also given to contemner. The cases of contempt are generally viewed against public at large. Along with the ordinary people advocates also enjoy certain safeguards. But a balance is always struck between safeguards and advocates professional commitment not to commit contempt of the court. As pointed out in *Ram Dayal* v. *State of M.P.*[139] the Supreme Court of India expressed the view that fair and reasonable comment is allowed but using this right a member of legal profession or anyone cannot cross its limits. In *State* v. *S.N. Dixit,*[140] the Allahabad High Court held the offence of contempt committed by an advocate who had statement based on vague information from irresponsible sources without proper verification. A note of caution was issued by the Supreme Court in *Pritam Pal* v. *High Court of M.P.*[141] The court said: "to punish an advocate for contempt of court, no doubt must be regarded as an extreme measure". Of course apology may present good defence is contempt cases.

139. (1978) 2 SCC 630.
140. 1973 All. L.J. 180.
141. 1993 Supp. (1) S.C.C. 529.

But apology has to be tendered *bonafide* there are a number of cases on the point. Thus, in *M.Y. Shareef* v. *The Hon'ble Judge of the High Court of Nagpur*,[142] a transfer application with charge of prejudice against the judges on the basis of some comment made by them was signed by two learned advocates. They were punished by the High Court for the contempt of court. In appeal they tendered unqualified apology to the Supreme Court and the High Court. The Supreme Court accepted the apology as a sincere expression of their regret for what happened in the court. It set aside the punishment and issued a strong admonition and warning to the two advocates for their conduct.

However, a person who offers a belated apology runs the risk that it may not be accepted for such an apology hardly shows the contrition which is the essence of purging of contempt. Unless apology is offered at the earliest opportunity and in good grace, the apology is shorn of penitence and hence it is liable to be rejected. In *Mulkh Raj* v. *State of Punjab*,[143] the contemner advocate offered the apology at the time when he found that the court was going to impose punishment. Supreme Court held that "it ceases to be an apology and his acts becomes an act of crining coward". However, where the court was convinced about the sincerity of apology asked by the contemner advocate at the time of the hearing the conviction made on the ground that the apology was not tendered at the earlier stage and was not in writing is not sustainable at law.

It appears that, it is open to the court to accept an apology in some belated cases but this will happen only in special circumstances.

Regarding the circumstances, wherein, an apology may be accepted, in a series of the decision, courts have considered the gravity of the offences. If the advocate had been cowing down the judge or judges by threats of character, apology must not be accepted. Thus, in *M.B. Sanghi* v. *High Court of Punjab and Haryana*[144] an advocate had made disparaging and derogatory

142. A.I.R. 1955 S.C. 19.
143. (1972) 3 S.C.C. 839.
144. (1991) 3 S.C.C. 600.

remark against a judge. It was found that the contempt proceeding had been initiated against the said advocate not for the first time but on an earlier occasion too. This time High Court was of the view that the appellant could not be allowed to get away by simply feeling sorry by way of apology as the easiest way. The Supreme Court agreed with the High Court and said, "with regard to apology in proceedings for contempt of court, it is well settled that an apology is not weapon of defence to urge the guilty of their offence, nor it is intended to operate as an universal panacea, but it is intended to evidence of real contriteness".

The observation of the Apex Court in *L.D. Jaikwal* v. *State of Uttar Pradesh*,[145] is worth mention. The Hon'ble Court observed:

> "We are sorry to say we cannot subscribe to the slap-say sorry—and forget 'school of though, in administration of contempt jurisprudence' saying sorry does not make the slapper taken the slam smart less upon the said hypocritical word being littered through the very lips which not long ago slandered a judicial officer without the slightest compunction. Apology should not be 'paper' apology and expression of sorrow should come from the heart and not from the pen. For, *it is one thing to 'say' sorry—it is another to 'feel' sorry"*.

The real problems in relation to contempt are: Whether the punishment provided under the Contempt of Courts Act are adequate to punish the exceptionally grave cases of contempt committed by advocates? Whether the power of the courts of records be limited to awarding of punishment given under Contempt of Courts Act?

As to the first issue it may be made clear that the maximum punishment for contempt of court is six months imprisonment or fine worth Rs. 2000. It is not sufficient in serious cases of contempt. The next issue relates to interconnected problem arising under constitutional provision and the ordinary law.

145. A.I.R. 1984 S.C. 1374.

Thus, controversial issue arises as to interrelationship between powers of the Supreme Court and High Courts as court of records read with Contempt of Courts Act, 1971 and power of the Bar Councils of States and Bar Council of India under Advocates Act, 1961. The moot question is; Have the Supreme Court or High Courts power to punish for their contempt with punishments given under Contempt of Courts Act only or they enjoy the power to a punish contemner Advocate also with punishments given under Advocates Act, 1961? The opinion of the highest court on the point has been shifting from one pole to another pole. Thus, in *Pritam Pal* v. *High Court of Madhya Pradesh*,[146] *in Re Vinay Chandra Mishra*[147] and *in re Ajay Kumar Pandey*,[148] the Apex Court took the view that Articles 129 and 215 are not subject to the Contempt of Courts Act and the jurisdiction of the Supreme Court and High Courts cannot be denuded, restricted or limited by the Contempt of Courts Act. Therefore, they may award punishment as they deem fit.

But the referred decisions had been superseded in the case of *Supreme Court Bar Association* v. *Union of India*.[149] In the instant case the Constitution Bench of the Supreme Court (consisting Mr. Justice S.C. Agrawal, Mr. Justice G.N. Ray, Mr. Justice A.S. Anand, Mr. Justice S.P. Bharucha and Mr. Justice Rajendra Babu) held that "the disciplinary jurisdiction of the Bar Councils to take action for professional misconduct is different from the jurisdiction of the courts to take action against the advocates for the contempt of court. The power of the Supreme Court to punish for contempt of court, though, quite wide, is yet limited and cannot be expanded to include the power to determine whether an advocate is also guilty of professional misconduct in a summary manner giving a goodbye to the procedure prescribed under Advocates Act".

Since the Supreme Court is the highest court of land and law declared by it is binding on all courts throughout the

146. 1993 Supp. (1) S.C.C. 529.
147. *Supra* note 138.
148. (1996) 6 S.C.C. 510.
149. (1998) 4 S.C.C. 409.

territory and it declares future law of the country, the decision of the Supreme Court in *Supreme Court Bar Association case* is law of the land. But, with due respect and in our humble submission it is bound to create some confusion as to the hierarchical structure of our constitutional law jurisprudence. *First,* Constitution is the basic law or *Grund norm* in Kelsen's terminology and no ordinary law should be allowed to overrule the basic norm. *Secondly,* what will happen to the overriding power of the Supreme Court under Article 142 or to say, when the power of the Supreme Court under Article 129 read with Article 142 of the Constitution is exercised with a view to render absolute justice? *Thirdly,* the *Supreme Court Bar Association case* decision may be treated as an example of hard cases creating bad laws. In this respect the opinion of the Supreme Court *in Re Vinay Chandra Mishra*[150] appears to be more convincing and in tune with our constitutional fabric where the court opined that if the Supreme Court of India can punish an advocate under its appellate jurisdiction under the Advocates Act, 1961 with any of punishments mentioned in Section 35(1) of that Act, there is no reason why the Supreme Court while exercising its contempt jurisdiction under 129 read with Article 142 cannot impose any of the said punishments. It may be said that the opinion of the Supreme Court in *Supreme Court Bar Association* case is bound to give many misgiving. If court chooses to declare judicial hands in cases of serious contempt after punishing with punishment in cases of serious contempt after punishing with punishment given under the Contempt of Courts Act there is no guaranteed of follow up action by the Bar Council. *Big fish may go out of net.* Here it may be made clear that in *Nandlal Balwani*[151] *case* the Bar Council took prompt action by removing the name of contemner from the State Roll of Advocates, after the Supreme Court had awarded punishment. But same was true in the case of *Sri Vinay Kumar Mishra.*[152] Thus, the control mechanism through contempt of court proceeds has not worked well and needs a serious look on the point.

150. *Supra* note 138.
151. (1999) 2 S.C.C. 315.
152. (1995) 2 S.C.C. 584.

IV. CRITICAL APPRAISAL OF THE MECHANISM PROVIDED FOR DISCIPLINING ADVOCATE

The earlier discussion regarding the mechanism to maintain accountability reveals that, in India though, the higher judiciary have certain powers, but the regulation of the conduct of the advocates is mainly through self-regulatory bodies, i.e. the State Bar Councils and Bar Councils of India. If we go through the scrutiny of these mechanisms we may find that there are two real problems: Firstly, the law[153] on which this system is based itself is not clear and reveals many anomalies and secondly, the actual working of the mechanism in India, are not satisfactory.

The first drawback of the self-regulatory system is that, complainant cannot actively participate in this system in holding the advocate or advocates accountable. Complainant can make a formal complaint that may initiate the disciplinary proceedings. Further, the general public lacks the expertise to contribute to the ethics and standards of the legal profession. Hence the legal profession itself decides what is in client's interest.

The regulation focuses only its attention on the standards of character. It punishes only such acts which come under the perview of profession and other misconduct. So, the self-regulatory system is disciplinary in nature and usually has no role to play in resolving dispute with clients about competence or standards of service. This is despite the fact that the majority of complaints about advocate concern with poor service to the clients.

It must be noted that the effectiveness of the legal system largely depends on the integrity and competence of the members of the Bar. David K. Malcolm opined that "disciplinary jurisdiction over lawyers should be extended to include both negligent and unethical conduct".[154] In countries like England and Australia, disciplinary offences are investigated and prosecuted by self-regulatory legal

153. See, Bar Council of India Rules, 1975.
154. David, K. Malcolm, The role of the profession and the regulation of the legal profession 55 A.L.J. 407 (1981).

professional associations and enforced in specialist tribunals dominated by practising advocates.[155] But in India, there is no investigation of disciplinary offences. The Bar Councils conduct only a preliminary inquiry either *suo motu* or on receipt of a complaint.[156]

In India, only in the case of extreme negligence an advocate may be punished for his lack of care and competence. Mere incompetence or deficiency in professional services is still not sufficient to amount to professional misconduct. In most of the cases the matters come to end due to non-establishment of a *prima-facie case against the advocate.* However in *N.G. Dastane* v. *Shrikant S. Shivde,*[157] the Hon'ble Supreme Court observed:

> "When the Bar Council in its wider scope of supervision over the conduct of advocates in their professional duties comes across any instance of such misconduct, it is the duty of the Bar Council concerned to refer the matter to its Disciplinary Committee. The expression "reason to believe" is employed in Section 35 of the Act only for the limited purpose of using it as a filter for excluding frivolous complaints against advocates. If the complaint is genuine and if the complaint is not lodged with the sole purpose of harassing an advocate or if it is not actuated by *malafides*, the Bar Council has a statutory duty to forward the complaint to the Disciplinary Committee".

By virtue of Section 24-A of the Advocates Act, 1961, entry regulation are attempted to ensure that only the people of good character enter the profession.. It means that in addition to LL.B. degree, the character of the person to be

155. Christine Parker, "Regulation of Ethics of Australian Legal Practice: Autonomy and Responsiveness", 25(3) U.N.S. W.L.J. 676, 680 (2002).
156. The rest of the disciplinary proceedings are similar to that of other countries, like the other contries the Supreme Court exercises an inherent jurisdiction to discipline lawyers. The court can interpret and enforce appropriate standards of conduct particularly in relation to the duty towards the administration of notice and resolve cost disputes.
157. (2001) 6 S.C.C. 135.

enrolled is also considered in India. However, it is important to note that under section 24-A disqualification cease to have effect after the expiry of the period of two years, since the person found guilty of offence. Further, the disqualification is not applicable to those people who having been found guilty are dealt with Probation of Offenders Act, 1958.

It is suggested that such proviso should be removed from the Section 24-A, otherwise even a criminal can become an advocate in India, after the expiry of the prescribed period of disqualification. The Advocates Act, 1961, provided for the establishment of the State Bar Councils as well as the Bar Council of India, with a view to ensure accountability of the members of the Bar. In fact, both the Bar Councils constituted under the Act, are itself a collective body of the members of legal profession. Hence, there are possibilities of pro-advocates bias in disciplining the members of the Bar. Though, some cases on the point have been discussed earlier in Chapter V, it is most desirable to make reference again in order to focus on the approach of the Bar Councils towards advocates' brethren.

In certain cases, Disciplinary Committee of the Bar Councils has taken a very lenient view. In a case,[158] before the Bar Council of India an advocate had appeared as a material witness for the opponent, while having been engaged by petitioner. That was clear violation of Bar Council of India Rules and was a gross negligence but he was simply reprimanded by the Bar Council of India. Likewise, in *A... complainant* v. *B... Respondent*,[159] an advocate had not filed suit and had misled the client to have filed it. The limitation period also had overrun. The client lost valuable property. The Disciplinary Committee of the Bar Council of India found him "guilty of gross negligence and dereliction of duty towards his client", but, awarded the punishment of only three months suspension from practice.

In *N.G. Dastane* v. *S.S. Shivade*,[160] the respondent advocate who were the advocates for the accused in a case where the appellant was the complainant sought reported adjournments

158. II, J.B.C.I. 275 (1973).
159. VII, J.B.C.I. 393 (1978).
160. (2001) 6 S.C.C. 135.

on flimsy or frivolous ground thereby abusing the process of the court. Even when the matter was brought to State Bar Council as well Bar Council of India, they shut their doors informing him that he did not have even *prima facie* case against the advocate.

Again in *Harish Chandra Tewari* v. *Baiju,*[161] an advocate had misappropriated money of the poor client, falsely claimed to return that money and also filed fraudulent affidavit. The Disciplinary Committee of the Bar Council of India awarded only the punishment of three months of suspension. In appeal the Supreme Court *depreciated the attitude of the Bar Council of India to treat a very grave profession misconduct in a comparatively lighter vein*.

The cases referred above are directly related with the client's interest; even in cases where the advocate shows disrespect towards judicial authority the Bar Council of India has taken a very lenient view. In a case, an advocate leveled high degree of corruption charge against the Assistant Income Tax Commissioner, but Disciplinary Committee of the Bar Council of India punished him only with reprimand.

In *P.B. Jog* v. *Bar Council of India,*[162] an advocate who was also a Deputy Mayor of the Poona Municipal Corporation and as such he used extremely vulgar and obscene language in a gathering at Pune. He was convicted under Sections 294 and 153 of the I.P.C. and sentenced to fine of Rs. 1000 which was enhanced by the appellate court to Rs. 3000. Thus, was guilty of other misconduct on *suo motu* action Maharashtra Bar Council suspended the advocate for a period of one month. The Disciplinary Committee of the Bar Council of India confirmed it. But it could not resist itself from making observation "may be if we have for the first time to impose punishment in the matter, we may, having regard to the heavy fine imposed, not ordered suspension for a month".

In a case,[163] where the advocate had even committed attempt of rape of a client's wife. The Bar Council of India

161. (2002) 2 S.C.C. 67.
162. DC Appeal No. 10/1970 JBC I 105.
163. Quoted from, Baxi, Upendra, "The Pathology the Indian Legal Profession, I.B.R. iii, New Delhi, 1986, p. 455.

held that it was the case called for drastic action of removal of name of advocate from rolls. However, it could not resist itself from clanging itself to a soft approach "It is always open to reinstate the advocate on prayer of that he is a changed man and fit to be admitted into profession".

The trend shown above is not very happy with respect to imposition of discipline among the advocates.

It is submitted that, the power to discipline the members should be with the Bar Council. But the power to ensure good conduct of lawyer should be retained by the Supreme Court.

V. MECHANISM FOR MAINTAINING THE ACCOUNTABILITY OF JUDGES

It is an acceptable fact that Indian Judiciary has enjoyed the highest degree of independence, and has been held least accountable wing of the Government. This is so because our judges are regarded as most honourable, dignified and honest men. But with the change of time and declining values, ethics, integrity, morality and propriety, the judges have also fallen in line with others.

Though, the Constitution of India provides safeguards to ensure, judiciary being manned by men of ability, honesty, experience and competence, but there are credible complaints against the judges of higher judiciary too, who are regarded as 'God'. "People talk with *nostalgia* of the not so distant past when, win or loss, the integrity of judiciary was never doubted.[164] A few years ago in the address to the Bar,[165] the former Chief Justice of India Mr. Justice S.P. Bharucha stated that more than 80 percent of the judges in the country were honest and incorruptible and the smaller percentage was bringing the entire judiciary into disrepute". It indicates that corruption has also invaded the judicial corridor.

Therefore, it would be idle to pretend that the general falling standards of public life had not affected judges of the Superior Court of India too. Allegations of misconduct by

---

164. Sachar, Rajendar, Judicial Accountability, available at www.pucl.org.htm, visited on 2.7.07.
165. (2002) 2 S.C.A.L.E. J.1.

judges are reported from time to time and tend to shake the confidence in the superior judiciary as a whole. To quote, another former Chief Justice in this regard that "there is no point in saying that there is no corruption in judiciary. No one is going to say it, much less accept it".[166]

Thus, the time has come to enact a credible mechanism to hold judges accountable. Till 1973, there were clashes between the Superior Courts' decisions on property and economic reform, but today no one speaks of judges being accountable for their judgement in economic or property matters, now it is the conduct of judges and the absence of any adequate disciplinary mechanism, which raises the question of accountability of judges.

In the Vedic days of Ancient India, the Monarch was the administrator of law and justice, but the monarch was not above the law but he was also under it.[167] The ancient Indian legal literature present five causes on which a monarch might be guilty and which a *propria vigora* gave rise to the charges of partiality against a judge (monarch) as the perceptions conveyed by those causes are incompatible with the concept of judicial independence,[168] viz.:

(i) 'Raga' (affection in favour of party),
(ii) 'Lobha' (greed),
(iii) Bhya (fear),
(iv) Dvesha (ill-will against a party), and
(v) Vadinoscha rahashrutihi (The meeting and hearing a party to case secrecies).

Accountability for judges is often traced from the sources such as, the traditional oath of office taken by judges which requires them to adhere to the constitution. Further judges are required to follow the Laws of the land as well as judicial decisions of the courts.

166. Shivani, "There's" Corruption in Judiciary it's Showing Now : J.S. Verma", available at www.expressidia.com. Visited on 05.06.06.
167. Gupta, Apar, 'Need to judge the judges, available at www.indlaw. com.visited on 26.10.07.
168. *Ibid*.

In India, apart from above, there exist following mechanism to dealt with the conduct of judges and ensuring accountability for the same.

(A) Impeachment Process

Impeachment is a proceeding in which accusations are brought by a legislative or executive branch of a government against civil official or, in some cases, private citizens.[169] Legally the term applies only to the indictment against judges or civil officials.

Impeachment process existed in ancient Greece, in a process called the *eisangelia*. However, the modern institution did not originate until the latter part of the 14th century in England and it spread throughout the world.

In India, as far as the lower judiciary is concerned, there is a lot of disciplinary mechanism provided by the Constitution[170] and also by the special Statutes.[171] The High Court can exercise not only judicial power but have also administrative control over the lower judiciary. Disciplinary action can be taken against a lower court's judge even to do with his judicial acts or omissions. The laws of contempt of courts are also applicable to the judges of subordinate or lower judiciary.

On the other hand with regard to the judges of higher judiciary i.e., High Courts and Supreme Court the Constitution of India provides only for impeachment procedure. Article 124(4) deals with the removal of a judge of the Supreme Court by following a prescribed procedure. Article 217(1)(b)[172] of the Indian Constitution, deals with the removal of a judge of a High Court from his office by the President in the manner provided in Clause (4) of Article 124 of the Constitution. The

169. In most countries impeachment is a device for removing civil official, namely, Chiefs of State, Cabinet Minister and judges, however in England, it also applies in the theory to private citizens.
170. Article 227 of Constitution of India.
171. See, The Contempt of Courts Act, 1971 and Indian Penal Code, 1860.
172. Article 217 (1)(b) runs as: Judge may be removed from his office by the president in manner provided in clause (4) of article 124 for the removal of judge of the Supreme Court.

manner of removal is the same both for the removal of the High Courts' judges and the judges of the Supreme Court.

The procedure prescribed under clause (4) of article 124 speaks in negative tone and thereby emphasizes the mandatory requirement to be fulfilled. It reads:

> "A judge of the Supreme Court shall not be removed from his office except by an order of the President passed after an address by each House of Parliament supported by a majority of the total membership of that house and by a majority of not less than two-thirds of the membership of that house present and voting has been presented to the President in the same session for such removal on ground of proved misbehaviour or incapacity".

It is equally applicable with respect to the removal of High Courts' judges as per Article 217 (1)(b).[173]

The above constitutional provisions make it clear that judges of either High Courts or the Supreme Court are to be removed only on the ground of proved misbehaviour or proved incapacity. The word "proved" used in the above Article makes the procedure so ticklish and "implies that the allegations have crystallized into conclusive proof pointing to the misbehaviour of incapacity".[174]

The word 'proved' used in Article 124(4) also indicates that the address can be presented by Parliament only after the alleged charge of misbehaviour or incapacity against the judge has been investigated, substantiated and established by an impartial tribunal.

The constitutional provision does not prescribe how this investigation is to be carried on. It leaves it to Parliament to settle and lay down by law the detailed procedure according to which the address may be presented and the charges of misconduct or incapacity against the judge be investigated and proved.[175]

173. Article 124(4) and 217(1)(b) of the Constitution of India.
174. M.P. Jain, Constitutional Law of India, 5th (ed.) (2003), p. 283.
175. Article 124(5), Constitutional of India.

The Parliament in pursuance of constitutional mandate enacted the Judges (Inquiry) Act, 1968, which regulates the procedure for investigation and proof of misbehaviour or incapacity of Judge for presenting an address by the Houses of Parliament to the President for his removal.

The Judges (Inquiry) Act, 1968 contains seven sections. It covers judges of the Supreme Court and High Courts including Chief Justice of both courts. Section 3 lays down the procedure for investigation into misbehaviour or incapacity of judges by committee.

A notice of a motion for presenting such an address may be given by 100 members of the Lok Sabha, or 50 members of the Rajya Sabha. Thereafter, the Speaker or the Chairman, as the case may be, may after consulting such persons, 'as he think fit', may admit or refuse to admit the motion. If it is admitted, then the Speaker/Chairman shall refer the matter to a committee consisting of three members, one each from the categories of:

(a) Chief Justice and other judges of the Supreme Court.
(b) Chief Justices of High Courts, and
(c) A distinguished Jurist.

If notices for the motion are given on the same day in both Houses, the Committee of Inquiry is to be constituted jointly by the Speaker and the Chairman. The Committee of Inquiry is to frame definite charges against the judge on the basis of which the investigation is proposed to be held and give him a reasonable opportunity of being heard including cross-examination of witnesses. If the charge is that of physical or mental incapacity, the committee may arrange for the medical examination of the judge by a medical board appointed by the Speaker/Chairman or the both as the case may be.

The committee, after investigation, would send a report to the Speaker or Chairman, as the case may be, stating its findings. The report of the committee is to be laid before the concerned House or Houses. If the committee exonerates the judge of the charges laid against him, then no further action is to be taken on the motion for his removal. If, however, the committee finds the judge to be guilty of misbehaviour, or suffering from an incapacity, the House can take up consideration of the motion.[176]

Section 6 of the Judges (Inquiry) Act provides for Consideration of the Report and refers the procedure for presentation of an address for removal of the judge. On the motion being adopted by both Houses according to Article 124 (as noted earlier), an address may be presented to the President for removal of the judge.

The procedures outlined above make itself clear that the procedure for removal of the High Courts and the Supreme Court judges is very cumbersome. Since adoption of our Constitution this procedure has been put in motion on only one occasion. Even that was impeded, and it did not reach its logical end, i.e. removal of the judge concerned could not take effect. The obvious result is that in nearly six decade functioning of our Constitution, not a single judge has been removed under the Article 124(4) of the Constitution of India. It does not mean that our judges are so capable and so honest and in India there are no need of provision for removal of judges of Higher Courts; rather it only means that procedure prescribed under Article 124(4) is cumbersome, flawed, dilatory and political.

Thus, due to dissatisfactory conditions of control mechanism envisaged under the Constitution and failure of removal process a different procedure was evolved to discipline the errant judges. It necessitated the evaluation of 'in-House' Procedure by the court itself.

(B) In-house Procedure

The adoption of in-house procedure has an interesting history. In 1995, the members of the Bar in Bombay High Court resorted to the extra-ordinary steps for disciplining the Chief Justice of the same High Court. The basis of the action of the Bombay Bar Association was financial irregularities alleged to have been reflected in the disproportionate amount of royalty received by Chief Justice Bhattacharjee from a foreign

---

176. *Supra* note 206.

publisher.[177] The Bombay Bar Association resorted to strike and passing a resolution against him to resign. While Justice Bhattacharjee resigned following an uproar, the Supreme Court emphasized the need to evolve a method of self-regulation by the judiciary in such cases of alleged misconduct.

The Judiciary chose to evolve a via media to satisfy both. It opined that:

> It is true that freedom of speech and expression guaranteed by Article 19(1)(a) of the Constitution is one of the most precious liberties in any democracy. But equally important is the maintenance of respect for judicial independence which alone would protect the life, liberty and reputation of the citizen. So the nation's interest requires that criticism of the judiciary must be measured, strictly rational, sober and proceed from the highest motives without being coloured by partisan spirit or pressure tactics or intimidatory attitude. The court must, therefore, harmonise constitutional values of free criticism and the need for a fearless judicial process and its presiding functionary, the judge. If freedom of expression subserves public interest in reasonable measure, public justice cannot gap it or manacle it; but if the court considered the attack, on the judge or judges scurrilous, offensive, intimidatory or malicious, beyond condonable limits, the strong arm of the law must strike a blow on him who challenges the supremacy of the rule of the law by fouling its source and stream. The power to punish the contemner is, therefore, granted to the court not because judges need the protection but because the citizens need an impartial and strong judiciary.

The threat of action on vague grounds of dissatisfaction would create a dragnet that would inevitably sweep into its grasp the maverick, the dissenter, the innovator, the reformer—in one word the unpopular. Insidious attempts pave way for

177. *C. Ravichandran Iyer* v. *Justice A.M. Bhattacharjee and others*, (1995) 5 S.C.C. 457.

removing the inconvenient. Therefore, proper care should be taken by the Bar Association concerned. First, it should gather specific, authentic and acceptable material which would show or tend to show that conduct on the part of a judge creating a feeling in the mind of a reasonable person doubting the honesty, integrity, impartiality or act which lowers the dignity of the office but necessarily, is not impeachable misbehaviour. In all fairness to the judge, the responsible office-bearers should meet him in camera after securing interview and apprise the judge of the information they have with them. If there is truth in it, there is every possibility that the judge would mend himself. Or to avoid embarrassment to the judge, the office-bearers can approach the Chief Justice of that High Court and apprise him of the situation with material they have in their procession and impress upon the Chief Justice to deal with the matter appropriately.

Therefore, where the complaint relates to the judge of the High Court, the Chief Justice of the High Court, after verification, and if necessary, after confidential enquiry from his independent source, should satisfy himself about the truth of the imputation made by the Bar Association through its office-bearers against the judge and consult the Chief Justice of India, where deemed necessary, by placing all the information with him. When the Chief Justice of India is seized of the matter, to avoid embarrassment to him and to allow fairness in the procedure to be adopted in furtherance thereof, the Bar should suspend all further actions to enable the Chief Justice of India to appropriately deal with the matter. This is necessary because any action he may take must not only be just but must also appear to be just to all concerned, i.e., it must not even appear to have been taken under pressure from any quarter. The Chief Justice of India, on receipt of the information from the Chief Justice of the High Court, after being satisfied about the correctness and truth touching the conduct of the judge, may tender such advice either directly or may initiate such action, as is deemed necessary or warranted under given facts and circumstances. If circumstances permit, it may be salutary to take the judge into confidence before initiating action. On the decision being taken by the Chief Justice of India, the matter should rest at that. This procedure would not only facilitate nipping in the bud the conduct of a judge leading to loss of public confidence in the courts and sustain public faith in the efficacy of the rule of law and respect for the judiciary, but would also avoid needless embarrassment of contempt proceedings against the office-bearers of the Bar Association and group libel against all concerned. The independence of judiciary and the stream of public justice would remain pure and unsullied. The Bar Association could remain a useful arm of the judiciary and in the case of sagging reputation of the particular Judge; the Bar Association could take up the matter with the Chief Justice of the High Court and await his response for the action taken thereunder for a reasonable period. In case the allegations are against Chief Justice of a High Court, the Bar should bring them directly to the notice of the Chief Justice of India. On receipt of such complaint, the Chief Justice of India would in the same way act as stated above qua complaint against a judge of the High Court, and the Bar would await for a reasonable period the response of the Chief Justice of India.

Thus, yawning gap between proved misbehaviour and bad conduct inconsistent with the high office on the part of a non-cooperating judges/Chief Justice of a High Court could be disciplined by self-regulation through in-house procedure. This in-house procedure would fill in the constitutional gap and would yield salutary effect.

In the aforementioned case evolving a domestic mechanism the Supreme Court said that instead of taking matter to press, staging *'bundh'* and boycotting the court, advocate should bring the matter before the Chief Justice of High Court, in the case of complaint against any judge of the High Court and in the case of complaint against Chief Justice of the High Court they should bring the matter before the Chief Justice of India.

Collaborating the benefits of this procedure the court opined that guarantee of tenure and its protection by the Constitution would not, however, accord sanctuary for corruption of grave misbehaviour. Yet every action or omission by a judicial officer in the performance of his duties which is not a good conduct necessarily may not be misbehaviour indictable by impeachment, but its insidious effect may be pervasive and may produce deleterious effect on the integrity and impartiality of the judge. Every misbehaviour in juxtaposition to good behaviour, as a constitutional tautology, will not support impeachment but a misbehaviour which is not a good behaviour may be improper conduct not befitting to the standard expected of a judge. Threat of impeachment process itself may swerve a judge to fall prey to misconduct but it serves disgrace to use impeachment process for minor offences or abrasive conduct on the part of a judge. The bad behaviour of one judge has a rippling effect on the reputation of the judiciary as a whole. When the edifice of judiciary is built heavily on public confidence and respect, the damage by an obstinate judge would rip apart the entire judicial structure built in the Constitution. Bad conduct or bad behaviour of a judge, therefore, needs correction to prevent erosion of public confidence in the efficacy of judicial process or dignity of the institution or credibility to the judicial office held by the obstinate judge.

This self-regulation is popularly termed as in-house procedure. Under the in-house proceeding, if the Chief Justice of the High Court is of the opinion that the allegation against a judge of the High Court needs a deeper probe, he shall forward to the Chief Justice of India the complaint and the response of the judge concerned along with his comments.

The procedure stipulates that after considering these, if the Chief Justice of India thinks that a deeper probe is required, he shall constitute a three-member inquiry committee of two Chief Justices of High Courts other than the High Court to which the judge facing the allegation belongs and one High Court Judge. The judge concerned would be entitled to appear before the committee and have his say. Under the procedure adopted by the Supreme Court, it would not be a formal judicial inquiry involving the examination and cross-examination of witness and representation by advocates.

Under this procedure, the committee may conclude and report to the Chief Justice of India that:

(i) There is no substance in the allegations contained in the complaint, or

(ii) There is sufficient substance in the allegations and

the misconduct disclosed is so serious that it calls for initiation of proceedings for removal of the judges, or

(iii) there is substance in the allegations contained in the complaint but the misconduct disclosed is not of such a serious nature as to call for initiation of proceedings for removal of judges.

Likewise in the case of a complaint against a Supreme Court judge, if the Chief Justice of India, in the light of the response of judge concerned, feels that it need a deeper probe, he would constitute on inquiry committee of three Supreme Court judges. The Chief Justice of India shall take further action based on the findings of the committee.

After receiving the findings of the committee under the in-house procedure, Chief Justice of India shall advise the judge concerned to resign or seek voluntary retirement. In case the judge refuses to do so, the Chief Justice of India shall advise the Chief Justice of the High Court concerned not to allocate any Judicial work to him, and intimate the President and the Prime Minister.[178]

The Supreme Court has experimented with its internal corrective mechanism, i.e. "in-house procedure" on three occasions. The scheme of in-house procedure, as spelt out by the Bench in the *Bhattacharjee case*[179] was tried out for the first time in the case of three judges of Punjab and Haryana High Court, for their alleged involvement in the Public Service Commission examination. As discussed earlier[180] in that case Chief Justice V.N. Kirpal recommended transfer of one of the tainted judges, Justice Amarbir Singh Gill, to the Guwahati High Court. However, said judge was never transferred because of opposition to the proposal from Guwahati Bar, which felt that the Guwahati High Court was being considered a dumping ground for tainted judges. With regard to other two judges, the in-house committee appointed by Chief Justice Pattanaik (who came in office in due time) had concluded that,

178. *Ibid.*
179. *Supra* note 209.
180. For details, see chapter VIIth.

judges misconduct did not warrant their removal. The committee exonerated Justice M.L. Singhal, while holding Justice Mehtab Singh Gill and Amarbir Singh Gill guilty.

However, it is noteworthy that, Justice Amarbir Singh Gill wrote to Justice Pattanaik that he would be taking leave, from December 16, 2002, until his retirement in May 2003. As Mehtab Singh Gill did not respond back to Justice Pattanaik on what he intended to do, Justice Pattanaik passed an order deprecating his misconduct. In his order he warned Mehtab Singh Gill to be careful in future, though, no further action was taken against all the three judges.

The "in-house procedure" was tried again in the matter of Justice Arun Madan, a judge of the Rajasthan High Court. A three judge Committee set-up in the case confirmed the involvement of Justice Madan in a proposition to a woman doctor to have sex with him in exchange for a judicial favour. Though, no disciplinary action was taken against Mr. Justice Arun Madan, but it is note worth that the Justice B.K. Roy committee report resulted into the resignation of Justice Arun Madan.[181]

The in-house procedure was tried again in case of a group of judges of the Karnataka High Court, however in that matter a three judge Committee headed by the Chief Justice of the Bombay High Court. Justice C.K. Thakkar was set-up to examine the alleged sexual misconduct of the judges. But the in-house procedure failed once again in that case and no damage was done to the judges of Karnataka High Court.[182]

Thus, it is clear from the above discussion that in order to maintain accountability of the Higher Court's judges, our judiciary always though to have a domestic mechanism, as in-house procedure. Although, under this procedure one thing may be appreciable in the sense that under this procedure alternative were given to the errant judges, either to quietly resign or to face impeachment proceedings, but this approach, however, is time taking, limited reach and same has not been working so well in every cases.

181. *Ibid.*
182. *Ibid.*

The failure of in-house procedure in the matter of allegation against Justice Nirmal Yadav is clear proof of the ineffectiveness of the procedure even if the in-house inquiry finds the actionable wrong committed by comes judges of the superior courts. To refresh our memory in allegation of 15 lakhs intended to be given to Justice Nirmal Yadav of Punjab & Haryana High Court. A Central Bureau Investigation (C.B.I.) investigated the matter and made out a case for prosecutting Justice Nirmal Yadav under the Prevention of Corruption Act. In meanwhile a three Judge in-house committee headed by justice H.L. Gokhley, Chief Justice of Allahabad High Court had found substance in allegation and recommended initiation of proceedings to removed from office. But due to otherwise advice of Attorney Genral Milon Banerjee, the proceeding was thwarted.

The ultimate result of the cases dealt under in-house procedure reveals that, this procedure may not be able to check the deviant behaviour of judges. Of late there has been a series of transfers of the High Court judges to another High Court, whenever some charges of malpractices are leveled against them.

It is humbly submitted that instead of dealing with the corruption, the judge concerned must not be transferred to another High Court. Continuing a judge found to be guilty of deviant behaviour by transferring him to another High Court is extremely unethical and highly objectionable, because of merely transfer in extreme cases is no punishment at all.

How can a judge found guilty of misdemeanor be foisted on the litigant public of another State? Therefore, it is submitted that, no option to transfer should be taken to those found guilty of misbehaviour. Though, the Supreme Court of India also adapted to Restatement of Values of Judicial Life, 1997, as 'in-house mechanism' but till now there has not been even a single case in which a judge has been removed from his office.

The main reason of failure of in-house mechanism in India is that, in fact this procedure is purely product of the judiciary and it does not have any constitutional or statutory basis. That is reason why there is an ultimate and urgent need of a statutory based mechanism for disciplining the judges of

Higher Courts, as in United State of America and other countries.

The unsatisfactory results of the impeachment process as well as the non-statutory nature of in-house procedure in India, the impropriety and misconduct of the judges seem to have ignited a public debate. There is growing acceptance that in India, there is a need to *Judge the Judges*. There exist various schools to though, as to means committed to the similar end of judicial accountability.

A very charitable view was shared by former Chief Justice of India, Mr. Justice Venkatachaliah, when he said, "my own feeling is that judges do not need a code of conduct in the strict sense. Rather, it is a restatement of those principles of judicial life and conduct which might come in handy for us, whenever we are in dilemma. The need for the code of conduct may imply that there is something wrong with the system and mechanism which dealt with the misbehaviour of judges. That may be well so because a system cannot be higher than the quality of the times in which it functions".

On the other hand, Chief Justice J.S. Verma expressed a quite opposite view. In his opinion "when moral sanction does not work, then legal sanction is required". Fears have been expressed that accusation of misconduct, before they have been established as credible—would affect the independence of the judiciary.

It is submitted with due respect that in our opinion judiciary like other institutions in a democratic set-up, must be open to receive a critical analysis and should be answerable. A former Chief Justice of Delhi High Court rightly wrote in his article that "the necessity of Council (which will be discussed later) is based on the undisputed fact that the judges do not come from another planet. They come from the same stock as the rest of society and subject to the same frailties. It is no secret that the antics of some of them do bring shame to judiciary. No protection is sought for them".[183]

183. Sachar, Rajendra, "National Judicial Council", available at www.pucl.org/law/judicialcouncel, visited at 5.3.2008.

The need of devising corrective means has gained favour with time. The coming discussion will focus on recent attempt towards ensuring judicial accountability in India.

(C) Recent Attempt Towards Ensuring Judicial Accountability

The general dissatisfaction with the procedure of impeachment and non-statutory in-house procedure in India, resulted into a voice of demand to establish a strong, efficient and adequate mechanism for maintaining accountability of judges of the higher courts.

In India, in this regard mainly two proposals have come out. Firstly, the formation of a National Judicial Commission, and secondly, a new law in place of existing, Judges (Inquiry) Act, 1968.

Though, the proposal for appointment of a National Judicial Commission was in fact first mooted by Mr. Justice P.N. Bhagwati,[184] but authoritatively it has been made by the Law Commission of India in its 80th report in the year of 1990. A Constitutional Amendment Bill, 1990[185] was also formulated in this regard by the Minister of Law and Justice, but the Bill lapsed on the dissolution of the 9th Lok Sabha.

Thereafter, the formation of National Judicial Commission was recommended by the *National Commission to Review the working of the Constitution*, its recommendation dated, March 31, 2002. It was proposed that, the commission will draw up a code of ethics for judges besides ordering transfer, postings and promotion of judges. It will also take disciplinary action against judges indulging in Malapractice.

Regarding the removal of judges and remedies for deviant behaviour, the Commission suggested[186] as under:

> "A Committee comprising the Chief Justice of India and two Senior-most judges of the Supreme Court shall be exclusively empowered to examine complaints of deviant

184. Quoted from Venkatesan, V., "A disciplinary mechanism on trial, available at www.hindu.com., visited on 26.10.2007.
185. 67th (Amendment) Bill, 1990.
186. See, Report, chapter VII, para 73.8.

behaviour of all kinds and complaints of misbehaviour and incapacity against judges of the Supreme Court and the High Courts. Their scrutiny at this stage would be confined to ascertain whether:

(a) there is substance at all in the complaint;
(b) there is a *prima facie* case calling for a fuller investigation and inquiry; or
(c) whether it would be sufficient to administer an appropriate advice/warning to the erring Judge or give other directions to the concerned Chief Justice regarding allotment of work to such Judge or to transfer to him to some other court.

If, however, the committee finds that the matter is serious enough to call for a fuller investigation or inquiry, it shall refer the matter for a full inquiry to the committee (constituted under the Judges (Inquiry) Act, 1968).

It is important to note that the Commission recommended also, certain changes in the Judges (Inquiry) Act, 1968, to make the system of accountability more effective.[187] The recommendations of the Commission provided that :

(1) The Committee constituted under the judges (Inquiry) Act, 1968 shall be a permanent committee with a fixed tenure with composition indicated in the said Act and not one constituted *ad-hoc* for a particular case or from case to case, as is the present position under Section 3(2) of the Act.
(2) The tenure of the inquiry committee shall be for a period of four years and to be re-constituted every four years.

The inquiry committee shall be constituted by the President in consultation with the Chief Justice of India. The inquiry committee shall inquire into and report on the allegation against the judge in accordance with the procedure prescribed by the said Act and submit their report to the Chief

187. *Id.*, para 77.9.

Justice of India, who shall place it before a committee of seven senior-most judges of the Supreme Court. The Committee of seven judges shall take a decision as to whether:

(a) Findings of the inquiry committee are proper, and

(b) any charge or charges are established against the judges and if so, whether the charges held proved are so serious as to call for his removal or whether it should be sufficient to administer a warning to him and/or make other directions with respect to allotment of work to him by the concerned Chief Justice or to transfer him to some other court. If the decision of the said committee of judges recommends the removal of the judge, it shall be a convention that the judge promptly demits office himself. If the fails to do so, the matter will be processed for being placed before Parliament in accordance with articles 124(4) and 217(1) proviso (b).

This procedure shall equally apply in case of judges of the Supreme Court and High Courts except that in the case of a Supreme Court Judge the Judge against whom complaint is received or inquiry is ordered, shall not participate in any proceeding affecting him. The matter of judges conduct inviting action was again taken up in 2003 and a suggestion to set-up a National Judicial Commission came under the Constitution (98th) Amendment Bill, 2003 but could not be passed.

VI. PROPOSAL FOR NEW LAW ON EXISTING JUDGES (INQUIRY) ACT AND FORMATION OF NATIONAL JUDICIAL COUNCIL

In the year of 2005, a major step towards ensuring judiciary accountable was taken up in the form of a proposal to set-up National Judicial Council to investigate the allegations of corruptions and misconduct against the judges of higher courts.

In this regard a bill namely, the Judges (Inquiry) Bill, 2005 was formulated and proposed to be introduced in Parliament but that could not be done, due to difference of opinion in judiciary. Former Chief Justice R.C. Lahoti said that he did not agree with the Bill in its current form. He also suggested several changes and recommended that the Law Commission's views should be sought by the Government". It is noteworthy that the Law Commission of India in its 195th report has dealt with the aspect of judicial accountability and made several suggestions for the improvement of the provisions. After a comprehensive study of the Bill of 2005 the Law Commission of India suggested 33 changes for a new law on the subject, including the inclusion of a whistleblower provision aimed at protecting those making complaints against judges.[188]

The Law Commission also recommended a total ban on the complainant or witnesses going public about facts and facets of the case, including allegations in the complaint, as well as the names of the complainant, witnesses and the judge concerned.

On the basis of the recommendations made in the 195th Report of the Law Commission of India on the Judges (Inquiry) Bill, 2005, a new Bill, namely the Judges (Inquiry) Bill, 2006 was prepared and placed before the Lok Sabha in 2006.

It may be recalled that the Judges (Inquiry) Act, 1968 was enacted with a view to lay down a procedure for removal for proved misbehaviour or incapacity of judges of the High Courts and Supreme Court by way of address of the Houses of Parliament by the President. The Law Commission of India in its 195th Report has examined the issue to judicial accountability in the light of the law laid down by the Supreme Court in its various judgements which relate to interpretation of Articles 121, 124 and 217 of the Indian Constitution.

(A) Object and Reason of the Bill of 2006

The proposed Bill aims at providing a statutory in-house mechanism to deal with the conduct of the judges of higher

188. "Judges Inquiry Bill 2006" may change, headlinesindia.com., visited on 7.11.2008. .

courts and to establish a statutory body for the same, namely National Judicial Council.

The object clause of the Bill states that:

> "The Bill, namely, the Judges (Inquiry) Bill, 2006 is based on the premise that judicial independence is one of the basic fundamentals of the Constitution. Judicial independence and judicial accountability are inseparable. Thus, there is an urgent need of legislation for establishing a National Judicial Council to look into the allegations of misbehaviour or incapacity of a judge of the Supreme Court or of a High Court, as the case may be, and to regulate the procedure for such investigation, inquiry and proof in a complaint procedure in addition to the earlier "reference procedure" as contained in the Judges (Inquiry) Act, 1968. In a complaint procedure, a complaint can be made by any person to the Judicial Council against judges of the Supreme Court (except the Chief Justice of India), Chief Justices and judges of High Courts. The Judges (Inquiry) Bill, 2006, *inter alia*, seeks to empower the National Judicial Council for imposing minor measures also. The Bill also seeks to repeal the Judges (Inquiry) Act, 1968".

(B) Changes Proposed by the Bill

In view of the lack of permanent authority to deal with the issues of misbehaviour and incapacity under the Act of 1968, the proposed Bill intends to bring many changes. Such changes include:

(1) It proposes for the first time to establish a permanent mechanism, namely, National Judicial Council, for the purpose of dealing with the misbehaviour or incapacity of judges.

(2) The proposed National Judicial Council will comprise of the Chief Justice of India, as a Chairman of the Council; two senior most judges of the Apex Court (recommended by the Chief Justice of India)

and two senior most Chief Justices of the High Courts nominated by the Chief of India.[189]

(3) Interestingly the New Bill has removed the place of 'distinguished jurist' from the Council and therefore assuring it to be purely represented by the Judiciary.[190]

(4) By establishing a new mechanism for the first time in India, the National Judicial Council is given the Status of a Civil Court for the purposes of conducting its proceedings of investigation and inquiry.[191]

(5) Like the American Statutes (Judicial Conduct and Disability) Act, 1980 and Judicial Improvements Act, 2002, the proposed Indian Bill provides the Council a full autonomy for the procedure to be followed during the inquiry.

(6) Though, the Bill has the same grounds for actions as earlier, but for the first time it has defined the terms. 'Incapacity' is defined as physical or mental incapacity which is or is likely to be of a permanent character, and misbehaviour to mean wilful or persistent conduct which brings dishonour or disrepute to the Judiciary, or wilful or persistent failure to perform the duties of a judge, or wilful abuse of Judicial Officer, corruption, lack of integrity; or committing and offence involving moral turpitude; and includes violation of code of conduct.[192]

(7) The Bill provides two procedures for disciplining the judges. In the first place it gave right to any person for initiating complaint against the judges of higher courts. However, under this procedure a common man cannot complain against the Chief Justice of India.[193]

---

189. Section 3 of the Judges (Inquiry) Bill, 2006.
190. *Ibid.*
191. *Id.*, section 35 of the Bill.
192. *Id.*, section 2(f).
193. *Id.*, section 8.

(8) The second procedure under the Bill is identical to the old statute. The Bill proposed for the first time power to take action against the judges in minor measure.

(9) The appeal can lie to the Supreme Court against the recommendation of the Council.[194]

(10) The Bill provides for inquiries by the National Judicial Council in cases of complaints against a Judicial Officer. Under the New Law, a judge against whom *prima facie* evidence of an illegal act is found would be asked not to attend courts pending the inquiry.

(11) The proposed law will make it easier to take action against a judge found to be guilty.

(C) Procedure Under Proposed Bill

The Judges (Inquiry) Bill, 2006 provides two procedures, i.e. complaint procedure[196] and reference procedure,[196] for initiating proceedings against the judges of the High Courts and Supreme Court.

(i) Complaint Procedure

Chapter IIIrd of the proposed Bill provides that a complaint may be initiated by any person for misbehaviour or incapacity of a judge. Clause 8(1) of the Bill runs as:

> "any person may make a complaint in writing involving any allegation of misbehaviour or incapacity in respect of a judge to the Council".

However, clause 8(1) makes it clear that in certain circumstances a complaint shall not be entertained and inquired. Those circumstances are:

(i) where the alleged act has taken place before the commencement of this Act;

194. *Id.*, section 30.

195. *Id.*, section 8(1).

196. *Id.*, section 11.

(ii) where the alleged act has taken place two years prior to the filing of complaint; and

(iii) where the complaint have made against a person who has demitted the office of a judge.

The proposed Bill also clarifies that the National Judicial Council is empowered to entertain application from any other sources also. However, no proceeding can be initiated against the Chief Justice of India by way of complaint procedure.[197] After receiving the complaint, first step provided under the Bill is to verify the genuineness of the complaint. If the Council is satisfied, after considering the complaint and after making such verification or where necessary, such preliminary investigation that complaint is frivolous or is not genuine, then such complaint is liable to be dismissed.

The Bill provides three grounds[198] for dismissing the complaint:

(i) that the complaint is frivolous or vexatious or is not made in good faith, or

(ii) that there are not sufficient grounds for inquiring into the complain, or

(iii) that the complaint relates only to merits of the judgement or a procedural order.

However, after the verification and preliminary investigation if the complaint is found to be genuine, the Council shall frame definite charges against the judge on the basis of which the inquiry is proposed to be held.

In inquiry the judge will be provided an opportunity to defend and such inquiry must be conducted in camera and it should be complete within six months. However, if reasonable cause has been shown then it can be extended further by six months. Clause 17 provided autonomy to the Council regarding the procedure. It says that the Council shall, while conducting a preliminary investigation or inquiry, have all the

197. Section 2(1) which deals with definition of a judge.
198. Section 20 of the Judge (Inquiry) Bill, 2006.

powers of a Civil Court trying a suit under the Code of Civil Procedure, 1908.

(ii) ***Reference Procedure***

Another mode for initiating the proceedings under the Bill is provided under Chapter IV. It is by reference, by any of the House of the Parliament. The procedure envisaged under chapter IV of the Bill is almost identical to the provisions of the Judges (Inquiry) Act, 1968.

It is important to note that by the Reference Procedure only removal of a judge can be effectuated. It will come into effect if after inquiry it is found that the case warrants removal of the judge. When complaint is under this procedure, then there is no preliminary verification, since ill intention can't be attributed to the Parliament and the matter directly steps into inquiry procedure. Like the complaint procedure, in this procedure also, the charges are communicated to the judge and an opportunity to defend himself is provided.

Clause 11 of the Bill provides for reference procedure. It reads:

(1) If a notice is given of a motion for presenting an address to the President praying for removal of a judge, on the ground of misbehaviour or incapacity signed :

(a) in the case of a notice given in the House of the People, by not less than one hundred members of that House; and

(b) in the case of a notice given in the Council of States, by not less than fifty members of that House,

then the Speaker or, as the case may be, the Chairman may, after consulting such persons, as he thinks fit and after considering such materials, if any, as may be available to him, either admit the motion or refuse to admit the same.

(2) If the motion referred to in sub-section (I) is admitted, the Speaker or the Chairman, as the case may be, shall keep the motion pending and refer the

> allegations on the basis of which the motion is based to the Council:
>
> Provided that where notices of motion referred to in sub-section (I) are given on the same day in both Houses of Parliament, no reference shall be made unless the motion is admitted in both Houses and where such motion has been admitted in both Houses, a reference shall be made jointly by the Speaker and the Chairman:
>
> Provided further that where notices of the motion as aforesaid are given in the Houses of Parliament on different dates, the notice that was given later shall stand rejected.

On receipt of a reference from the Speaker or the Chairman under Sub-section (2) of Section II, the Council shall frame definite charges against the judge on the basis of which the inquiry is proposed to be held.

Every such inquiry shall be conducted *in camera* by the Chairperson and the members of the Council sitting jointly.[199] The Council will have power to regulate its own procedure in making the inquiry. However, Council must give reasonable opportunity to the judge of cross-examining witness, adducing evidence and being heard in his defence.[200]

(D) Findings of the Council

On the completion of inquiry Council may make any of the three findings:

(i) Where Charge Not Proved

If, after inquiry in respect of complaint, the Council is satisfied that no charge has been proved, it shall dismiss the complaint and no further action shall be taken against the judge, and the judge and the complainant shall be informed accordingly.

---

199. *Id.*, section 14.
200. *Id.*, section 15.

(ii) Where the Charge is Proved but does not Warrant Removal

Under the proposed Bill the Council can recommend minor measures if after inquiry in respect of a complaint, the Council is satisfied that all or any of the charges in regard to misbehaviour or incapacity have been proved but in the opinion of Council the charges proved do not warrant removal of the judge. In such circumstances the Council may impose all or any of the following minor measures:

(i) issuing advisories;
(ii) issuing warnings;
(iii) withdrawal of judicial work for a limited time including cases already assigned;
(iv) request that the judge may voluntarily retire; and
(v) censure or admonition, public or private.

However, these minor measures can be taken in case of complaint procedure only and not in the case of Reference.

(iii) Where the Charge is Proved and Warrants Removal

The Council have power also to recommend for the removal of the judge where the Council is satisfied that all or any of the charge in regard to misbehaviour or incapacity have been proved and that they are of serious nature warranting his removal, it shall advice the President accordingly. Council may arrive to this conclusion in either of the procedures in each case the procedure to be followed for removal of a judge is through a resolution in both the Houses of the Parliament.

The President on receipt of advice under sub-section (3) shall cause the findings of the Council alongwith the accompanying materials to be laid before both Houses of Parliament.

On lying of the advice of the Council the Government shall move a motion in either House of Parliament for presenting an address to the President for the removal of the said Judge.

If the motion is accepted in both the Houses as mentioned under Article 124(4) read with Article 218 of the Indian

Constitution, then the proposal is passed to the President, who in turn orders removal of the judge. Clause 23 of the Bill enumerates other consequences of removal. It says: where the recommendation of the Council for removal of a judge is accepted by the Houses and removal order is passed by the President; the judges shall be disqualified for:

(i) any diplomatic assignment, appointment as an administrator of a Union territory and such other assignment which is required by law to be made by President by warrant under his hand and seal;
(ii) employment to any office of profit under the government of India or the government of a state;
(iii) to act as an arbitrator in any arbitration proceedings; and
(iv) to pursue chamber practice.

VII. CRITICAL APPRISAL OF THE PROPOSED MECHANISM FOR DISCIPLINING JUDGES

The perusal of the provisions of The Judges (Inquiry) Bill, 2006 reveals that it has made sufficient improvement upon the Judges (Inquiry) Act, 1968 and has also made effort to provide the procedure for dealing the cases requiring action short of removal. The proposed Bill will fill in and remove certain infirmities to be found under 'in-House' procedure. It is to be noted that the Apex Court itself had pointed out the special significance of 'in-House' procedure, when it observed "It would thus, be seen that owing gap between proved misbehaviour and bad conduct inconsistent with the high office on the part of a non-cooperating Judge/Chief Justice of a High Court could be disciplined by self-regulation through 'in-House' procedure. This 'in-House' procedure would fill in the constitutional gap and would yield salutary effect". But the functioning of 'in-House' procedure for a decade exposed its unsatisfactory position due to lack of statutory basis and therefore, non-obligatory nature. Complaint procedure given under the proposed Bill will remove this infirmity by providing statutory and obligatory basis.

If after inquiry in respect of a complaint the counsel is satisfied that charges against the judge concerned regarding misbehaviour or incapacity are proved but do not warrant removal of the judge it may impose the measures in form of advisories warnings, withdrawal of judicial work for a limited time censure or admonition, public or private. It may also request that Judge may voluntarily retire.

The proposed Bill also shows improvement upon the earlier Judges (Inquiry) Act, 1968. *Firstly,* on the line of Advocates Act, 1961, requiring the disciplinary action purely by the advocates themselves, it provides for the establishment of National Judicial Council consisting of all the members of the judiciary itself. It has dropped the membership of a 'distinguish jurist' and has also increased the number of members in the Council. To make it specific the inquiry expected to be constituted under judges (Inquiry) Act, 1968, consisted of three members including one member, as 'distinguished jurist'. Now the proposed National a Judicial Council will consist of five members i.e. Chief Justice of India as Chairman, two senior most Judges of the Supreme Court and two Chief Justices of the High Court as members. Chief Justice will have the dominant role as he will be Chairman and will nominate the other four members, *Secondly,* it has taken full care of maintaining judicial independence without leaving any chance of prosecution through Media, as, inquiry is to be conducted *in camera* by the Chairperson and the members of the Council seating jointly. *Thirdly,* the proposed Bill tries to safeguard the interest of the complainant by keeping identity confidential from all persons in general and also the judge against whom the complaint is made in particular along with such protections as the Counsel deems fit. *Fourthly,* the proposed Bill also disqualifies, the removed judge from getting any further employment to any office of profit under the Government of India, or Government of States, any diplomatic assignments or other appointment required to be made by the President, acting as an arbitrator in any Arbitration proceedings and pursuing chamber practice. *Fifthly,* with a view to minimize or avoid complaints false, which are frivolous, vexatious, not in good faith or with an instant to hares the judge against whom such complaint is filed, are made punishable. *Sixthly,* the proposed Bill also recognizes right to appeal and provides that an aggrieved Judge may prefer an appeal to the Supreme Court against an order of removal by the President, or a final order passed by the Council imposing one or other 'minor measure' on the basis of the complaint. *Seventhly,* with a view to keep the stream of justice pure the proposed Bill aims at issuing of code of conduct containing guidelines for the conduct and behaviour of judges. And *lastly,* the proposal regarding inclusion of the intimation of assets and liabilities by the superior court judges to their respective Chief Justice may have good effect with a view to attract the public confidence in the judges.

Despite the above narrated merits and improvement upon the earlier measures on the point, the proposed Bill is not completely free from blemishes. *First,* it is not intended to entertain complaints with respect to any act or conduct constituting misbehaviour which took place before the commencement of the Judges (Inquiry) Act (when it will come into force after becoming an Act of Parliament). Likewise it does not intend to entertain any complaint against a judge constituting misbehaviour which has become more than two year old. Similarly, no complaint is intended to be entertained against a judge who has demitted the office. Thus, in all such cases the errant judges will go unnoticed and unpunished.

Second, the position regarding impractibility of removal of the superior courts' judges will remains as it has been earlier, because after the Inquiry and its conclusion it will have to follow the same procedure of Article 124(4) of the Constitution of India. It may justify the comment putting old wine in new bottle. In addition, it will require Constitution of 15 members joint committee to be constituted by the nomination of 10 members by Speaker of Lok Sabha and 5 member by the Chairman of Council of States which is likely to make the procedure further complicated and unworkable.

Third, the proposed Bill is not intended to cover the Chief Justice of India under the complaint procedure and thereby leaves free Chief Justice of India from the clutches of disciplinary action short of removal. It is common knowledge that, the conduct of some of Hon'ble Chief Justices has also been called in question.

The study in the present chapter has shown the inefficaciousness or failure of control mechanism intended to discipline the errant members of the bench and the bar.

9

Conclusions

The book began with the note of the desirability of the order and security as vehicle of justice. The importance and essentiality of justice being recognized throughout the vein of the ordered and civilized society it was discussed how the courts of justice have been vehicle of justice with the help of learned counsels and dignified justices. It had also been shown how the purpose of administering the impartial justice can be achieved only with cooperation of honest, learned, hardworking, intelligent and men of character on the Bar and impartial, full of integrity, righteous and fair-minded persons adorning the Bench. Chapter 1 presented the study of the judges as trustee of the social welfare through their honest and incorruptible image. It also showed how justice had been done sometimes by saving the life of innocent individual from the hands of wicked people.

Chapter 2 of this book dealt with the historical account of legal profession and prime notion of maintaining the high tradition of Bench and Bar for the administration of justice. The study concluded that in early England the idea of justice possessed high value and to provide or help in justice, was regarded as pious work and therefore, it had an ecclesiastical touch and *Clergymen* took active part in administration of justice. The dress of barristers and now advocates are still reminder of that fact. By and by with the growing complexity of common law, professional pleaders came into existence. Different Inns of the court were established for training the apprentice in law. Such persons were trend by the Inns and were subject to visitorial jurisdiction of judges and in certain respect autonomous societies. Gradually the job of training and teaching law went into the hands of law colleges and universities; and a dignified profession developed in that country.

In United States of America the legal profession developed in some what different way but its institutional and doctorinal foundation could be found in monasteries and Universities as well as in ecclesiastical and Royal Households of Western Christiandom. The American legal profession was broadly based on British pattern and by and by the competent professional lawyers' begain to arrived from England to the United States. In United States too independent status of Bench and Bar was established. The professionals came to be the creation of 'Langdell-Pound' system and law graduates adopted the legal profession. The Bar Association became to contract the legal profession with a view to maintain the dignity of the profession.

In India Justice had prime value, but the study has shown that though in ancient India the quality of good Judge was narrated but there had been no reference to professional lawyers.

In Muslim period the high tradition of justice was to be found during the regime of Balbon and Mohammad Bin Tuglak but it did not show the system of learned person in law. As a matter of fact, the present system is the result of British regime which prescribed qualification for persons appearing before the court and qualification of the justices. Various attempts had been made to improve upon through different Legal Practitioners' Act. Attempt had also been made towards the autonomy and unification of Bar which could be materialized only in real sense in post-independence era in India. The study revealed how Advocates Act, 1961 was envisaged to have unified Bar on the all India basis with guarantee of the autonomy of Bar. It also provided for qualification for persons practising before the court and decorum to be maintained by them.

The study in Chapter 3 dealt with the high tradition and present status of legal profession. It outlined the necessity of legal profession and status and nature of legal profession as a profession of high tradition, learned profession, noble profession and dignified profession. These qualities attract the confidence of the people in administration of justice due to the very wide and analytical knowledge of lawyers about the all facts of life in light of knowledge gathered from the learning of different subjects. The study also revealed the falling standards of legal education and thereby adding bad name to the profession.

The study of Chapters 2 and 3 proves that though the legal profession has been regarded as a noble, honorable and the profession of high tradition throughout the world, the members of the profession are not always held in high esteem. No doubt the tradition of legal profession has inspired and received admiration for its great contribution in administration of justice and rendering socio-legal service to the society, but lawyers as a class have been adversely commented upon. Plato said that "It was a sign of intemperate and corrupt Commonwealth where lawyer abounded". Bentham himself a lawyer described his uncle as "one of the gentlest of all human being though a lawyer by profession".[1] Lawyers are now viewed as seekers of the service and they have become fortune seekers. Sometimes lawyers have been described as unavoidable scoundrels and necessary evils. Tailing a lie and using ambiguous terminology has been attributed to the lawyers.[2]

1. Quoted from Prasad, Anirudh, *Principles of the Ethics of Legal Profession in India*, 2006 ed., p. 53.
2. Sorabji, J. Soli, "Lawyers as Professionals", A.I.R. (J) 2004, p. 4.

The study also revealed how once upon a time only the law graduates from reputed universities were allowed to practise before the courts of law. Despite the LL.B. degree being made an essential qualification for enrolment as an advocate, the very genuineness of the law degree is being called in question. No doubt the highest court of the land from time to time has tried to make the law study meaningful by disallowing the enrolment of a student who obtained a degree of law in two years as a private candidate and did only third years course as a regular student[3] and a student who completed legal education without regular attendance in the classes. It is also proved that some Institutions like National Law Universities are doing well, but such Institutions and the products of such institutions are a drop in the ocean. Bulk of law degree is awarded and distributed by colleges having no well trained teachers and proper arrangement for teaching. The mushroom growth of colleges is causing great damage to the academic standard of legal education. The study in Chapter 3 has revealed how the number of Universities conducting teaching in law department has increased from seven in 1950 to one hundred nineteen in 2007 and how the number of affiliated colleges conducting law teaching have increased 36 in 1950 to 687 in 2007. The table given in the study showed that between 2000 and 2007 the number of advocates increased above three lakhs and five thousand. The country is producing approximately fifty thousand advocates every year. The quantity has demolished the quality. Not only this the self-financing law colleges have added fuel to the fire of deteriorating condition of teaching as they are nearly money-making institutions, with Motto of *less investment more and more profit*.

The offshoot of the mushroom growth is that the colleges are acting as law graduate manufacturing factories. The tension and not upto mark behaviour is bound to bring disrepute and affect the purity of the stream of administration of justice. The incidence of unbecoming conduct of advocates as well as justices has become common news in the papers.

3. *Baldevraj Sharma* v. *Bar Council of India*, A.I.R. 1989 S.C. 1541.

The study in Chapter 4 revealed that how the image of judiciary once adorned not only due to the power of contempt of court but due to the public confidence in high traditions and impartiality of justices has gone eroded in the span of times. Once it was thought that the authority of the court has to be respected and protected at all costs as it insures peace and tranquility in society. The standard of conduct is expected to be higher than what is expected of a layman. But now-a-days the confidence in judiciary has not remained as it had been few decades earlier. The factors like delay in justice, illusory system of trial proceeding and not upto mark behaviour of justices has foreshaken the confidence of people in judicial system.

With a view to appreciate the real problems behind the gap in expectations and reality the study in Chapter 5 had been devoted to the state of professional ethics in administration of justice and Bench Bar relation. The study revealed how the high tradition of Bar and Bench required adherence to certain standards of right and honorable conducts by members of learned profession in their dealing with one another and in protecting the interest and handling of affairs in relation to administration of justice. To achieve this purpose Bar Associations of different countries have adopted certain rules of etiquette and code of conducts to be observed by the members of the Bar. The Bar Council of India has issued certain code of conducts necessitated by the experience and pressing need of the time. The court had appreciated such needs in *R.D. Saxena* v. *Balram Prasad*[5] when it observed: "It is high time for the legal profession to join hands and evolve a code for themselves in addition to mandate of the Advocates Act, Rules made thereunder and Rules made by various High Courts and this court, for strengthening the belief of the common man in the institution of judiciary in general and in their profession in particular. Creation of such a faith and confidence would not only strengthen the rule of law but also

4. *Aparna Basu Mallik* v. *Bar Council of India*, A.I.R. 1983 Cal. 461.
5. (2007) 7 S.C.C. 264.

result in reaching excellence in the profession. It has been essential for making advocate liable to disciplinary action if he departs from the high standards which the profession set for itself and conducts himself in a manner which is not fair, reasonable and according to law. The study revealed the duties of advocates to the client, to the court, and to others. The study also revealed propriety of the judges needed to inspire cordial relation with the Bar, to give patient hearing, to remain courteous and to ensure the autonomy and independence of the Bar. It also pointed out the necessity of judicial propriety to inspire confidence of society in administration of justice. A number of suggestions have been put forward through the Re-statement of Value of Judicial Life, Bangalore Draft principles and the Oath for Affirmation by Judges, etc. However, the study in this Chapter did not result into clear conclusion as to certain controversial issues regarding brief.

The tradition of bar requires that no accused should be left unattended and an advocate should not refuse to represent even the accused of anti-national and terrorist activities. But, this tradition is not clear in practice. In *Parliament attack case*[6] the counsels of the accused had to face fury and strong reaction of some people. In *Ayodhya blast case*[7] the counsel of the accused was expelled from the membership of bar by the District Bar Association, Faizabad.

Another such issue relates to the position of strike by advocates more and often and that too on national level on one pretext or the other is most disturbing. The judiciary has made effort to curb them but the incidents of strikes in violation of even the direction of the Supreme Court is not healthy tradition. Bar Council has failed to deal with such strikers advocate en-masse. It indicates the clear picture of the failure of the system. The requirement of code of conduct both for the Bench and Bar is essential for maintaining the high tradition of the administration of justice. But its failure might prove injurious to the health of the administration of justice

6. See Chapter Vth.
7. *Ibid.*

inspiring public confidence. Therefore, two subsequent chapters had been devoted to the conducts of errant members of the Bench and Bar. The study conducted in Chapter 6 revealed diverse cases of professional misconduct including misconduct in relation to client like dereliction of duty, changing the sides and negligence; misconduct in relation to money like financial misappropriation, misuse of blank signed papers, charging improper fee, taking undue advantage of position, champertous bargain, advertisement and solicitation, carrying on other business, touting and seeking money from the client to bribe the Judge; misconduct in relation to the court, misleading the court, corrupting the administration of justice and disrespect to court; other misconducts including obscene behaviour, criminal conduct, sexual misbehaviour, physical assault, abuse of privileges, political activities and civil disobedience, etc. It also exposed the cases of showing disrespect or scandalizing court popularly known as contempt of court committed by advocates. To narrate; imputation of partiality, allegation of corruption, unsavory language, threatening, unbecoming behaviour, strike and boycott, disturbing court proceedings, influencing the judge by private communication, etc.

Likewise Chapter 7 dealt with the unbecoming behaviour of the judges and revealed tendency of corrupting administration of justice on the part of judges unbecoming behaviour of judges and contempt of Court, unseemly behaviour against advocates, abusing decorum of the court, insubordination, influencing another judge, attributing bias on superior court's judge. The study in that chapter also dealt with the controversial and important but unresolved issue of the contempt of court on the part of honorable Justices of the superior courts like the High Courts and the Supreme Court.

There is a good case proving tendency towards the need of inclusion of superior court judges too in the definition of 'Judge' under the Contempt of Courts Act. The plain meaning, rule and grammatical, literal and natural meaning of the expression 'Judge' goes in the favour of including all judges from bottom to the top. Judiciary has put artificial limitation on the scope of section 16 of Contempt of Courts Act, using expression 'Judges and Magistrate' and thereby arriving at conclusion that the judges of the courts of record could not be held liable for the contempt of court. The study proved that such restricted interpretation is not very much convincing and conducive to the confidence in administration of justice by reposing unequalled faith in and respect for the superior court judges merely with the help of unwritten norms of English tradition prevailing at the time of the commencement of the Constitution or Statutory Provision of the Contempt of Courts Act. It has been interesting to note how the conduct of the honorable Judge of Patna High Court during the proceeding of the Court in *Harishchandra Misra* v. *the Honorable Mr. Justice S. Ali Ahmed,*[8] could be justified or appreciated. In that case the learned judge had not only threatened advocate Mr. Sadanand Jha to get him arrested but on his expressing a word of sorrow his reaction was *"you should be sorry and you would be sorry. You will suffer and you are doomed. Do not think with the attitude you will flourish or prosper.*[9]

The majority decision of the five judge bench exonerating the learned judge from the contempt of courts by four to one majority did not appear to be legally convincing by giving restricted meaning to Sections 9 and 16 of the Contempt of Courts Act. *Firstly,* the Supreme Court and High Courts were said to be immune from contempt proceedings in view of their being court of record respectively under Articles 129 and 215 of the Constitution merely on the ground that courts of record in England had never been subject to contempt of court. We have written Constitution and statutory provisions in the term of the Contempt of Courts Act, 1971. *Secondly,* the superior courts judges' immunity from contempt of court was said to be justified because absolute freedom and independence of such judges was necessary for the administration of justice.

8. A.I.R. 1986 Pat. 65.
9. *Id.,* p. 69.

It is submitted with due respect that if it is so the absolute freedom and independence of subordinate court also ought to be ensured. *Thirdly*, at the time of enforcement of Contempt of Courts Act the judges of the superior court were said not to have been charged for having committed contempt of the court. It is also not very much convincing because of the specific provision using the term 'Judge' and not expressly granting immunity to superior courts' judges. *Fourthly*, the immunity of the conduct of judges from being discussed in Parliament and State Legislature or removal process also did not appear to be very attractive because no such specific provision has been made in the Constitution itself. *Finally*, the reasoning of the majority that such things had happened in the court room in the past as well but they had been burried in the sprit of forget and forgive also does not prove to be of any avail, as bad precedent could not be treated as good precedent. For the reasons discussed here the dissenting opinion of Mr. Justice Virendra Prasad Sinha appeared to be more convincing and in accordance with the call of the time. The highest court of the land otherwise did not allow a petition against the former Chief Justice of India, E.S. Venkataramiah without expressing any view on the issue whether contempt proceeding could lie against the superior court justices or not.[10] The issue had arisen out of an interview given by the learned former Chief Justice exposing the reasons for deterioration of standards due to the role of lavish party and Whiskey bottle in judicial appointments. He had exposed that in every High Court there were at least four to five Judges who had practically been out every evening, wining and dining either at a lawyers' house or a foreign embassy.[11] The honorable Court silenced the issue by reminding Chinese proverb "as long as you are upright do not care if your shadowed is crooked". The highest Court also avoided contempt proceedings against *Mr. Justice V. Ramaswamy* in *Sub-Committee of Judicial*

10. *Viswanath* v. E.S. Venkataramiah, (1990) Cr.L.J. 2179 (S.C.).
11. *Ibid.*

Accountability v. *Justice V. Ramaswamy*[12] for having written a letter to members of the inquiry committee set-up under Judges (Inquiry) Act, 1968 making reckless allegation against the judiciary as a whole. The Supreme Court like earlier case[13] did not touch the issue whether contempt proceeding could lie against the superior court judges or not. The same judicial attitude continued in State of *Rajasthan* v. *Prakash Chand*[14] where Justice Sethna had chosen to issue contempt proceedings against the Chief Justice himself because the latter had transferred a writ petition from the board of Mr. Justice Sethna to a division bench. The Apex Court again choose to *sail on the same boat*. In *Tarak Singh* v. *Joyti Basu*,[15] which represented unholy nexus between duty and interest of a High Court judge, wherein the judge concerned had stayed allotment in Salt Lake City but had got a corner plot allotted to himself out of Chief Minister's discretionary quota. The Supreme Court noted that, the learned judge had misused his divine judicial duty as liveries to accomplish to his personal ends. He had betrayed the trust reposed in him by the people. But the court did not think it proper to proceed under Contempt of Courts Act in spite of false affidavit submitted by the learned judge.

The silence of the court in successive cases is bound to create a background in which the court will break its silence and bring the contemptuous conduct of superior courts' judges within the preview of the Contempt of Courts Act. The court is likely to do it in view of no specific exemption granted either under the Constitution or under the Statutes. The rule of interpretation evolved in *Superintendent and Remembrancer of Legal Affairs, W.B.* v. *Corporation of Calcutta*,[16] wherein while dealing with the issue whether state is bound by its own statute the Supreme Court had said that it is bound unless it

12. (1995) 1 S.C.C. 5.
13. *Sikanker Khan* v. *Ashok Kumar Mathur*, (1991) 3 S.C.R. 236.
14. A.I.R. 1998 S.C.1344.
15. (2005) 1 S.C.C. 1.
16. A.I.R. 1967 S.C. 997.

is excluded expressly or by necessary implication may serve as torch bearer.

The study conducted under Chapter 8 dealt with control mechanism enforcing accountability of the Bench and the Bar and its efficacy. It revealed that the accountability of the advocates have been statutorily envisaged through the instrumentality of the State Bar Council with provision of first appeal to the Bar Council of India and the ultimate appeal to the Supreme Court of India. The study proved that the self-regulatory proceedings of the Bar Council put some check on the recalcitrant activities of the advocates but they have not proved to be very satisfactory. Different punishments by the way of reprimand, suspension or striking off name from the roll proved to be not so effective. One of the reasons being that the complainant had no active participation in the self-regulatory procedure where legal profession itself decides the interest of the client. Here the fourth thesis is approved and the self-disciplinary control mechanism ensuring discipline among advocates through the State Bar Council and the Bar Council of India has not achieved its intended aim as only in extreme cases of negligence, an advocate may be punished for his lack of care and competence. Mere incompetence and lack of care or deficiency in professional services is still not sufficient to amount to professional misconduct. In most of the cases the matters come to an end due to non-establishment of a *prima-facie* case against the advocate. Section 24-A of Advocates Act ensures the enrolment of men of character, with LL.B. degree but disqualification is not applicable to person found guilty of the Crime to be dealt with the Probation of Offenders' Act, 1958 and disqualification seizes to have effect after two years and even a criminal can become an advocate after the expiry of the prescribed period of disqualification.

The Bar Council has not proved to be effective and upto mark in some of the cases like the case of appearance as witness for the opponent while having been engaged by petitioner. The punishment of simple reprimand by Bar Council of India for such a gross negligence or non-filing of suit, misguiding the client, resulting into loss of valuable property being punished only with three months suspension from practice or ignoring of the recurring adjournment on flimsy or frivolous ground and abusing process of the court or the punishment of three months suspension against an advocate who had misappropriated money of the poor client, falsely claimed to have returned money and had filed fraudulent affidavit or the punishment of only reprimand for the act of levelling high degree of corruption charge against the Assistant Income Tax Commissioner or the confirmation of one month suspension by the Bar Council of India with respect to advocate-*cum*-Deputy Mayor using extremely vulgar and obscene language in a gathering and having been convicted under Sections 294 and 153 of Indian Penal Code with fine of three hundred Rupees. The Bar Council of India did not resist itself from making observation "may be if we have for the first time to impose punishment in the matter, we may having regard to heavy fine imposed not ordered suspension for a month", show the attitude of Bar Council to deal with brother advocates. If such approach prevails what would be significance of "other misconduct" used under Section 35 of the Advocates Act in addition to the "professional misconduct"? Similar message is conveyed through the observation "It is always open to reinstate the advocate on prayer of that he is a changed man and fit to be admitted into profession" with respect to punishment of the removal of name from roll for having committed rape of a clients' wife. Such incidents are neither happy nor conducive to inspire the confidence in the functioning of the Bar Council.

The study of control mechanism with a view to ensure accountability of judges also formed the subject matter of inquiry in Chapter 8. It dealt with the efficacy or otherwise of the 'in-house' procedure and the impeachment processes alongwith a critical and evaluative control mechanism envisaged under the proposed National Judicial (Inquiry) Bill 2006.

The study has proved that the self-regulatory in-house-procedure evolved by the Supreme Court in *C. Ravichandran Iyer* v. *Justice Bhattacharjee*,[17] has not proved to work well. With great hope the Supreme Court had added the special

17. (1995) 5 S.C.C. 457.

significance of 'in-house' procedure using the expressions "it would thus be seen that owing gap between proved misbehaviour and bad conduct inconsistent with the high office on the part of a non-cooperating Judge/Chief Justice of a High Court could be disciplined by self-regulation through in-house procedure. This 'in-house' procedure would fill a constitutional gap and would yield salutary effect". But the later experience of the scheme of the 'in-house' procedure in case of three judges of Punjab and Haryana High Court for their alleged involvement in Public Service Commission Examination and in the case of Mr. Justice Arun Madan facing the allegation of a proposition to a woman doctor to have sex with him in exchange for a judicial favour and the case of a group of the judges of the Karnataka High Court has proved to be total failure. It is more so in view of the lack of constitutional or statutory provisions to deal with errant judges facing charges short of impeachment.

The constitutionally envisaged procedure for removal of the High Court and Supreme Court Judges has proved to be impracticable and therefore, a total failure. The experience of the failure of impeachment motion in relation to Mr. Justice V. Ramaswamy speaks a volume of things regarding the impracticability of the removal process and the procedure proposed under National Judicial (Inquiry) Bill, 2006 is no exception.

The Judicial accountability has got underscore in view of the overriding value of independence of judiciary and unwritten norms appeared to prevail over the written norms under the Constitution or the Statutes. As advocates' autonomy has got precedence in the form of the self-regulatory disciplinary procedure through the members of Bar itself even without tolerating the participation of outsiders like Attorney General or the Justices, so is the case with the courts. The proposed Bill has done away with the participation of distinguished Jurist and all thc members of the council are to be from the judiciary itself. Likewise, in cases before the Supreme Court involving the errant conduct of the superior court's judges, the Supreme Court's attitude has been very soft. The court has given under importance to written norms.

It has chosen the value of insuring of the independence of judiciary through special protection granted to the justices in preference to the value of punishing the errant judges so as to ensure faith and confidence of people reposed in them through the Constitution and other Statutory provisions. The issue still remains: will the country be benefited by giving special benefit to the justices with a view to ensure independence of judiciary or by dealing with them properly and thereby reposing confidence in the famous principle of natural justice that *justice is not only to be done, it should manifestly appear to have been done*?

The study in the book has revealed many if and buts, drawbacks, thought provoking, unresolved issues necessitating redressal at earliest. With a view to ensure the dignity of the legal profession and unchallengeable faith in administration of justice through courts the following suggestions are proffered:

1. It is high time to ensure the quality of legal education with a view to make honest and fearless advocates and Judges above board. It is felt that in spite of the periodic inspection by the Bar Council of India the condition of Law colleges is very vunerable. Colleges have become advocate producing factories without proper training and education through unqualified teachers or sometimes without arrangements for the teaching. It is experienced that the mushroom growth of self-financing Law colleges are putting threat to the standard of legal education under the present system. Commercialisation has completely undermined the standards of teaching through admission and examinations without teaching. Care should be taken of this fact and self-financing courses should not be allowed in any case.
2. Section 24-A of the Advocates' Act needs a fresh consideration. Proviso (1) of this section should be deleted as it allows disqualification after two years of the completion of punishment by way of dismissal or removal for a charge involving moral turpitude to

witheraway. To allow such unwanted person to practise after some time will not be conducive to the image of pure and clear administration of justice.

3. Though legal profession is a learned profession dependent on the personal ability of individual, the appropriate fee should be fixed with a view to avoid exploitation of clients at the hands of some of Advocates charging exorbitant fees.
4. In view of the increasing number of advocates day-by-day and technicalities of issues involved there is necessity of allowing advocates to practise even before the tribunals, etc. With a view to make the services of experts counsels available, Section 30 of the Advocates' Act should be immediately brought into force. Many problems are arising due to non-enforcement of this provision which envisages the practice of advocates in all courts, before tribunals or person authorized to take evidence or other authority.
5. A thorough study and inquiry of the functioning of Advocates' Act, 1961 is very essential in view of the fast changing society and ever increasing number of advocates. The Central Government should immediately set-up a high power committee to review the Advocates' Act and to suggest changes with a view to inspire the confidence of the clients and general people in the efficacy of the disciplinary procedure given under the Act. It is high time to think whether disciplinary committee of the State Bar Council or National should comprise only of the Advocates or some members from outside the Bar may be included in such committee.
6. With a view to ensure transparency and effectiveness of the disciplinary proceedings the code of ethics should be made mandatory and they should not remain merely recommendatory as some of the rules given under Bar Council of India Rules are at present. The specific code of conduct needs to be added as to accepting of briefs. At present, there is

utter confusion. Should the Bar punish those advocates who accept the brief from persons accused of anti-national and terrorist activities? Since the advocates only aid in administration of justice and it is their duty to see that procedural injustice is not done to any accused, the duty of advocate is not to decide the case but to assist in deciding the cases and therefore it should be insured that no accused of any crime is left unattended on merely emotional appeals.

7. The delay in administration of justice is tarnishing the image of administration of Justice. Most of the cases of delay are due to the callous attitude of the advocates and therefore, the advocates demanding adjournment on frivolous grounds should be properly dealt with.
8. It is common knowledge that the new entrant in profession are coming without knowledge of any decorum, decency or tradition of the Bar. Some sort of training is felt essential and therefore, the Supreme Court decision allowing enrolment without apprenticeship needs a fresh and practical re-thinking. The Parliament should nullify the effect of this decision by adding appropriate provision in the Advocates Act.
9. In view of the requirement of transparency in every walk of life it is not appealing why the honorable judges of the superior courts should enjoy immunity from contempt proceedings. Though the Contempt of Courts Act does not specifically grant such immunity the judicial interpretation has recognized it. Therefore, there are two options, first, the Supreme Court should give natural meaning to the expression 'Judge' used under the Contempt of Courts Act and include the Judges of the Superior Courts within its preview, or second, the Parliament should amend the Contempt of Courts Act making it clear by using the expression "Judges including the Justices of the High Courts and the Supreme Court". Not only this judges

should also be required to declare their assets before assuming the office. The recent developments and the Delhi High Court decision declaring Chief Justice of India covered under R.T.I. Act further strengthen suggestion.

10. The faith in Judiciary is the backbone of our system. Judges may be said to be as honest as an ordinary person of the society. It is the only speciality with a Judge that he invites confidence due to his training of impartiality, giving reasoned decision and his impeachment in some rare cases of misconduct. If a Judge acts on extraneous consideration and does not give convincing reasons for decisions or gives decision against the law and norms laid down by the superior courts, he should also be dealt like common citizen, because independence of judiciary does not allow arbitrary exercise of power for personal ends as could be found in the case of honorable Judge of Calcutta High Court in getting plot allotted in "Salt Lake City".

11. Recently in Gaziabad judges scam allegedly involving 26 honourable judges, the Supreme Court has expressed the view that judges should not be examined as other persons charged of similar offence. Even the *amicus curiae* Mr. Anil Diwan did not appear to subscribe such view. It is not advisable that the judiciary should adopt the attitude of *touch me not* in all the cases. The requirement of faith in administration is otherwise. The persons who are more learned and law knowing should be required to be more responsible. Exemplary treatment is required to ensure the stream of Justice pure and clear.

12. In the similar vein it is suggested that the honourable Judges need not be spared if they file false affidavit before a Court of Law (as Mr. Justice A.C. Banerjee of Calcutta High Court was charged to have done) because they are learned person in law and if filing of false affidavit is criminal acts for

others why it should not be such for the person well versed in law?

13. No person should be treated above law and the proposed Judges (Inquiry) Bill, 2006 should be amended to include Chief Justice of India also under the jurisdiction of the complaint procedure before the Judicial Council.
14. The defect in the proposed Judges Inquiry Bill regarding not entertaining of complaint with respect to misconduct of a Judge which would have taken place before the commencement of the Act or the conduct of misbehaviour which has taken place before two years of the filing of complaint or complaint of misconduct against a person demitted the office of a Judge needs to be removed and no alibi should be allowed in the cases of misconduct.
15. The attitude about 'in-house' or self-regulatory measures needs drastic change. If something goes wrong with the justices of the superior courts, why it should not be made a public issue and include personnel from the others public walk of life instead of leaving the matter strictly to the honourable justices. It should not be made *closed shop*. Therefore, the provision relating to the constitution of Judicial Council under the proposed Bill needs appropriate amendment to allow some high dignitaries like Prime Minister and Vice-President of India to participate in the process of impeachment. In this regard serious thought should be given over the matter of appointment of some high dignatory like Ombudsman also to inquire into the conduct of judges.
16. The impracticability of removal process remains as it was earlier. Therefore, Article 124 itself should be appropriately amended as to make the impeachment procedure practicable, though with some difficulty, but not impracticability.
17. Anyway Judge (Inquiry) Bill, 2006 should not be allowed to meet the fate of many Bills by being allowed to lapse. It should be passed immediately.

18. The Judges should also be covered under the Information Act so as to maintain faith in judiciary and ensure it to remain beyond suspicion like Caesar's wife.
19. Justice Saumitra Sen incidence necessitates disclosure of all information about incumbent before his joining as Mr. Justice.
20. Last, but not least, the views of Hon'ble Chief Justice of India, K.G. Balakrishnan expressed before press persons at Kochi on 09.08.2008 that a time may come when videography of court proceedings may be allowed is most timely and welcomed. It is suggested that it should be allowed in the interest of justice making more transparent and objective.
21. A serious consideration is needed with respect to appoint the superior court justices though Judicial Appointments Commission on the pattern of South African J.A.C.

Bibliography

Books

Aiyer Krishna Swamy, Professional Conduct and Advocacy, IIIrd Edition, Oxford University Publication, New York.

Anand, C.L., General Principles of Legal Ethics, 1965 Edition, Law Books Company, Allahabad.

Anand, C.L., Professional Ethics of The Bar, 1987 Edition, The Law Books Company, Allahabad.

Cacnegem, R.C., Judges, Legislatures and Professors, 1985 Edition, Cambridge University Press, Cambridge.

Chagala, M.C., Roses in December, 1974 Edition, Wadhwa and Company, Nagpur.

Chaudhary, V.K.S., The Ivory Tower, 2002 Edition, Universal Law Publishing Company (Pvt.) Ltd., Delhi.

Clark, Great Saying by Great Lawyers, North-Holland Publishing Company, Amsterdam, New York.

Clive, Richard, The Law and Conduct of Legal Profession, 1963 Edition, The Law Book Company of Australia Pvt. Ltd., Sydney.

Das, Cyrus, Judges and Judicial Accountability, 2005 Edition, Universal Law Publishing Company Pvt. Ltd., Delhi.

Gururajachari, K., Advocacy and Professional Ethics, Ist Edition, 2000, Wadhva and Company, Allahabad.

Iyer and Iyer, The Duties of the Advocates to His Clients and Legal Ethics, 2001 Edition, Eastern Book Company.

Iyer, V.R.K., Law, Lawyers and Justice, 1989 Edition, B.R. Publishing Corporation, Delhi.

Jain, M.P., Indian Constitutional Law (Vol. I and II), Vth Edition, 2003, Wadhwa and Company, Nagpur.

Janak Raj, J., Assault on Judiciary and the Role of Parliament, 1977 Edition, Associated Legal Advisors (Pvt.) Ltd., New Delhi.

Kapoor, J.D., Contempt of Court, 2004 Edition, Universal Law Publishing Co. Pvt. Ltd., New Delhi.

Khanna, H.R., Neither Roses Nor Thorn, 1990 Edition, Eastern Book Company, Lucknow.

Mahanty, Indrajit, Selected Judgements on Professional Ethics, 2002 Edition, Bar Council of India Trust, New Delhi.

Mehrotra, V.K., Contempt of Court, VIth Edition, 2002 Eastern Book Company, Lucknow.

Parker, Stepha, Samford Legal Ethics and Legal Practice, 1985 Edition, Clarendon Press, Oxford.

Prasad, Anirudh, Principles of the Ethics of Legal Profession in India, 2006 Edition, University Book House Pvt. Ltd., Jaipur, Rajasthan.

Rai, Kailash, History of Courts Legislature and Legal Profession in India, 2005 Edition, Allahabad Law Agency, Published from Faridabad, Haryana.

Shetreet, Shimon, Judges on Trial, 1976 Edition, North-Holland Publishing Company, Amsterdam, New York.

Singh, M.P., Outlines of Indian Legal and Constitutional History, 2007 Edition, Universal Law Publishing Company, New Delhi.

Sinha, B.P., Reminiscences and Reflections of a Chief Justice, 1985 Edition, B.R. Publishing Corporation.

Subba Rao, D.V., Sanjva Row's The Advocates Act, VIIth Edition, 2005, Butterworths, New Delhi.

Tripathi, S.C., Indian Legal and Constitutional History, Ist Edition, 2006, *Central Law Publication*, Allahabad.

Articles

Bhatt, Jitendra (J), The American Bar Assciation (2001) S.C.C., pp. 18-22.

Clive, J., Lid-off the Pandora's Box of Judicial Corruption, *The Lawyer*, January 1991 at 25.

Crally, Bimal, A Miniscule Profile of Lawyers and his Profession, *A.I.R.* (J), 2000 at 205.

David (J), Lawyer's Duties to the Court, *114 L.Q.R.* 63 (1998) at 6.

Desai, D.A., Research for Justice, *3 Lex Juris* (1988) 24.

Desai, D.A., Role and Structure of Legal Profession *J.B.C.I.*, 1981 at 117.

Dhavan, Rajiv, Litigation Exploitation in India (1986) *C.I.L.R.*, Vol. 4:6 at 987.

Gaur, K.D., Professional Responsibilities of Lawyers (1) Co., *U.L. Rev.* 297 (1985).

Geethisha, G., Professional Misconduct by Advocates, *Cochin University Law Review,* 2003 at 204.

Gupta, Apar, Need to Judge the Judges, Available at www.indlaw.com., Visited on 25.7.08.

Howard, J. Chirlin, Judicial Appointment in America, J.I.L.I. Vol. 9(3) at 521-530.

Iyer, V.R.K., The Patchy Indian Judicial Record, *The Hindu,* dated 6.9.07 at 5.

Iyer, V.R.K., The Indian Lawyers; His Social Responsibilities and Legal Immunities, Vol. 15, *Indian Law Review,* (1988) at 123.

Jethamalni, R., Courage and the Lawyer, Vol. (2) 1973, *JBCI,* 33.

Kelu, Nambiar T.P., Bar Bench and Gap (2002), *S.C.J.* at 39.

Lahoti, R.C., The Culture of a Judge, available at www.Judicial Academy, nic. In visited on 2.7.06.

Malcalm, David, The Role of the Profession and the Reinlation of the Legal Profession (55), *A.L.J.* (407) 1981.

Pandya, Asim, How is a Judge Expected to conduct himself in Temple of Justice, *A.I.R.* (J) 2001, p. 154.

Parker, Chiristne, Regulation of Ethics of Australian Legal Practice: Autonomy and Responsiveness 25(3), *U.N.S.W.L.J.* 670 (2002).

Paul, Radha, Vinod, Professional Ethics, *A.I.R. (J)* 1961 at 67.

Prasad, Nageshwar, Professional Ethics, *A.I.R. (J)* 1962 at 42.

Rao, M.N., The Advocate and Judges, 1993 (2), *A.L.T. (J)* at 1.

Roy, Mantosh, Evaluation of the Indian Legal System and the Administration of Rule of Law in India, *A.I.R. (J)* 1970 at 21.

Sachar, Rajendra, Judicial Accountability, available at www.puclorg.accountability.com. visited on 2.7.06.

Sorabji, Soli J., Lawyers as Professionals, *A.I.R. (J)* 2002 at 4.

———, The Law of Contempt, Some Anomalies, *The Indian Advocate*, 17 at 19.

Tulsi, K.T.S., Legal System in India and America : A Comparative View, *A.I.R.(J)* at 81-85.

Veera, Raghvan, A.N., Legal Profession and the Advocates, Act, *J.I.L.I.*, Vol. 94 at 231.

Venkatesh, V., Judging Judges; Available at www.hindu.com, visited on 2.7.2006.

Verma, J.S., The Role of the Bar in the Preservation of the Role of Law (1985), *S.C.J.* 11.

News Papers and Magazine

Frontline.

India Today.

Outlook

The Hindu

The Times of India

Index

Abusing the Decorum of the Court, 355
Administrative Tribunal's Act, 1985, 136
Advocates' Act, 60, 164, 284
Quantum of Punishment, 405
Advocates' Duty to:
Court, 197
The Client, 175
Towards Country, 208
To Opponent, 209
To Colleagues, 209
Community, 210
Advocates:
Misconducts Committed, 277
Contempt of Court, 287
Political Activities and Civil Disobedience, 285
Mechanism Provided for Maintaining Accountability, 380
Professional and other Misconducts, 225, 231
Administration of Justice and Bench-bar Relations:
State of Professional Ethics, 151
Advertisement and Solicitation, 261
Allegation of Corruption, 292
All India Bar Committee and the Law Commission:
Recommendations, 58
American Bar Association, 32
American Revolution, 25
Anand, A.S., 143
Anand, C.L., 107, 214
Anti-corruption Act, 340
Appeal Before the Supreme Court:
Procedural Aspect, 414
Appelate Jurisdiction of the Supreme Court, 312
Attributing Bias on Superior Judges, 367
Award of Punishment, 398

Balakrishnan, K.G., 139, 144
Bangalore Draft Principles, 221
Bar Council Act, 1926, 164
Bar Council of India:
Procedure to be Followed, 398

Bar Councils and Its Committees:
  Disciplinary Proceedings, 381
Bar:
  Problem of Over-crowding, 109
Bench and Bar in India:
  Mechanism for Maintaining Accountability, 379
Bharadwaj, H.R., 317
Bharucha, S.P., 143

Carrying on Other Business, 266
Chagala, M.C., 265
Chamier Committee Report, 53
Champertous Bargain, 259
Charging Improper Fee, 250
Class of Advocates, 61
Client's Interest:
  Duty to Protect, 188
Company Courts System:
  Position of Legal Profession, 45
Contempt during Conducting Cases, 318
Contempt of Court:
  Conduct of the Superior Court Judges, 370
Contempt of Courts Act, 1971, 128, 317
Contempt Proceedings, 417
Corrupting the Administration of Justice, 275, 332
Criminal Conduct, 279

Delay in Justice, 134
Dereliction of Duty, 231
Desai, D.A., 153
Dhavan, Rajiv, 140
Disciplinary Powers of the Bar Council of India, 393
Disciplinary Powers of the State Bar Councils, 84
Disciplinary Powers Under Appellate Jurisdiction, 396
Disciplining Judges, 454
Disrespect to the Court, 277
Disturbing the Court Proceedings, 326
Duty not to Mislead the Court, 204
Duty of Advocates, 174
Duty to be Respectful, 199
Duty to Fairness, 191
Duty to Maintain Public Estimation, 202
Duty to Maintain Secrecy, 196
Duty to Return Documents, 195

England:
  History of Legal Profession, 17
Ensuring Judicial Accountability:
  Recent Attempt, 443
Exercise of Appellate Jurisdiction, 416

Fillon, John F., 106
Financial Misappropriation, 244
Formation of National Judicial Council, 445

Gaur, Babulal, 341

Hart, H.L.A., 172
Herbert, A.P., 139
High Traditions and the Image of Judiciary, 116
Historical Account of Legal Profession, 15
Hussan, Gulam, 284

Ill Health of the Judiciary, 331
Impeachment Process, 431
Imputation of Partiality, 290
India:
  History of Legal Profession, 34
    Ancient India, 34
    Muslim Period, 39
    British India, 41
Indian Bar Council Act, 1926, 54
Indian Evidence Act, 1872, 238
Influencing Another Judge, 365
In-house Procedure, 434
Insubordination, 358
Iyer, Sundaram, 166
Iyer, V.R. Krishna, 108, 135, 171, 309

Jaiswal, K.P., 35
Jolly, Jullius, 36
Judges and Contempt of Court:
  Unbecoming Behaviour, 347
Judges and Judicial Conduct:
  Criticism, 306
Judges:
  Seat of High Traditions, 122
  Seat of Great Respect and Dignity, 126
Judicial Life:
  Restatement of Values, 219
Judicial Officers:
  Behaviour, 143
Judiciary:
  Necessity and Role, 117
  Status and Image, 122
  Deterioration in Image, 133
Justice Frankfurter, 127

Kane, P.V., 37
Kangle, R.P., 35
King's Court System:
  Position of Legal Profession, 42

Lahoti, R.C., 223
Law:
  A Noble Profession, 90
  Profession of Great Honour and Dignity, 92
Law Institutions:
  Mushroom Growth, 102
Learned Profession, 87
Legal Education:
  System, 96
Legal Practitioners' Act, 1879, 164, 229
Legal Practitioners' (Women) Act, 1923, 55
Legal Profession:
  Falling Standards and Degradation, 94
  Status and Nature, 82
  Lack of Service Spirit, 105
  Impact of Legal Practitioners' Acts, 47
  High Traditions and Present Status, 76
Legal Service Authorities Act, 1987, 136
Life of Judges and Expectations, 129
Lord Hailshman, 214

Mechanism Provided for Disciplining Advocate, 425
Mechanism for Maintaining the Accountability of Judges, 429
Members of Bench and Bar:
  Professional Ethics, 173

Menon, N.R. Madhava, 208
Mill, Johnstuart, 172
Misconduct in Relation to Money, 243
Misleading Court, 273
Moreland, W.H., 40
Mukhargi, Sabyasanchi, 38, 235

Nature of Disciplinary Proceedings, 401
Necessity of the Legal Profession, 78
Nyay Chala Nirdhan Se Milane, 142

Oath or Affirmation by Judge, 223
Obscene Behaviour, 278
Original Jurisdiction:
  Disciplinary Powers, 393

Paradoxes in Administration of Justice, 11
Persons Who Preferred Appeal, 413
Physical Assault, 283
Prasad, Anirudh, 172
Professional Ethics, 154
  Meaning, 154
  Sources, 159
Professional Misconduct in Relation to the Court, 272
Professional Misconduct, 226
  Meaning, 226
Profession of High Traditions, 85
Property of Judges, 212
Property to Ensure:
  Autonomy and Independence of the Bar, 216
Property to Remain Courteous, 215

Punishment:
  Deterrent Approach, 407
  Reformatory Approach, 410

Qazi-ul-Qazat, 39

Ramaswami, V., 147
Ram Janambhoomi, 187
Rao, M.N., 145
Ray, B.C., 337
Reddy, Chinnapa, 338
Right to Practice, 64
Rocher, Ludo, 35
Rules of Professional Ethics:
  Problems in Framing, 170

Seeking Money from Client to Bribe the Judge, 270
Sen, A.P., 181
Setalvad, M.C., 59
Sethi, R.P., 166
Sexual Misbehaviour, 282
Should Judges be Leftout of the Information Act, 149
Singhal, P.N., 108
Sinha, B.P., 215
State Bar Council and its Disciplinary Committees, 382
State Bar Council:
  Procedure, 385
Strike and Boycott of Court, 321
Sudder Dewani Adalat, 46

Thakkar, C.K., 440
Thomas, K.T., 144
Threatening, 299
Titus, Harold H., 158, 169

Touting, 268
Transfer of Property Act, 1882, 164
Trial Proceedings:
Illusory Systems, 140

Unbecoming Behaviour of Judges, 303, 331
Unification of the Bar, 61
United States:
History of the Legal Profession, 24
Unsavory Language, 296
Unseemly Behaviour Against Advocates, 349

Varadachariar, P., 35
Venkatachaliah, M.N., 37
Verma, J.S., 161